THE POSTCOLONIAL ANIMAL

 AFRICAN PERSPECTIVES 

Kelly Askew and Anne Pitcher
Series Editors

Gender, Separatist Politics, and Embodied Nationalism in Cameroon
Jacqueline-Bethel Tchouta Mougoué

The Postcolonial Animal: African Literature and Posthuman Ethics
Evan Maina Mwangi

Developing States, Shaping Citizenship:
Service Delivery and Political Participation in Zambia
Erin Accampo Hern

African Print Cultures: Newspapers and
Their Publics in the Twentieth Century,
edited by Derek R. Peterson, Emma Hunter,
and Stephanie Newell

Unsettled History: Making South African Public Pasts,
by Leslie Witz, Gary Minkley, and Ciraj Rassool

Seven Plays of Koffi Kwahulé: In and Out of Africa,
translated by Chantal Bilodeau and Judith G. Miller
edited with Introductions by Judith G. Miller

The Rise of the African Novel:
Politics of Language, Identity, and Ownership,
by Mukoma Wa Ngugi

Black Cultural Life in South Africa:
Reception, Apartheid, and Ethics,
by Lily Saint

Nimrod: Selected Writings,
edited by Frieda Ekotto

The Postcolonial Animal

African Literature and Posthuman Ethics

Evan Maina Mwangi

University of Michigan Press
Ann Arbor

Published in the United States of America by
the University of Michigan Press
Manufactured in the United States of America
Printed on acid-free paper

First published September 2019

A CIP catalog record for this book is available from the British Library.

ISBN 978-0-472-07419-8 (hardcover : alk. paper)
ISBN 978-0-472-05419-0 (paper : alk. paper)
ISBN 978-0-472-12570-8 (ebook)

ACKNOWLEDGMENTS

To become what it is, this book has passed through the hands of many editors, anonymous readers, students, and collaborators in different institutions, and I have therefore accumulated numerous debts along the way. I would like to extend my sincere gratitude to the editors at the University of Michigan Press for seeing the potential in the project even when the manuscript needed a lot of work, as it did when they first looked at it. I would like to specially thank Ellen Bauerle, Susan Cronin, Marcia LaBrenz, and Sarah Dougherty for their support and patience throughout the revisions.

Susanna Sacks and Ari Bookman read the early drafts several times. Their comments were extremely useful in helping me answer some of the questions the project raised. Susanna painstakingly read later drafts multiple times, and I thank her for her generosity. Delali Kumavie, Ernest Waititu, Cajetan Iheka, Besi Muhonja, Serah Kasembeli, Charles Rono, and Eddie Ombagi also read various drafts of the manuscript and offered much-appreciated feedback and honest advice on how to make parts of the manuscript clearer. Delali, Scott Newman, Carla Marie Nicole Bertrand, Peter Gachanja, and Nahashon Nyangeri offered a second opinion on my translations, while Daniel Otis assisted with copyediting.

I tried out some of the ideas in this book at several institutions, including the University of Illinois at Urbana-Champaign, Stellenbosch University, Harvard University, and the University of Nairobi. I'm grateful to the seminar attendants who gave me valuable feedback about the project. Parts of the presentations and research were funded through the Carnegie African Diaspora Fellowship Program and Mellon Foundation's Critical Theory in the Global South Project. Malek Nicolas Assi graciously helped me transcribe some of the materials used here. The staffs at various libraries, especially the special collections at the Jomo Kenyatta Memorial Library at the University of Nairobi and the Melville J. Herskovits Library of African Studies at Northwestern University were extremely resourceful. I particularly want to thank Florence Mugambi and Esmeralda Kale for getting me all the materials I needed for the book.

I continue to thrive with the intellectual support of Northwestern University, where much of the book was written. The students in whose classes I taught some of the texts discussed here helped me see things in a different way through their probing questions and luminous insights. I thank Laurie Shannon, Kathy Daniels, Susan Manning, and Myriah Harris for ensuring that I got all the funding I needed to complete the book. My colleague and friend Nitasha Tamar Sharma had excellent ideas on how to make sure I was steadily writing, especially toward the end of the project.

Ernestine White, Nancy Dantas, John Peffers, Rahiem Whisgary, and Elroy Bell helped me with access to images at very short notice. I also thank Jane Alexander for the rights to use her *Butcher Boys* in the book. Wangechi Mutu also graciously allowed me to use her *Intertwined* as the cover image. Bright Gyamfi traveled all the way from Evanston to Kumasi, Ghana, to get me one of the images used in the book after trying without success to get it through other means. I thank Bright for his cheerful generosity.

Finally, special thanks to Jim Fuhr for not only lending his editing and proofreading skills to the manuscript at various stages, but for preparing the index.

I alone am responsible for any lapses and errors that readers may find in the book.

—*Evan Mwangi*
Evanston, 2018

PREFACE

The Postcolonial Animal offers an Africanist perspective on animal rights and welfare as represented in literary texts from Africa and its black diaspora. The book seeks to introduce various strands of critical animal-human studies and postcolonial African studies to one another. This is necessary because there is a paucity of studies analyzing the interface of animal studies and postcolonial studies, in spite of the shared concerns in these fields of scholarship. There is also a tendency to see animal and environmental concerns as the preserve of white writers and activists. Yet there are animals all through African literature; indeed, one of my dilemmas has been which texts to include in my discussion, because almost all African texts qualify to be part of our critical analysis. Therefore, given the pervasive presence of animality in African art, this book is not an exhaustive examination of the animal question in African literature; I only use a few examples to illustrate my claims in the hope that more studies will be done on the topic. Sometimes I allude to texts from other cultures (e.g., Māori literature) for comparative purposes.

This work grows out of both personal and academic interests. The rapid changes that a Western-style meat industry has brought to African countries have made me keenly and personally aware of the need for a marked change in how we understand and treat animals. I read expansively across African literary texts and cultural expressions to theorize from within, so that, while I engage with scholarship and cultural theory from the Global North, I also examine the philosophical positions within the African texts themselves. Rather than asking how texts represent the animal, I ask how the animal shapes texts, and I reframe the human within a broad planetary approach.

Veganism (the belief that people should not use animals in any way) is also a germane approach to the study and practice of animal rights, as we cannot genuinely claim to care for animals while killing them for food, laboratory specimens, and clothes or using them for labor and entertainment. However, I explain in chapter 1 why I have avoided imposing my veganism on my readers and the texts under analysis. Most African authors seem, at the moment, to see nothing wrong in people using animals as long as we are responsible and humane to those animals. I explain their position and recognize throughout the book the societies' gradual and encouraging espousal of less use of animals in ways that hamper an animal's right to flourish at the hands of human beings.

I have divided this book into five interrelated chapters. In the introductory chapter, I argue for the need to take seriously the representation of animals in postcolonial texts, because reading some of these texts from a perspective of existential rights offers interpretations that earlier readings had missed. The second chapter, "Re-Animating Precolonial Ecological Practices," evaluates the treatment of animals in precolonial philosophies, using the case study of *ubuntu*. I read Bessie Head's *Maru* from this perspective as suggesting that there is an innate alliance between animals and the underprivileged sections of society.

In the third chapter, "Not Yet Happily Ever After," I examine the representation of animals in certain oral performances and children's texts based on oral literature. I draw mainly from East African texts because I can access in them in their original languages. Resisting the tendency to idealize folklore, I use published works by Yuda Komora, Ngũgĩ wa Thiong'o, and Henry ole Kulet that borrow from oral narratives; these writers energetically critique human behavior toward animals by reworking traditional stories to express contemporary postcolonial conditions in Africa. Using Patrice Nganang's *Dog Days*, which is told using a dog narrator, I examine the agency that speaking animals enjoy in African texts. I argue that the authors avoid the exuberant hope of traditional oral literature to suggest to the reader the depth of the problems humans and animals face in contemporary Africa because of bad policies and poor governance.

The fourth chapter focuses on the representation of small animals in the context of natural forces such as storms and hurricanes to argue that, even when colonialists are presented as insects in anticolonial texts, the works suggest that insects should be spared violence. In that chapter, I also reexamine Charles Mungoshi's story about the killing of a crow, which is traditionally interpreted to be an anticolonial nationalist story. The vitality of small animals signifies and emphasizes that humans do not have complete control of the universe; the representation of insects as symbols of nonnormative sexuality also reveals the acceptance of the existence of these practices in societies that have suppressed nonheterosexual identities.

Chapter 5 discusses a difficult topic in postcolonial African studies: sex with animals. I am intrigued by the reticence of African texts regarding human-animal sex. I ask why these otherwise progressive works, which seek to demolish unfair binary oppositions and existential hierarchies, adopt a stance toward human-animal sex that borders on bigotry when compared with their Western and some Asian counterparts. Drawing on texts that represent interspecies sex and outlining the methodological difficulties involved in treating this transgressive sexuality, the chapter suggests that postcolonial African writers are neither opposed to animal-human intimacies per se, nor are they enamored of heteronormativity; rather, they are careful not to base human liberation on what might be considered animal abuse. These texts reject penetrative coitus only because their authors believe humans to be incapable of comprehending sexual consent among animals. In this context, I examine *The Whale Caller* by Zakes Mda of South Africa (not to be confused with *The Whale Rider* by Witi Ihimaera of New Zealand) and *Secrets* by Nuruddin Farah of Somalia, while surveying other works in which human-animal sex is suggested or portrayed

In the coda, I briefly enlist the aid of Jan Carew's *Black Midas* (1958) not only to summarize the main arguments of my book, but to appreciate the use of animals and nonhuman agents as a deus ex machina device in works from Africa and its black diasporas. In these works, animal-induced coincidences are mobilized to propel the plot forward, to resolve conflicts, and to suggest the affective power of organic and inorganic matter over human destiny.

CONTENTS

Digital materials related to this title can be found on the Fulcrum platform via the following citable URL https://doi.org/10.3998/mpub.9955521

CHAPTER 1

Being Animals, Becoming-Africa

I have no utopia to propose, no critical denunciation to proffer, no revolution to hope for.
—Bruno Latour, *Politics of Nature* (2004, 163)

In his *Game Changer* (2012), the environmentalist Glen Martin captures a mindset prevalent among European settlers in Africa. Black people like me, they contend, have no interest in animals, except when we view wild game instrumentally, in the service of our "gastronomic" functions and desires. The insinuation is that the conservation of African wildlife is best left to Western conservationists and philanthropists. To such Westerners, we are just a bunch of meat-eaters from whom animals should be protected. I personally have never had an appetite for meat, and Martin is right to laugh at Euro-Americans who have formed the opinion that Africans are carnivorously incapable of wildlife conservation. This book is intended as an appreciation of the complexities that the figure of the animal adds to contemporary African texts and to posthuman ethics embedded in the use of animal motifs in such texts. (I define "posthuman ethics" below). The book emerged from courses I taught that derived from the interface between animal studies and postcolonial literatures (texts about colonialism and its aftereffects), and in particular the representation and treatment of animals in African cultures. I developed these courses (and this book) in part to address the dearth of materials on the role of animals in contemporary postcolonial literature, a deficiency deriving from critics' preoccupations with humanistic anticolonial themes. When I first started thinking about animals in African literature, it was primarily in terms that interpret the presence of animals in a text as symbolizing human-human relations. In its current form, my book views animals as representing their own need for recognition and rights as sentient beings.

There are also parallels, especially in scholarship since the 1980s, between the treatment by humans of nonhuman others and the way colonialists view the colonized natives. Similar parallels exist between the way humans treat animals and the manner they treat human minorities. While appreciating the rich texture the figure of the animal brings to a particular narrative or poem, I use animals in African literature to consider the intersections of oppressions in the societies presented.

The purpose of this introduction is to bring together these two strains of cultural analysis—postcolonialism and animal studies—through an anticolonial rethinking of what it means to be human in African societies still grappling with the legacies of Western colonialism. Considering the paucity of systematic conversations between African literary criticism and critical animal studies, the aim of this introduction is to perform a simple and necessary task: in addition to describing the preoccupations of my book and its methodology, I seek to introduce animal studies and postcolonial studies to one other by reviewing major statements in critical animal studies and postcolonialism to pinpoint the shared interests of the two subfields. I start by interrogating the absence of black African perspectives in animal studies in general, in spite of pervasive animality in postcolonial theories and literary practices. I proceed to explain why African authors adopt an incremental approach to animal rights, as most African texts avoid radical vegan positions (those that, preliminarily defined, condemn the use of animals as a source of food, clothing, or labor of any kind). In the Western-dominated critical animal studies, such a welfarist approach to animal experiences and conditions (a perspective that accepts that we can kill animals as long as we minimize their suffering while doing so) has been criticized as reactionary.[1] I particularly elaborate on contextual issues that, in spite of myself, nudge me from such absolutist vegan responses to African literature. The next section defines the book's central terms and explains the relationship between posthumanism and postcolonialism in African contexts. I close the introduction by emphasizing a point made throughout this chapter—that we need to study animals in African literature from interdisciplinary and intersectional perspectives because the experiences of animals in these texts are analogous to the experiences of other marginalized groups in African colonies and postcolonies. Without disregarding human experiences, African writers urge us to avoid thinking about animals and the environment in ways that privilege humans at the expense of the nonhuman others. Therefore, considering animals in African literature does not mean that we overlook human beings, because the authors use animals not only to meditate on the rights of nonhuman others, but to disrupt established or persecutory frameworks of power among humans in the societies depicted.

The Postcolonial Animal becomes, then, a way of refiguring both the animal and the human, in a postcolonial context, against European traditions of humanist thought. I view postcolonial African writing through a posthuman lens to reject humanist ideals that failed to incorporate the African subject. Instead, posthumanism allows us to take a position that rejects anthropocentrism and the attendant human hierarchies. *The Postcolonial Animal* seeks to uncover noncolonial attitudes toward, and responses to, animality in African literary texts as part of a broader project to account for entwined, planetary problems created through anthropocentric thought. Bringing together postcolonial, posthumanist, and animal studies helps us engage with alternative approaches to the animal, decentering the human in our worldviews.

Readers will notice my indebtedness to Rosi Braidotti's idea of the posthuman. However, to me, posthuman Africa is not a postindustrial utopia teeming with such artificialities as robots, genetically modified bodies, or military drones, as posthumanism would be in Western contexts. Most of the African societies discussed here do not have such technologies, though a few science fiction writers (e.g., Nnedi Okorafor and Lauren Beukes) have started to imagine their potential use. Therefore, I use the figure of the animal in African folktales, religious texts, philosophy, and anticolonial statements, as well as literary sources, to argue for an ethos that calls into question all thought systems based on human primacy over nature. In my view, postcolonial African writing is particularly well suited to this type of investigation, for three reasons. First, archival resources for postcolonial animal studies as practiced in the Western academy today are limited; the archives are comprised primarily and predictably of writings by white authors. Second, the Western definition of "human" has underwritten colonization and exploitation. And third, contemporary ecological writing tends either to celebrate the flora and fauna of the Global South while demonizing its human residents or to uncritically idealize "natives" as perfect environmentalists. My approach to African literary texts helps to position postcolonial studies at the interface of ecology, globalism, ethics, and representation.

THE ABSENCE OF AFRICANS IN ANIMAL STUDIES, OR AFRICANS AS NONHUMAN HUMANS

I write this book against a background of stereotypes circulating in African societies about animal rights activists as hypocrites and mostly white racists who pretend to love animals to assuage their guilt for hating fellow humans, especially to mask their deeply ingrained dislike for black people with a façade of philanthropic animal welfare causes. Animal rights concerns are misrepresented as the preserve of affluent white people and their elite black lackeys trying to use the plight of animals to raise funds from gullible Western human-hating animal-lovers.[2] The primary aim of this book is to expand the canon of human-animal studies by including rarely read African texts. But beyond that, given the complaints that the animal rights movement replicates within itself some of the hierarchies it seeks to dismantle (Deckha 2018, 280; Greenebaum 2016, 358; Harper 2010, 5; Nocella 2012, 142), it is time we considered human-animal studies from perspectives other than those of predominantly white authors in order to appreciate the different ways African texts demonstrate the intricate interconnectedness between humans and nonhumans and how the authors acknowledge indigenous societies' innate capacity to change.

Animals occupy a central place in African everyday life and in the African definition of the human. While he notes that animal motifs are present in other cultures, Allen F. Roberts remarks on their preponderance in African contexts: "Zoomorphic imagery still appears in a great many contexts of leadership, healing, divination, problem-solving, rites of passage, and rituals. Animal allusions are woven or dyed into the patterns of women's fabrics . . . , incised on pots, scarified on bodies, braided into hair, and painted into houses" (1995, 6). In these cultures, Roberts further notes, animals are used as mirrors of the human in identity formation, as they are similar to humans yet at the same time different from us. They are also "common subjects of both verbal and visual arts, often portrayed in dynamic interactions as a comment on the nature of social relationships" (Roberts 1995, 176). However, despite the centrality of animals in much of African writing and in key texts of postcolonial theory, African literature and African thinkers remain conspicuously absent from the field of animal studies. Critics seem to believe that focusing on animals tends to stereotype Africa as the symbol of uncultivated nature vis-à-vis the West as the epitome of civilization and culture. In fact, Philip Armstrong has speculated that postcolonial studies' apparent lack of concern for animal studies derives from an impression prevalent among its scholars that "pursuing an interest in the postcolonial animal risks trivializing the suffering of human beings under colonialism" (2002, 413).[3] I have proposed an intersectional approach that addresses this fear by showing that African literary texts regard human and animal interests to be intertwined.

It remains a fact that critics have focused on postcolonial studies' interests in other forms of oppression, ignoring the elision of the animal in a field that seeks to expose power differentials occasioned by European colonialism.[4] Yet there is a rich body of literature on the colonialist projection of animality on non-Western cultures. Such works include canons of postcolonial theory (e.g., Edward Said's *Orientalism*, Aimé Césaire's *Discourse on Colonialism*, and Frantz Fanon's *Black Skin, White Masks*). It is animal studies scholars who, by focusing only on texts of Western high modernism, have ignored the postcolonial animal. Even when Western animal-studies scholars consider work from postcolonial societies, they see only white writers, such as J. M. Coetzee and Barbara Gowdy.[5] But as Maneesha Deckha observes, race and colonialism are deeply imbricated in the animalization of the colonized. Comparing colonial subjects to animals "helped justify imperial land seizure, eugenics, and other 'civilizing projects,'" as "violence was enacted against colonized human beings through the differentiating logic of animalization, racialization, and dehumanization" (Deckha 2012, 539). Under colonialism, the "cultivation of ideas of race, culture, gender, and species was thus interactive and mutually constitutive" (Deckha 2008, 252).[6] Deckha (2012) is right to point out that the West, even today, stereotypes non-Western cultures as insensitive to animals while continuing its own violence against nonhuman others. Therefore, what needs attention today is not the use of animals in Western cultures to figure non-Western subjects in colonialist high modernism, but how African postcolonial cultures, for example, have used animals to address their hopes and anxieties and, furthermore, to address the rights of animals in the real world.

To demonstrate how recognition of the intersections of animalization and colonialism have been at the heart of anticolonial African writing, let us consider two quick examples from classical postcolonial theoretical texts, both published in French in the 1950s: Albert Memmi's *The Colonizer and the Colonized*, first published in 1957, and Frantz Fanon's *Black Skin, White Masks*, first published in 1952. In these works, postcolonial theorists recognize Western colonial thinking as based on what Agamben (2004) calls an "anthropological machine," in which the concept of the human is established by setting a human being against the animal. In such schematization, the West is seen as privileged space for the production of the human, whereas non-Western subjects are considered animals in human form.[7] In this scheme of things, to use Syl Ko's language, the African is a "nonhuman human," a being that is not quite human (2017, 85). Suggesting this crisis of humanity, in which nonwhite people under racist colonialism are excluded from the realm of the human, Fanon shows the damage that such antihumanism has done to the colonized subject. To Fanon, the colonized can only regain their humanity through violence against the colonizer who has reduced them to animal status. The alleged animality is associated with other negative terms of reference: "The Negro is an animal, the Negro is bad, the Negro is wicked, the Negro is ugly" (Fanon 2008 [1952], 93). This statement imitates the stream of consciousness of a colonialist's child afraid of black people because "the Negro's going to eat me" (93). Throughout the treatise, Fanon demonstrates how "the white man is convinced that the black man is an animal" (147). One of the tactics that the colonized use to restore their humanity, as we shall see, is to use animals as allies against the violence of colonialism without animalizing the colonialists to justify causing harm to the animals used as avatars of the colonizer.

Like Fanon, Memmi emphasizes the naturalizing tendencies of colonialism, in which race is used to rationalize the dehumanization of the colonized: "To observe the life of the colonizer and the colonized is to discover rapidly that the daily humiliation of the colonized, his objective subjugation, are [sic] not merely economic. Even the poorest colonizer thought himself to be superior to the colonized" (1965 [1957], xii). Memmi also recognizes that, as a form of advanced capitalism, imperialism is primarily exploitative: "A qualified worker existing among the colonizers earns three or four times more than does the colonized, while he does not produce three or four times as much, either in quantity or in quality" (1965 [1957], 80). This need to exploit the colonized feeds into the ultimate animalization of the nonwhite subjects. For Memmi, "the traits ascribed to the colonized are incompatible with one another, though this does not bother his prosecutor" (1965 [1957], 83). The colonizer systematically dehumanizes the colonized because "one does not have a serious obligation toward an animal or an object" (86). Animalization is not just metaphorical; it is also physical. The natives are "driven like game toward huge cages," producing an occasion for humor to a colonial journalist; the journalist does not question any of this because "the spectacle had contained nothing human" (Memmi 1965 [1957], 83). In this context, it is not surprising that postcolonial literature uses the animal as a cultural signifier, both as a metaphor of the condition of the colonized and as an ally against colonial antihumanism.[8]

While it is tempting to focus, as Memmi and Fanon do, on the animal as negating humanity, I resist those readings to emphasize the animal as a figure for resistance and alternative social formations. In this sense, I claim an affirmative response to these texts and the animals in them. I view affirmative readings of African literature as those that, while interpreting dark texts, do not degenerate into nihilist promotions of racism, speciesism, misogyny, ableism, homophobia, and/or environmental degradation. They might acknowledge positive liberation in an anticapitalist nationalist statement against colonialism but criticize the same statement if it radiates gender bias, homophobia, or discrimination against animals.

THE VEGAN UNCONSCIOUS

We cannot engage with animal rights fully without considering the question of veganism, the belief that humans should not use animals in any way, including as food, laboratory specimens, entertainment in zoos and circuses, or in making clothes. But this concept needs to be put in African contexts to be useful in the study of African literature, where the texts do not even openly espouse vegetarianism (where animals can be used, except as a source of meat). Coined in 1944 by Donald Watson and Elsie Shrigley (cofounders of the Vegan Society) to name a nondairy vegetarian diet (Bulliet 2005, 16), the term "vegan" was defined later by Leslie Cross to stand for "the principle of the emancipation of animals from exploitation by man" (Cross 1949, 16). When the Vegan Society was registered in 1979, its Memorandum of Association defined veganism as a "philosophy and way of living which seeks to exclude—as far as is possible and practicable—all forms of exploitation of, and cruelty to, animals for food, clothing or any other purpose; and by extension, promotes the development and use of animal-free alternatives for the benefit of humans, animals and the environment. In dietary terms, it denotes the practice of dispensing with all products derived wholly or partly from animals."[9] From this definition, it is apparent that veganism recognizes itself as aspirational and it considers the practicability of some of its proposals. I will consider the practicability of its tenets when assessing the treatment of animals in the African societies presented in the texts.

The animal rights theorist pattrice jones encourages us to see "veganism as potentially a central component of decolonization" (2010, 197). To jones, it is the most marginalized people (e.g., black lesbians, in her case) who would most passionately embrace practices such as veganism that consciously avoid harming other groups as much as possible. Yet of the authors I discuss in this book, only two—J. M. Coetzee and Benjamin Zephaniah—openly embrace veganism. Most of the other anticolonial African writers and literary critics see nothing wrong in Africans eating meat for ceremonial, ritual, and dietary reasons. They only call for fair treatment of animals and the conservation of the environment to allow the animals to flourish so that humans can have an ample supply of meat, milk, and skins the next time we need these animal products. Therefore, strictly speaking, few African texts are vegan. In fact, when starting to write this book, I did not know what the word "vegan" meant. I became aware of the concept way into the third draft when reviewing work related to mine. I looked around, but I could not find African-language equivalents of "vegan."[10] Most of my readers at that time (mainly students and colleagues in US and African universities) viscerally resisted my use of the term. They found it inappropriate in African contexts. I see their point and I will not impose my veganism on the texts under analysis for reasons I outline below.

Although they do not openly advocate vegan ethics, African authors grapple with the possibilities of alternatives to meat eating and encourage us to minimize animal suffering as much as possible. That is, postcolonial animal-consuming cultures are presented in African texts as shifting toward an embrace of cultural and political practices that avoid the use of animals. The texts suggest that, as readers, our duty is to accelerate the process, as the societies are themselves evolving toward it in discrete actions that condition other interrelated processes. We see this, for example, in Wangari Muta Maathai's memoir *Unbowed* (2006). A veterinarian by training, Wangari was better known for her work at the Greenbelt Movement than as an advocate of animal rights. She led the grassroots environmental conservation group, established in 1977, to plant over fifty-one million trees in her native Kenya. She was the first East African woman to earn a doctoral degree and the first African woman Nobel Peace Prize winner. In certain passages in her memoir, Wangari signals a personal and communal evolution toward a vegan ethics, even if she is more concerned with preserving plants than animals. The society she presents to the reader is governed by a vegan unconscious. I use this term in a way that parallels what Caminero-Santangelo, following Lawrence

Buell, has termed "environmental unconscious" (Caminero-Santangelo 2014, 113).[11] While Buell (2001) views the environmental unconscious as an expression of a lack of awareness of the need to conserve the environment, we can understand the vegan unconscious as an affirmative expression of potential. That is, there is a latent possibility that the societies portrayed in the text will embrace a future where animals will not be killed to satisfy human needs. They suggest that the society advocates sparing animals from being exploited, especially being indiscriminately killed for food. In *Unbowed,* Maathai suggests that modernity and forest conservation go hand in hand with vegan ethics. One interesting passage describes her earliest days in school: "I had a slate, an exercise book, and a pencil to write with and a simple bag made from animal skin. Later on, my uncle gave me a cotton bag from the shop he owned" (Maathai 2006, 40). As she enters deeper into the vestibule to modernity that formal education symbolizes, Wangari abandons the use of animal products. It may not be a conscious vegan choice on the young Wangari's part; it simply appears to have been the natural thing to do.

Although *nyama choma* (roast beef) remains a popular food item in Wangari Maathai's Kenya, she suggests that veganism is a potential force in the community that she depicts. Earlier in the autobiography, we see her society evolving from the wearing clothes made from animal skins as it ushers in the modern era: "as the crops changed, so did the tools used for agriculture and cooking: corrugated iron posts replaced earthen ones, plates and cups replaced calabashes, spoons replaced fingers and sticks. Clothes of animal skin were put aside in favor of cotton dresses for women and shirts, shorts, and trousers for men" (Maathai 2006, 11). The syntactical parallelism used to describe the replacement of nonanimal implements and cutlery is replicated when she writes about the replacement of animal-skin clothes with cotton clothing. This demonstrates a natural progression of the community away from the unnecessary consumption of animals. In the autobiography, Wangari Maathai criticizes modern lifestyles that have led to the destruction of habitats, and the abandonment of these forms of animal exploitation is not something she regrets.

Most texts analyzed here tend to imagine a world where animals are not abused or used as a source of food, clothing, or labor. I interrogate the texts for instruction in how we might act responsibly and how we should relate to others (including nonhuman others) to ensure a world free of oppression, a world in which humans do not use animal products or services. I distance myself from Western approaches that fetishize human-like higher sentience in animals. The African texts I examine suggest that respect for animals should not be based on whether they share human traits; it should be based on the need to create an equitable world where even those who are utterly foreign to us are accorded respect. The result is a world where we recognize the rights of all marginalized groups, including all animals, regardless of the level of their sentience. To borrow from Edward Said in *Culture and Imperialism* (1993), Caliban, in recognition of the interconnectedness of various forms of oppression, speaks for all the subjugated subaltern categories in society (women, queer, ethnic minorities, outcasts, the disabled, the impoverished, nonhuman animals, etc.). In calling on postcolonial scholars to take on Caliban's mantle, Said notes the dangers of the identitarian privileging of one group over another: "The dangers of chauvinism and xenophobia ('Africa for Africans') are very real. In ideal circumstances, Caliban sees his own history as an aspect of the history of *all* subjugated men and women, and comprehends the complex truth of his own social and historical situations" (Said 1993, 210). Said offers a strong case for the need of the intellectual to speak on behalf of the subjugated groups.[12] It is also apparent from his position that postcolonial critics should condemn any efforts to achieve the rights of one group at the expense of those in any of the other groups. A good feminist cannot support colonialism. Nor could I praise neoimperialist support of animal rights in order to justify the dispossession and denigration of local communities.

AGAINST ETHICAL ABSOLUTISM

Killing of animals has deep symbolic value in Africa, as the rituals are not only aesthetic and anticolonial but they connect the living with the dead (Éla 2009 [1988], 20; Shipton 2007, 188). In such contexts, to abandon animal sacrifices is to accept the colonial erasure of African cultures. Going by Michael Glover's account of objections to attempts in 2015 to introduce veganism in a South African institution, where such traditional practices as the Zulu *Ukweshwama* (animal ritual sacrifices to celebrate a new harvest) are still held dear by the black majorities, veganism can in some situations be seen as an "inherently racist" imposition on black Africans if vegan advocacy models ignore cultural contexts (2017, 185). Therefore, I would like to explain further why we need to contextualize veganism in African literary studies, especially considering the socioeconomic facts in the societies depicted in literary texts and the emergent research that shows plants to also be sentient, even if not to the same level as animals. While Kathryn Paxton George (1994; 2000) regards vegetarianism as a Western practice that Euro-Americans should not impose on non-Western subjects, I grew up almost completely vegan in rural Kenya, not for any ethical reasons but just because I don't like the taste of animal products (I could tolerate only beef, which wasn't very available in my peasant family).[13] I was unaware until recently that as a vegan I need to take supplements to stay healthy. I wrote some of the earlier drafts of this book while ill and fatigued, needlessly fearing that the book would be my last. For a while, I foolishly avoided seeing the doctor I had been referred to, because her online profile indicated that she was a specialist in a terminal illness that my diagnoses mimicked. However, mine was a simple case of B12 deficiency that was cured with a single vitamin shot. I was well within ten minutes, and I experienced a world I had missed for much of my life. I know that some of the life-and-death medications people take are not vegan. I am also aware that the vitamin B12 supplements I take cost five times more in Nairobi than in Chicago, that they are sold in upscale specialist stores, and that I could probably not afford them if I were still teaching in a Kenyan university. And as Lori Gruen and Robert C. Jones (2016) urge us to remember, veganism is an aspiration; the fruits, vegetables, and grains I eat in an American city in the age of late capitalism are produced using methods that involve the killing or harming rodents and insects. The flu shot I got this morning is not vegan (the nurse talked about allergies to eggs), and its "vegan" alternative, I learn, is made from insects—and is not yet available. This means that as I write this sentence, nonvegan substances are circulating in my body. Therefore, I must avoid an absolutist stance: becoming-vegan should be considered aspirational, a process rather than an end in itself.

After watching, in disbelief, the spread into African nations of Western practices of industrial animal breeding, I am now convinced that veganism should be practiced ethically. Why then do I condone texts that fall short of a radical rejection of meat-eating and that promote welfarist utilitarian attitudes, whereby the authors of such texts accept the society's use of animals as long as the customs or practices governing animal use are allegedly humane and sustainable? In accepting this difficult position, I put into consideration the reality that African writers are aware that it is counterproductive to hector people who have been denied their rights to be vegan or equating them with villains of the Western world because they use animal products. Through my analysis of African texts, my main interest here is to encourage compassionate treatment of animals in their natural environments and to assert that animals have the moral right not to be killed and eaten or otherwise consumed. Although I am aware of the criticism of the low-bar tolerance approach to minority issues, I accept what I would call the bare minimum for marginalized groups. In this paradigm, we first agree, despite differences of opinion, that animals in the postcolonial world deserve as much respect for their intrinsic worth as we accord to other members of the planetary environment.[14] My near-term acceptance of the basic minimum is not a problematic position to take in an African context because most African societies reject violence against animals. In addition, putting animals to work in literary representations comes with qualifications about the uses that animals should be put to in general. W. J. T. Mitchell (2003, ix–x) has noted the "resistance and anxiety" aroused by calls for animal rights, but such anxieties are absent in postcolonial literature and theory, most of which—with the exception of a few works such as Jomo Kenyatta's *Facing Mount Kenya*—advocate the humane treatment of both animals and the environment. Even if close readings of this literature sometimes reveal uncomfortable subtexts of self-righteousness among the conservationist characters or a misplaced understanding of animals, environmental degradation is largely seen to be exported from the West into Africa through imperialism and its destructive technologies.

Anthropologists such as Gabriel Bannerman-Richter (1982) and Adam Ashforth (2005) have independently demonstrated that personhood, in everyday African life, involves relations not only with and among human individuals, but with a large set of visible and invisible beings (e.g., water, plants, rocks, the landscape, animals, soil, minerals, spirits). That is, a human being is interconnected with agencies inherent in substances, animals, images, and objects. These nonhuman others may be real, imaginary, or mythic but they fundamentally destabilize the dualistic view of animals vs. humans that is privileged in Western societies.[15] This is not to say that animals in African societies live in perfect harmony with humans, but the animal/human divide found in Western societies is much more porous in African cultures.

The instability of the animal/human dichotomy is seen in such configurations as, for example, the man-leopards of Central and West Africa, which Deleuze and Guattari include in the list of ways of "becoming animal" in black Africa (1987, 247). Western writers (e.g., Edgar Rice Burroughs in his 1935 *Tarzan and the Leopard Men*) depicts the practice of humans imitating animals as an expression of innate African atavism. However, African writers such as Chinua Achebe in *No Longer at Ease* (1960) regard the Western fascination with such cults as serving a civilizing colonialist agenda "to bring light to the heart of darkness, to tribal headhunters performing weird ceremonies and unspeakable rites" (121).[16] Although documented in historical and anthropological texts, Achebe goes so far as to suggest that such cultic behaviors are figments of a racist imagination.[17] Their absence in African literature can therefore be read as writers attempting to avoid reinforcing Western stereotypes of African societies as practitioners of violent human sacrifices. Whatever the case, we should point out that figures such as the men-leopards do not represent benevolence in the nonhuman animal they identify with in occult practices. They imagine the leopard to be destructive and malevolent toward humans, and they imitate it to destroy fellow human beings, not necessarily to protect actual leopards. As I show in the next chapter, in African societies, the leopard and other ferocious animals are seen as part of human life, not as destructive, as the leopard-men imagine them to be.

This book moves beyond questions of representation to develop animal-oriented perspectives on postcolonial narratives. Considering the entanglements of oppressions, I therefore ask: What new interpretations are available to critics who consider animal rights in the readings of African cultural texts? What theoretical advantages might we obtain from reading African and postcolonial cultural practices using a posthuman prism?[18] What would critical human-animal studies be like if we considered African writers and their colleagues from the Global South, not just the studies a few white authors that animal studies scholars usually base their analysis on? What would the humanities look like if we incorporated postcolonial animal studies, and what methodological challenges should we expect when engaging in such a project? African criticism itself would also benefit from posthuman ethics that shifts focus from a postcolonial version of the European Man to marginalized groups within postindependence African nations. As currently practiced, postcolonial criticism is largely interested in either nationalist (vis-à-vis colonialist) writing or is limited to transnational flows among diverse postcolonial African elites.[19] The nonhuman animal and locally produced texts about human-animal relations are rarely part of postcolonial scholarship.

ANIMAL RIGHTS IN CONTEXT

Related to the concerns above is the need to put animal rights in African contexts without using African cultural values to justify continued mistreatment of animals, as African literary texts prepare us to expect those cultural values to be dynamic and responsive to changes and new knowledges. Some young Kenyans with whom I shared the claims in this book asked me tough questions that I probably have not fully answered, but that have affected my outlook in analyzing African literary texts. The questions had to do with poverty in African societies and the essential nature of carnivores. Can we convince a poor man in a Nairobi slum, for example, to stop wearing his only pair of shoes, bought from a second-hand dealer who imports such old shoes from Western societies after they have been thrown away by their original users, just because those shoes are not vegan? Would a pastoralist who owns only one goat and has no formal employment be ready to get rid of that goat because it is against vegan ethics to keep animals? Richard Twine (2014) advises us not to universalize veganism because "there is much diversity within veganism and it should not be assumed it is always a choice of nonviolence" (192). I have suggested that my hesitation to adopt an absolutist position is that I recognize that one cannot be completely vegan. Although abolitionists such as Gary Francione are opposed to incremental changes and would prefer an immediate stoppage of the consumption of animal products, I have avoided such a militant approach because it is also likely to backfire in postcolonial societies. I have adopted Chris Abani's sentiment, expressed in a TED talk, that "the world is never saved in grand messianic gestures, but in the simple accumulation of gentle, soft, almost invisible acts of compassion" (2008). Attempts to impose radical changes on African societies are likely to flop, especially if they are enforced from outside or by the elites. African literary texts suggest that the changes need to be gradual and carefully negotiated. Instead of telling our hypothetical leather-wearing poor man to throw away his shoes and belt, we could ask him to ensure that the next jacket, belt, and pair of shoes he buys are vegan. Small gestures such as avoiding eating animals might be more effective as a start.[20]

If the man has a carnivorous pet (e.g., a dog), should he feed it on *sukumawiki* (kale) to avoid the killing of animals that such a pet would have to be fed on? Should we compel other animals to be vegan? What if animal products are from an animal that has died of natural causes, not killed by selfish humans? Novels such as Nganang's *Dog Days* suggest that it is unethical to force carnivorous animals to be vegetarian. For the time being, I think it is best to work toward stopping all human consumption of animal products, whether the animals died of natural causes or through an accident. It is hard to verify how the animal whose products we use died, especially if the products are bought from the mass market. Following Rosa Luxemburg's Marxism, Rosi Braidotti has abundantly shown us the cunning ways that advanced capitalism uses to naturalize everything. If we allow capitalism some wiggle room regarding the human use of animals as a source of food, it will generate situations that create the impression that the animals die in the humane way we want them to die.[21]

The skeptical readers also asked me: if, as I demonstrate in this book, some texts, such as Ngũgĩ's *Njamba Nene and the Flying Bus* and Jan Carew's *Black Midas*, suggest that plants are as sentient as animals, don't we need to stop eating altogether and starve ourselves to death and extinction, instead of victimizing plants in an ontological dualism that prioritizes animals over nonanimals? Indeed, several theorists have noted that nonanimals should be treated with as much respect as animals. For example, discussing the sensations of plants that enable some of them to defend themselves from predators, Catriona Sandilands observes that "understanding plants as part of the complex enmeshments of biopolitics allows us to consider not only the ways in which plants are treated as objects of various forms of extraction, production, consumption, and manipulation, but also the ways in which different plants' specific capacities are a crucial part of their diverse involvements in the multispecies relations of, say, imperial display and neo-liberal exchange (giant water lilies and petunias do particular things in particular contexts; so do corn, kudzu, and clover)" (2016, 228–29).[22] The fact that we cannot solve all the problems in the world does not mean we should not try to solve those that we can at the moment. There are no life-sustaining alternatives to not eating at all yet, but at least it is easy to find replacements for things we misuse animals to achieve (e.g., food, labor, clothing, entertainment, etc.) and leave animals to flourish in their natural environment. In my discussion, I have avoided the argument that the reason we should not mistreat animals is because they are similar to us. Although it is hard to eliminate one form of oppression, it does not mean that we should allow other oppressive practices to continue.

RETAINING THE "HUMAN" IN AFRICAN POSTHUMANISM

I use the term "posthuman" in an affirmative way, building on Rosi Braidotti's use of the term to express the demise of a humanism in which most African subjects have never been included.[23] Her mobilization of the term goes further than "antihumanism," the poststructuralist demonstration of the decline of humanist moral ideals of man in the wake of genocides, world wars, and intense anti-Semitism. Seeking to conceptualize the human subject without privileging humans, Braidotti's approach not only seeks to bring on board categories that capital-letter Humanism of the West has strategically left out or treated with disdain, entities such as "non-white, non-masculine, non-normal, non-young, non-healthy, disabled, malformed or enhanced peoples." It also collapses ontological divides between humans and the rest of the cosmos, including animals, plants, and nature (2013b, 67).[24] Therefore, marginalized Africans are part of the posthuman as I, following Braidotti, conceive it.

Treating "zoomorphic others" as genuine subjects requires a close connection to the social world they inhabit. Of the three elements that Jill Didur (2003) has identified as constituting posthumanism, I am only peripherally interested here in techno-scientific and transgenetic transformations, because the ontological flesh-and-blood animal question is remote from those texts' central themes. As such novels as Zakes Mda's *The Whale Caller* demonstrate, technology is an extension of the capitalist enhancement of human exceptionalism and the human mastery of nature, not a regenerative disruption of man/machine dualism that Jill Didur's formulation of posthumanism assumes. I therefore focus on Didur's other tenets of posthumanism: the recognition that the arbitrary human/animal and nature/culture ontological binaries, used to rationalize the killability of nonhuman others, are untenable; and that humanism, which materially, discursively, and institutionally regards the human species as unique, distinct, and exceptional, can no longer serve as an ethical model for the way we relate to nonhuman others.

In postcolonial cultures, nonhuman animals are bound up with larger historical issues, such that it is difficult to consider the animals seriously without considering human conditions as well. The available criticism centered on animals does not treat them as hermetically separate categories; they are tied to human concerns and predicaments. For example, Jennifer Wenzel demonstrates aptly the human-animal interrelation in *Bullet Proof* (2009b), in which she reads from an interdisciplinary perspective how the Xhosa culture relies on animals for its economic, political, and spiritual existence. She shows that events of the past involving killing cattle to cleanse the land of colonialism imbricate with the later anti-colonial struggles. From her reading, it is clear that history is as open-ended as the boundary between humans and their nonhuman environment is porous. If one uses a methodology similar to Wenzel's in reading the animal figure in postcolonial literature, it would be difficult to separate animal issues from larger ecological and political concerns. Such an interdisciplinary approach also ensures that we do not ignore the conditions of real animals as we study the artistic representations of nonhuman others.

It is in recognizing the need for interdisciplinary engagement with texts that students of nonhuman others, such as Byron Caminero-Santangelo, insist on a holistic reading of texts to consider sociopolitical human conditions signaled in the representation of the nonhuman others. Constructing an African ecocritical reading, Caminero-Santangelo notes that, unlike in Western ecocritical visions of the world, the environment in formerly colonized societies cannot be divorced from human existence: "Concerns with environmental policy are couched in terms of their connections with economic inequality, social justice, and political rights and in terms of how they impact lives—the homes, livelihoods, and health—of the impoverished and disenfranchised" (2014, 7). In the same vein, the study of animal interests should not be at the expense of the powerless in postcolonial societies. Postcolonial texts suggest an intricate relationship between the powerless and the nonhuman others. What we should be careful about is not that we can easily ignore the human in reading animals; more immediate is that we might treat animals as mere appendages of the human, whereby they primarily serve human interests as analogues of human predicaments without interests of their own in the real world.

I discuss interspecies intimacies in chapter 5, but it is worth noting in a preliminary way that postcolonial artistic expression emphasizes interdependence in ways that undermine the human/animal binary. Take, for example, Wangechi Mutu's *Intertwined*, a collage and watercolor on paper that suggests interspecies interdependence as well as interdependence of sexual orientations. In this painting, Wangechi Mutu imagines animals that are also humans and vice versa. Here the portrayal of positive emotions suggests negative ones as well. The protruding tongues may evoke in the human contemplator fear of the animal's greed, but they also symbolize erogenous desire for one another, as their sexuality is fluid, and it is suggested that they enjoy a same-sex erotic attachment. The relationship seems interracial and possibly interspecies. One wears clothes and the other does not. This calls attention to their hybridization of different modes of living. The leggings one of the animals wears recall a giraffe and a cobra at once in ways that gesture to the proliferation of identities in a single being. We are also reminded that what could have brought such animals into existence is sex taboo between humans

Figure 1: Wangechi Mutu, *Intertwined*, 2003. Collage and watercolor on paper 20 x 16 in. Courtesy of the Artist and Susanne Vielmetter Los Angeles Projects.

and other species. The animals are ready to shake up the ontological binaries that divide one species from another.

In the rural Kenya where I grew up, I not only interacted with domestic animals daily but I occasionally shared my bedroom with goats and sheep, a common practice in African societies (Maathai 2010, 52). Indeed, in most of Africa, fences that separate animals from human beings are a Western invention. Therefore, any approach to animal rights and animal studies that ignores the human is deficient in African literary studies. In fact, the European who comes to Africa to see animals without regard for Africans is a common source of ridicule in African texts.[25] One of the reasons Africanists are wary of the term "posthuman" is that it poses the risk of scholars downplaying the importance of humanity in a Eurocentric approach that creates unnecessary binaries between humans and animals.[26] The animal question will need to be looked at alongside the problems facing human minorities because of the shared vulnerability among animals and marginalized social groups. I do not seek to partition human from posthuman considerations; rather, I am interested in how the conception of the human is linked to the presentation of nonhuman agents in cultural texts or that of interspecies relationships between humans and nonhumans. In critiquing humanist ideals, Braidotti does not seek to dehumanize people; in her view, "to be posthuman does not mean to be indifferent to the humans, or to be de-humanized" (2013, 190). She rejects the cynical antihumanism of advanced capitalism that uses emerging technologies (e.g., drones) for the destruction of human life.[27] It is important to note Braidotti's insistence on new normative values that reject the privileging of human beings; she recuperates humanness and criticizes the forces that destroy life forms for profit.[28] Despite the anthropocentrism that governs environmental practices in Africa, as Kai Horsthemke ably illustrates in *Animals and African Ethics* (2015), postcolonial African literature demonstrates that societies that tend toward environmental ethics also consider the rights of animals. In the Anthropocene (the era that began when humans developed capabilities to alter geologically significant conditions and processes), we, as humans, should accept responsibility for having destroyed the environment and be ready to rectify the current condition as humans, not as some science-fiction ethereal beings yet to exist in this world.[29] Therefore, posthumanism includes the human, nonhuman animals, and the planet as a whole.

IS THE "POST" IN "POSTCOLONIAL" THE "POST" IN "POSTHUMAN"?

The engagement with posthumanism in African literature, particularly as it stands against European humanist thinking, naturally evokes postcolonialism. However, their temporal positions and theoretical investments may conflict with one another, forcing us to ask how their "post" investments relate. Therefore, I must clarify the relationship between the "post" in "posthuman" and the "post" in "postcolonial," especially in the wake of Braidotti's pronouncements against postmodernism, and Gary Steiner's eloquent critique of postmodernism as being incapable of offering firm ethical positions on the moral status of nonhuman animals that derive from its fascination with ambivalence and indeterminacy. Steiner disapproves of literary critics in North American institutions, including the animal studies stalwart Cary Wolfe, who use Derridean deconstruction to disavow ethics in the study of animals. Steiner views postmodernism as lacking coherence because of its commitment to irreconcilable positions: a "commitment to the indeterminacy of meaning and a sense of justice that presupposes the very access of determinacy that postmodern epistemology dismisses as illusory" (2013, 4). For Steiner, postmodernism privileges aporia and evasiveness toward the simple recognition that "we *ought* to care for other beings who share the condition of mortality with us" (2013, 166). However, most of the postcolonial African texts that use animal motifs are experimental, revealing an affinity with vagueness and opposition to closure or a monochromatic vision.[30]

The ethical positions of these texts are rarely clear, as the texts are open-ended and raise multiple possibilities without directly determining the issues under debate. While many animal rights activists would be frustrated by such ambivalence, ambiguity, paradoxes, contradictions, and vagueness, I am prepared to accept the protocols of the genres I am dealing with and concede that a creative writer does not have to illustrate a moral argument in glib didactic statements. Granted, most postcolonial theorists share a view similar to Steiner's. While recognizing postmodern elements in postcolonial literature, they also feel that the postmodern emphasis on semantic slippage and linguistic play erodes the power of literature to transform the material circumstances of the oppressed or undermines a recognition of the gritty realities of horrors and resistance as depicted in art. The "post" in "postcolonial," as Kwame Anthony Appiah urges us to understand, is nuanced differently from the "post" in "postmodernism," as postcolonial writers meld postmodernism with a depiction of the realities of colonialism.[31]

Braidotti also raises the issue of an unnecessary duality between language and materiality, and in so doing too hastily rules out signification from the constitution of the posthuman. In her view, "the posthuman subject is not postmodern, because it does not rely on any anti-foundationalist premises. Nor is it poststructuralist, because it does not function within the linguistic turn or other forms of deconstruction. Not being framed by the ineluctable powers of signification, it is consequently not condemned to seek adequate representation of its existence within a system that is constitutionally incapable of granting due recognition" (Braidotti 2013b, 188). These concepts celebrate experiences that those subjected to European colonialism would abhor, yet scholars from these communities find some aspects of those descriptions useful for analyzing specific cultural expressions.[32] Similarly, poststructuralism is far removed from the antithetical critiques of liberalism.[33] It can be repurposed so that cohesion or solidarity among denigrated groups does not become equated, to use Katerina Kolozova's (2014) words, with "totality, fixity, and exclusiveness" (20) or with "fixedness, stability, and continuity (non-transformability)" (79).[34] What Braidotti rejects in her disapproval of deconstruction is overcorrection, wherein we critique a unitary subjectivity in such a way that reality and solidarity become "bad words" that intimate "oppressive political values" (Kolozova 2014, 79). In my view, then, it is possible to examine morally ambivalent texts ethically by reading them against the grain to recover the experiences of the oppressed subjects they portray.[35]

It is essential that we read affirmatively, because even the most seemingly progressive texts often contain ethically ambivalent nuances. Writing about a rich range of texts from East Asia, Karen Thornber (2012) has detected ambiguities and paradoxes about nature in texts that purport to advance green politics. She notes that "creative writing often makes matters more confusing by remaining silent about its uncertainties: many narrators and characters are unaware of the discrepancies they depict or exhibit" (434).[36] Like Thornber, I consider it axiomatic that it is in the nature and even the responsibility of literature to call attention to human contradictions about the nonhuman world, and to do so through dramatic irony, paradoxes, and ambiguities.[37] In the postcolonial world of Chinua Achebe, Ayi Kwei Armah, and Ngũgĩ wa Thiong'o, however, such experimental vagueness is a solipsistic exercise that any serious writer can ill afford. The stylistic experiments are regarded as art for art's sake, which Achebe declared to be "deodorized dog-shit" (1975, 19). Indeed, only a member of privileged groups would derive pleasure from a work that is ambivalent about rape, racism, and discrimination against individuals with disability, or that is in sympathy with characters who perpetrate such evils.

So far, it might be clear in this book that I am governed, in a new materialist context, by a premise popular in postcolonial studies since the late 1960s: Ngũgĩ's pivotal declaration that "literature does not grow or even develop in a vacuum; it is given impetus, shape, direction and even area of concern by social, political and economic forces in a particular society" (1972, xv). This means that even the most antirealist texts about animals have a bearing on the realities of animal lives in abusive quotidian practices. It is not likely that we will ever encounter a forty-two-year-old, speaking porcupine like the one that narrates Alain Mabanckou's *Memoirs of a Porcupine*. Yet a consideration of facts about real porcupines and the way they and other animals are treated in everyday practice in Congo would help us comprehend Mabanckou's bizarre novel. Social constructivism is important in helping us understand stereotypes about animals, but those animals also exist in a material and natural reality outside of human imaginative constructs.[38] I therefore agree with Jane Desmond's observation that even when we encounter figurative representations of animals in literary texts, "we must not let the figure of the metaphorical animal, the idea of the animal or its extended ideological deployment of 'animality,' be decoupled from living, or once living, animals" (2016, 22).[39] It is only by coupling the fictional animal, such as the whales in Zakes Mda's *The Whale Caller,* with similar animals in the real biological world that we can begin to understand the irony with which an otherwise sympathetically drawn character is ultimately presented to the reader as a self-aggrandizing exploiter of whales.

INEVITABLE INTERDISCIPLINARY ASSEMBLAGES

My approach to animal studies in African contexts is inevitably intersectional, and I therefore do not recognize any advocacy for the rights of one set of minorities that allows discrimination against other minorities.[40] That is, we cannot endorse anticolonial struggles that encourage discrimination against women or animals. In my view, becoming-Africa is exemplified in Ngũgĩ wa Thiong'o's 1986 revision of *A Grain of Wheat* (1986b [1967]). Here, he expunged an earlier celebration of fantasized and actual rape of white women and the unapologetic killings of dogs belonging to a colonialist (Ngũgĩ 1967; Ngũgĩ 1986).[41] The dogs slaughtered in Ngũgĩ's revisions retain their status as symbols of white privilege in colonial Kenya, but the character who kills them tries to rationalize his actions by claiming that he loves dogs and that he would not have killed them had they not been used to attack native Africans. Nothing justifies killing these dogs, but the text's revisions indicate the author's positive change of perspective regarding wanton killing of dogs. Because becoming-minority is a never-ending process, the question remains: why did anticolonialists not liberate these dogs from the colonizers who used them to terrorize the colonized?

African texts also suggest that we need to nuance our conception of intersectionality to study African animals in a way that does not trivialize the suffering of other minorities in an anthropocentric world. When Kimberlé W. Crenshaw advanced the theory of intersectionality in "Demarginalizing the Intersection of Race and Sex" (1989) and "Mapping the Margins" (1991), she highlighted the ways in which systems of oppression based on identity (class, gender, race) impact an individual or a set of victims (in her case women of color).[42] She observes the need of specificity in identifying the experiences of marginalized women of color. Crenshaw's point, emphasized by postcolonial feminists since the 1980s, is that the conditions of white women do not equate to or represent experiences of women of color. The "focus on the most privileged group members marginalizes those who are multiply burdened and obscures claims that cannot be understood as resulting from discrete sources of discrimination" (Crenshaw 1989, 140). In her view, race intersects with gender to marginalize black women relative to white women.[43] However, despite the focus on distinctiveness, we can expand her formulation to include the ways in which oppression of one marginalized group enhances the oppression of another, such as when the oppression of women promotes the oppression of animals and vice versa. Even if the suffering of a particular animal is specific to the condition of that animal, it is also analogous to conditions produced in similar oppressive practices among other groups of people or animals. These forms of oppression intersect with and intensify one another because, as Ange-Marie Hancock (2016) explains, while intersectionality foregrounds the specificity of experience, it shows us "how to connect with one's experience away from and in relationship with others in the world" (126).[44] In a same way, the experiences of individuals and groups in the postcolony are specific to postcolonialism itself, but one needs to examine how a particular group shares certain experiences with other marginalized groups. My sense of intersectionality is inclusive and rhizomic. This means that if multiple different systems of marginalization malleably interact with one another to augment the oppression of a single individual or social category, then such systems can best be undermined by using similarly morphing and mutually coconstitutive symbiotic assemblages.[45]

The interlocking nature of oppressions is the very reason that it is essential to be attentive to the rights and treatment of animals, all as part of the broader question of addressing and eliminating oppression in human communities. In the preface to Cary Wolfe's *Animal Rites,* Mitchell usefully mocks the hierarchies we institute to justify the neglect of animal rights that derives from the lack of respect for human rights: "First let us get our own house in order and create a humane world civilization that does not treat vast populations of human beings as if they were sheep to be shorn, cattle to be slaughtered, or vermin to be exterminated. Then we can talk about animal rights" (Mitchell 2003a, x). Looking at African literature from an intersectional perspective, I see the well-being of humans as intricately fused with that of the environment; the rights of animals are bound together with those of humans. In addition, cynics, as Mitchell conceives them, argue that "in the meantime, an obsession with animal rights is nothing but the ultimate form of liberal guilt, the kind of self-indulgent breast-beating that encourages moralistic, sentimental posturing while doing nothing about the lot of animals" (2003a, x.). Echoing Mari Matsuda's argument that "no person is free until the last and the least of us is free" (1996, 65), several scholars have analyzed the interface of animal oppression and injustices perpetrated by humans against other humans. They demonstrate, in Laura Wright's words, that "oppressions are linked, intersectional, and codependently reinforcing" (2015, 15).[46] We should also note that respect for the rights of animals will not reverse or impede the respect for the rights of humans. Therefore, even if, as Mitchell's hypothetical cynics conclude, "animals are simply the latest candidates in an endless procession of victims—women, minorities, the poor—clamoring for rights and justice, or just a modicum of decent treatment" (2003, x), I contend that to acknowledge the rights of these "latest candidates" would enhance the rights of all previous candidates as well as the rights of others to come in the yet-to-be-compiled list of victims.[47]

Therefore, when Benjamin Zephaniah writes about animal rights in the poem "We People Too" (2001, 59–60), it is in contexts that suggest interconnections of the abuse of animal rights, police harassment of black people, and abuses of power at the expense of minorities in England, present and past.[48] Similarly, Oswald Mtshali's "Pigeons at the Oppenheimer Park" (1971) and Katleho Kano Shoro's "Animals of Colour" (2017) present segregationist policies in South Africa in terms of animal defiance against the apartheid system. Mtshali celebrates the birds' refusal to follow apartheid edicts by making love across what, in human contexts, would be racial lines. In such texts, resistance takes many forms. When Shoro (2017) rewrites Mtshali's poem in "Animals of Colour," she suggests that the animals are discriminated against, as are nonwhite citizens of South Africa. The policeman in Shoro's poem does not leave the lovebirds on their own as he does in Mtshali's poem; he chokes and arrests the birds. As indicated in Mtshali's and Shoro's poems, resistance takes different forms. Therefore, a focus on animals also requires a consideration of gender, class, disability, and other forms of marginality.

Outside an intersectional framework, a study like this one runs the risk of appearing to play down the problems African human populations have suffered under slavery, colonialism, and neocolonialism. The concern Philip Armstrong notes to be the probable reason postcolonial critics show little interest in animal studies—the fear that they would be seen to be trivializing human suffering—is best addressed through an intersectional approach. This is where the interests of animals are intertwined with those of the humans, plants, and the entire ecosystem. It is particularly important to remember the centrality of colonialism in African writing; even when we adopt new methods and theories of reading, we should not sweep colonialism under the carpet. To consider the representation of animals in African literature from a posthuman perspective is to understand colonists' treatment of Africans as colonial others.[49]

Attention to animal interests must, then, extend to global concerns. The texts suggest that we should acknowledge the place of the human broadly, and the postcolonial subject more particularly, as constituted through their relationship to the environment. Karen Thornber has recommended that literary studies consider global environmental issues even in local texts that "have not travelled far themselves, neither intertextualized, discussed, or even available in more than one literary space" (2012, 435). Some of the texts discussed in this book are not in wide circulation. Nevertheless, they illuminate local communities' attitudes toward human-animal relationships and toward ecology in general. These small texts also show that they share the same concerns revealed in better-known texts. Furthermore, emphasizing the gravity of the global-warming crisis, Chakrabarty calls on "academics to rise above their disciplinary prejudices, for it is a crisis of many dimension" (2009, 215). The same can be said about the plight of animals, much of which results from the very activities that cause global warming. Therefore, I conclude this section with an emphasis on the need to appreciate the mounting resistance against animal abuse among minority groups. We have so far seen that various feminist, postcolonial, and animal-rights activists and scholars have recognized intersectionalities among marginalized groups. In evoking similar alliances, I turn to precolonial philosophies (particularly *ubuntu*) in the next chapter to examine views on how we should treat animals in formerly colonized societies.

CHAPTER 2

Re-Animating Precolonial Ecological Practices

The Case of *Ubuntu*

Ukama makore hunopfekana. (Relationships are like clouds; they interpenetrate each other.)
—Shona proverb (qtd. in Murove 2004, 197).

Icalo bapata abantu, ba mwena kunkoko. (How humans treat their chicken says a lot about that community.)
—Mbeba proverb (qtd. in Kaoma 2013, 101).

Nature—and in particular, the wild—feeds our spirit, and a direct encounter with it is vital in helping us appreciate it. For unless we see it, smell it, or touch it, we tend to forget about it, and or souls wither.
—Wangari Maathai, in *Replenishing the Earth* (2010, 87).

In an Institut National de l'Audiovisuel (INA) documentary interview from 1980 titled *Les animaux ont une âme* (Animals Have a Soul), the Senegalese philosopher and statesman Leopold Sédar Senghor (1906–2001) expressed his love for animals as lyrically as he does in his negritude poetry. Senghor is best known in literary studies as one of the pillars of negritude, a movement begun in the 1930s by Francophone intellectuals known for the rejection of Western rationality.[1] Negritude is rarely read in animal rights discourse. Yet its thought is founded on similar notions of interdependent posthuman energies. Senghor's poetic and philosophical writing is informed by a totemic belief system that undermines the distinction between humans and nature; it gains its vitality from numerous references to animals and the cosmos that emphasize that humans cannot reach their potential without animals and nature. He believes that "Dieu a donné la force vitale non seulement aux hommes, mais encore aux animaux, aux végétaux, voire aux minéraux. Par quoi ils sont. Mais cette force a pour vocation croître" (God has given vital force not only to man, but also to animals, vegetables, even minerals. By which they exist. But it is the purpose of this force to multiply/make thrive/grow; 1993, 19). In its reference to the strict meaning of the verb to be, Senghor's expression "par quoi ils sont" here suggests ontology, and when he uses the word "coître" in the next sentence, it is to indicate the processes multiplying and ripening. From the context, then, he contends that it is from nonhuman forces that humans are able to multiply, grow, and mature. He thus suggests that the nature of being, though it may appear on the surface as fixed, is caught up with an external life force/vitality which impels beings to grow/ripen/mature, such that humans cannot thrive or come to fruition without interaction with the nonhuman world.

Similarly, in the INA interview, Senghor says that like Aristotle and Pierre Teilhard de Chardin, he believes that animals have souls.[2] In the interview, he asserts that Africa is the cradle of civilization and that animals are our ancestors: "I chose them because they are good companions; birds and animals are our parents. It is also very important for a continent like Africa—you know that it is in Africa that man emerged from the animal five million and five hundred thousand years ago—since there is a symbiosis, an intimacy between man and nature, especially between animals and man." While Senghor's abiding love for other-than-human components of the universe is ironically proved through his reference to how he has imprisoned animals in real life, his interview—and his poetry—nevertheless testifies to the value placed on nonhuman life and interests in African philosophies and worldviews.[3] Although often ignored as "precolonial" and thus historically displaced, I argue in this chapter that these philosophies in fact continue to permeate African attitudes toward animals, as evidenced in anticolonial writing from the twentieth century.

In parallel with Senghor, I examine here precolonial ideas about culture and the environment, because those cultures animate how animals are understood in postcolonial texts. Rather than focusing on Senghor's totemism—which suggests human-animal hierarchies—I focus on *ubuntu* as a case study both to illustrate how its ideas about universal relationships animate literary texts and to uncover its limitations. My aim is not to idealize *ubuntu*, whose tenets and applicability some Africanists have questioned. I intend to show that some of its proponents' ideas are not viable in the contemporary world, but that it can be transformed to address current ecological conditions.[4] While *ubuntu*, focused as it is on the human, might appear antianimal on the surface, it actually allows us to appreciate the web of relationality that interconnects humans with the more-than-human universe.[5] Using *ubuntu* as a case study shows us that African indigenous practices need as much reform as Western institutions. Therefore, we need to question the duality between *ubuntu* and its supposed animal opposite. To do this, after my examination of the philosophical tensions within *ubuntu*, I read Bessie Head's *Maru* as showing that animals exhibit *ubuntu* more spontaneously that humans. I close the chapter with a summary of other Africanist philosophies related to *ubuntu* (the Shona's *ukama*, Senghor's negritude, and Nkrumah's consciencism) to demonstrate that the core of *ubuntu* is shared by practices and beliefs it is sometimes thought to compete against. This comparative approach will thus lay the groundwork for my readings of both popular and canonized texts in future chapters.

PRECOLONIAL PRACTICES AND THE NATURE-CULTURE CONTINUUM

Several studies relate precolonial philosophies to strong environmental ethics and respect for animals.[6] In African contexts, several scholars have emphasized the traditional African respect for animals and environments. Two examples will suffice: Kofi Opoku's and Kapya Kaoma's coupling of the African with ecological awareness. For Opoku, "our African forebears regarded themselves as an inextricable part of the environment, and their lives were interconnected with all living things. They found themselves to be in neighborly relationships with the created order of things, such as the earth, trees, animals and spirits . . . the environment was not dead or inert but was populated by beings, just like ourselves, and the existence of these beings presupposed relationships between us (humans) and them" (2006, 351). This means that even if the African used the animals and the environment for food, clothing, and medicine, humans considered these nonhuman beings as companions. For his part, Kaoma's theology of the environment proposes that "African worldviews uphold the belief that all biota [are] part of the sacred web of life, with sacred links to the ancestors and the Supreme Being. For Africans, how the land is treated says much about the nation or community's values" (2013, 101).[7] In these styles of thought and everyday practice, precolonial African societies display affinities with what Matthew Calarco would call "indistinction," seeking "to establish a relevantly similar moral identity between human beings and animals" (2011, 42). Neither these studies nor Calarco's construct are based on the evolutionary theories of Darwin or the philosophies of Agamben and Deleuze, in whose thinking the world is animated by what contemporary ecocritical and posthuman theorists term the "nature-culture continuum" (Braidotti 2013), suggesting that in traditional cultures around the globe (European societies included), animals, plants, and humans were all considered to be part of the same web of life, completely interdependent with one another.[8] These communities viewed the Cartesian logic that sets humans apart from animals and rationalizes the destruction of other members of the planetary habitat as a modern deformation of the world. The need to care for human life correlated with the imperative of responsibility to nonhuman animals.

Environmental activists such as Wangari Maathai suggest that the ecological crises we are facing today could be reduced if we reanimate precolonial practices, which are anchored in belief systems that protect the environment and the animals. She calls on us to harness the animistic and shamanistic practices of precolonial Africa, which colonialism could not fully erase, and synthesize them with modern spiritual values (e.g., the biblical beliefs that Christianity brought to the continent) to heal the wounds mankind has inflicted on the earth (e.g., desertification and soil erosion). For Maathai, the boundary between the secular and the spiritual in African environmental conservation is fluid, just as spiritual and material realities on the continent are intertwined.[9] In *Replenishing the Earth* (2010), she points out that her Kikuyu community lived close to domestic animals, even sleeping in the same room with them. This not only sheltered animals from predators and bad weather, it kept at bay some parasites that would attack humans (e.g., chigoe fleas). Strict taboos protected the animals from abuse by humans. One could not kill an animal arbitrarily; permission had to be sought from the spirits. According to Maathai, "because the Kikuyus lived close to their animals, they grew to know their idiosyncrasies and responded well to their needs. . . . Permission to kill was sought from the Creator and the ancestors. To protect the animal from the trauma of instant death, it would be denied air and blood to the brain before a knife touched its body" (53). It is worth noting that Maathai's account of an ideal spiritual world indicates that even if the Kikuyu culture protected domestic animals from abuse, it still sanctioned their killing. The "Creator and the ancestors" would seldom turn down the request to kill an animal. As I point out throughout this book, to assume that animals led perfect lives in these ancient cultures or that humans lived in perfect harmony with other agencies in the universe is to romanticize an ecologically noble savage who may never had existed.[10] Animals were consumed as food and clothing, sacrificed to the gods, used in wars, abused in blood sports such as cock fighting and bull fighting, and used as targets in archery. Rosi Braidotti notes that "since antiquity, animals have constituted a sort of zoo-proletariat, in a species hierarchy run by the humans. They have been exploited for hard labour, as natural slaves and logistical supports for humans prior to and throughout the mechanical age" (2013, 70). The West is not alone in this. Modern postcolonial texts depict these ancient traditions sympathetically and also indicate deeply ingrained ambivalence toward violence, especially toward animal and human others.[11] The value of references to such cultures today lies in the fact that they reveal how far we have veered away from the ideal.

Although it is only one indigenous philosophy among many others, *ubuntu* illustrates the tensions between human-animal relations in some strands of indigenous thought.[12] Braidotti includes *ubuntu* alongside Édouard Glissant's poetics of relations, Paul Gilroy's planetary cosmopolitanism, Avtar Brah's diasporic ethics, Homi Bhabha's subaltern secularism, and Vandana Shiva's antiglobal neohumanism among the concepts we could employ to salvage the study of humanities in the West (Braidotti 2008, 7–8; Braidotti 2013a, 18; Braidotti 2013b, 46–48). In its multifarious strands, *ubuntu* considers the shared experiences of various marginalized groups in ways that empower humans as well as animals, marking a posthuman ethics that sees the world as having a complexity beyond anthropocentric interests.[13] This genre of ethics is based on the Xhosa proverb "*Umuntu ngumuntu ngabantu*" (I am because you are, you are because we are), and the word *ubuntu* is a Xhosa and Zulu word often translated as "humanity" or "being human."[14] The maxim emphasizes not only the need to safeguard one another's interests but also to remain connected with one's ancestors and the cosmos, for, as Molefi Kete Asante observes, "those who uphold the principle of *ubuntu* throughout their lives will, in death, achieve unity with those still living, thus completing the circle of life" (2015, 254–55).

To Buntu Mfenyana, *ubuntu* is "a communal way of life which says that a society must be run for the sake of all. This requires cooperation, sharing, and charity" (1986, 18). Unfortunately, and possibly because they are still struggling to come to terms with what it means to be human after decades of being treated like animals, African students of *ubuntu* such as Mfenyane tend to introduce into *ubuntu* an unproductive human/animal hierarchy in which a human being is considered fully human *because* he or she is not an animal. For example, while viewing *ubuntu* as standing in "direct opposition to the hierarchical, discriminatory, separatist and systemic class warfare of apartheid," Samuel A. Paul follows Mfenyana in arguing that *ubuntu* "is the quality that distinguishes a human creature from an animal or spirit. When you do something that is not human then you are being like an animal" (Paul 2009, 6).[15] But as we learn from African literary texts, Africans do not accept rigid dichotomies between humans and animals in practice. These texts extend kindness and generosity to nonhuman animals, but they do so without minimizing humanness or human suffering. As Villa-Vicencio notes, the concept of *ubuntu* is inseparable from the rest of the world of ideas (126).[16] It can be brought into negotiation with animal studies.

ENOUGH *UBUNTU* TO GO AROUND

In its postcolonial African form, *ubuntu* is inclusive, cosmopolitan, and egalitarian. Although it is sometimes denigrated within the South African academy as anthropocentric in contrast to other philosophies, Mogobe B. Ramose insists that it is "the root of all African philosophy" on which "the fundamental ethical, social, and legal judgment of human worth and human conduct is based" (2005 [2002], 270).[17] The values it espouses, based on communalism as opposed to capitalistic individualism, are encouraged in most African cultures. Granted, Western cultures also encourage respect for others, reconciliation, generosity, honesty, truth, and unconditional hospitality. But it is in the communalistic cultures of precolonial societies that values are practiced in their purest form. Under colonialism, African societies view the Western espousal of these virtues as hypocritical, as the colonizers only pay lip service to the moral ideals they expect the world to be governed by. However, if we make the mistake of viewing it in its colonial- and apartheid-era stages of development as a South African nationalist concept, we might dismiss *ubuntu* as a form of reverse racism because it tends to exclude white people. For instance, the South African land-rights activist Anika Claassens was surprised by the nuanced use of *ubuntu* to suggest that white people are not human:

> Most of us recognize that *abeLungu* is a Zulu word for white people and that *abantu* is the Zulu word for people. Learning Zulu, I had always used *abantu* in that sense, people; people in a crowd, people of the world. But I began to notice that this can cause confusion with Zulu people. *Abantu* sometimes has another meaning, which is black people, white people not being included. It is necessary to specify who in the world before one can continue to call everyone there *abantu.* Otherwise when you mention that that one of these *abantu* was called Oliver Twist people look skeptical—*abantu* don't have names like that. (Claassens 1986, 18)

It is not because of their race that white people under apartheid are excluded from the realm of the human. Claassens discovered that white people are not *bantu* (human beings) because "there has been a terrible shortage of *ubuntu* in white people's behaviour towards blacks" (1986, 18). In its apartheid-era mutations, and in response to the dehumanization of black people under white minority rule, *ubuntu* excludes white people, who are called *AbeLungu* or *abaMhlope* to distinguish them from the human *abantu*. The whites relinquish their *ubuntu* when they assume and accept privilege over other human beings. In this sense, Mfenyana insists that privileged white people under apartheid are not *abantu*:

> Strictly speaking it's not possible to refer to the people who came in 1652 with a different way of life and took our land as *abantu*. We distinguish those who came after 1652 with the words *AbeLungu* or *abaMhlope*. This distinction could not have carried on if the new arrivals hand shared the land and way of life in a humane way. (Mfenyana 1986, 19)

In this mutation of the term, white people become human only as an afterthought. With the end of apartheid and the need for interracial reconciliation, this exclusion is no longer valid or acceptable.[18] If, during apartheid, privileged whites were thought to exist outside the realm of *ubuntu*, its proponents in postapartheid Africa present *ubuntu* as an inclusive philosophy. Even Claassens's Oliver Twist can be worthy of *ubuntu*. A music club in Cambridge, England, styling itself as a prototype of *ubuntu*, claims it is "the only club in the world you can't join because you are already in." In a more formal context, Desmond Tutu rejects revenge and reverse hatred as a projection of *ubuntu*. A person imbued with *ubuntu* is, according to Desmond Tutu, "generous, hospitable, friendly, caring and compassionate" (1999, 34). Such affirmation of others, in contemporary *ubuntu* logic, means recognizing that one "belongs in a greater whole," creating a connection between each human and a broader affective ecosystem. Many anti-Eurocentric environmentalists view non-Western societies as being more sensitive to the environment and to animals than their Western counterparts,[19] occasionally to the point of romanticization.[20] I do not idealize the Global South's treatment of animals. For example, most of its fiction presents nonvegan habits and practices that are very far from ideals to be emulated by the rest of the world. In these texts, the philosophy of *ubuntu* (humanness), as documented so far, tends to regard humans as being distinct from animals. However, non-Western societies provide a useful foil to what is viewed as Western cynicism toward nonhuman others.[21] Working within *ubuntu*, and using novels imbued with *ubuntu* as our guide, the remainder of the chapter will lay out an antianthropocentric model of interaction through which to read animals in postcolonial fiction.

ANIMALS AND THE AFRICAN STRUGGLE TO BE HUMAN

A reductive interpretation of *ubuntu* might lead us to conclude that it is anti-animal because the word's denotative antonym is *ubulwane*, related to the word *isilwane* for animals. But contextually, the *isilwane* in *ubulwane* is not an actual animal because the category *isilwane* encompasses all animals, including admired ones, such as cows and goats. Therefore, *ubulwane* is an evil spirit that causes one to behave inhumanely toward animals and people alike. A person suffering this affliction would need to visit a healer to *ukukhipha isilwane* (exorcise the bad metaphysical animal), and to sacrifice an actual *isilwane* as purification from the bad spirit. Therefore, the bird in Charles Mungoshi's story "The Crow" (discussed in the next chapter) is an *isilwane* (animal) without *ubulwane* (negative animalness). The boys who kill the Crow are the ones who display *ubulwane.* Relating the Heideggarian principle of dwelling to the question of justice, Drucilla Cornell suggests the importance of *ubuntu* in our understanding of how to relate honorably to the environment and one another (2009, 151). Cornell understands *ubuntu* as residing in those "indigenous ideals" that have resisted destruction by modern colonial laws and forcible removals. In Mungoshi's story, the boys' violence shows that they lack the rudiments of *ubuntu,* that "internal state of being or the very essence of being human" (Chinkanda 1994, 1). The narrator recognizes this in the feelings he displays later, in which he questions his and his brother's actions. Similarly, Credo Mutwa, a South African traditional healer (*sangoma*), writes in his book, *Isilwane, the Animal* (1996), that "Africans did not hunt animals for fun. They were hunted for food and for other religious reasons" (Mutwa 1996, 19). This does not necessarily make hunting ethical today. In the southern African precolonial world that Mutwa presents in his work, humans did not consider themselves superior to animals; dogs and cats were even considered to own the humans they lived with. Although *isilwane* (animal) is usually considered as the opposite of *umuntu* (human), Mutwa cites proverbs to support the communal worldview that the natural environment should be preserved and the lives of animals respected.[22]

Above all, *ubuntu* is holistic, a human practice related to the environment and fellow humans. Therefore, in spite of lapses in the concept of the human as that which defines itself by its differences from animals, it is incorrect to view *ubuntu* as a purveyor of anthropocentrism. Ramose considers *ubuntu* as the capacity to perceive "being, or the universe, as a complex wholeness involving the multi-layered and incessant interaction of all entities." The nonhuman animal is not excluded from this wholeness: Ramose insists that "caring for one another is the fulfilment of the natural duty to care for the physical nature as well" in the sense that *ubuntu* is "the constant strife to strike and then maintain a balance between human beings and physical nature" (1999, 155). Similarly, in relating precolonial ecological practices to *ukama*, ethicist Munyaradzi Felix Murove understands *ubuntu* as "an existential reality that permeates everything that exists" (2004, 197). He quotes the Shona proverb we have used as our first epigraph in this chapter to insist that the interrelatedness between phenomena is perpetual and that these relations endure even when the phenomena are separated in space, time, or both. Moreover, Murove argues that colonialism and slavery animated the feelings of *ubuntu* among Africans because of the inherent inhumanity of the practices. Africans and wild animals were forcibly moved from their habitats and placed in enclosed reserves. To regain the humanity that colonialism and slavery suppressed in the African, there was a need to reconstruct wholeness and solidarity among Africans. Building on Henri-Philippe Junod's 1938 study of Bantu totemism, Murove also observes that in African beliefs "there inheres conviction that umuntu [person] was not only related to other abantu [people], s/he was also related to the natural environment" (Murove 2014, 44). Desmond Tutu says of *ubuntu* that "anger, resentment, lust for revenge, even success through aggressive competitiveness, are corrosive of this good" (1999, 35). Even if actual animals as such are not expected to display *ubuntu*, humans cannot be excused from embracing this life-affirming worldview, which includes respect for animals.[23]

Proponents of *ubuntu* include the environment in their ethics because, as Lovemore Mbigi observes, "African religions are emphatic on affirming our brotherhood with animals" (1997, 70). He reminds us that "one of the primary functions of the African religious mythology is to reconcile our waking consciousness with the mysteries of nature . . . [as] God is everywhere and the individuation of his spirit can also be found in rocks, caves, forests, rivers, and animals" (143). This means that a follower of the kind of *ubuntu* Mbigi advocates in postcolonial Africa, especially in postapartheid South Africa, should hold nature and animals in reverence. Other proponents of *ubuntu,* such as Mfuniselwa J. Bhengu in his manifesto of *ubuntu,* emphasize the imperative of refraining from violence against the environment (2006, 76). There are moments when Bhengu's perspective acquires a Darwinian tone. In his view, one of the primary qualities and capacities that identifies us as human is the recognition that "our status as creatures is interconnected with the existence of other creatures: our being is one minute and integral part of a unified cosmic process of being" (85). Although verbal language is a uniquely human capacity, Bhengu recognizes that "our symbolic intelligence and language are shared by other creatures" (85). Despite his regenerative posthuman politics and ecologically progressive views, at some points Bhengu sounds retrogressive with regard to animal rights. His position is largely utilitarian in that he believes humans can use animals as long as they do not cause extinction of any of the species being exploited: "All things, living or not, deserve moral consideration. The life-centred ethic would make us morally obliged to preserve all types of living thing, whether animal or not, though it would allow use of them provided the use did not lead to destruction of [sic] of their species type" (Bhengu 2006, 77). He accepts that animals deserve moral consideration but insists on humans' right over animals' bodies. This is the view that most postcolonial writers—including vegans such as Benjamin Zephaniah—espouse. They reject selfish overexploitation of natural resources, but nevertheless see animals as resources rather than as wholly independent agents.

The debate over *ubuntu's* anthropocentrism reveals its dual reputation: as a philosophy, it is either affirmative, based in union and connectivity, or negative, based on the need to act against some members of the society. Adam Ashforth identifies "negative *ubuntu*" with witchcraft and occult violence and shows that, although *ubuntu* is associated with social harmony, the same principle can be used to rationalize injustice and violence. Ashforth writes that "A person is a person through other people . . . because they can destroy you" (2005, 86). Therefore, in African communities where people survive only to the extent that others do not destroy them, the chances are high that people will engage in preventive violence against those whom they either know or imagine to be threats. Stories that use the witchcraft motif suggest that the sorcerer is antihuman and needlessly violent against fellow human beings. For example, in Alain Mabanckou's *Memoirs of a Porcupine*, a sorcerer uses a porcupine to kill his adversaries. His behavior is seen throughout the work as abnormal, even by the companion porcupine that narrates the story.

Ashforth also notes that *ubuntu* is impractical in modern societies and that elites who praise *ubuntu* as the essence of Africanness never live by its ethics in urban environments. If we are to accept *ubuntu*, then, we must note that it is not an immutable philosophy, but one living tradition among many others on the continent. Attributed to the Zulu, it may be rejected by other societies who have borne the brunt of Zulu hegemony in the past. Non-Bantu African cultures might also refuse to be lumped together in a one-size-fits-all-Africa notion of humanism; indeed, some of the proponents of *ubuntu*, including Bhengu, treat all Africans as the same across the continent, ignoring the diversity of African communities and individuals. Drucilla Cornell has posited that in *ubuntu* there is "a benevolent paternalism" regarding women, who are "treated as if they were minors under the care of their husbands." Yet she also accepts that customs are "dynamic" because "there are sources within the practice of social custom itself that can be imagined and reimagined so as to reconfigure the norms of the customary law" (Cornell 2012, 329).[24] Instead of dismissing *ubuntu* because it does not fully fit into humanistic Western conceptions of law and philosophy, a better strategy would be to update its less-productive aspects to bring them into alignment with contemporary ideas of freedom for all, including animals.

It is true that some proponents of *ubuntu* believe that the traditional values of African society are incompatible with modern ideals of equality and human rights. In Bhengu's world, abortion is evil and polygamy is allowed. Moreover, even if *ubuntu* is seen to reject class warfare and what Bhengu calls "a voracious global corporate economy" produced by Western education and ideals (215), some of the trappings of traditionalist *ubuntu* would be inaccessible to an ordinary African. For example, while trenchantly criticizing exploitation, Bhengu and Mbigi imagine *ubuntu* as a business paradigm enabling African companies to make profits. Mbigi's Afrocentric paradigm accepts using clothes made of animal skins and killing animals in modern business practices that mimic traditional African rituals. The luxuries nature and cultural heritage offer should not be reserved to foreign and white tourists; local black populations should enjoy access to animals and performances hitherto reserved for foreigners (Mbigi 1997, 142–44).[25] However, it goes without saying that spaces such as the Las Vegas–style Lost City that Mbigi praises are a model of heritage tourism beyond the reach of ordinary Africans. Such tourist paradises are, as Njabulo Ndebele has argued, "the ultimate 'leisuring' of colonial history that has remained relatively untouched in the discourse of freedom" (2007 [1999], 99). Conducting *ubuntu* business activities in these tourist spaces replicates white colonial practices and encourages the new black elite to take part in what Ndebele would call "colonial leisure" (101). We must remember Ndebele's observation that, as signifiers of "the success of conquest," leisure tourist resorts "are the concrete manifestation of the movement of the dominant culture across time and space, and its ability to replicate itself far away" (100). Tourist paradises (exemplified by game lodges in Ndebele's example) are foreign to the ideals of *ubuntu*. Ndebele explains that in those lodges one expects "isolation, unobtrusive personalised care, campfire camaraderie and pre-dinner drinks with a small number of fellow guests in the evenings, a dinner presided over by the managers, and late-night or early-morning game drives" (99). As part of the advanced capitalism that converts everything into a commodity, the tourist paradises dehumanize the poor. Ndebele's view of the elite black patrons in the game reserves is that they "see the faceless black workers and instinctively see a reflection of themselves" (101). Like humans looking at animals they have evolved from, the black patrons "may be wealthy or politically powerful, but at that moment they are made aware of their special kind of powerlessness: they lack the backing of cultural power" (101–2). Reference to animals in postapartheid *ubuntu* arguments are usually made in terms of excess and superfluity, and are only meant to emphasize human exceptionalism. Bhengu, for example, argues that "unlike an animal, man has acquired history by entering fundamentally on something that would be bound to appear to the beast of prey as senseless and grotesque—namely, on responsibility, and thus on becoming a person with a relation to the truth" (2006, 80). Yet African texts such as Bessie Head's *Maru* (discussed below) do not necessarily portray human beings as responsible or animals as irresponsible; most reverse this stereotype. Decency requires that we accept the ideals of *ubuntu* (generosity, civility, humility, respect, dignity, et cetera). The main question is, how can we achieve *ubuntu* practically? Certainly, it will not be by ignoring the rights of animals.

HUMAN OUTCASTS AND THE *UBUNTU* OF ANIMALS

Philosophers have used the compassion of animals to turn our attention to the brutality of human interactions. For example, Emmanuel Levinas documents an extreme case in which a dog showed more compassion than the Nazis who incarcerated the author and his fellow Jews in a concentration camp. The animal was the only being that offered the prisoners comfort. The dog received the Jewish prisoners as "men" at a time when the Nazis had stripped them of all their humanity. We are not shown the stray dog, Bobby (as the prisoners name the dog), undergoing any training to respond to the downtrodden detainees with compassion; it is apparent from the context that it is in dog's nature to be kindhearted. The sentries chase the dog away because they do not want Bobby to recognize the humanity of the prisoners in the camp. Levinas suggests that the dog doesn't know what it is doing in the way that person does, but it is clear that the Nazis, who can decide to be compassionate because they are human, operate beneath the level of a dog. We do not expect much compassion from Nazis to begin with, but Bobby's response to the prisoners emphasizes the compassion of an animal vis-à-vis the brutality of the Nazis. Nevertheless, Levinas, at the end of the story, denies this dog moral status.[26] This denial is based on human biases, not on any data from Bobby's actions. Similarly, Martha Nussbaum (2012 [2009]) has demonstrated that actual animals display more altruistic compassion than humans. She uses Theodor Fontane's *Effi Briest* and Tolstoy's *The Kreutzer Sonata* to argue that these authors suggest that their sympathetic characters, in times of conflict with others, should expect compassion only from animals. Humans may well be cold and cynical in such cases, abandoning their own kind in times of crisis. Nussbaum also believes that in the actual world, animals display a higher level of empathy than humans, concluding that humans have much to learn from animals to become more humane to one another than they are at present.[27]

The heartlessness of certain sociopolitical groups toward others is a common theme in postcolonial literature. In these texts, animals often display *ubuntu* with greater intensity and spontaneity than humans. The hierarchy governing the relationship between humans and animals is given prominence early in the Bessie Head's *Maru* (1971), a story of a love affair between Margaret Cadmore, an outcaste woman, and Maru, a chief in the Batswana royal family. Following European colonialists, the dominant Batswana pejoratively dismiss the indigenous group from which Margaret comes as "Bushmen" to justify the minority group's dispossession and enslavement. These so-called Bushmen are the first nation of Southern Africa, whose territories span not only Botswana (the setting of Head's novel) but also Namibia, Angola, Zambia, Zimbabwe, Lesotho, and South Africa. Bessie Head wants to show how their treatment parallels the discrimination against black people in whites in apartheid South Africa: "the astonishing similarity between racial prejudices" (1986, 46). To the Batswana group, Margaret's community is no better than animals or things. They are denigrated as "Masarwa" in the text (not even "Basarwa" or "San", two equally depreciatory terms) to signify that post-independence Botswana does not consider this minority group human; in the dominant Bantu language, the "ma" in "Masarwa" suggests lower-class beings or even "things" without rights. Yet Margaret's community displays more humanity toward their fellow human beings and animals than do the communities that reserve that quality exclusively for themselves. Moreover, as further evidence of their humanity, the "Bushmen" are natural vegans. Unsanctioned by mainstream society, the marriage between Margaret and Maru results in their being exiled to a remote place where, it is suggested, they will establish a utopian world, free from racism.[28]

Exploring the absurdities of racism outside a formal apartheid setting, where Africans discriminate against fellow Africans, Head uses animals in the novel to undermine notions of supremacy and hierarchy. At the beginning of the story, a white woman rescues a Masarwa orphan, whom she names after herself: Margaret Cadmore. She takes the young Margaret to a missionary school, and the girl eventually becomes a teacher in Dilepe village, where she is forced into low-caste status despite her modern education. She and Maru fall in love and marry, but this marriage does not recover her agency. At the very beginning of the story, the elder Margaret explains the Batswana's low opinion of the Masarwa, who they derisively compare to animals. Either group is vulnerable to scorn: "In Botswana they say: Zebras, Lions, Buffalo and Bushmen live in the Kalahari Desert. If you can catch a Zebra, you can walk up to it, forcefully open its mouth and examine its teeth. The Zebra is not supposed to mind because it is an animal" (1995 [1971], 7). Margaret as a white woman is outraged that the Masarwa are treated like animals, but not because we owe justice to both humans and animals or because neither animals nor humans should be mistreated. In the next sentence, scientists invoked racist theories to justify the humiliation of the Masarwa:

> Scientists do the same to Bushmen and they are not supposed to mind, because there is no one they can still turn round to and say, "At least I am not a—" Of all things that are said of oppressed people, the worst things are said and done to the Bushmen. Ask the scientists. Haven't they yet written a treatise on how Bushmen are an oddity of the human race, who are half the head of a man and half the body of a donkey? (7)[29]

Neither is the use of animals in laboratory experiments the subject of the white woman's righteous anger. Her displeasure focuses on the implication that it would be legitimate to mistreat the donkeys and spare the Masarwa. The elder Margaret is basically a colonialist, a maternal imperialist fighting for the liberation of girls from ethically marginalized groups, but only in Western terms. The younger Margaret's education does not include the mores or values of her people, who ultimately send her into exile. The "Bushmen" would not condone the abuse of animals that the elder Margaret takes for granted. The community is largely vegetarian, "far more dependent on plants than meat for their sustenance—gatherers more than hunters" (Reader 2011, 249).[30] In Bessie Head's novel, their "mealie pap" diet is the butt of jokes among the young Margaret's classmates (13). As a teacher, Margaret's diet is largely vegetarian: ironically, the Margaret-Maru wedding is celebrated with meat-eating because, as the novel suggests, the Masarwa woman is being assimilated into the dominant culture. She has accepted a new colonizer, and the novel links the heteropatriarchal structures, in which she is now subsumed, with the oppression and abuse of animals. Her identity as a Masarwa remains unacceptable even in the utopian future that the novel gestures toward.

The narration is nonchronological. The narrative begins in medias res, with Maru and Margaret already married. There is a threat of drought, a symbol of looming strife in the new community that they intend to establish. Although the novel's ending appears optimistic, its overall chronology requires that that optimism remain guarded. The community is surprised that Maru, a member of the royal family, would marry a Masarwa woman. The plot ends in puzzlement. The Masarwa are happy for the recognition, but memories of being compared with animals linger:

> As they breathed in the fresh, clear air their humanity awakened. They examined their condition. There was the fetid air, the excreta and the horror of being an oddity of the human race, with half the head of a man and half the body of a donkey. They laughed in an embarrassed way, scratching their heads. (122)

The analogy reminds us of the observation by the elder Margaret Cadmore about the Batswana treatment of the Masarwa. A generation later, the Masarwa are still regarded as half-animal. Although a superficial reading would identify the Batswana society as anti-Masarwa because they invoke animality to denigrate the ethnic subgroup, the elites in power are also antianimal and antiwoman, suggesting Bessie Head's disillusionment with postindependence Botswana leadership for perpetuating race-based discrimination and hegemonic masculinist practices. Moleka, a figure of cold masculine arrogance in the novel, is the terror of both humans and animals as he drives his car furiously around Dilepe, scaring goats and humans alike: "First one goat jumped out of the road. Then six, seven or eight more. People jumped. Both people and goats looked outraged. He kept on smiling. He was royalty, the son of a chief. He'd grown up making goats and people jump" (24). The same response is repeated later and tied closely with his treatment of the women who are in love with him: "At the end of a love affair, Moleka would smile in the way he smiled when he made people and goats jump out of his path, outrage in their eyes" (30). Bessie Head suggests parallelism between Moleka's strong masculinism and speciesist behavior, equating his cruelty to women with his misuse of technology to dominate and terrorize animals.

There is a remarkable relationship between the goats and the Masarwa woman. The goats are Margaret's kindred spirits. From the center of Margaret's consciousness, the narrator names the goat Queen of Sheba and her kid the Windscreen-wiper. They are humanized and given human speech:

> She led the way up the slope with animated footsteps. The child cried: 'Mme, mme, don't walk so fast. I can't keep up with you.' His mother paid no heed. She was intent on making a breakthrough. It wasn't every day that there was

an opportunity to collect gossip. She was old as goats go and age brought wisdom and boldness. (91)

It is young Margaret who reports the language of the goat. Whether she is making it up or not, it shows her closeness to animals. Her generosity to the goats is altruistic; she does not expect anything in return from them. We do not see her drinking its milk, as do the cynical characters in Mda's *The Whale Caller.* She does not even know who the owners of the animal are: "The funny thing was that the owners of Sheba and the Windscreen-wiper never seemed to bother about their comings or goings or how they spent their days or what they ate" (83). Margaret does not romanticize the goats, for "goats, like people, know whom they can take advantage of and, as far as the mother goat and her child were concerned, they had arrived to stay" (92). However, they do not exploit the Masarwa woman; they offer her companionship that the human society withholds.

But in her relation to animals, Margaret is somewhat like her foster mother. She establishes unnecessary hierarchies among them. She considers the goats "civilized" because they appear to have acquired human behaviors, just as the colonialist would see the Africans as civilized because they have assimilated the values of the West: "They were indeed becoming very superior goats. The Windscreen-wiper had learned the ways of civilized human behaviour and now made his puddles and dropped his pills outside" (108). Her comment ratifies the stereotypes that brand other goats as inferior. Like the elder Margaret Cadmore, who only assists her daughter—a single Masarwa girl—instead of focusing on the whole community, the younger Margaret extends her generosity only to one goat and its kid:

> The Queen of Sheba and the Windscreen-wiper had started having trouble with their diet. . . . From a miller in the village, Dikeledi had purchased a bag of husks for Sheba and her baby and they continued to swell with fat and happiness while the other village goats were reduced to lean skeletons, eating bits of dried, wind-blown paper in their desperation. (94)

Margaret's generosity extends only to this pair, not to goats in general. Although her gesture is as altruistic as that of her foster mother, it has the potential to alienate its beneficiary and reinscribe a sense of superiority of one set of animals over others.

BECOMING-HUMAN: *UBUNTU* AND OTHER AFRICANIST VIEWS

Margaret's generosity toward both animals and humans in Head's *Maru* makes her a model for empathy, a symbol of the power of altruism to break boundaries. But if her actions represent *ubuntu* ethics, the novel needs to depict her acting in concert with others as part of a collectively-becoming whole. Tom Bennett and James Patrick interpret *ubuntu* in Levinasian terms: as a call for recognition that one cannot survive by oneself alone. But they describe it as a "dynamic and interactive process of *becoming*" (in a way that also echoes the Deleuzian process of being part of an organic assemblage of different components, especially because for them, *ubuntu* expresses an aspirational mindset in search of social justice and equality (Bennet and Patrick 2011, 240). Although the philosophy is based on traditional practices that may not embrace certain concerns in currency today (e.g., animal rights and gay rights), it is malleable and adaptable. It is a category of situational ethics that Joseph Fletcher describes as "many sided and wide aimed, not one-directional" (1966, 89).[31] But is *ubuntu* a new form of speciesism that, while criticizing colonialism, slavery, and apartheid retains exceptional privileges for select humans and animals? The moral philosopher and animal liberationist Peter Singer defines speciesism as "a prejudice or attitude of bias in favour of the interests of members of one's own species and against those of members of other species" (2009 [1975], 185), and Joan Dunayer asserts that new speciesists "advocate rights for only some nonhumans, those whose thoughts and behavior seem most human-like" (2004, 77). These partitions represent a critical limitation that Kai Horsthemke (2015) locates in the *ubuntu* view of particular species. Fortunately, Horsthemke finds in *ukama* a platform on which to base a holistic perspective on the environmental issues that is lacking in *ubuntu*.

A considerable amount of literature establishes the consensus that precolonial practices are more ecologically conscious than modern-day practices. In spite of his condescension toward African "savage" ethics, the Russian zoologist and geographer Pyotr Kropotkin notes the reluctance of the precolonial African to disrupt the social order in a way that would anger not only fellow human beings and ancestors but also "some animal tribe: crocodiles, bears, tigers, etc." (1924 [1922], 77). Animals are thought to enjoy personhoods, and they must not be violated. The code of custom demands communality that brings together not only different kinds of people but animals as well. As an evolutionist, Kropotkin believes that Africans have not yet evolved to the same level of individualism as Europeans, but he sees positive value in the way Africans relate to nonhuman others. Without reducing Africans to noble savages, other scholars, including local intellectuals, point out a similar respect for the environment. For example, calling for a holistic ecological approach that includes Western rationality as well as African perspectives, the theologian Bénézet Bujo posits that from "an African point of view, a being can simultaneously be animal, plant and mineral" (2009, 296). In Bujo's view, an independent, bounded category of the human that separates itself from other animate components of the universe is moot. Ali Mazrui also characterizes ancient African civilizations as making "no great distinction between the past, the present, and the future; no great distinction between the kingdom of God, the animal kingdom and the human kingdom; the crocodile could be the god" (1994; 195).[32] According to these views, to be African is to be environmentally conscious.

While practices across the continent differ in many ways, ecological consciousness and communal regard are at the core of a wide range of African philosophies of which *ukama* and *ubuntu* are parts. We do not have space to explore all these philosophies in depth, but Nkrumah's consciencism and Senghor's negritude can serve as examples. We have explored the tension between *ubuntu*'s holistic vision of the world and the antianimal attitudes of some of its prominent philosophers. That tension is evident in Margaret's behavior toward goats and humans in *Maru*. Her behavior suggests that humanity might be enriched by empathy toward animals, but it fails to consider animals' experiences and needs in themselves. Bearing these tensions in mind, the philosophies of human-animal relations put forward by Kwame Nkrumah and Léopold Sédar Senghor illuminate some of *ubuntu*'s positive contributions to modern animal ethics and posthuman theories.

Writing in the 1960s, Nkrumah noted the absurdity of Western rationalism's denigration of animals and its blurring of distinctions between humans and animals. In *Consciencism* (1964), he offers a convincing critique of Western philosophies of humanity, indicting the Aristotelian and Cartesian insistence on human superiority based on rationality.[33] Nkrumah rejects the Cartesian dualism that posits an immutable division between mind and body, between the human and the animal:

> The suspicion that living things exhibit non-apperceptive response is not new. Indeed, Descartes thought that the response of all non-human animals was non-perceptive. He therefore denied that non-human animals possessed

> souls, remaining content to believe that all the actions of such animals could be given a mechanical explanation which is complete. But even humans are not entirely above non-appreciative response. (85)

Nkrumah views colonialism as based on a similar mindset that sees some races as weaker than others; to the colonialist, Africans are non-apperceptive (unable to think, learn, and feel): "Colonialism requires exertion, and much of that exertion is taken up by the combat of progressive forces, forces which seek to negate this oppressive enterprise of greedy individuals and classes by means of which an egotistical imposition of the strong is made upon the weak" (99). As Nkrumah perceives it, colonialism, in its advanced capitalist practices, thrives on such distortions. He therefore calls for a judicious approach to Euro-American and Islamic beliefs in Africa. While these two systems of thought are integral to contemporary Africa, Nkrumah urges us to subordinate them to the pursuit of indigenous precolonial egalitarianism that abolishes Western philosophical dualities and establishes the unities necessary to any ecologically sensitive philosophy.

Although Senghor's negritude movement embraces similar unitarian approaches to the environment, it often portrays the precolonial as perfect. In "Elements constructifs d'une civilization d'inspiration negro-africaine" (1959 [1976]), Senghor states that the West's separation of humans from the environment has resulted in destruction. His view is not based on capacities for emotion, which he elsewhere attributes to Africans; it is based on "science" that warns of catastrophes facing the world as a result of human disturbances in natural balances. In Senghor's Africa, there is no separation between human beings and their environment. "A certain tree or animal from the local fauna or flora," Senghor observes, "is identified with the clan." In a preceding paragraph, he noted that the clan is the African concept of what the West views as family. Although African totemism may appear "unnatural" to a Western observer, in Senghor's philosophy, "what is really unnatural and inhuman is to isolate man from his environment and to domesticate animal or tree" (44). Negritude is "essentially relation with others, an opening out to the world, contact and participation with others" (2010 [1970], 478). It is not surprising that Senghor was among the first modern African writers to meditate on nonhuman animals and to propose proper ways of relating to them. However, in his imagery, he seems to accept precolonial utilitarian practices, because he is more interested in presenting an ideal Africa than in championing universal freedom:

> Art does not consist in photographing nature but in taming it, like the hunter when he reproduces the call of the hunted animal, like a separated couple, or two lovers, calling each other in a desire to be reunited. The call is not simply the reproduction of the Other; it is a call of complementarity, a *song*: a call of harmony to the harmony of union that enriches by increasing *being*. (2010 [1970], 482)

As a metaphor relating art to society, Senghor presents hunting as a natural practice, a "harmony of union" that increases general wellness. Never mind that it is a form of violence against animals. Senghor's generation of writers (who reached prominence in the '60s) idealized culturally marginalized groups (e.g., animals and women) without bestowing them with agency in the real world. We would not expect postcolonial writers or philosophers to hold similar views in the twenty-first century. In fact, the cultural nationalist movement among African writers started to wane in the late 1960s after intellectuals became disillusioned by the failure of independence leaders to deliver on their promises to improve people's lives.[34]

The contradictions in Senghor's views can be found in the writings of other scholars from that period. A similar attitude is evident in John S. Mbiti's defense of African traditional religions. He was among the first Anglophone African scholars to defend in his theological work on traditional African religions against the charge that they were primitive. In the 1960s, Mbiti's mission was to demonstrate that traditional African religions are not antithetical to Christianity; Mbiti views Christianity as indigenous to Africa and not an import by European missionaries. He rejected the term "animism" and other popular descriptors of African religions as being "inadequate, derogatory and prejudicial" because they locate African religions at the bottom of the sociocultural evolutionary ladder. But he does not reject animism per se; he is critical of the prejudicial way the term is used, noting that social evolution theory denigrates African belief systems because it "fails to take into account the fact that another theory equally argues that man's religious development began with a monotheism and moved towards polytheism and animism" (1990 [1969], 7). Although he sounds unnecessarily defensive, Mbiti's views on animism are similar to those expressed by a wide range of researchers on non-Western cultures—e.g., Descola, Marshall Sahlins, and Graham Harvey, among others—who critique Western ontological dualism in favor of a more ecologically friendly animistic monism that disrupts the nature-culture dichotomy.[35] To Mbiti, postcolonial religions denigrated by the West are as complex as Christianity. He goes so far as to argue that African religions have "done the donkey work" on behalf of Christianity in creating a foundation of religiosity that Christianity can build on (Mbiti 1971, 8). African religions are therefore in the service of Christianity. Regrettably, Christianity is one of the religions that, in contrast to Buddhism, Hinduism, and various African religions, most blatantly overlooks animal subjectivity and sentience.[36]

Like a transhuman experiment using nonhuman elements to enhance human vitality, Mbiti's defense of African religions supports the spread of Christianity in Africa by demonstrating how traditional religions can be co-opted to revitalize proselytizing missions. Examining African societies through a Judeo-Christian lens, he paints African cultures in purely anthropocentric terms: "Animals and plants constitute human food" (50). There are no references to the many attempts to conserve the environment that are found in later works on precolonial African societies, such as the poetry of Tanure Ojaide about the Delta region of Nigeria or Zakes Mda's novels about the Xhosa and the Khoikhoi of South Africa.[37] Mbiti asserts that animals' "importance is obviously great" because they satisfy the requirements of both human religion and nutrition (50).

Despite his Christiocentric anthropocentrism, Mbiti's own name signals his community's belief in the ecological interconnectedness between humans and other animals. Through such naming, humans merge with their environment in a mutually reinforcing symbiotic relationship wherein human beings are extensions of nature, not separate from it even in its more repulsive manifestations. Mbiti's name connotes an exhortation to the cosmos to spare the bearer of the name from death after the demise of the siblings born before him: the "mbiti" (hyena) in his name is meant to scare death away. Therefore, the animals that his community subjugates have cultural value. In this context, Ernest Hemingway's graphic and enthusiastic descriptions of his hunting and killing of animals and the presentation of his Kamba companions' celebration of a hunt in *Green Hills of Africa* is "unconvincing" to Kamba readers (Kitunda 2011, 133). The Kamba people would not approve of killing a "mbiti" or any other animal in the way Hemingway describes, because "within the Kamba lore, the killing of hyenas and similar species of animals was practically taboo" (Kitunda 2011, 133).[38] In a discussion of *ubuntu*, Johann Broodlyk explains that although it is "acceptable" in Western cultures to "hunt animals with firearms for the pleasure of hunting" and that society at large sees nothing wrong in that practice, "in Africa this practice is regarded as grossly inhuman" (2006, 20). Normally the Kamba would regard

Hemingway as inhuman for killing animals just for the pleasure of killing. Therefore, it is likely that either the Kamba's enjoyment of hunting with Hemingway is staged, or that the community was laughing out of puzzlement at the Westerner's life-destroying practices, or that Hemingway had managed to co-opt some wayward locals in practices that would traditionally have been sanctioned against within the culture.

WEAKNESSES DISAPPEARING OVER TIME

Fabien Eboussi Boulaga (2014 [1977]) is one of the African intellectuals who have reminded us about the futility of seeking an unpolluted African past and the dangers of what he calls "blind loyalty" to harmful traditions, some of which Boulaga sees to have even facilitated colonialism and slavery (130). He suggests that, in contemporary Africa, we have no choice but to "enact traditions through their reinterpretation and reinvention" (238). Attempts to recover a pure past also assume that precolonial African societies were static and perfect. Most creative works about that the beauty of the past that colonialism destroyed do not hesitate to at the same time point out the foibles of precolonial Africa. While defending African traditions, Ngũgĩ's *The River Between* (1965) shows the inefficacy of such practices as female genital mutilation among the Kikuyus; in his *Is It Possible?* (1971) and *To Become a Man* (1972), Henry ole Kulet has suggested that it is no longer necessary for a Maasai *moran* (young man) to kill a lion with bare hands to prove his valor and manhood to society; women writers, such as the Ugandan Jane Bakaluba in *Honeymoon for Three* (1975) have satirized traditional virginity testing as retrogressive in modern Africa; and Achebe similarly casts a disapproving gaze at the killing of twins among the precolonial Igbos in *Things Fall Apart* (1958). Even if they denounce colonialists for demonizing Africans without putting these customs into a larger social context, African writers indicate that we should not repeat or go back to certain practices when we seek to resurrect African customs. In other words, going back to precolonial practices is generative because, as Jean Comaroff and John Comaroff explain, "it is often a mode of producing new forms of consciousness; of expressing discontent with modernity and dealing with its deformities" (1999b, 284). But more urgent for these writers is that we should be selective in the customs we readopt from the past.

Indeed, writers themselves do evolve over time. Mbiti's earlier positions shift as his project of anticolonial nationalism develops. Unlike the environmentalist Wangari Maathai, whose memoirs detail her fight for ecological justice in Afrocentric and indigenous contexts, the early Mbiti's aim was to offer a corrective to Eurocentric misunderstandings of Africa. Initially he seemed unaware of his subjectivity's extension to the world around him. By contrast, Wangari Maathai is writing at a time when the twenty-first century postcolonial intellectual no longer needs to emphasize her humanity vis-à-vis the European Man. It is now urgent to confront internal colonialism, through which one postcolonial component of the universe unjustly dominates another. She idealizes the precolonial world as one in which humans did not colonize the environment, writing that she was taught early on that only stepping on the tail of a leopard would prevent it from attacking her. The leopard was to be considered and treated as her companion and as a rational actor. She suggests that in precolonial cultural thought, animals become violent only when provoked. She laments the fact that "many people in Kenya these days get so scared when they see a large wild animal that they overreact and frighten it, which in turn may lead to an attack" (Maathai 2006, 43). Unfortunately, even government officials charged with taking care of animals do not know how to handle them. Offering an anecdote from real life, she explains that instead of tranquilizing an animal in dangerous human-animal encounters, the game rangers choose to shoot the animal dead: "This sad state of affairs is caused by a lack of understanding of animal behavior, something my mother's generation seemed to grasp" (44). She suggests that modern society has lost the precolonial sensitivity to the well-being of animals—a sensitivity that I argue can be reclaimed through a deeper attention to indigenous philosophies.

Blindsided by Christianity and the anticolonial nationalist project of trying to reform Eurocentric church ideologies, Mbiti's conceptions of African traditions generally fail to grasp the importance of animals. Fortunately, as his writing progresses, there is still some hope of becoming-animal. At the heart of his philosophy is a yet-to-be-activated connection between the Africans and their natural world, a connection in which "human life" is "mystically tied up with that of other animals" (Mbiti 1991 [1975], 138). Such connections are vividly expressed in his literary writing even as they are muted in his philosophy. The verses in his *Poems of Nature and Faith* (1969) ring with this belief in human-animal interconnectedness even if individual poems remain largely anthropocentric. The final poem features monkeys as representing human foibles that are specific to different regions of the world: "Eastern monkeys are thieves / Northern monkeys are liars / Western monkeys are greedy / Southern monkeys are lazy" (Mbiti 1969, 62). The repetition of "monkey" complements the title in foregrounding the animal as a metaphorical vehicle to illustrate human weaknesses. The next two stanzas are spoken in the monkeys' voices. The animals decide to climb the tree and eat fruit "and swing our tails / eating nuts nuts / and laughing" (1969, 62). The monkey's vegetarianism becomes a source of joy, connected by the repetition of "nuts" and "laughing." If the monkeys follow this path, they will "forget to steal / and forget to lie / and learn to give / and learn to work" (Mbiti 1969, 62). Their redemption is not yet been fully realized, but there is hope that it will be.

In *Concepts of God in Africa,* Mbiti's position further softens in the chapter titled "God and Animals" (1970, 98). If Lévi-Strauss views natural species as ubiquitous in cultural expressions and beliefs because they are "good to think with" (1963, 89), in Mbiti's philosophy, animals are not only useful for food and religious sacrifice, they are also regularly called on to inculcate moral values.[39] Mbiti notes that in numerous African societies, animals feature in folklore to indicate the depth to which they and humans are interlinked. Mbiti opens with the claim that, among the Barotse, there is the belief that "originally God gave animals to the first men to be their brothers, forbidding men to eat them" (98). God withdrew Himself from the world because of human violence against animals—a story consistent with certain Christian readings of Genesis, which claim that Adam, as the caretaker of all animals and plants, must have been vegan. Mbiti also presents a story about the Nandi wherein the dog curses humans for denying it food. The dog's curse is vindictive, but the story warns the community away from arrogance toward animals and humans of low status. After offering a long list of the ways different animals are treated in various African cultures, Mbiti, remaining anthropocentric, acknowledges that the place of animals needs to be researched further.

Writers have demonstrated that, even if the precolonial past is preferable to the exploitative capitalist present, we should not even dream of being able to reverse time to that remote past. The past itself was not perfect. Like negritude and other Africanist modes of thought, some earlier strands of *ubuntu* have their weaknesses. But we have demonstrated that *ubuntu* is a malleable philosophy that can evolve with the times. *Ubuntu*'s emphasis on unity may be particularly useful in theorizing a vegan ethics of becoming in postcolonial novels. Given this unanimity of thought about precolonial Africa, it is not productive to dwell on perceived weaknesses of *ubuntu*. What is even less useful is interscholastic hairsplitting over interpretations of the term or its practice, in place of an examination of its ethics itself through, for example, analyses of artworks. We have shown that advocates of *ubuntu* who earlier understood the concept in purely anthropocentric terms are now ready to adopt animal rights issues. Robert Peterson concludes that although Africans seem to believe that animals are made purposely for human use, they do not advocate Western anthropocentrism, in which "humans as the center of the universe believe they can do whatever they please with the rest of the creation." Equating African humanism with Western anthropocentricism obscures "the fact that African beliefs, such as the world and its various creatures being created for the sake of human beings, are couched within a communal rather than an individualistic utilitarian ethos" (2000, 127).

Some of the criteria that Western theorists in human-animal studies use to argue for animal rights (e.g., that animals are capable of higher thought and emotions than ordinarily believed) are irrelevant in an African context. Whether animals can appreciate art is immaterial; we respect them as part of an ecological unity regardless of whether they can read books or interpret a painting. This enables us to respect the natural environment holistically because it too is believed to have cognitive capacities. Barbara Smuts is correct when she concludes that "relating to other beings as persons has nothing to do with whether or not we attribute human characteristics to them. It has to do . . . with recognizing that they are social subjects, like us, whose idiosyncratic, subjective experience of us plays the same role in their relations with us that our subjective experience of them plays in our relations with them" (118). Most African artists see fellow humans, animals, and the environment at large as social subjects to whom we should relate to with sensitivity and decency. Destructiveness, in the view of these artists, is a vice of the West that its cronies in the Global South embrace. *Ubuntu* has its critics, but we should not to relapse into the cynicism of the white-dominated South African academy, which would privilege *ukama*, a foreign black philosophy, over *ubuntu*, as if the two were unrelated. *Ubuntu* is an aspiration, not necessarily an ideal already in place. In the next chapter, I critique precolonial folklore to show that even if it embraces *ubuntu* and the potentials of veganism in the future, the texts are shot through with hegemonic subtexts. This does not minimize the importance of either veganism or *ubuntu* as strategies for relating to the environment.

CHAPTER 3

Not Yet Happily Ever After

Orature and Animals

Until the lions have their own historians, the history of the hunt will always glorify the hunter.
—Chinua Achebe (1994)

In encounters with literary animal characters, the distinction between the representation of human values and the respect for animal interests blurs; promoting norms that treat animals as literary agents will inevitably further their treatment as rational actors in the material world. And it is in African orature and children's books based on oral literature that animals find their fullest expression as creative beings. They speak and dance and solve dilemmas that are too complicated for humans. These folktales use animals allegorically in stories about human morals, treating the nonhuman characters as simpler subjects and humanoid stand-ins. As I will argue in this chapter, the inclusion of animal subjectivities in folktales and fables also forms the basis for cross-species empathy as explored in twentieth- and twenty-first-century African literature. Braidotti asserts that "animals have long spelled out the social grammar of virtues and moral distinctions for the benefit of humans" in "moral glossaries and cognitive bestiaries that turned animals into metaphorical referents for norms and values" (2013b, 69). Their images can be commercialized in the entertainment industries of advanced capitalism and used to spread stereotypes about certain species. Nonetheless, folktales, children's books, and orature help, in Braidotti's terms, to "displace the notion of species hierarchy and of a single, common standard for 'Man' as the measure of all things. In the ontological gap thus opened, other species come galloping in" (2013b, 67). Therefore, in reading such animal metaphors in African oral literature, it is important to remember Karen Barad's warning that "we would be remiss if the acknowledgment of the differential constitution of the human in relation to the nonhuman only served to refocus our attention, once again, exclusively on the human" (2011, 123). Without downplaying human suffering compared with that of animals in order to justify their abjection, we should be attentive to the instances in which metaphors performatively call on us to accept the "unquestioned killability of nonhumans" (Barad 2011, 123). That is, the animals have their own interests and intrinsic value beyond serving as metaphors of the human condition.

I begin this chapter with a brief discussion of the role animals play in African oral literature from the perspective of modern writers. I further discuss oral literature's representation of the powerless, including its reactionary portraits of women and animals, and then I explain the use of animals in anticolonial writing, such as Jomo Kenyatta's *Facing Mount Kenya* and Yuda Komora's children's book, *Usininyonye.* The ideal world in Komora's story is one in which animals do not eat or oppress one another, but it promotes the view that humans are superior to animals and that we can use animals for labor and as a source of food. I proceed to examine the rewriting of oral narratives in a short story by Grace Ogot and a children's book by Rebecca Nandwa, in which the authors use animals and nature to address feminist themes. In these works, animals and nature are allies of women in the fight for gender equality. I follow this with a discussion of Henry ole Kulet's novel *Vanishing Herds* as an example of ecofeminist transformations of orature in modern African writing. To acknowledge the complexities that modern Africans face in the fight against postindependence dictatorships that are difficult to overthrow, I end the chapter with a discussion of the deployment of animals as narrators in modern writings that reject the kinds of happy endings we find in traditional orature.

It needs to be mentioned at the outset that the use of animals as literary characters can appear simplistic on the surface. John Simons refers to the representation of animals as humans in children's books and fables as "trivial anthropomorphism" because, while troubling the boundary between human and nonhuman animals, such representations do not "press against us to question the reality of that boundary" (2002, 119). Children are the ideal audience for these performances, and the artists demand that the children see humans as no different from animals. Even if they make few demands on adult readers, the texts do reveal social attitudes toward animals. The manner in which they represent animals is likely to have an effect on the way those animals are treated in the real world. This is especially true in oral and written texts for young people: these works instruct children in ways to treat different categories of animals, thus integrating the reader or audience into the social habitus or as, Bob Dixon puts it, "catching them young" (1978) to treat animals as instructed in the story.

By "orature" (also "oral literature") I refer to what Austin Bukenya and Jane Nandwa define as "those utterances, whether spoken, recited or sung, whose composition and performance exhibit to an appreciable degree the artistic character of accurate observation, vivid imagination and ingenious expression" (1983, 1).[1] The attitude toward animals in the texts is usually communal. For example, the uniqueness of individual performances, such as that of Norpisia in Henry ole Kulet's *Vanishing Herds* (2011; discussed below), serves the interests of the whole community, to which they are subordinated. Following the literary artists that I discuss, I do not intend to idealize the world represented in orature. That would promote the image of an ecologically noble savage, who never existed in reality. Instead, I seek to understand how orature imagines and analyzes human-animal relationships in contemporary literary texts. Through an examination of stories by Yuda Komora, Rebecca Nandwa, Grace Ogot, Henry ole Kulet, Patrice Nganang, I conclude that these texts repurpose oral literature to draw parallels between the plight of animals and the condition of powerless individuals and communities in an African nation, asking if there is hope for the oppressed to break free from persecution. Rather than privileging authorial intention in my reading of these texts, as has been common in postcolonial studies, I focus on the texts' cultural situations and sensitivities to understand how they address preexisting social norms.

In responding to orature's figuration of animals, Wanjiku Mukabi Kabira notes that in most oral narratives, girls are presented "as easily cheated, chatty, shallow, pre-occupied with external looks, dependent, and vulnerable" (Kabira 1993, 273), while wives are seen as "unreliable, dishonest, stupid, liars, dependent, [and] dishonest" (1993, 274). Moving beyond the nationalist paradigm, Kabira specifically urges us, "while promoting our cultural heritage" through the study of orature, to "not be blind to these forces that promote gender discrimination and ideologies of oppression" (Kabira 1994, 84). Some of the stories discussed here carry in them a speciesist and misogynistic bias that needs a critical response.

ANIMAL AGENCY IN ORATURE

In her study of gender inequalities in the orature of her Gĩkũyũ community, Wanjiku Mukabi Kabira uses a method she explained in a handbook developed with Masheti Masinjila called the *ABC of Gender Analysis* (Kabira and Masinjila 1997). They wrote the pamphlet for use in schools to foster gender sensitivity, even in math and science classes. The authors' assumption is that "each and every text book and all learning materials tell a story about people; how they relate to one another and the environment within which they live" (9). The goal is to make sure that "none" of the students "will feel alienated" (11) from the lessons because of the gendered illustrations used (11). Echoing Mieke Bal's *Narratology* (1990 [1985]), Kabira is interested in ways of analyzing orature to assess the distribution of gender agency in a narrative: "who focalizes? . . . who acts? . . . who talks? . . . who sees? . . . who has power?" (Kabira 1994, 61). Like Bal, by the focalizer Kabira means the character through whose perspective the narrator views other characters, situations, feelings, events, and phenomena presented in the story. She asserts that, through masculinist focalization, oral performances in some instances have "been used to perpetuate a negative image of women and has in the images it represents legitimised the need to control women" (1994, 83).[2] The same can be said about the representation of animals, although in some instances, male animals are represented more positively than females. This results in a hierarchy based on both species and gender.

Borrowing heavily from oral literature, magical realism is a prominent mode of writing in postcolonial cultures. In magical realism, we encounter "the general instability of the perceived world, and the nature and range of the blurring of boundaries between the animal and the human world" (Quayson 2002, 730).[3] In reading European children's books that exploit magical realism, Erica Fudge observes that in such performances, "we cannot enjoy the tale and simultaneously doubt the world in which it takes place: to do so would be to destroy the narrative altogether" (2003, 72). However, I find such texts rewarding in the ways they unearth contradictions and aporias that Fudge foregrounds to expose the anthropocentrism of the narratives. Children are usually aware that what they are hearing is a fictional story, yet they actively participate in the construction of meanings rather than take the story as a documentation of reality.

The study of the representation of animals in orature is beneficial because it has been largely ignored by scholars, and because it forms the basis for the representation of animals in other modern genres. In response to claims that the ethics of care is the provenance of neocolonialists and ecotourists, Zakes Mda writes:

> Caring about animals and telling stories about them cannot be a "white thing" because these are the very animals that featured as characters in the stories that my grandmother told me when I was a little boy, stories that had been passed to her by previous generations of grandmothers long before white people came to South Africa. (2018, 51)

Mda made these comments in 2009 at the African Literature Association annual conference to remind Africanists of the need to consider animals and the landscape seriously in the study of African literatures. He believes that black people in postapartheid South Africa are mistaken when they assume that the government's interest in environmental protection is an extension of the white apartheid colonialism.[4] He suggests that the natural world is an integral component of indigenous cultures themselves, and it is only the black elites that would be indifferent to the ecological crises facing the nation. In *The Whale Caller* (discussed in chapter 5), Mda satirizes groups of black people who view conservation of the environment as antithetical to indigenous people's interests.

Other African scholars have taken a similar stand, making links between humans and the broader ecological world portrayed in folk art. In *Penpoints, Gunpoints, and Dreams* (1998), Ngũgĩ wa Thiong'o emphasizes the codependence of humans and nature in orature: "Pre-colonial orature in Africa reflects the interdependence of forms of life in the fluidity of movement of characters through all the four realms of being and their interactions in flexible time and space. Plants, animals, and humans interact freely in many of the narratives" (1998, 117). Here Ngũgĩ identifies a unifying commonality between nature, the oppressed, and popular oral forms of representation. In *Decolonising the Mind* (1986a), Ngũgĩ suggests that literature about animals is a product of the human need to understand and master the natural environment. The presence of animals and nature in literary texts also suggests to Ngũgĩ the underdevelopment of the world signified or producing those texts. Echoing Marx and Engels, whom he later criticized for looking down on peasants in favor of industrial workers, Ngũgĩ states that unlike Europe, "the pre-colonial African world . . . was on the whole characterized by a low level of development of productive forces" (65).[5] He uses words such as "incomprehensible," "unpredictable," "unknowable," "hostile," and "largely cruel" to describe nature, which dominates what he sees as underdeveloped precolonial Africa and was "only knowable through ritual, magic and divination" (65). Orature about the environment, to Ngũgĩ, provides a means of coming to terms with a world that the African could not comprehend: "This world was reflected in the literature it produced with its mixture of animal characters, of half-man-half-beast and of human beings all intermingling and interacting in a co-existence of mutual suspicion, hostility, and cunning but also occasional moments of co-operation" (Ngũgĩ, 1986, 65). Earlier he had indicated that the stories of animals reflect the class struggles in human society. We identify with the hare because it is small and represents the downtrodden.

> We identify with him as he struggled against the brutes of prey like lion, leopard, hyena. His victories were our victories and we learnt that the apparently weak can outwit the strong. We followed animals in their struggle against hostile nature—drought, rain, sun, wind—a confrontation often forcing them to search for forms of co-operation. But we were also interested in their struggles among themselves, and particularly between the beasts and the victims of prey. These twin struggles, against nature and other animals, reflected real-life struggles in the human world. (10)

Ngũgĩ presents the unity between humans, animals, and the environment in his children's stories where nature is presented as sympathetic to local struggles. For example, in his *Njamba Nene and the Flying Bus* (1986c), anticolonial struggles are presented in metaphors that signify the Gĩkũyũ community's attitude toward animals. The small book was originally published in Ngũgĩ's mother tongue, Gĩkũyũ, in 1982 as *Njamba Nene na Mbaathi ĩ Mathagu* (Njamba Nene and the Bus with Wings; Ngũgĩ 1982b). It addresses most of the postcolonial themes also found in Ngũgĩ's essays, fiction, and drama: the wanton brutality of the colonial government, the inevitability of armed conflict to dislodge colonialism, the importance of respect for local cultures and knowledge, and the need for Africans to use and retain their indigenous languages. As part of the "Njamba Nene" series, *Njamba Nene and the Flying Bus* describes the experiences of the eponymous Njamba Nene and his schoolmates in a strange forest after their bus is involved in what appears at first to be an accident caused by reckless driving, but that instead becomes a fantastic journey to a dangerous forest.[6] The students are on their way to the national museum in Nairobi when their bus (named "*Go after Money*") is involved in an accident as it competes with another bus (called *"Money Matters"*). As a critique of runaway capitalism, the Gĩkũyũ edition of the story gives the two competing buses synonymous names that express colonialism's hunger for money.[7] The bus turns into an animal—a cross between a horse and a bird—and flies the children into a forest filled with dangerous animals before bursting into flames.

In this tale of self-reliance, Njamba Nene leads other students out of danger. The first theme that Ngũgĩ addresses in the children's book is the language question. Ngũgĩ has argued, especially in *Decolonising the Mind* (1986a), that literatures from the Global South should be written in indigenous languages as opposed to the hegemonic languages that colonialism injected into non-Western societies. In *Njamba Nene and the Flying Bus,* the language debate appears in an early section of the story. Njamba Nene is derided for his knowledge of his mother tongue. Kĩgorogoru, his brainwashed teacher, laughs at the boy for his command of Gĩkũyũ: "You really know how to speak Gĩkũyũ! When will you learn to speak English? When hyenas grow horns?" (2). Ironically, even as the teacher derides Gĩkũyũ, the reference to hyenas growing horns is itself a Gĩkũyũ stock phrase. Often the animals in this phrase are domestic—hens, hares, dogs, and the like. The change he makes to the stock expression underscores Kĩgorogoru's underlying wild animality as an agent of neocolonial pedagogy and knowledge production. The metaphor of a hyena with horns emphasizes that the status referred to can never be achieved. In other words, Kĩgorogoru (whose name connotes a huge Adam's apple) believes that Njamba Nene will never learn English and become civilized. The metaphor also betrays that Kĩgorogoru is more familiar with hyenas than the domestic animals that would ordinarily feature in the idiom. This signifies that he is no different from the community that he views as crass and primitive.

In a culture striving to reclaim its humanity after a long period of animalization, it is understandable that even narratives about animals would be anthropocentric. Anthropocentrism does, after all, have its benefits. As Jane Bennett writes in *Vibrant Matter* (2009), "maybe it is worth running the risks associated with anthropomorphizing (superstition, the divinization of nature, romanticism) because it, oddly enough, works against anthropocentrism: a chord is struck between person and thing, and I am no longer above or outside a nonhuman 'environment'" (120). Ngũgĩ's human-centered ethics also undermines the priority we usually uncritically assign to humans vis-à-vis animals and the environment. Told largely from an anthropocentric perspective, *Njamba Nene and the Flying Bus* is ambivalent about animals, presenting them as both dangerous and tamable. It justifies animals being killed for food; Njamba Nene slaughters an antelope for the rest of his class. But it also indicates that animals may help society understand itself. While other students are acquiring alien colonial geographies that focus on European localities and physical features, Njamba Nene's mother has offered him an organic education that emphasizes local knowledge. In her lessons, she inserts perspectives on animals, indigenous viewpoints that have been erased from the modern Eurocentric school's curriculum.

In the forest, Njamba Nene's classmates cannot tell where they are. But he knows they are in a forest called Ngaindeithia (Gĩkũyũ language for "God, help me"). He also knows that the forest bears that name because "there are a lot of wild animals in it. Some are very fierce, and others not so fierce. But the fierce ones are the majority" (25). The suspense that the children's vulnerability generates as they try to find their way out of the dangerous forest is heightened through references to these ferocious wild animals. The animals are not necessarily fighting for their rights within their habitat; they seem to only be endangering human lives. Njamba Nene's heroic stature resides in his ability to tame these fierce animals. In parts of the story seen through his eyes, we are told that he has acquired mastery over animals through the natural education his mother offered him, a form of anticolonial indigenous instruction that integrates the child into the environment, as opposed to the formal colonial education that alienates humans from nature: "Mother Wacu had taught Njamba Nene the habit of differentiating wild animals; how they walked, how they howled, and even how to distinguish one from the other by their smell" (30). Although the story is told by an omniscient narrator, it is largely filtered through Njamba Nene's perspective. Through this voice we come to understand that he knows more than the other students. To contrast modern education with the informal education he received at home, the story promotes the belief that all crises can be resolved through proper applications of indigenous knowledge, knowledge that enables Njamba Nene to tame animals: "His mother Wacu had taught him that there was no animal so wild that it could not be tamed. All he had to do was to pet it and show it affection. And above all one must never show fear. Most animals were harmless to those who were friendly to them" (30). In contrast, their teacher, a brainwashed Kenyan native who goes by the British-sounding name "John Bull," does not understand his own country, as he "knew nothing about its trees, rivers, animals, mountains, languages, or anything else for that matter" (32). He views

Africans' alleged nonhumanity in animal terms: To him, African freedom fighters look like wild animals with their unkempt hair" (37). He is the complete opposite of Njamba Nene in that he understands very little of the wild, although he is quick to assign wild animality to people he dislikes. Good education, then, is that which organically teaches the child to be a living part of his environment. It is this knowledge that Njamba Nene employs to save his peers: "As each animal came by, Njamba Nene sang to it as best as he could, until each one of them quietened down. The animals came closer, drawn by his gentle voice. They lay near him" (30).The environment is presented with a vitality that the school lacks. In the Valley of Tears, trees have human-like emotions: They "were weeping, actually shedding tears, just like people do. Their tears seemed to water the trees at the same time" (32). The trees are presented as "actually" weeping, and we have no reason to believe that this is a misreading of the environment on the Njamba Nene's part.[8] The unity of the human and nonhuman in Ngũgĩ's story is not a metafictional conceit in a fiction about fiction; it is an actual part of existence in the Global South. Ngũgĩ's Njamba Nene story thus reads environmental ethics as part of human experience, urging its school-age readers toward a deeper awareness of and unity with the natural world and nonhuman animals.

UNNECESSARILY FIGHTING BACK, OR PITFALLS OF ANTICOLONIAL NATIONALISM

The tendency to give priority to individual performers and writers emanates from a need to prove colonial ethnologists wrong in their assertion that orature is nothing more than the unoriginal collective art of "primitive" societies. Denigrated by colonialists and missionary scholars, orature is usually studied in postcolonial societies from a nationalist perspective, in which its images are romanticized as representations of an ideal world in which all conflicts are resolved, evil is banished, virtue triumphs, and good people live happily ever after. Among the most famous of these defenses is Jomo Kenyatta's 1938 ethnographic study, *Facing Mount Kenya*. Written as part of Kenyatta's studies at the London School of Economics, the anthropological treatise also became an important declamation of anticolonial nationalist sentiment, in part because of its satire.

Halfway through *Facing Mount Kenya,* Kenyatta digresses to poke fun at the relationship between the colonizer and the colonized by way of an animal fable that echoes Aesop's tale of a camel that pushed a hospitable Arab from his own tent on a cold desert night (Aesop 1882, 67–68). Instead of Aesop's Orientalist representation of a far-off place, Kenyatta's story comments on the colonialist dispossession of the Gĩkũyũ people in the Kenya of his time. In Kenyatta's fable, Mr. Elephant is searching for a place in the hut of his friend, a human being, to shelter his trunk from a severe thunderstorm. Once the trunk is inside the hut, Mr. Elephant gradually squeezes his entire body into the hut, forcing the man out. The elephant claims that humans have thicker skins than elephants and are therefore better equipped to withstand the weather, a preposterous argument to justify its colonialist usurpation of the hut. The irony is clear: the elephant has turned logic upside-down by claiming to be more vulnerable to a thunderstorm than humans. The law of the jungle assumes priority over human welfare. When the lion overhears the commotion between the man and the elephant, a commission of inquiry is set up to investigate the man's dispossession. However, the commissioners are all animals, and the man loses the case. Whenever he builds a new hut another animal takes it over, and the animal-run commission rules against him every time he lodges a complaint. Thus, the animals, in turn, take over every house. The man decides to build a house on a grand scale, and the animals fight with one another to occupy it. As they squabble with one another inside the house, he sets it on fire, killing them all. The human being triumphs over the animals, and the story turns out to be an etiological tale about how humans became superior to other animals. It is also a morality tale presenting nonhuman animals as colonialists, and an allegory warning people against ceding their space to larger forces. Kenyatta enlists animals as what Armstrong would call a "blank slate for the inscription of human meanings and values" (2008, 102). Beyond representing the tension between the colonizers, the animals have no interests of their own.

Writing in this allegorical mode, Kenyatta clearly establishes the anticolonial context of his story in that readers can easily discern that the animals in the story represent forces of colonialism.[9] The chapter in which the story is offered concerns the dispossession of the Gĩkũyũ people by colonialists, who have annexed arable land and disrupted the indigenous land tenure system. The author announces that he is using the story as an analogy for how British colonialists have acted against the interests of the colonized. The inclusion of the story constitutes a form of structural excess, reiterating the argument in a secondary form without furthering that argument directly. Yet presenting it as coming from the repertoire of folk expression, Kenyatta suggests as well that the story long predated colonialism, and that it simply illustrates the folly of ingratitude acted out against extended hospitality. Kenyatta changes the story to give the oppressive characters British titles ("Mr.," "Rt. Hon.," etc.) and to mock colonial legal and constitutional practices, such as setting up commissions of inquiry to investigate banal matters.[10] It is clear from the outset that the story is not about the relationship between Kenyatta's Gĩkũyũ people and their ecological environment; it is about "the relationship between the Gikuyu and Europeans" (Kenyatta 1978 [1938], 47). Indeed, Chinua Achebe reads Kenyatta's story as a "parody of British imperialist practices" and notes that when it was first published, contemporaneous critics condemned it as a "subversive and seditious document" (2000, 67).[11] Achebe enjoys it as an anticolonial text that uses animals to satirize British imperialists.

In *The Language of Allegory*, Maureen Quilligan argues that allegories are about the processes through which they are self-reflexively produced: "allegories are about the making of an allegory . . . they all signal that they are about language by using methods that have remained remarkably constant over the centuries" (1992 [1979], 15). In using animals for his nationalist purposes, Kenyatta stereotypes them as ungrateful. Yet his folktale departs from much African orature, where animals are mostly presented as democratic and cosmopolitan. I indicated in the previous chapter that I do not find nationalist critiques of colonial writers productive at this stage in postcolonial African studies. Such polemics may have been useful in the 1930s when Kenyatta wrote *Facing Mount Kenya*, but more urgent today is the plight of marginalized groups, especially those who are vulnerable to the destruction of their livelihoods through the destruction of the environment in postcolonial nations. The inhumane treatment of animals is a result of colonialism, and we should assess how nationalists used this fact during the fight for independence and afterward.[12] Moving forward, then, I ask how folklore and mythology work together to uphold potentially oppressive social norms, and I examine how individual authors have used them to resist the same norms.

ONCE UPON A TIME . . . KOMORA'S EDENIC PAST

In a reading of the role of myth in justifying the oppression of women, Wanjiku Mukabi Kabira remarks that "the nature of myth is such that they claim a sacred quality, demand to be believed in, and sound like statements of fact. They therefore can justify the control of women in society" (1994, 79). This echoes Barthes's view that "myth does not deny things, on the contrary, its function is to talk about them; simply, it purifies them, it makes them innocent, it gives a natural and eternal justification, it gives them a clarity which is not that of an explanation but that of a statement of fact" (1972 [1957], 143). Even as Barthes suggests that we accept the edicts of a myth without questioning the obvious contradictions of the fabrication, he urges us to identify politically charged ideological components in texts that present themselves as depoliticized statements about the past. With Barthes, Kabira observes that Gĩkũyũ myths present subjective male ideological positions as incontestable facts in order to entrench stereotypes that women "need to be controlled because they are incapable of running their families, because they are disloyal and easily cheated" (81). Animals are often used to fulfill this agenda. For example, in Ngũgĩ's *The River Between*, Chege utilizes such a myth to explain why gazelles are not afraid of women, yet the myth's purpose backfires in the literary context of the novel (discussed below), revealing the form's adaptability in changing cultural contexts.

Myths thus reflect the tensions, contradictions, and inequities of social realities. To recover precolonial traditions that colonial modernity threatens to erase, postcolonial artists often integrate oral narratives into their writing, transforming these works into commentaries on the postindependence moment. The Wapokomo community on whose oral literature Yuda Komora draws is largely agriculturist. Its staple food is rice, supplemented with bananas and sorghum. Residents of the Tana River delta in Kenya, the Wapokomo also rely on fishing and hunting.[13] Then, it is clear that this community kills animals for food. But it also practiced sustainable ecology, even protecting crocodile eggs from destruction. Komora's treatment of the Wapokomo marks a departure from that of earlier scholars, who fail to recognize this Bantu community's attachment to its environment. C. W. Hobley (1894) describes the people as "the lazy Wapokomo" because they "do not care for the labour of clearing away the woods in order to make plantations" (99). Looking at Africans and their land in purely extractive capitalist terms, Hobley fails to understand that the Wapokomo's reluctance to clear forests could reflect the community's uncomplicated desire to preserve their environment and natural resources. Equally blind to the neighboring Wakauma community's conservationism, the ethnologist Alice Werner derides her native informant for thinking that finches are not pests destroying ripening rice, but are just "playing" on the rice fields without doing "any harm to the crops" (1913, 382).[14]

Yuda Komora's Kiswahili fable *Usininyonye* (meaning "Suck Me Not" or "Don't Exploit Me," 1970) deals with exploitative habits in postindependence East Africa. Without advocating a radical abolitionist position regarding animal rights, the fable enlists oral literature to imagine a world where no animal eats the flesh of another. Instead, in *Usininyonye*, eating other beings is symbolic of aggressive colonizing and neocolonizing tendencies.[15] The story is didactic. At the time of writing the book, Komora was a UNESCO board member (1972 to 1976) and a prominent educator in Kenya. Around the same time, he served as Kenya's assistant minister for education and was a senior official in the Ministry of Tourism and Wildlife. Although he was not an animal rights activist as such, the conservationist David Western describes him as "kindred spirit," a person "who had grown up among wildlife and pastoralists" (1997, 164). *Usininyonye* addresses the theme of oppression by imagining an ideal world in which animals remain under the control of humans, which aligns him with Stephen Budiansky, who argues that the domestication of animals is benign and beneficial for animals (1992, 61). Komora suggests that animals have benefitted more from domestication than the humans who exploit them for labor and food.[16]

Like most fiction meant for African schools in the first decades of independence, Komora's story is not about animals as animals; it uses animals to allegorize the vicious circle of exploitation in postcolonial societies, where people liberate other people from colonizers only to become colonizers themselves. Komora's fable enables him to indirectly criticize the man-eat-man capitalistic tendencies of the Kenyan postindependence regime. The story opens in an Edenic world. In the ideal exploitation-free animal environment that Komora conjures at the beginning of the narrative, none of the inhabitants of the universe ate flesh until things started falling apart. Eating flesh emerged as a consequence of oppression, as animals found ways to punish their oppressors. Small insects such as ants and ticks were trampled by large mammals such as elephants. In violent retaliation, the ants declare war on these oppressors by relentlessly biting their persecutors.[17] The suggestion here is that the best way to combat colonial violence is to be more violent than one's oppressors. But even after the universe has fallen from its ideal, the animals recognize the need not to eat others. The Edenic world in *Usininyonye* is vegetarian:

> Hapo kale vyumbe vyote vilikua vikila vyakula vya matunda, mboga na nafaka. Hakukuwa na hata mdudu, mnyama, ndege au binadamu aliyekula nya-

ma ya kiumbe kingine. Tena, nyakati hizo, binadamu, wanyama na viumbe vyote walikua marafiki walioishi pamoja katika hali ya amani, umoja na udugu (Komora 1970, 1)

(In the past, all creatures used to eat fruits, vegetables, and grains. There was not even an insect, animal, bird, or human who would eat the flesh of another live being. Furthermore, in those times, humans, animals, and all creatures were friends who lived together in a state of peace, unity, and brotherhood.)[18]

The story disrupts the biological food chain as we know it. But it is not calling for animals, including carnivores, to be vegetarians. It is an allegory asking humans to stop exploiting one another. It is only after the animals stop eating one another in Komora's story that they are able to live in perfect harmony. This motif is found in several other texts based on oral literature that imagine a modern Africa where privileged Africans do not exploit their marginalized colleagues.[19] Mourning the fall from this Edenic past, Kaka Nyati (Brother Buffalo) observes that no one has the right to suck another's blood or trample on their rights: "Na hakuna haki mataifa ya kupe kutusumbua namna hii, sawa na vile ambavyo watu wakubwa kama sisi hatuna haki ya kusumbua watu wa ukoo wa wadudu" (5). (There is no justice in the nation of ticks bothering us this way, just as much we big people have no right to bother people from the clan of insects). Here the animals see themselves as *watu* (persons) and condemn the mistreatment of other nonhuman beings.

Later in the story, the past is remembered with nostalgia. As Babu Ndovu (Grandfather Elephant) puts it, "maisha ya zamani yalikua mazuri sana" (life in the past was very good, 20), and all animals were united. But now there are all sorts of diseases, and animals die in large numbers (20–21). Insects such as "kupe, chawa, kunguni, papasi na mataifa yote ya asili hizo" (ticks, lice, bed-bugs and other nations of that nature) have stopped eating "mboga na natafaka" (vegetables and grains) and started "kujilea kwa kunyonya damu za mataifa ya wale waliokua wakiwakanyanga" (nourishing themselves by sucking the blood of nations of those who had been trampling on them) (3). The repetition of "kunyonya damu yetu" (sucking our blood) "usiku na mchana" (day and night) in direct speech accentuates the mammals' complaints against the insect pests. This is not only to emphasize the exploitative habits of certain members of the cosmos, but to anchor the story in Swahili oral culture. It is intended to be read more as an oral narrative around the fireplace than as a scripted narrative. It primarily addresses the foibles of human beings, not the plight of animals. Therefore, words such as *mataifa* (nations), *watu* (human beings), *bwana huyu* (this gentleman), and *jamaa huyo* (that human individual) are occasionally used by the animals in the story when they talk about each other. At the same time, these references suggest that human and nonhuman subjectivities are entangled with each other such that there is no firm boundary between them.

In the struggle between the parasites and other animals, the narrator sides with the mammals. The narrator uses words we have heard among the mammals, such as *usiku na mchana* (day and night) and *dhiki kuu* (great trauma), to describe the extreme discomfort that the insects inflict on the mammals. As the plot unfolds, all exploitative animals are equated with ticks. The *wimbo mtamu* (sweet song) one of the female donkeys teaches the other mammal addresses the tick as symbols of exploitation:

Wewe mlaghai Kupe
Wacha kungojea vya bure
Ukizururazurura mitaani na misituni
Ama kuvizia kwa chuki na makini
Kwa ulafi wa damu ya bure. (70)

(You, untrustworthy tick
Stop relying on freebies
Loitering in the suburbs and forests
And trawling with hatred
Because of your greed for free blood.)

The tick, who represents all parasites at this point, symbolizes neocolonialism, and consequently is later declared *mfisadi* (corrupt). The story tacitly accepts violence as a solution to social problems, but the attacks animals launch against one another are not arbitrary. As the story progresses, we are reminded of the rationale the small insects and arthropods give at the beginning of the story to justify their attacks on some animals but not on others. Even when he uses the tick to represent all arthropods and insects, Komora refuses to lump all the mammals together into a single category, thereby insisting on their heterogeneity. The list of the different animals is long, possibly as a way to teach young audience the names of the various animals: "chui [leopard], duma [cheetah], fisi [hyena], mbwa mwitu [fox], mbweha [jackal], simba mangu [caracal], mondo [serval], paka [cat], fungo

[African palm civet], kanu [genet], nguchiro [mongoose], kicheche [striped polecat], nyegere [honey badger]" have been spared attacks because "walikua waangalifu walipotembea nchini mwao" (they were cautious in the way they walked in their country) (9). The long inventory in Komora's narrative underscores the diversity of the animal world. At the same time, the pervasive listing of different animal species in the story demands recognition of the kind of heterogeneous ontological status that Derrida calls for. This differs from the tendency to lump all animals together as the Other of the human.[20] But as I will demonstrate shortly, this heterogeneity is cancelled in the dénouement because the story places humans at the top of the hierarchy.

The leopard is demoted and kicked out of the animal kingdom because of his carnivorous appetites. To emphasize the fable's reality, the narrative takes an etiological turn, claiming that the results of the animals' punishment of the offending leopard can still be seen today on the skin of the flesh-eating offender: "alama za mawe na udongo waliomtupia hata sasa zaonekana katika ngozi ya chui" (the markings of stones and soil that the animals threw at him can be seen on the leopard's skin) (13). Jemadari Duma (General Cheetah) and Kapteni Fisi (Captain Hyena) are caught red-handed eating the flesh of Bwana Nyumbu (Mister Ass). The narrator sides with the victims against these military animals and their newfound carnivorousness. They are described as "hawa wahalifu wawili" (these two criminals) (14). The word *wahalifu* connotes both destructiveness (as it can translate to "those who destroy") and the thuggish proclivities of the meat-eating animals, thereby distancing the reader from those animals and their habits.

Despite the story's use of animals, the author's investments in human politics makes it ultimately anthropocentric. This focus becomes quickly apparent as the plot unfolds. When the lion starts eating meat, other mammals such as cows, goats, and sheep seek help from *binadamu* (son of Adam, that is, a human being).[21] In its representation of domestication as equivalent to the protection of animals, Komora's story aligns itself with the common assumption that domesticated animals reap benefits from their human masters.[22] But Komora fails to consider whether this protection of animals is altruistic or an extension of the exploitation inherent in the human domestication of animals. In Komora's fictional narrative, the animals appreciate human protection from aggressive carnivores and pests. This echoes Budiansky's conclusion that "freedom from predators, from starvation, and from parasites are not advantages to be dismissed casually" (144). As they beg him for help, the animals in Komora's story recognize the *binadamu* (human being) as the *mkuu wa viumbe wote* (master of all creatures) (15). To the chagrin of the insects considered pests, the human being protects the animals by spraying them with insecticides.

At the beginning of the dénouement, the narrator summarizes: "Basi hali ya maisha ikawa ngumu kwa kila kiumbe" (therefore, life was hard for every creature) (26). In this the narrator underscores the moral lesson of the narrative with a Kiswahili proverb also found in Ngũgĩ wa Thiong'o's *A Grain of Wheat:* "kikulacho ki nguoni mwako" (that which eats you up hides in your own clothes) (Komora 1970, 28; Ngũgĩ 1986 [1967], 15, 152). In Ngũgĩ's story, the traitors among African anticolonial movements are people close to the freedom fighters. In Komora's story, those who exploit others in postindependence Africa are no longer foreigners, they are greedy individuals and forces within the nation itself. In the proverb, the enemy within is portrayed as insects that live in human hair, clothes, and bedding (e.g., fleas, lice, and bedbugs). I show later how the parasite motif is extended to women, who are considered undesirable exploiters (chapter 5) or to sexual and ethnic minorities whom the rest of the society wants to exterminate (chapter 4). In Komora's story, the narrator goes so far as to reveal the allegory as a commentary on humans who exploit fellow humans in the same society:

> Kwa bahati baya walizaliwa binadamu ambao mara nyingi huonelea wanaweza kupata maisha rahisi kwa kuwanyonya wenzao kama kupe ama chawa wafanyao. Watu kama hawa wanawasaidia kupe, kunguni na wadudu wengine kama hao katika vita hivi vya maisha kati ya binadamu na vyumbe vingine. (29)
>
> (Unfortunately, some humans came into being who most of the time prefer to lead an easy life, exploiting others the way ticks and lice do. People of this nature act in cahoots with ticks, bedbugs, and other insects like those in the war between humans and other animals.)

This statement is an auto-interpretation of the story, in which the oral narrator summarizes the lesson for the audience. This is clear from the story not only because we have already seen carnivorous humans exploiting the other animals, but because the rest of the story illustrates human behavior analogous to that presented in the animal world. The narrator presents a teacher, Bwana Moto (Mr. Moto, or Mr. Fire), who invites people to a pub for a beer and then escapes through the back door without paying. Instead of being a good host to his friend Yusuf, Bwana Moto "alimnyonya kwa hila baya" (exploited him in a bad way) (30). In fact, Bwana Moto has been treating other friends the way he treats Yusuf, exploiting them by luring them to a pub and leaving them to pay the bill.

Although the story presents itself as a commentary on human behavior rather than the human exploitation of animals, the conclusion is that all forms of exploitation should be eliminated. Long-time human adversaries are urged to unite against nonhuman forces that have taken advantage of their ignorance. The society elects to educate one of the children to find a *dawa* (medicine or panacea) that will end all forms of *unyonyaji* (sucking, exploitation), which is carried out by *binadamu* (humans), *wanyama* (animals), *ndege* (birds), *samaki* (fish), and insects. The child would also come up with a solution against *viini* (microbes) that cause diseases.

The domestic animals in the story and the narrator believe that, despite the undesirability of confinement in homes and zoos, nonhuman animals in human captivity have a higher chance of survival than those in the wild.[23] Similarly, some historians believe that European colonialism is beneficial to colonized cultures. The impact of colonialism was "both positive and negative, with positive aspects far outweighing the negative ones" (Boahen, 1987, 94).[24] In Komora's story, the narrator justifies exploitation of animals in similar terms to those used by scholars who justify colonialism. The logic in the story's opening is discarded to justify human consumption of animals. It is because of attacks by "kunguni, chawa na funza" (bed-bugs, lice, and fleas) that humans start eating domestic animals (17). The animals become fatalistic, accepting their destiny as victims of the humans as God-ordained. They reason:

> Pale Mwenyezi Mungu akuwekapo ni lazima upakubali. Kila tulipokimbilia tulipatwa na matatizo ya namna nyingi. Lakini afadhali hapa tulipo sababu tunapata ulinzi wa binadamu. Atupa chakula kila siku. Hutupa dawa na pahali pa kulala, na hutulinda kutokana na hatari ya wanyama wa porini. (18)
>
> (You must accept the place where God places you. Everywhere we ran to, we were confronted with many problems. But we are better off where we are now because we can get security from the human. He gives us food every day. He gives us medicine and a place to sleep, and he defends us against danger from wild animals.)

The other animals that sucked the blood of the newly domesticated animals in the past "hawakutufanyia jambo lolote" (will not harm us at all) (18). However, the narrator recognizes that this human habit of eating animal flesh is not universal. The animals that sought help in the Asian continent "walipata bahati kubwa" (were extremely lucky) because "wahindi wengi" (most Indians) are religious and vegetarian. Animal submission to humans even has some gendered implications. When the parasite-tormented Mbwa (dog) flees the wild seeking work as a guard in a human dwelling, the narrator's language suggests that the man is both a boss and a husband. The dog flees "porini" (the wild) to receive "ulinzi" (protection) and "matunzo" (care) from the "bwana wake mpya" (new boss) (19). The word *bwana* means both "husband" and "master." We are taken full circle. In the beginning, animals lost their freedom to another; in the end they surrender their freedom to humans.

FEMINIST ANIMALS FROM *TERRA NULLIUS*

The 1960 publication of Albert B. Lord's influential *Singer of Tales* gave rise to a consensus among folklorists that oral performances are a process of dynamic evolution that is dependent on the performer, the occasion, and the audience. Each performance of an oral text is, in this view, a new iteration of that text. The text's aesthetic power remains constant; the same story can be heard many times and continue to fascinate because of the artist's stylistic innovations. As Ato Quayson observes regarding the use of folklore in modern Nigerian novels, materials from orature always adapt to reflect the anxieties of their times.[25] It is worth examining how animals signal these transformations in stories that insert nonhuman characters in the plot to show the inhumanity of humans and to express a desire for a utopian world in which animals rule. A case in point is the reference to animals in Rebecca Nandwa's *Mnyama Mwenye Huruma* (*A Merciful Animal*, 2005), a rewriting of Grace Ogot's popular short story "The Bamboo Hut" (1969). A children's book, *Mnyama Mwenye Huruma* locates itself at the outset in the realm of orature, complete with an opening formula that is a familiar cue to child audiences that they are about to encounter a fictional narrative set in a sublime fantasy world: *"hapo zamani za kale"* (Once upon a time, in the very remote past . . .). On the other hand, "The Bamboo Hut" presents itself as a modern story, but it borrows heavily from Luo orature, which Grace Ogot adapts to emphasize feminist themes. Ogot's story revolves around Achieng', one of the nine wives of Chief Mbago. She is forced by circumstances to abandon her female twin baby in the wilderness to please her husband and bring home only the male twin. For over twelve years, the chief has been waiting for his wives to bear him a male heir. As an incentive, and acting from the belief that women can determine the gender of the children, he has promised the titular bamboo hut to the wife who gives birth to a boy. When Achieng' gives birth to twins, a boy and a girl, she abandons the girl, Apiyo, and brings home the male child, Owiny. The abandoned Apiyo is brought up in exile. Years later, in the son's search for a wife, it happens that the girl he wants to marry is the twin sister that his mother discarded.

Nandwa's story follows a similar pattern. While Ogot's story in English tries to imitate Dholuo speech patterns in the narrator's voice and the character's dialogue, Nandwa's narrative is told in idiomatic standard Kiswahili. It is the story of the brutal King Hodari, who demands from his ten wives "watoto wa kiume ambao wataniletea heshima, sifa na utajiri" (male children, who will bring me honor, fame, and wealth) (2). As in Ogot's story, the first wife (unnamed throughout the story to symbolize her marginality in society beyond being the king's wife) gives birth to twins, a boy and a girl. Like Ogot's Achieng', the woman abandons her daughter (Waheelwa) and returns home with the son (Wafula). From this point in the story, she is called Mama Wafula (Wafula's mother) to emphasize the importance attached to giving birth to a boy. In Nandwa's folktale, the wife is in the company of other women when she leaves Waheelwa in the bushes. Thus, this version of the story has less to do with the complicity of women with patriarchy than with the violent suppression of women's agency in a patriarchal society. The women would openly protest their condition, but they are vulnerable to their patriarch's violence. In Ogot's story, women compete with one another to occupy the coveted bamboo hut; in Nandwa's story, the narrator focuses on the women's sorrow and shame as they unwillingly leave Waheelwa to her fate in the wild. Furthermore, Waheelwa's mother does not erase her from memory as Achieng' does with Apiyo. We sympathize with her more than Achieng' because when Achieng' abandons Apiyo, she does so from self-interest.

Looking at the world from female perspectives, Ogot and Nandwa do not idealize the precolonial African societies they represent. The bamboo hut that Achieng' and her cowives compete for is the symbol of rewards given to women by the patriarchal power-wielders to perpetuate their own oppression. In Ogot's story, Achieng' at least is allowed to occupy the bamboo hut together with her daughter and her newborn son. Although it does not criticize patriarchy as strongly as Nandwa's, Ogot's story shows the weaknesses of the patriarchal system in which Achieng' dwells, and portrays the wilderness as a space of possibility in which the girl is safely delivered back to her family, thus defeating the patriarchal system that rejected her.

As Stacy Alaimo (2010) argues in the context of queer identity, in an oppressive world, homosexuality can only thrive in the wilderness. Wilderness, to Alaimo, is therefore queer. In Ogot's and Nandwa's stories, wilderness is markedly feminist, contrasted with the domestic space that is destructively patriarchal and constricting to women. Ogot's narrative carves out for the girl a sociological space that Mudimbe, in his theory of the postcolony, calls *terra nullius* (nobody's land). Mudimbe's *terra nullius* is a principle activated by colonialism to dispossess natives of their land and to impose their religion and economic and political will on new territories (1988, 45; 1994, 35). Such deterritorialized spaces, in Deleuzian terms, offer sites for multiple becomings and creative potentials. Apiyo is not portrayed as a colonialist who turns the *terra nullius* into personal property.[26] She is taken there to acquire female power, and returns to her society to reclaim her rightful position therein. However, the *terra nullius* in "The Bamboo Hut" is imaginary. We know Apiyo grows up in a real family because even if her mother believes that a witch takes care of the girl, the story suggests that the mother has created that witch in her imagination. But the no-man's-land is a site where becoming-female, for example, is possible. Even if it is only imagined, it gives the girl immense potential.

Like Ogot, Nandwa does not idealize nature; the narrative's humans do not seek to relocate to the natural environment where Okunani dwells. Instead, at the end of the story, they harness natural resources to restore their physically and morally moribund society. Granted, this social resuscitation begins at the point of the girl's redemption in *terra nullius*. An animal saves the girl, and is real in the story, although it does not exist in the material world:

> Mtoto wa kike alieachwa kichakani hakufa kama walivyodhania. Mnyama mmoja kwa jina Okunani—alieyekua mtu sehemu ya juu, na sehemu za chini mnyama, [sic] alikua akipita karibu na hicho kichaka. Okunani pia alikua na uwezo wa kujigeuza akawa mtu kamili au mnyama kamili. Lakini sababu ya kuishi misituni, alizoea kuvaa sura ya mnyama. (7)

> (The girl-child left in the bush did not die as expected. An animal by the name Okunani—who was human in the upper body and animal in the lower body, happened to be passing near that bush. Okunani had the ability to change into a full human being or a complete animal. But because of living in the wild Okunani was accustomed to putting on the looks of an animal.) [my translation][27]

It is imperative to note Okunani's ability to change seamlessly from human to animal and vice versa. Through the figure of the half-beast, Nandwa seeks to erase the differences between humans and animals, but she does not blame humans for creating such a figure. It is already part of the assemblage of nature. When it is humans who try to become animals, they are criticized. Okunani too is able literally to convert herself into a human, but not with the destructive intention by which the king becomes animalistic.

In the Luhya oral literature on which Nandwa's story is based, *okunani* (ogre) stories employ the beauty-and-the-beast motif, in which a beautiful girl encounters a handsome suitor who later turns out to be an evil ugly ogre. In Nandwa's story, Okunani is half-human, half-animal in a way that suggests, to use Tiffin's words in a different context, "both a repelling distance from ourselves and, troublingly, some similarities" (2014, 154). In Luhya folklore, the ugly being is usually a male *linani* (ogre). In fact, in most societies the ugly *linani*-like animal is most often male: "the Beast has been primarily identified with the male since the earliest forms" (Warner 1994, 279). However, Nandwa's story makes changes that accommodate the humanism of women and animals. In traditional folklore, *okunani* is a malevolent force. The word *okunani* is the augmentative form of *linani* (an ogre; plural *amanani*). To the child-audience, *okunani* is supposed to be bigger and scarier than the ordinary human-eating *linani.* Even in its less frightening form, *okunani* is a dangerous and wily character. With a huge appetite for beautiful girls, a *linani* can disguise himself as a handsome young man to lure girls into his lair and devour them. It is an *okunani* who kidnaps Simbi, the vain girl in another Luhya story who turns down all suitors, waiting to marry a man who does not defecate, a "man without an anus" in one version of the story (Kabira and Adagala, 2). Indeed, in Nandwa's 2007 Kiswahili children's book, *Kibuyu cha Miujiza* (*A Miraculous Gourd*), Okunani is a woman-eating male.

However, Nandwa presents a different kind of ogre in *Mnyama Mwenye Huruma* (*Merciful Animal*). Indicating the infinite possibilities of redemption, Okunani here is female, kind, and motherly. She is similar to Mammy Wata, the half-woman, half-fish creature who protects humans from destructive forces in Véronique Tadjo's children's book, *Mammy Wata and the Monster* (1997 [1993]). To humanize animals and to foreground the king's animal-like qualities, Nandwa features prominent references to animals at the beginning narrative. The king is named Hodari (the gallant one), but the stories about his conquests over animals are revealed to be lies:

> Hakuogopa chochote, wala yeyote. Kulikuwa na uvumi wa kila aina kuhusu ushujaa na ukatili wake. Wengine walisema kuwa akiwa kijana, aliwaua simba na chui peke yake, kasha akaula moyo wa simba, ndipo akachukua sifa za mnyama huyo mkali. (1)
>
> (He feared nothing and nobody. There were rumors of all kinds about his courage and inhumanity. Some said that when he was a young man he would kill lions and leopards all by himself, and then eat the heart of the lion, so he acquired the qualities of that ferocious animal.)

The passage emphasizes that Hodari (apparently not his real name) is not a gallant man. His masculinity is constructed through fictional narratives about his adventures in the wild. In a story that transports the child listener to a fantastical world in the hills where no humans live, it is remarkable that the omniscient narrator suggests that he or she cannot verify the king's credentials. This is to imply that details about his past are false, and that he has resorted to propaganda and fear to consolidate his authority and dominance over the society. As if this were not enough, animals are invoked in the next paragraph to indicate that the king has been exaggerating his power over animals:

> Wengine walieneza uvumi kua aliweza kuishi msituni na wanyama wakali bila ya kusumbuliwa nao. Vile vile kuna waliodai kuwa wanyama walipomkaribia, walitishwa na ukali wake na walitoroka. (2)
>
> (Others spread the rumor that he used to live in the wild with fierce animals, without the animals bothering him. Also there are some who claimed that when animals came near him, they were scared of his fierceness and fled.)

His relations to animals and powerless humans are different from those of Ngũgĩ's Njamba Nene, who has an amicable rapport with animals in the forests. The king in Nandwa's story is frightening to animals; he kills and eats them. The narrator skillfully nudges young readers not to identify with such a ruthless person. The details of his prowess are indicated as *uvumi* (rumors) and the reporting verb is *dai* (to claim) to inform the young reader or listener that the chief is a liar. He has spread his propaganda so as not to be held accountable to the citizens because he does not want the people to correct him for his mistakes.

Although Nandwa's story remains anthropocentric, it suppresses abuse of animals that similar stories like it usually celebrate as the normal order of things. It is good to remember that stories of this nature are notorious for inserting the food motif as a Pavlov-style trick to keep the young readers alert. Fat bulls are usually slaughtered, and honey flows freely. But Nandwa does not serve food in her story, even on occasions that call for feasting, such as when Wafula is born or when Waheelwa is reunited with her family. Okunani, normally portrayed as cannibalistic, does not eat Waheelwa. The sublimity that the story evokes lies not in its acknowledgment of the "apparent almightiness of nature" that Kant saw as a condition for the sublime (Kant 1951 [1790], 101). It resides instead in Nandwa's belief in the recovery of human innocence wherein even creatures who are worse than ogres are capable of righteousness and where brutal leaders come to their senses and become humane and gender-sensitive men. The story is more about the need to change humans to treat one another better than about the need to be compassionate to animals. At the end of the story, Okunani is disposed of as superfluous to create a happy ending from a human perspective. The medical skills that Okunani taught the girl are used to cure the king. Waheelwa and Okunani's biological child move in with the king's family.

The moral of Nandwa's story is explicit and consistent with the closing formulas of East African folklore. Waheelwa recalls a Swahili proverb from Okunani: "wema hauozi" (virtue never rots).[28] But Okunani is not rewarded for her virtuousness. It is for humans, after penitence, to enjoy utopian happy endings. Okunani does not die to provoke fear and pity for the tragic end of a hero; rather, the story encourages the audience to feel grateful that the human race has been restored to wholeness with the ogre's death. In spite of her benevolence, she dies at the end of the story like any other *linani* or *okunani* in Luhya folklore. She is a sacrificial surrogate who can easily be abandoned for the benefit of humans. All the same, she suffers less than ordinary *linani* in Luhya folktales, who usually die at the ends of these stories. Here, Okunani dies of natural causes. Nandwa suggests that the killing of animals is unnecessary, especially if we have benefitted from them at some point. Even if we do not like those animals, the story suggests, we could just bide our time, patiently and cynically waiting for them to die of a natural cause.

TOWARD ECOFEMINIST TRANSFORMATIONS

As evidenced by its use in these children's stories, the mode in which orature is transmitted has changed from being passed along by word of mouth to modern written forms as well as digital storage and circulation. Isidore Okpewho explores the various ways that orature is represented in modern African writing, arguing that authors use precolonial expressive forms to "demonstrate that traditional African culture is not obsolete but [is] relevant for the articulation of contemporary needs and goals" (1992, 293).[29] In much modern African literature, oral texts are more numerous than scripted texts because the narrators are nonliterate and the narrative assumes an audience of listeners rather than readers. Modern African writing that features animals as characters and narrators belongs to an established tradition of animated and spontaneous unscripted oral performances that are sometimes antagonistic to the written discourse, which is considered alienating and pretentious.

Of course, as Ato Quayson and Eileen Julien assert regarding folklore in modern postcolonial writing, African writers do not passively reproduce the stories borrowed from their precolonial cultures. Just as a traditional artist reworks a well-known text from the cultural repertoire to adjust it for different audiences and occasions, postcolonial African writers modify materials from oral traditions to address contemporary fears and desires.[30] In my view, the changes that the artist makes in these narratives say the most about the artist's ideology. For example, in *The River Between* (1965), Ngũgĩ wa Thiong'o draws on an allegory that expresses the notion that gazelles are not afraid of women because the animals were, once upon a time, the property of women. He does this to subtly point out the unfair treatment of women in his Gĩkũyũ community. Chege tells the story to his son Waiyaki, the protagonist in the novel, to illustrate why women are autocrats and poor managers:

> Long ago women used to rule this land and its men. They were harsh and men began to resent them their hard hand. So when all the women were pregnant, men came together and overthrew them. Before this, women owned everything. The animals you saw were their goats. But because the women could

> not manage them, the goats ran away. They knew women to be weak. So why should they fear them? (1965, 15)

Here, nature and animals in their natural habitats are summoned in myths to bolster self-serving patriarchal attitudes. The young man who hears this story is being indoctrinated against questioning the marginalization of women, even those close to him, such as his own mother; yet we know the story is a fiction without any basis in reality, as gazelle are likely never to have been dometic animals in the past.[31] Not expected to imagine himself in the situations of women, Waiyaki is being primed by his father to view the world in feudal masculine terms and to accept economical dispossession as the natural state of women.[32] Chege's rhetorical questions signify, as irrational as the story is, that its contents are not open to debate. Nevertheless, Ngũgĩ's story shows that Waiyaki is more gender-sensitive than his father, and that the narrative awakens Waiyaki to the disempowerment of women: "It was then [that] Waiyaki understood why his mother owned nothing" (15).[33] In a novel about the need to synthesize traditional African worldviews with developments that colonial modernity brought about, Waiyaki's reflection about his late mother's dispossession suggests that the new generation of men will not be disposed to uphold myths by which the patriarchal society rationalizes its discrimination against women.

Written in the critical realist mode that Ngũgĩ abandoned a decade later, *The River Between* (1965) draws on oral narrative to reflect an unfair reality about women and nature without overtly seeking to change that reality. But it replicates the unfairness in its own form. Most of the story is focused on and imagined through men. When the same folktale is repeated in a different context in Ngũgĩ's next novel, *A Grain of Wheat* (1967), it is to subtly link Queen Victoria's colonial rule to her gender. The colonial queen is no different from the improvident, autocratic women in the oral narrative. She deserves to be overthrown in an armed struggle and, in the early editions of the novel, raped. In contrast, when the Maasai writer Henry ole Kulet constructs a similar narrative in *Vanishing Herds* (2011), there is less emphasis on gender bias, though it is not eradicated. Women's animals escape to the wild not because the women are negligent but because the animals need certain minerals when they become pregnant, compelling them to search for certain fruits. Therefore, animals flee to the wild in the season when they become pregnant. The unlikely possibility that all women would get pregnant at the same time and crave the same *isanangurrurr* fruit is used to justify the economic dispossession of women. In ole Kulet's story, the oral narrative suggests that women are more likely than men to consider as divine the duty to defend the environment. In the world that ole Kulet creates, it is women characters—most notably the modern activist Eddah Sein and the Maasai traditional healer Norpisia—who spearhead the efforts to "resuscitate the degraded environment" (ole Kulet 2011, 165). As in Ngũgĩ's *The River Between*, the Maasai cultural past and the advances occasioned by modernity combine synergistically in human efforts to conserve the environment.

Whereas men are portrayed as destroyers in Kulet's novel, women represent forces that will restore both the environment and the culture. In a country where reading for entertainment is minimal, the novelist is definitely written with an eye toward Kenyan schools, where the text, if included in curricula, would offer instruction not only on the characteristics of literary works, but on gender and environmental justice.[34] The novel follows templates of oral narratives. It includes legends and proverbs and is linear and largely didactic in nature. In the story, Eddah Sein is a Christian with a modern education who tours the area in a four-wheel-drive vehicle, but she is still faithful to indigenous knowledge of her nomadic community. Whether educated like Sein or traditional like Norpisia, women are portrayed as the ones who will save the nation from the masculinist destruction of the environment. It is through the two women that the most overt environmentalist messages are relayed. Observing the Erereti trading center in a passage presented through her stream of consciousness, Eddah Sein notes:

> It was now a fact that the wantonly destroyed forests were no more, and the timber industry had been brought to a halt. The elephants, rhinos, cheetahs, leopards and other games had been poached to near extinction . . . charcoal burning being the only other business available after the timber industry had collapsed—until they found out that the lengthening spell of dry weather had dried up the only river that was the source of drinking water. (164)

The statements may sound simplistic, but they allow the author to locate agency in his female characters. The women's actions are denounced for not observing the vegetarian ideal. Norpisia has domesticated four wildebeests. This would violate the kind of land ethic that J. Baird Callicott espouses, in which "a herd of cattle, sheep, or pigs is as much or more of a ruinous blight on the landscape as a fleet of four-wheel-drive off-road vehicles" (1989, 30). Callicott views the domestication of any animal as morally wrong because it transforms natural phenomena into man-made artifacts.[35] Norpisia's family not only keeps cattle, but she goes so far as to domesticate wild animals. Within the intradiegetic context, the domestication of the animals shows that it is possible to erase hierarchizing boundaries between the highly valued male-owned dairy animals and the wild animals owned by women. In this narrative, the society should value both types of animals and conserve the environment in which the wild animals are found. Nature is presented as dimorphic and unpredictable. It protects and destroys, and its victims may include those who are trying to defend it. At the end of the novel, all the animals this exemplary couple owns drown in a flash flood. Norpisia loses the four wildebeests that she had domesticated and that were being used as a tourist attraction. It is possible that the animals have survived, but they are no longer under human control.

The powers that enable Eddah and Norpisia to defend the environment come at a cost to traditional, patriarchal social norms, and the men who tell their stories never fully endorse women's ecologically noble capabilities. Unlike other women, Norpisia has acquired military skills, but mainly for "self-defense, self-reliance" after losing her siblings at the hands of (probably male) bandits. Norpisia is also a storyteller: "she was clear and precise with exemplary word choice, accompanied by evocative gestures" (171). Her stories are about the restoration of the environment. In one of these stories she divulges "her grandmother's wish that she join wild animals to fight human beings who destroyed their habitat" (171). The stories are thus different from those that her husband Kedoki tells. Kedoki, from whose perspective Norpisia's griot skills are described to the reader, emphasizes style more than experience. He is poetic in the dramatic personal oral testimony he delivers before Norpisia's narrative orations, but his performance sets up animals as the foil of the heroic Kedoki, the autobiographical protagonist. He narrates how he gallantly survived the dangers that "had lurked everywhere with crocodiles waiting to rip off those who crossed the rivers, the trumpeting giant elephants hurtling down hills like cannons" (170). However, when we encounter the animals in their natural habitat, they are not as violent as Kedoki has portrayed them. As Norpisia observes earlier in the narrative, the enemy of human beings is not animals, but "fellow" human beings (70). Even when, later in the novel, Kedoki lies wounded but still alive, vultures do not attack him. The woman's position is clear in the narrative: if humans restore the natural resources they have overexploited, "this would naturally help the return of the wild animals to their habitat and minimize human and animal conflicts" (172). The author seems hesitant to show people who contravene land ethics as successful even when they are well-meaning heroines.

In its dénouement, the story avoids a happily-ever-after resolution in which the government showers the heroines with medals and trophies. Furthermore, though neither the narrator nor any of the characters criticize the eating of meat or the keeping of animals as a form of other-species enslavement, the frequency of eating "appetizing" meat (13) diminishes as the narrative develops and the community embraces environmental conservation. Granted, the narrative never criticizes meat-eating. Meat is a good source of nutrition for Kedoki after he is injured. He eats "six healthy he-goats" and takes "mugfuls of soup" before he can recover enough to proceed with his journey (95). The reduction in meat-eating as the plot develops is not so much an embrace of vegetarianism as it is a natural consequence of environmental stewardship. As the story reaches its end, the community's conservation efforts are rewarded with a bull to slaughter. The feast is even joyful: "the throng of men, women, and children chatted and laughed merrily as they feasted on large quantities of roasted, fried, and boiled meat" (201), emphasizing a welcome abundance and variety of meat dishes as the story gestures toward a happy ending and a celebration of the restoration of the forests. But the apparent drowning of the livestock owned by Kedoki and his wife implies that animals both wild and domesticated should be left in the wild. We are not sure whether the cows and wildebeests died in the flood, but it is clear they are no longer under Kedoki's or Norpisia's control as domestic animals or tourist attractions. Kulet uses Kedoki's and Norpisia's conflicting versions of the female herder folktale in these final moments to emphasize the story's message about environmental conservation and the natural order. The two never agree, but they do not need to. Instead, the wider narrative conveys the tale's message in print, to Norpisia's audience, to Kedoki's audience, and to future schoolchildren and readers.

AUTHORIAL PESSIMISM AND THE AGENCY OF AN ANIMAL NARRATOR

Contemporary African writers who use animal narrators, such as Patrice Nganang in his *Dog Days*, have credited orature and other forms that evoke oral texts (e.g., newspaper cartoons), in which animals speak, for inspiring them to do so. Although animals speak in traditional African oral literature, as seen above, rarely are they narrators.[36] The narrating animal is a departure from orature to give animals more agency and to free them from a traditional anthropocentric gaze. Reminiscent of characters in oral literature, the dog in Nganang's *Dog Days* is either telling the reader the story of his experiences or listening to humans tell stories in an oral setting. The feature of narrating animals is not confined to African literature; several Western texts use it to good effect.[37] As Yves Clavaron notes in a discussion of *Dog Days,* while the use of speaking animals is common in world literatures (including European literature, such as Aesop's tales), they are "typical" in postcolonial writing because the art "aims at reclaiming an oral tradition that had been muzzled by colonization for a long time, as well as at appropriating Western literary genres" (2012, 554).[38] We should add that what distinguishes this kind of narrator in African writing is the use of the speaking animal to expose both the plight of nonhumans and that of the African postcolonial subject experiencing the legacies of European colonialism. The condition of the animals also signifies the problems of the society depicted in the story, such that under colonialism and its aftermath both humans and animals are seen to experience similar conditions. Through the dog narrator, Nganang's *Dog Days* comments on Cameroonian politics under Paul Biya, whom the novel presents as a despot who has curtailed human rights so much since he came to power in 1982 that it would be difficult to overthrow him. His regime has conditioned the people to accept him as unassailable and to be cynical about the possibility of change. The novel is set between 1989 and 1990 and signals both the resistance against the one-party state in Cameroon and the public's complicity in their own oppression. Like the narrating dog, Cameroonians sometimes reject avenues to freedom from Biya's stranglehold on power. At the same time, while commenting on the inhuman conditions Cameroonians live in, the dog's story also foregrounds animal rights. I argue that the use of an animal narrator does not always result in agency for the speaking animal; in the novel, the author manages to use the dog to show the dehumanization of everything under a cynical postcolonial regime. But it is the responsibility of humans to recover that agency for the dog.

The dog is the most important component of the novel. Without its narrating dog Mboudjak, *Dog Days* would not be a terribly original book in African literary contexts. The Congolese Sony Labou Tansi's *In Life and a Half* and the various dramas by the Anglophone Cameroonians Bate Besong and Bole Butake have captured in an equally satirical forcefulness the predicaments facing the postcolonial nation that Nganang's novel presents. But none of these works is narrated from the perspective of a dog. Through the dog, the novel captures vividly the despondency of a nation in the grip of an authoritarian regime. The deployment of a dog narrator in Nganang's novel is not merely an absurdist conceit to keep government censors from banning the book (some of the things the novel says through its narrator and characters are libelous and would definitely attract he wrath of the government so ruthlessly satirized, as has happened to other works critical of the Cameroonian regime).[39] Attempting to capture the political condition in the late 1980s as Cameroonians pressured the authoritative government of Paul Biya to allow multiparty democracy, the novel chronicles a dog's encounters with animals and humans in a Yaoundé working-class neighborhood called Madagascar. A literary individual, Mboudjak has read the works of Jacques Rabemananjara and underlines that the "Madagascar" he comes from is different from the one praised in Rabemananjara's artistic works (9). Massa Yo is Mboudjak's master and owner. The man is a civil servant, but he loses his job. He becomes violent toward the dog, and he escapes to the street, where he shares the seedy conditions of city life with stray dogs. Of his own volition, Mboudjak returns to Massa Yo's home because he considers himself a special dog. The dog survives an attempted hanging by his master's son but voluntarily returns to his master's home. In the meantime, Massa Yo sets up a bar he calls The Customer is King in the hope of making ends meet as conditions worsen. It is at the bar that the dog encounters the lumpen class of Yaoundé, who come there to drown their sorrow. He relays to the readers the stories and rumors patrons like Panther and Crow tell about the sociopolitical conditions they face. He also experiences the political upheavals happening in Cameroon as the country adopts multiparty democracy. In a use of the self-reflexive *mise-en-abyme* technique, we learn that the Crow is a novelist who is writing a book about Cameroon that is also titled *Dog Days,* indicating that dogs have no agency; it is humans who tell animal stories to allegorize human experiences.

Nganang regards his writing to be part of *écriture preemptive,* a tradition of postcolonial writing that considers itself committed to preventing the continent from repeating the mistakes it has made before. In such art, creative writing tries to preempt the problems that affect the society, not waiting until the problems have grown out of control. In preemptive moves, we need the kind of irony Mboudjak evinces because, as Mariana Valverde proposes, when thinkers and political movements "lose their irony, their sense of humor," they become "uncomfortably similar to the powers they seek to challenge" (2002, 86). Although marginalized groups are, as Valverde points out, more likely to be the victims of injustice at the hands of powerful groups, they should be aware that they are capable of committing injustice as well, especially against other minorities. The oppressed Cameroonians Nganang's novel presents are therefore not mere victims; instead, the novel suggests they are complicit or participants in injustices toward one another or other animals. Furthermore, according to Laura Brown, one of the characteristics of the canine narrative subgenre is "the grounding but problematic premise of canine access to human discourse or human processes of thought, the transgression of foundational structures of order, the engagement with the diversity of human experience, and the trip beyond the accepted and the regulated world of here and now" (2010, 142–43). Yet by exposing a world we are still not happy about, the author is not urging us to lose hope; rather, he calls for the kind of theoretical consciousness Amilcar Cabral demanded from anticolonial nationalists in the 1970s; according to Cabral, a revolution is likely to fail if it is indifferent to theory.

ANIMAL SPEECH AND SELF-ASSERTION

"I am a dog," declares the rollicking and gossipy canine-narrator in *Dog Days* to underline his humility and marginalization in a human-dominated world (2006, 7). Central as a marker of his identity is his species: Mboudjak emphasizes that he is a dog. Humans deny him agency and maltreat him as abjectly as the Cameroonian government mistreats its citizens. The well-known dog in Honwana's *We Killed the Mangy Dog* represents the marginalized blacks under Portuguese colonialism in Mozambique; Nganang's Mboudjak is a symbol of the downtrodden in postindependence Cameroon. In Honwana's story, humans (analogs to colonialists) consider the dog a "shit of a black" (108); he is killed by colonial government officials, who seem ready to extend similar violence to the black narrator, himself a diseased mangy dog in the eyes of the privileged characters. Although he has a soul and a subjectivity, the mangy dog in Honwana's story does not speak; in Nganang's story the dog is the narrator.[40] But does getting to speak give the dog agency, especially when we remember the injunction from postcolonial theorists that visibility in identity politics is not enough, as one can be present and visible but remain powerless?[41] In this context, how animals are made visible and what they articulate through their visibility is what matters most. We would expect Mboudjak to forge an alliance with the oppressed animals, but he remains enamored of the humans who oppress him. The only redeeming quality in Mboudjak is that, as he engages in one act of self-humiliation after another, he does not seek to ingratiate himself with the reader. He seems uninterested in our approval of his actions or thoughts, hence revealing some level of intratextual independence, a freedom within the story-world where he defies the expectations of everyone. But throughout the novel, Mboudjak's condition does not improve. If a postcolonial reader were to examine the text from the perspective of a dog, Mboudjak's account would be more escapist than agential. The novel encourages us to grapple with the extent to which telling the story from the perspective of an animal empowers that animal. I argue that the satire is directed at humans; we are the ones to reform and stop subjecting Mboudjak and his kind to the humiliation that he goes through. Mboudjak uses human language, yet as the philosopher Catriona Sandlands reminds us, "human language about nonhuman nature can never be complete; only by acknowledging its limits is the space opened for otherworldly conversations" (1999, 185). We should recognize those limits without forgetting that we should strive to feel the world the way animals perceive it. That is, it is strategic to acknowledge the level of effort needed to achieve that. The narrative privilege given to the animal who speaks in the story does not translate to ideological power within the internal dynamics of the plot. For example, in Nganang's *Dog Days,* the narrating dog speaks, listens, and smells. It is through his consciousness that all the developments in the story are sifted to the reader, even when his presence in the story is unnecessary. But the dog remains hopelessly powerless as an animal. Such animals' prominence in nonhuman-narrated texts reminds us of the situation highlighted in the 1980s, whereby women featured in texts by male writers but had no agency.[42] The same could be said about animal characters in postcolonial texts, because the characters allegorize human predicaments but do not address animal rights. It is not a surprise, then, that in the most nuanced and theoretically sophisticated reading of Nganang's story, Moradewun Adejunmobi (2014) does not focus on animal rights because, to her, "the presentation of the socially subordinate as victim persists in works focused on subordination due to race and gender" (450). Seen this way, Mboudjak has no individuality as a dog, but instead represents human forms of victimhood. Although Adejunmobi is correct to take this position in relation to *Dog Days*, we need to critique such animal characters and pay attention to animal rights as well in relation to the welfare of marginalized human categories. We can spare the author from criticism because his intentions might not be recoverable from the story, but the society and the characters presented need to be critiqued for the negligence of animal rights.

Germane here is Laura Brown's premise that "by using or ventriloquizing human language, by occupying human-centered roles of literary protagonist, by wandering through the diverse world of human experience, by occupying the place of the displaced or the dispossessed as well as that of privilege or fashion, and by undercutting claims to genealogical hierarchy and social regulation, the imaginary dog creates a unique cultural opportunity to consider an alternative to the structures and limits of the present day" (2010, 138). In Nganang's novel, the marginality of Mboudjak echoes the subaltern status of the Cameroonian population and the possibilities of the people seizing power from a draconian regime, though that agency is still limited in the material world of systematic disempowerment. I consider that agency in the section that follows, in which I read the Cameroonians and the narrating dog as zombies.

THE ZOMBIE NARRATION OF A ZOMBIE NATION

Dogs have come to prototypically represent human-animal relations. As Wendy Woodward points out, dogs are "represented as socially and historically located" in contemporary literature in ways that "enable writers to structure notions of human identities and to incorporate broader ecological views of the relationship between human and nonhuman animals" (2008b, 235). As the dog explores the world in which the work of art is set, its experiences form a critique of the postcolonial condition and the attendant ecological dangers the corrupt postcolonial regime poses. Taking the reader with him from one place to the other within the city, the canine in Nganang's *Dog Days* exposes the rot in the postcolonial Cameroonian nation. In Africa, dogs as domestic pets were a creation of the colonial middle class (Woodward 2008a, 91), and in postcolonial writing they "may function as ciphers of racialized privilege" (Woodward 2008b, 235). Mboudjak in Nganang's novel is a symbol of privilege when compared with the stray and sometimes disabled dogs in the streets, who consider him, like colonial European-owned canines, a "petit bourgeois dog" (11). But he leads a horrible life, which indicates the deterioration of the nation after independence; even symbols of privilege under colonialism seem to have lost their luster in this postindependence era, where the history of the nation is what Mbembe would see as "an aggregate of dead things, of masks, of a sense of horrors that . . . produce figures that are half-human, half-animal, whose essence is to devour themselves" (2004, 12). I want to suggest here that the dog and other characters in Nganang's novel are dead, having consumed themselves and one another to death. The story is told to us by a zombie, a symbol of a life-after-death being with superhuman powers to triumph beyond Africa's modern necropolises to imbue in the reader what Braidotti would term "futurist self-confidence" (2013b, 105). Although the novel is dark, the fact that it is told by a dead dog signals posthuman possibilities beyond the current realities of an inhuman postcolonial world. At the same time, its death urges the reader against notions of developmentalism and a romantic attachment to imagined African potentials.

The dog narrator is different from the porcupine narrator in the Congolese Alain Mabanckou's *Memoirs of a Porcupine,* because Mabanckou's character was a double of a forty-two-year-old human being called Kibandi, from Sekepembe village. Mboudjak has no genealogical links with humans. His animal-human links are purely as a victimized servant-dog. There is a chance that the porcupine could be dead, because it is customary for an animal double to die at the same time, but the porcupine gives a plausible explanation that he is alive. In Nganang's *Dog Days,* it is hard to believe that Mboudjak is alive because of the way he undermines his own agency. The first way he fails to take charge of his destiny is in his choice of a natural language. Defying linguistic theories,[43] Mboudjak tells fictions, admits to telling lies, and reflects on the language humans use to name him.

> I swear, never again will men catch me in the trap of their sordid sympathy and their useless games. From now on it is I who will determine the field for defining things. It is I who will give names to things and beings. Yes, I alone will interpret the world around me. I'll do it in their language, of course, but all the same, I'll use their words and phrases only to simplify things for myself. I alone will tell my story and that of innumerable mysteries of life. Let me make myself clear: I alone will succeed in resolving the enigma of humanity. (26)

In this declaration that echoes the language debate in African literature, Mboudjak offers to seize agency using a natural language other than his own. This recalls the position Achebe takes that African writers may use European language but in a way that changes the language to capture local experiences (Achebe 1965, 347). But Mboudjak does not seek to portray the complexity of a life as a dog; he wants to solve the problems of humanity and will use the language to "simplify" things for himself. With such an attitude, it would be hard for him to solve any complex problem facing him and his species. He uses a human language, but humans cannot understand his barks. This reflects the dilemma of African writers who have chosen to write in European languages but are still devalued within the European-language canon. Indeed, his human language is not considered a language among the humans; they just hear incomprehensible "barks." He is like Spivak's well-known subaltern widow, who speaks, but the dominant categories of people do not allow her to have any political agency.

Mboudjak enjoys some narratorial agency even when it is humans speaking in the story. Because humans cannot comprehend him even though he claims to speak their language and can understand what they are saying to one another, Mboudjack acts as what Melba Cuddy-Kearns calls an "auscultizer" (the agent who listens in a narrative), granted agency through his ability to listen and filter the information presented to the reader. He possesses the narrative agency as an auscultizer because without him the voices of the human characters would not reach the reader.[44] Within this agency, however, Mboudjak has no choice but to accept the tags humans have given him. He does not name the characters he listens to, not even those who later bear fictional names such as Panther and Crow; he prefers the nomenclature that the humans give these characters. The word "dog" appears in quotes at the beginning of the narrative to suggest the difficulties the animal narrator faces in telling his life story using the terms humans have conventionalized to name him. But as the story develops he accepts that term as the natural descriptor for him.

The story reveals the parallelism between human abuse of the dogs and the horrors of chattel slavery. Unlike in the Angolan Pepetela's *O Cão e os Caluandas (The Dog in Luanda)*, in which the narrative is told using different voices, including the sections about the adventures of the eponymous dog, Mboudjak's experiences are narrated in the dog's voice throughout—even when the dog is unconscious. In most African first-person narratives, when the narrator loses consciousness, the plot makes a leap forward to the time the narrator has regained it. In such a scenario, another character reports to the narrator, and by extension the reader, about the events that happened when the character was unconscious. We see this, for example, in Omondi Mak'Oloo's *Times Beyond.* When Waweru Njuhia, the narrator in the novel, falls unconscious like Nganang's Mboudjak does in *Dog Days*, the events that immediately follow before he regains consciousness are narrated through reports to him by other characters. While this technique is a fairly common stylistic choice for circumventing the shortcomings of a first-person eyewitness narration, in postcolonial works, the technique is tied to a commentary on the relations between the Northern and Southern Hemispheres of the globe. In Mak'Oloo's novel, the narrator blacks out and hits the canvas in a boxing match with a white competitor in Hungary, where as an immigrant he has had to join a dangerous sport to earn a living. It is not just Africans who are reduced to this predicament; we learn that Arabs face a similar fate in Europe. Unlike Mboudjak, who sees himself as a special dog, Waweru views himself as representing his race in a racism-soaked Central European nation. In a stream of consciousness technique, Waweru addresses himself in the second-person voice to remind himself of the racial circumstances that circumscribe his life in Hungary and why he needs to beat his white competitor: "all of them down there are seeing this as White against Black. Ask any of them and if he's honest he'll tell you he wants Horvath to win, not because they love Horvarth so much but because Horvarth is white" (198). The fans shout "anti-nigger" slogans (198). Coming from a black man, the N-word is not as offensive in African literature as it would be in Western contexts, but in Hungary it signifies the charged racial atmosphere in the stadium. We have already been told that white people look at Waweru as if he were "an animal in a zoo" (98), while others think he came from Africa "covered with animal skins" (59). Even when a girl calls a white man a "primitive animal" (102), it is in response to how Hungarians see Waweru. In using the N-word, the narrator is also likely to be echoing the word as it reaches him from the white spectators; it has been used liberally in the novel from the very first page, given to white characters, who are made to sound like Fanon's white child in *Black Skin, White Masks,* who finds the "nigger" quite "ugly" (Fanon 2008 [1952], 93); Mak'Oloo 1991, 1).

In Mak'Oloo's novel, Horvarth wins unfairly by hitting Waweru's genitals. This suggests castration and the absolute emasculation of the black man in an unfair world of black immigrants in a communist country. Like Mboudjak in Nganang's *Dog Days,* it appears that the downtrodden masses, represented by the spectators, will join the exploiters in tormenting fellow workers who do not belong to the mainstream race. When the narrator regains consciousness, the information about his fainting is relayed to him (and to the reader as well) through television news that his white friend Erika has watched. The agency is in Erika. The TV station, part of the capitalist exploitation of black people in a communist country, is the source of the information she sees broadcast live about Waweru's collapse. Here the subaltern cannot speak directly. His white friends, his doctor, and the TV commentators are the ones with a voice.

However, in Nganang's *Dog Days* Mboudjak retains his agency even when he becomes unconscious after Soumi, his master's ten-year-old, hangs him from a rope on a tree branch to punish him for eating his food. The narrative goes on without any break:

> I thought I saw him dancing around my suspended body. I was blinded by the pain. My eyes bulged out of their sockets. My tongue hung down to the ground. I couldn't even bark out my suffering. Overcome by a coma, I couldn't voice my distress. I was doomed to silence by that razor-sharp rope cutting into my throat, breaking my neck, slowly killing me. I struggled wildly. A mortal chill was gripping my body. (19)

The narrative leaps to the present through Mboudjak's contention that he does not know how he survived the hanging. But Mboudjak could in fact be dead already, speaking to us as his ghost:

> Or maybe no one bothered to take me down from my branch because each was waiting for the people from the Sanitation Department to do their job. But, as always, they never came. You never know, maybe I'm still hanging from that tree, with my eyes fixed in an empty stare, surprised to have been caught unawares by death, and with my mouth open to the void, surprised to have fallen silent before it could bark out my pain. (19)

The use of *maybe* indicates uncertainty about his current ontological status. The last sentence suggests that there is a possibility that he is dead and that he is telling us the story from the netherworld. He could be an ineffectual zombie in a "mutual zombification" relationship with both the state and the humans who oppress, if we may use Achille Mbembe's famous term. With the term "mutual zombification," Mbembe explains that in the postcolony, the oppressor and the oppressed collude in sapping agency from each other because each of the two groups (the oppressor and the oppressed) "has robbed the other of vitality and left both impotent [*impouvoir*]" (2001, 104).[45] The status quo is therefore likely to continue.

The zombie is also a figure of disillusionment. Jean Comaroff and John Comaroff note the prevalence of the zombie in postapartheid rural South

Africa: "The end of apartheid might have fired utopian imaginations around the world with a uniquely telegenic vision of rights restored and history redeemed," they write. "But South Africa has also been remarkable for the speed with which it has run up against problems common to societies, especially to post-revolutionary societies, abruptly confronted with the prospect of liberation under neoliberal conditions" (1999a, 19). There is a similar euphoria in the Cameroon presented in Nganang's *Dog Days* as the nation ushers in multiparty politics, but soon the oppressed realize that in a neoliberal order, efforts to preserve the status quo possibilities of liberation are doomed to fail. Certainly, animals will not be beneficiaries of any change in society.

The narrator and the whole environment reek of death. In one of the longest sentences, we are given a catalogue of stinking things, including the narrator's body, suggesting that he is dead as well:

> At first I thought I was being shocked by my own body's bad breath. Then I convinced myself that the haunting stench came from the neighborhood all around: from the thousand garbage piles, crumbling houses, busted-up streets, ammonia-filled bars, and leaky crap-ridden sewers, from the moldy restaurants, drugged-out cars, open-air outhouses, and wells dug into shit, from the streams battling with piles of garbage, from the filthy beds, and the living dead. (134)

The use of the word *haunting* together with *living dead* at the end of the sentence underscores the zombification of Cameroon. Everyone is dead spiritually, even if they are alive biologically. Reading the novel vis-à-vis Mbembe's sense of apparent pessimism, Moradewun Adejunmobi uses James Scott's (1990) concept of "hidden transcript" to see forms of indirect resistance in the society, explaining that in this hidden transcript, "subordinated groups execute and rehearse hidden acts of insubordination while awaiting an opportunity for open rebellion against domination" (2014, 441). I want to suggest that Nganang does not cheer this form of unspoken resistance because it is based on cynicism and the oppression of minorities within the resisting oppressed groups. In *Dog Days,* possibilities of open resistance against Biya or oppressors of animals are extremely limited. The characters fully comprehend the politics in which they participate, and Adejunmobi is correct to note, following Scott's critique of Gramscian theories of hegemony, that the character's attitude toward their oppressors is not based on false consciousness (Adejunmobi 2014, 449). They are not resigned to their fate and do not volunteer for further abuse because they are ignorant of the structures of oppression to which they are subordinated. There is no indication that they will one day openly resist. In fact, the ultimate tragedy in Mboudjak's narration is that although the characters' "recoil from domination," to use Adejunmobi's apt expression (449), this is not because of their ideological failure to understand what is going on. They are pervaded with a sense of fatalism cloaked as exuberant hope for freedom in some indefinite future. Actual opportunities for resistance slip through their fingers because they prefer futile fabulation about a better future to concrete action. From the very beginning, we see Mboudjak squandering every opportunity to resist human domination; so do the oppressed masses in Biya's Cameroon as the narrative unspools through Mboudjak's point of view.

When Francis B. Nyamjoh (2005) uses the term "mutual zombification" in a study of domestic workers in Southern Africa, he sees the workers as paralyzed, while the state remains indifferent to the worker's sordid circumstances. For Nyamjoh, the ignored insecurities and dehumanization of the workers "demonstrates not only that the nation-state is deaf and blind to the sounds and images of difference, but also that like a workman whose only tool is a giant hammer and to whom every problem is a nail, the nation-state lacks the creative flexibility to be entrusted with the task of managing a world marked by ever more flexible mobilities" (Nyamjoh 2005, 182; Nyamjoh 2006, 207). Ironically, there is no mobility in the Madagascar Mboudjak paints in *Dog Days.* The atmosphere is similar to that in the absurdist theatre of Bate Besong's *The Most Cruel Death of the Talkative Zombie* (1986), in which any change must be for the worse or else be located in an indefinite future. As in the case that Nyamjoh highlights, the Cameroonian nation-state in Nganang's *Dog Days* is a zombie. It only springs into action to safeguard the status quo. Although there seems to be a government agency in charge of animal welfare, there are stray dogs on the streets. Most of these animals are disabled and their movement is limited. The three-legged dog who has declared himself a communist lost his leg when crossing the street. His owner threw him out because, in the dog's disability, he is said to look "laughable and ugly" (13).

REJECTING FREEDOM

Even if one were to agree with Stephen Budiansky in *The Covenant of the Wild* (1992, 61) that animals benefit from domestication, Mboudjak's narration suggests that, in at least one instance, the dog's life was not improved through domestication. The prestige the dog has enjoyed among other dogs on account of his domestication is illusory, based on the now-confessed pretense that he is more privileged than the stray dogs that envy him. The narrator says that the stray dog is jealous of other dogs with homes as pets or service dogs. In what appears to be a broadside at the negritude movement, the stray dog declares that the myriad problems facing the canines stem from their rejection of their own "canitude" (13). Despite his militant "canitude," he is eventually offered as a sacrifice (135). This reminds us of the argument in Robert Garner's *A Theory of Justice for Animals,* in which he asks us not to bother arguing "against the claim that the differences between 'normal' adult humans and adult animals *are* morally significant" (2013, 15). To him, it is hard to believe that we can morally justify treating animals differently from the way we would like to be treated as humans. Like Julian H. Franklin in *Animal Rights and Moral Philosophy* (2005), Garner's major complaint about John Rawls's theory of justice is that it excludes animals from state-protected rights (Garner 2013, 24); Rawls sees human obligations to animals as moral, not legal. Thus, Garner prefers the terms of legal justice in animal rights discourse to moral arguments. But legal protection of animals, especially in the disintegrating contemporary state that Nganang presents to the reader, is ineffective. Ethical obligation might be more meaningful in such circumstances, because the state does not respect even human rights, despite its legal commitment to protect them. The animal in the postcolony is, like us, an individual whose rights are ignored; it is therefore more useful to see animals as mutual sufferers at the hands of the state.

I follow the tenets that Rosi Braidotti upholds, whereby ethics "is not confined to the realm of rights, distributive justice, or the law, but rather it bears close links with notions of political agency and the management of power and of power-relations" (Braidotti 2006, 12). In spite of laws that favor animals, nonhuman animals such as Mboudjak continue to experience abuse. *Ubuntu* (endorsed by Braidotti as a non-Western perspective the humanities can take advantage of; discussed in chapter 2 of this book) would be ideal for thinking about animals in a nonlegal context because "it emphasizes responsibility rather than right" in a setting where "responsibilities become more important than individual rights" (Bennett and Patrick 2011, 227). Written in the 1960s, the Cameroonian penal code has criminalized cruelty to animals "not only because of any desire to protect and promote 'animal rights' but also because the law-giver considers such conduct revolting to public decency" (Anyangwe 2011, 291). Anyangwe puts "animal rights" in scare quotes probably because the society does not believe that animals have intrinsic rights. The sentences are relatively light (imprisonment for fifteen days to three months, a fine, or both), and as captured in Section R369 (1) of the Cameroonian Penal Code, the law protects animals from human harm only as property: an "animal or beast belonging to someone else" (Federal Republic of Cameroon 1965, 95). But in *Dogs Days* we do not see anybody punished—even though Mboudjak and the other maimed dogs are covered by these legal statutes. Anyangwe notes that the law includes causing harm to animals through "excessive speed" and "bad driving" (2011, 292). Yet this is precisely what happens to the three-legged dog, having "lost one of his legs crossing the street, and his owner had kicked him out because his wife found him laughable and ugly" (2006, 13). From the many unpunished instances of animal abuse, it is apparent that good laws exist only on paper; they do not translate into material protection of animal or human rights. Yet even the abused humans mistreat animals instead of protecting them as fellow members of the group of the wretched of the earth.

The world that Nganang presents in the novel is defined by stasis; recalling the failed suicide attempts in Beckett's *Waiting for Godot,* even hanging a dog to death seems impossible. The Sanitation Department, mentioned four times in the story, is the organ that would offer Mboudjak an environment free of abuse. But the fear that viscerally runs through Mboudjak whenever the state agency is mentioned suggests that the organ would probably eliminate him as a way of keeping the environment clean for humans. To be sure, it is not lost on him that Sanitation Department agents do not show up to save him when he is on the verge of death after Soumi hangs him (19).

The Crow, the artist writing a book also titled *Dog Days,* is himself a zombie. Although Mboudjak foregrounds him at Massa Yo's bar, we are told he could be an "invention" that has been "ripped straight out of a rumor" (81). When he first appears, he wears a "cadaverous smile" (80) which is supposed to create in our mind the image of death. Like the cigarette hawker and push-cart man, who mentions "cadavers" to draw people's attention, Mboudjak mentions corpses, carcasses, and rotting cadavers throughout the story to draw our attention to the corruption and despondency eating at the vitals of the Cameroonian nation. Mboudjak emphasizes his feeling that the writer is long dead: "I looked at him in shock. I just couldn't believe that his filthy silhouette, that his carcass, now leprously perched on an upturned crate, had once housed a poet. As if roused by the memory of his very different youth, this poet of ours who'd been assassinated by life ordered another Guinness for the man in black" (83). The expression "this poet of ours" is sarcastic, because Mboudjak does not feel any affiliation with or affection for the Crow. Yet the Crow's story, said to be based on his observations of Madagascar, seems to exude hope. In the passage that we see from his notebook, he celebrates what James Scott (1990) would see as the "hidden transcripts" of resistance and the boundless humanness of the downtrodden: "The neighborhoods are the forge of mankind's creativity. The wretchedness of their surroundings is but an illusion. It conceals the profound reality of the unknown which remains to be discovered: the truth of History in its creation" (82). The use of capital H catches the attention of the tavern patrons as well as the reader. It signals the mistakenness of the poet, who is deluded in thinking that there is a fixed, single truth. If both the Crow and the dog Mboudjak have written stories about the same place that bear the same title yet project different visions, whom do we agree with? Mboudjak is unreliable as a narrator. But we can observe that Mboudjak gives cues when he is about to lie. In this instance, either the drunk poet does not exist or is completely mistaken about the agency of the downtrodden in Madagascar.

Mboudjak appears superficially to have agency, because the story is told from his perspective. But he remains powerless throughout. As in the colonial conception of Africans, Mboudjak has no history beyond being Massa Yo's dog. We don't know his parents or siblings. The details of his capture into slavery are not mentioned. As the narrative enters the dénouement, Mboudjak stops where he began—as Massa Yo's downtrodden dog. He participates in demonstrations against the authoritarian government in the last pages of the story, but his antiestablishment enthusiasm seems misplaced; he should be protesting the humans who curtail his potential as an animal. He is the only dog who seems to support humans' political activities. More devastating is that his narrative agency comes at the expense of his political agency. It would be understandable for him to be given agency at Massa Yo's house and bar, because from his perspective we can learn about the problems facing the Cameroonians. He is not only a narrator, but he also serves as auscultizer, listening to stories being told at The Customer is King and relaying them to the reader. But to tell us about events that happen outside this setting, he has to get lost and wander the streets, looking for Massa Yo's bar. Earlier, he had more instrumentality, when he left his master's house to live among stray dogs. But he gets lost and tries to find his way back toward the end of the story, when we expect him to be more streetwise. It is also remarkable that he has to be helped by a vulgar human (the pushcart pusher) because all other animals fail him, laughing cynically at him.

We must concede that in the act of giving narrative agency to a possibly dead narrator, the narrative symbolizes hope that the authoritarian government cannot suppress the submerged voices forever. The deaths of protesters at the hands of the police are not in vain. They are likely to inspire more-vocal opposition in a country that has all along been resigned to the fact that nothing can change because "Cameroon is Cameroon" (49). Interestingly, although the novel mocks communists and Afrocentrists, it takes on the socialist realist format of imbuing the ending of the narrative with some optimism. This could also derive from oral narratives, which usually have a happy ending. But in *Dog Days,* we do not experience the kind of optimism we find in Marxist novels, such as Pepetela's *Return of the Water Spirit,* Sembène's *God's Bits of Wood,* or Ngũgĩ's *Devil on the Cross* (1982a) and *Matigari* (1988). In these novels, even if the narratives are idealistic, their exuberant optimism about the end of the capitalist order is organic to the dynamics of the story. The characters grow ideologically from their earlier naiveté to become admirable revolutionaries. In *Dog Days,* the introduction of optimism comes abruptly in the plot and toward the last few pages. Mboudjak does not change throughout the story, in spite the experiences he has gone through. The animals remain divided even toward the end of the narrative, as poultry and the cat exemplify when Mboudjak asks them for guidance. The animals, including Mboudjak, are cynical about the conditions of the poor, laughing at workers. Massa Yo might change after a prostitute steals his million francs, but nothing is definite about that. There are protests about the student Takou's death, and Cameroonians feel that "BIYA MUST GO," but this remains an empty slogan because it is not based on solidarity. They are against Biya, without being clear-minded about what alternative they should have. Their resistance is in the mode of self-cancelling resentment; even if they were to remove Biya from power, they are too fragmented along ethnic lines to be altruistic in choosing an alternative. Putting our noses to the ground for signs of hope, we might want to see, using Franz Karl Stanzel's model of narrative mediation, a distinction between the narrating *I* and the experiencing *I* in the story. That is to say that in such a situation, there is a difference in ideology and perspective between the mature narrating dog speaking to us now and the dog that experienced the events he is telling us about. There are moments in which Mboudjak makes fun of his naiveté and conceitedness. But there isn't a lot of evidence that he has changed, at least not in the melodramatic way he joins street protests. There is no mediation between the younger Mboudjak in Yaoundé's seedy neighborhood of Madagascar and the Mboudjak telling us the story. The problem with an autobiographical narration that does not distinguish the experiencing *I* and the narrating *I* is that it rarely contrasts the narrator with other characters who have transformed more positively over time than the egoistic narrator. The dramatic irony is also lost because we are not sure if the narrators in such stories are laughing at their earlier naïve selves. The chances that the melodramatic dog and other characters he narrates about will fundamentally change for the better, in spite of getting angrier at the political system, are extremely slim.

But Mboudjak seems quite aware of this, self-consciously exposing his own weaknesses, parallels to which he sees in humans. Adejunmobi is, then, correct to argue that *Dog Days* belongs to an emerging cluster of African narratives in which "social subordinates are no longer always innocent victims of unjust power as they had been in earlier works" (2014, 440). In affecting Nietzschean cynicism, Mboudjak is not a completely admirable character. At times, he is unreliable as a narrator, not because he is naïve and ignorant, as would be the case in a child narration, but because he is a conceited liar trying to entertain us to death with his cynicism. He is also a showoff. But more disturbing is his tendency to place animals in hierarchies. Even if he does a superb job of showing us that humans are not the intelligent and civilized beings they are cracked up to be, he is also chauvinistic and bigoted in his view of other animals, including fellow dogs. The chickens are portrayed as gluttons, and there is no sympathy throughout the story for dogs with disabilities. "I admit that I am just a dog, yes, a dog whose wanderings have never taken his paws beyond the borders of Yaoundé's neighborhoods. And yes, I concede that for my canine intelligence, Yaoundé's city limits are those of Cameroon, and Cameroon itself is the center of the world" (186). The dog affects inarticulateness and ignorance, but is adept at acute observation and inventiveness. The more the dog becomes powerless, the more agency he is given, as he seems to communicate to the reader when dead. He has a life after death that not only decenters the present human life, but reminds readers that they occupy a space in between life and death.

Then, can the animal really speak? The use of an animal narrator in *Dog Days* crystallizes the thin boundary between humans and animals. Inherent in the use of the narrating animal is strong support for the belief that animals and humans are incarnations of each other. Therefore, to abuse an animal is primarily to contravene the rights of that animal, not those of its owner. But we have also observed that the narrative agency that the dog is given in the story does not amount to material improvement of dogs' welfare. Karla Armbruster (2013) is correct to point out that animal autobiographies are mostly based on "a yearning to genuinely know the otherness of nonhuman animals," but the desire to understand this nonhuman otherness is "sometimes almost completely overshadowed by or absorbed back into [the] human tendency to gaze—whether lovingly or critically—at our own reflection when we look at other animals" (19). We hear our own voice when we listen to Mboudjak's story, yet that does not deny him agency.

Like the eponymous dog in Anton Chekov's "Asthana" (1887), Mboudjak rejects opportunities to obtain freedom from his abusive master, preferring to return to his house. This on the surface seems to deny the narrating dog agency and to suggest that Cameroonians under Biya behave toward him like blindly loyal dogs. But as Laura Brown articulates, "the diversity of experience that the canine world provides emerges through the dog's connection with prosperous masters on the one hand, and with beggars, Gypsies, minstrels, soldiers, and other itinerants on the other hand" (134). Mboudjak's initial escape from home enables him to bring to the reader details of the dire conditions other dogs live in. The most political dogs in Nganang's story stray in the streets, nomads without a home. The only problem with them is their negativity toward fellow animals. Unlike Chekov's Asthana, Mboudjak helps us see the deteriorating conditions in the human world that he has returned to. As presented in Mboudjak's story, humans cannot be the masters of the universe; they lack the individuality they deny animals.

NO NEED TO WRESTLE WITH NATURE

We need to remember that the constant presence of folkloric techniques in modern art arises from the fact that, while the predominance of orature does not mean the society is unsophisticated, "the most technologically advanced races of the world still cherish, treasure and share their oral literature" (Bukenya et al. 1997, 4). The question we should be asking is what the elements of orature do in the work; we should not see their presence as signaling a pristine world. I have argued above that when oral narratives contain negative images of women, the language portraying those images is likely to be transmitted to the real world to justify the mistreatment of women. The situation is slightly different with the images of animals, because when the character is an animal, we know immediately that we are being presented with a fable. We have noted that when Ngũgĩ wants to draw parallels between the events in an oral narrative and the reality of the actual world, it is, for example, mentioned that Waiyaki's mother does not own any property, as is the case with the women represented as bad managers in the oral narrative. But, immersed in a fabulist world, we know that the animal is not likely to do the bad things it is said to have done in the story. The stigma is not as strong as it would be if the story were about a human category. In the proverbial language of the Waswahili, for example, it is emphasized that only a *mjinga* (fool) would take a *fumbo* (riddle, fable, allegory) literally. The *fumbo* is supposed to be taken as a commentary on human behavior, not the behavior of the animals in the story. Although some animals might be stigmatized in the way they are represented in stories, only a fool would seek retribution from an animal for what it is supposed to have done in a fictional presentation. Therefore, even negatively presented animals (e.g., the chameleon or the hyena) are still protected from abuse in the real world. (I noted the protection of the hyena among the Akamba in chapter 2).

Most oral narratives undermine anthropocentrism without supporting full abolition of human control of animals. In this setup, animals are to be respected, but they can continue be exploited and hierarchized, such that some animals are declared superior to others, because they are characters that represent either a human virtue or a human foible. However, written texts that use orature risk transforming the traditional materials that seek to interpolate audiences into a social habitus that tacitly encourages listeners to see animals as inferior. Wanjiku Kabira has noted that despite the perpetuation of the "the ideology of control" in the works of some artists, "there must be forces of resistance among other artists who struggle within the same genre to address gender-based oppression" (Kabira 1994, 84). Nandwa's story discussed above exemplifies resistance against negative images of women. Most of the violence in the story comes from men, while women restore and heal the society. Nandwa also shows that there is no need to wrestle with nature. The humans in her story do not have to kill Okunani to get the child they had abandoned. This is common in postcolonial texts, and is also in line with Braidotti's call for less confrontational and disputatious politics, because we are likely ourselves to be parts of the system we want to get rid of.[46] Illustrating the same idea in the context of the representation of the colonized as a small animal, in the next chapter I examine their representation, especially in written literature about imperialism.

CHAPTER 4

Winds of Change and the God of Small Animals

Mdudu eeeee, mdudu eee, kaingiaje?

Mdudu eeeee, mdudu eee, kaingiaje?
Mdudu ndani ya koko ya embe, kaingiajeee?

(The insect eeee, insect eee, how did it enter?
The insect eeee, insect eee, how did it enter?
How did the insect get into the core of a mango seed?)
—a *taarab* song by Zuhura Swaleh

The insect in this song by Zuhura Swaleh is an enigma. It is at the core of a mango seed without leaving any mark on the skin of the mango or the shell of the seed. The *taarab* singer asks: how did it get there? As a literal being, the insect is unfathomable, but as a figure of speech it is a pest that needs to be eradicated. Much of the study of insects considers them as pests, but the song suggests that small animals have powers we cannot fully understand.[1] Titled "Mdudu" (Insect), the taarab song wonders how the small animal manages to achieve this feat.[2] In the song, the insect is symbolic both of the problems facing the woman speaker, who has been abandoned by her man, and of her resilience. The poet wonders how the figurative insect (the man who oppresses the female persona) managed to get to the core of her heart, but this is captured with reference to literal insects that mysteriously get into the middle of a fruit. She pronounces *kokwa* (the shell of the mango seed) as *koko* (skull) to draw attention to the analogy between the insect getting into the seed and its penetration of her mind. The *mdudu* suffers and enjoys what Harrison King, in a reading of the representation of ants in Rabbinic literature, calls a "dialectical image of aversion and fascination" (2016, 157). The *mdudu* is loathsome in the way it has penetrated the fruit and destroyed it, but it is at the same time amazing in managing to pull off such an astounding achievement; the lingering question that the song asks in its refrain is about the skills of an insect that allow it to go so deep into the core of a fruit.

The figure of the insect and such allied arthropods as the spider and the scorpion is a common feature in global literatures, from the Gilgamesh epic, Plato's *Phaedrus,* and Ovid's Arachne tale to Franz Kafka's *The Metamorphosis,* Samuel Beckett's *Molloy,* James Joyce's *Finnegans Wake* and *Ulysses,* and Arundhati Roy's *The God of Small Things.*[3] Roy's novel, whose title I allude to in the title of this chapter, presents insects, especially moths, as more capable than humans of destroying colonial institutions and their archives.[4] In polemical commentaries and ripostes to Western theorists and artists, postcolonial theorists have complained of being treated as downtrodden insects. For example, the reason Sembène Ousmane does not like the ethnographic films about traditional African life that Jean Rouch and Rouch's fellow Euro-American Africanists make is that they freeze Africa in a putative unchanging past: "What I hold against you and the Africanists is that you look at us as if we were insects" (Sembène 2013 [1965], 96). A socialist realist who is also considered the father of African film, Ousmane prefers a more nomadic view of Africa: an assemblage of cultures and practices in constant flux. He rejects neocolonialism and affirms the humanity of the African people.

A society that thinks its members are seen as insects may, in turn, identify with those insects and use them to depict its problems. Incidentally, Rouch does not see anything wrong in treating Africans like insects. Citing Jean Henri Fabre (1823–1915), the French scholar famous for his study of the behavior and anatomy of insects, Rouch defends Euro-American Africanists because some, as he says, see from their detached studies the commonality between cultures: "I will defend the Africanists. They are men that can certainly be accused of looking at black men as if they were insects. But there might be Fabres out there who, when examining ants, discover a similar culture, one that is as meaningful as their own" (Sembène 2013 [1965], 96). Thus, to Roach, even if films dehumanize the Africans by presenting them as the exotic "other" of Europe, they are legitimate because they tell Europe about itself. Should we then allow the humiliation of animals in projects that help us understand ourselves? Can't we obtain such knowledge from the study of human beings without having to seek analogies to animals?

Harrison King has opined that although insects are figures of disgust, "the spatial and behavioral proximity of humans and insect bodies constantly undermines any attempts to ignore these entomological others or avoid contact with them" (2016, 157). Even as anticolonial intellectuals decry colonizers' identification of the colonized with insects, they also represent themselves as small animals and are hesitant to advocate destroying insects with impunity. This chapter examines the representation of small animals—insects, arthropods, birds—in the context of nonhuman forces such as storms and hurricanes. I start with a reading of Charles Mungoshi's story "The Crow," which is traditionally read as an anticolonial nationalist story. I argue that consideration of the mistreatment of a bird yields different meanings. I then examine the representation of colonialists as butterflies and locusts, observing that, intriguingly, anticolonial writers do not call for the destruction of these insects. The vitality of the insect emphasizes that humans do not have complete control of the universe, while a reading of insects as symbols of nonnormative sexuality reveals an acceptance of the existence of nonnormative practices. I include with a brief discussion of *chewa,* a mythical leviathan in Ibrahim Hussein's play *Mashetani* (Devils), because, although it is a big animal, it echoes the representation of the frog in Swahili poetry, which instead of *chewa* uses small animals to suggest the power of ordinary people to change society.

BEYOND NATIONALISM: HUNTING FOR NEW MEANINGS

Although postcolonialism is cited as one of those areas that can revitalize the humanities (Braidotti 2013a), in its current practice, postcolonialism largely ignores animals and their capabilities, focusing more on human nationalists as the actants with the greatest agency to determine the fate of the nation. We need to recharge postcolonial studies with ideas that draw energy from units other than the nation. Reading the human treatment of small animals changes how we read certain texts that were earlier read through a nationalist lens. First published in the early 1970s, Zimbabwean Charles Mungoshi's short story "The Crow" (1987 [1980]) has been read as a composition about the transition from boyhood to manhood, and as a narrative about the stakes involved in asserting one's masculinity as an anti-colonial gesture. According to these readings, fellow men need to confirm the boy's masculinity before he can take his own masculinity seriously.[5] Related to this interpretation is the reading of the story as a national Bildungsroman about Zimbabwe's breaking away from colonial shackles as the country matures gradually into postindependence nationhood in the 1980s. In the story, the narrator and his brother, Chiko, refuse to follow their parents' instructions to go to church one Sunday morning. They decide instead to go hunt and kill a crow. "Chiko" is short for "Chikomborero" (Shona for "blessing"). This name provides one of the signals of the irony in the story: the character so named is the reverse of a blessing, in that he refuses to go to church and behaves irrationally toward animals in a culture where, in the spirit of *ubuntu*, the killing of an animal "is only excusable if it is for the purpose of feeding people" (Broodryk 2006, 20). In the story, food is not part of the reason Chiko and his brother kill the crow; rather, the boys engage in a wanton display of violence.[6]

This story describes a gruesome killing of the crow that risks entrenching the stereotype that Africans are by nature atavistic. Simon Gikandi has noted the moral predicaments confronting the student of African literature trying to explain the violence embedded in some of the most foundational postcolonial texts. The question Gikandi finds difficult to answer when it is raised by his students has to do with why the people presented in the stories are "so cruel" (2001, 5). We must remember that the texts do not endorse violence, including cruelty to animals. Are African children as atavistic and antianimal as the boys in Mungoshi's story? Their violence toward the crow might be justifiable if the crow were read as a symbol of colonialism. But it is not; the animal is an innocent victim of human destructiveness. Moreover, the children go against the wish of their parents, and they are not following an example of an adult foil to their parents; the story does not cue us to distance ourselves from the children's church-going parents as symbols of subservient colonial natives. That is, even if the parents themselves may be going against the Shona traditions by attending church, the children receive no guidance from a traditional authority to justify their action. In this it is unlike other stories of Mungoshi's, which elicit complete sympathy for the child protagonist under the tutelage of a traditional sage. It is not clear if the church-going parents are to blame for abdicating their role in socializing the children into an *ubuntu* mindset, but the narrator does not seek to excuse his and his brother's action against a harmless bird. His only redeeming grace in the story is that he, at the time of narrating the events, seems to regret the past act of violence. It is implied that he would treat the crow differently today.

The hunt for big game is a well-worked field in postcolonial criticism, but "The Crow" involves the hunt for a relatively small animal, a bird.[7] In the competition to kill the crow, the boys seem to be seeking each other's approval; it is the fear each boy feels about what his companion will think of him that fuels the violence against the bird. The narrator emphasizes the fear that governs the boys' action and their feelings toward each other and the environment: "We were both afraid but it was a code between us not to show each other that we were afraid" (29). Though not in so many words, at the current moment he is narrating about his actions, Mungoshi's child narrator seems to be laughing at the folly of killing the innocent crow.

Some critics (e.g., Muponde 2006, 84) see the story as a celebration of defiance against an oppressive order that the Christian parents have imposed on their children. In contrast to the alienated parents, the narrator and his brother, according to this interpretation, aspire to an Afrocentric life that would liberate African cultures from the shackles of European domination that the church represents in much of African literature. Indeed, that the boys have refused to go to church can easily be read to suggest that the boys' actions have anticolonial overtones. However, the story may also be read as a statement about the futility of human rites of passage that involve killing animals. At the moment of narration, the narrator casts doubt on the reliability of his intuition when he and his brother assaulted the crow. He even wishes someone had stopped them from their "obsession" to kill the crow:

> But what made us want to kill that crow in its nest by the river I still do not know . . .
>
> We were getting tired but we were all of a sudden very serious about hitting it. We were quite soaked with sweat and this running had ceased to be fun. It had become something which had to be done: the killing of the crow. We would have been glad if somebody had come along and told us to stop all this madness and go home. But there were only the two of us, our obsession, our fears and the crow. (28–29)

The narrator indicates that with proper guidance the boys would not have assaulted the bird. The sentence "But what made us want to kill that crow in its nest by the river I still do not know" stands out in the narrative because it forms a one-sentence paragraph at the beginning of the narrative. It is the third paragraph in the story, suggesting to the reader at the outset that we should not expect a rational explanation for the killing of the bird. The contrastive conjunction with which the sentence-paragraph opens indicates that the reasons for the killing of the crow given in the previous paragraph were phony. Furthermore, the syntactical inversion with which the narrator expresses this incomprehension about his and his brother's "obsession" to kill the crow indicates that he understands that the attack on the bird was pathological. In other words, today the narrator would not repeat that act because, as he tells the story now, he seems to know better than he did when he participated in the violent deed. He is laughing at himself for having done what today appears to him as utter absurdity. Like Achebe's Okonkwo, he does not confess his mistakes in public, but there is in this narrating character a distinct difference between his earlier self (when he participated in killing the crow) and his present self (now as he tells his story).[8]

The tension between resisting colonialist church teachings and respecting *ubuntu* teachings about the connectedness of life erupts in brutal violence at the culmination of the boys' hunt. We may therefore interrogate the hunt itself as a site of resistance—whether positive or negative. Gary Varner has outlined three forms of hunting: therapeutic, subsistence, and sport hunting. The boys in Mungoshi's story are practicing sport hunting, which, in Varner's words, is "aimed at reenacting national or evolutionary history, at practicing certain skills, or just at securing [a] trophy" (1998, 101). But it is notable that the boys do not obtain any pleasure when the hunt is over; it causes more distress than they had when they began. Varner defines therapeutic hunting as "motivated by and designed to secure the aggregate welfare of the target species, the integrity of its ecosystem, or both" (100). The boys' hunting expedition is not meant to achieve any of these "therapeutic" goals. Could we, defining therapeutic hunting differently to mean that which has a curative effect on the hunter, say then that what the boys do to the crow can be forgiven because, stressed by the colonial condition, the colonial subjects are relieving pent-up emotions? Maybe this point is moot, because colonialism is over at the time of reading the story; if one could be forgiven for violence because of the pressures of the colonialism in colonial Zimbabwe, the kind of violence visited on the bird is completely unnecessary today. How about committing violence elsewhere and in other times to relieve tension under circumstances similar to colonialism? The short story is skeptical about the wisdom of such violence. Certainly Mungoshi (and to some extent the narrator) is, like Tom Regan, against hunting. While Regan criticizes all forms of hunting because people can be vegetarian and avoid eating animals (2004 [1983], 354–55), in Mungoshi's story the hunting is reduced to a pointless act of self-assertion that disregards the welfare of other species.[9]

Ironically, the boys in Mungoshi's story are not hunting the crow for food. They are not like the ancient Opanyin Yaw Poku in Nii Ayikwei Parkes's *Tail of the Blue Bird,* who confesses that he must "kill beasts so I can eat" (2009, 155). We do not see *ubulwane* (animal-ness) in the crow; it is the boys who exhibit a hegemonic, masculine, and destructive violence. As the Zimbabwean critic Rino Zhuwarara notes, "the violence that the boys inflict on the innocent crow is not only excessive but morally wrong; it reveals the darker and menacing side of mankind which more often than not lies hidden in seemingly innocent-looking children" (2001, 32).[10] I have indicated that I would be ready to reluctantly forgive the killing of animals if the primeval society, in its ignorance, believes killing the animals is beneficial to the society at large. Most African writers hold that position; they do not condemn precolonial societies that kill animals, but they celebrate the way those societies at the same time tried to protect the ecosystem—a form of hunting encapsulated in Varner's "therapeutic" hunting, which we have already seen does not apply in this case.

Contextually, the killing of the crow is, then, unjustified because it serves no economic purpose. The crow is not a competitor to the boys for economic resources. Its death does not enhance their chances in life in any way. At the time that the events in the story happen, the Shona society is not a hunter-and-gatherer economy, from which it transitioned between 2000 BC and 1 AD (Beach 1977, 39). The reference to the church indicates that the setting of the story is post–nineteenth century because, although Portuguese Jesuit missionaries tried to set up churches in the region as far back as the sixteenth century, it is in the nineteenth century that the church became a common icon of Western influence. To the Shona of the late nineteenth century, hunting was not a critical economic activity; it "provided a valuable addition to the diet of the Shona, but it was not central to the Shona economy, and could offer only a limited support to subsistence during famines" (Beach 1977, 40). In fact, we are not shown in the story any reason the boys would be hunting for a crow, except the irrational excuses they give.

It is imperative to follow Clare Palmer's contextual ethics for a moment and look at things from an indigenous Shona perspective. Let us, then, assume that the society from which the children in Mungoshi's story come allows hunting for food. Even with this assumption, we have to remember that this does not mean that because the Shona ancestors used to hunt in the precolonial past, hunting is justified today. As Gary Varner would note, although human predation on other animals was natural at a certain stage in human evolution, it no longer can be justified. At some point, Varner notes, it was "natural for us to make stone tools and defecate in the woods, but no one argues that we should continue to do these things just because they are natural. Showing that something is natural in this sense does not suffice to show that it is morally permissible, let alone in some sense morally obligatory or at least exemplary" (2002, 119–20). To Varner, then, accepting the killing of animals because it has been the tradition of a people is like arguing that racism, sexism, and other forms of bigotry are justified today because there was a time they were considered natural.[11] Thus, to Varner, "acknowledging that hunting is in one sense natural for humans [to justify hunting today], implies nothing compelling about the morality of hunting" (2002, 120).[12]

Without endorsing the boys' action, some critics have regarded these characters as avatars of African traditions vis-à-vis Christianity.[13] Since its spread across Africa alongside colonialism in the nineteenth century, the church in Africa has, like the school, been regarded as a part of the European "civilizing mission" used to justify the destruction of African mores. The institution is thus seen in African literature, without much qualification, as an anathema to precolonial beliefs. By refusing to go to church, the boys in Mungoshi's story are to some extent resisting the colonial order that has imposed a foreign religion on their society. Unlike their parents, who have acquiesced to Christianity, the boys are symbols of resistance against European culture and its institutions. Furthermore, we may join Robert Mupondi (2006, 85) in celebrating the boys as having broken from the ranks of idealistically drawn prelapsarian innocent children by resisting the dominance of their parents.[14] Mupondi notes that in Mungoshi's story, the boys are not "pure, artless, fresh, virgin, immaculate," as we would expect them to be in tales of innocence (2006, 85). Yet in all of these readings, it is the crow—and not the boys—that is a figure of innocence, suffering the sexual aggression of the pubescent boys. They turn the bird into an Other—a woman, a figure with a disability—and proceed to violate its rights to flourish.

It is also instructive to consider Mungoshi's narrator, as Wayne C. Booth (1961) would see him, as largely unreliable. According to Booth's well-known definition, an unreliable narrator is one who cannot be trusted because he is biased or has limited knowledge of the subject matter presented. As a child, the narrator lacks the knowledge of African traditions to be an authority on them. The story is for adults and probably adultist in its view of children, in that they are criticized for going against the instructions of their parents although Mungoshi has upheld rebellion against parents in other stories. Even when we look at the narrator from a child's perspective, we only take him seriously if he attributes his statements about traditions to an authority of that culture.

In hunting the crow, the boys do not respect traditions. The Shona display a lot of respect for the crow, as expressed in the proverb *Dai pasina nyimo, makunguo aizodyei?* (If there were no roundnuts what would the crows eat?). The proverb is used to show that animals like the crow should be accorded hospitality and generosity, because they, like the seemingly low-value *nyimo* (Vigna subterrane or Bambara groundnuts), serve a purpose. Indeed, according to Masaka and Makahamadze's discussion of this particular proverb, its "deeper meaning" is that "life needs people who are kind-hearted so much so that they would assist the needy members of society. A society that does not have such benevolent, philanthropic and sympathetic members is not a normal society because the existence of deprivations in the universe would imply the need for a sector that addresses these problems. This proverb is normally brought up to implore people to be thankful to *Mwari* [the Supreme Being or God] that there are kind-hearted people among them who are prepared to help the needy" (2013, 138). As opposed to the readings that see them as avatars of tradition, in acting the way they do toward the crow, the boys go against the edicts of the traditional Shona religion, where they are supposed to care for the less powerful members of the cosmos.

While Tom Regan allows for the killing of animals in self-defense, the crow in the story has not attacked the boys. There is no evidence that this bird is a "thief," as accused. We do not see it preying on chickens or other domestic animals. The boys use the thievery charge against the crow only to justify their irrational behavior toward it. They are Othering the bird to justify oppressing it in a way similar to how colonialists presented Africans as the Other to rationalize plunder and murder. Although the boys in the story are definitely of subordinate rank and represent resistance to normative practices and beliefs, they come through as representatives of a new form of colonialism because, as Anias Mutekwa (2013, 357) notes, their act of coming together "to oppress the crow (representing nature) mimics the nature of the colonial state in which whites oppress blacks."

It is remarkable that Mungoshi's story opens with an indication that the boys had not shot birds before. They had seen this crow and its mate before, but it had not occurred to them that they should kill them. If the crow is a symbol of witchcraft, why is it important to kill it today, except if, like Oduche in Achebe's *Arrow of God*, the boys are Christian believers out to eliminate all symbols of heathen behavior and beliefs? Another crow also appears on the scene, but the boys do not go after it. In fact, we do not see them killing any other animals, as the story focuses on their obsession with this particular crow. With the benefit of hindsight, the narrator indicates that their hostility to the crow was irrational: "we don't eat crows, and birds and animals that people do not eat are associated with night and witchcraft in our country" (28). This sentence indicates that the embedded audience for the story is a person who does not come from this country and probably would be able to appreciate the absurdity of the action in the context of the beliefs of the community the boys come from. The use of present tense in the story ("I don't know why . . .") indicates that the narrator is still baffled by his decision to kill the crow and probably regrets it. He only falls short of confessing that what he and Chiko did was wrong.

At the time of killing the crow, there was no differentiation between the boys. The narrator does not want to appear different from his brother: "There was no more fun in proving myself tougher than he was, so to be equal I threw my catapult after Chiko's into the river. I suddenly smelled hot blood in my nose but I wasn't bleeding. It is the way I feel when everything goes wrong and I am afraid" (32). But today, at the moment the story is narrated, the boy sees himself as having outgrown his violent former self, differentiating himself from the laughably still-violent Chiko. Chiko, who is most aggressive in fighting the crow, is portrayed as hysterical even when it comes to violence against other animals: "When Chiko is angry with anything—say a slow ox—he hits it with everything he's got—hands, head, legs, sticks, stones—and all the time he makes a sound in his throat, and if the ox won't move he bursts into tears and you can hear him cursing through his tears and hitting the ox, getting madder and madder with each whack until he bursts into real bawling as if he had been hit" (32). The story reverts to the present tense to give this part of narration a sense of immediacy. The tense also indicates that the narrator and his brother are still children. Chiko still continues with aggressiveness against animals, but the narrator seems to have outgrown it. With this description of Chiko, it is apparent that violence against animals victimizes not only the animals in question but the human aggressor as well. In the passage, Chiko undergoes great pain from his violence against the ox. He comes off as foolish.

I want to offer a few examples from African writing to further suggest that Mungoshi's boys are not symbols of African traditions, as claimed by Rino Zhuwarara (2010). In modern writing, African traditions are portrayed as protective of the environment and small animals; it is the colonial and industrial modernity that degrades nature.[15] For example, in the opening of

Camara Laye's *The African Child,* a novel that presents an idealized precolonial Africa, the first lesson the child-narrator receives from his blacksmith father in the story is that he should not kill a snake, which is named the totem of his community.[16] Similarly, in the equally negritudist "Le Totem" by Leopold Sedar Senghor, the persona has an "animal guardian," an expression that challenges the Christian notion of a guardian angel. In Achebe's *Arrow of God* (1986 [1964]), it is the boy who has converted to Christianity, Oduche, who fancies killing snakes. He uses the Bible to justify the thought of harming the pythons, considered sacred in his community. Although Achebe's novel points out early in the story that snakes usually bite and scorpions sting, we do not see them do so in the whole novel. We know from the story that the kind of python Oduche violates is different from an "ordinary snake" (205), the killing of which would not cause a stir in the community. But we do not encounter these other snakes in the novel. In fact, Oduche, a symbol of Christian-inspired alienation in the story, wants to violate snakes that he knows are innocent. The part of the narrative is focalized through his center of consciousness to indicate to the reader that he knows that these animals do not deserve the action he is contemplating carrying out against them. This is underscored in the way the narrator absolves the snakes of their alleged mischiefs:

> At that moment Oduche took his decision. There were two pythons—a big one and a small one—which lived almost entirely in his mother's hut, on top of the wall which carried the roof. They did no harm and kept the rats away; only once were they suspected of frightening away a hen and swallowing her eggs. Oduche decided that he would hit one of them on the head with a big stick. He would do it so carefully and secretly that when it finally died people would think it had died of its own accord. (50)

Although in this passage there are none of the elements found elsewhere that indicate stream of consciousness through Oduche's perspective, the first sentence in this paragraph indicates that the snakes are presented to us from Oduche's perspective. He knows they are harmless. There have been allegations that they eat eggs and scare domestic animals, but this does not go beyond suspicions. The snake does not interfere with Christian missionary work. We have been told in a previous paragraph that "nobody here has complained . . . that the python has ever blocked his way as he came to church" (50). As a member of the Umuaro community, a person of Oduche's age is supposed to know better than to kill a python: "Every Umuaro child knows that if a man kills the python inadvertently he must placate Idemili by arranging a funeral for the snake almost as elaborate as a man's funeral" (60). Oduche willfully violates the snakes in order to overzealously enact alienating church teachings, but it is suggested that even the church itself would not call for this level of foolhardy violence.

Even if we were to agree with Peter Singer that "it is not arbitrary to hold that the life of a self-aware being, capable of abstract thought, of planning for the future, of complex acts of communication, and so on, is more valuable than life of being without these capacities" (2009 [1975], 20), it is clear that neither the python in Achebe's story nor the crow in Mungoshi's belongs to the lower rung that the utilitarian in Singer assigns to animals. The crows are presented preparing for the future by building a next. They also communicate with each other. In contrast to Chiko's hysteria, the main crow in the story is intelligent and patient. It manages to elude the boys a number of times before they catch up with it. The boys in Mungoshi's story could be envious of the crow, which the Zimbabwean critic Musaemura Zimunya argues "represents élan vital, that eternal flicker which taunts mankind's curiosity and exposes his vulnerability endlessly" (1982, 63). In outlining his concept of *élan vital* (vital impulse) in *Creative Evolution* (1907), Henri Bergson tried to demolish the distinction between intellect and impulse, arguing that evolutionary survival depends on both. Human intelligence on its own is unable to access the essence of life. According to Bergson, we overcome the numerous hindrances in life through the use of intuition. If Bergson is right, then, we can argue that the boys are driven by an instinct to survive. They have no evidence that the crow is malevolent, but they imagine it is and proceed to act on the basis of that suspicion. But it is the crow that embodies the will to live, as the story presents the boys' sense of control of the environment disintegrating as the plot unfolds. From the very beginning, the boys find it difficult to hit the bird using their catapults. When they eventually hit the crow, it does not die as expected. They have to throw it into the river together with their weapons, unsure if they have fulfilled their mission. Like most of Mungoshi's narratives, this is a story of disillusionment. Instead of bringing relief, killing the crow leaves a feeling one gets "when everything goes wrong" (32). The end of the story emphasizes that the situation did not improve after the killing of the crow, if the crow died at all. Even if it is physically dead, the crow is still alive in the fears of the boys. Furthermore, its mate is still alive. All signs are that the boys have biologically killed the crow, having reduced it to a "bloody mess" (31) followed by Chiko's throwing it into the river to drown. But symbolically the crow is still alive, and its vitality vibrates throughout the story.

THE IRONY OF HARMLESS COLONIALISTS

Although rarely discussed in postcolonial animal studies, insects and other arthropods are a recurrent motif in texts that explore colonial experiences. Indeed, modern ethology (the study of animal behavior) is presaged in the work of the Afrikaner poet and naturalist Eugène N. Marais, whose groundbreaking research related humans not only to primates but to insects. Marais demonstrated in essays published between 1923 and 1925 (published in 1925 as a book, *Die Siel van die Mier*, and in English translation in 1937 as *The Soul of White Ants)* that insects share quite a lot with humans, including what he sees as an intricate symbolic form of communication analogous to human language. He presents insects as having a memory and as capable of expressing pleasure and pain, just like the so-called higher mammals. The product of a Darwinian intellectual milieu, Marais may be wrong in some of the attributes he gives insects, but he shows that we can learn a great deal from them.[17] He also criticizes Western ideas about insects, insisting on insects' value on their own terms, rather than on anthropocentric ones. For instance, he presents termites that are "destructive to wood of all kinds" (1971 [1925], 16), but he does not advocate their destruction. Instead, he marvels throughout at the complex social structures in which the insects are organized—their nests resemble the body of a mammal, such as a human being.[18] In other words, in Marais's work, we are not learning about insects to destroy them but to help us understand ourselves better. It is also apparent that although Marais sees the monarchy as the ideal constitutional organization, as reflected in the hierarchy among termites (Rodgers 2008, 124), he does not endorse the notion of one insect or group of insects within the same species imposing its sense of order on another community of insects.

In human-animal studies, Charles Darwin is celebrated for his role in reminding us about the link between animals and humans. But in postcolonial societies, Darwin is also a villain. His theories of evolution have been used in racist discourses to suggest that non-Western societies are intellectually underdeveloped. In cultures socialized to believe that they are at the pinnacle of civilization or belong to the topmost rung in the evolutionary process, insects may cause revulsion because they remind humans about their lowly primordial earlier selves. In postcolonial societies, however, writers are sympathetic to insects as part of the subordinate other; at least the writers do not display the kind of negative attitude toward insects seen in Western societies, especially when the postcolonial artists explore the ravages of colonialism. For example, while North American discourses offensively present the Mexicans as cockroaches (Hollingsworth 2006, 273), Mexican journalists such as Elena Paniatowska use the same metaphor in a nonoffensive sense to express the marginalized and denigrated status of the wretched of the earth. Paniatowska's metaphor is even hopeful in comparing the downtrodden with cockroaches, which are hard to exterminate in spite of what the journalist sees as the West's dehumanizing and genocidal policies toward non-Westerners.

In postcolonial African writing, the use of insects as metaphors is not confined to sympathetic representations of the colonized wretched of the earth. It is also turned back against the colonists themselves. Ordinarily, one would expect the representation of colonialists through the image of insects in anticolonial literature would be founded on disgust for insects,[19] but the use of insects to represent colonialism suggest that Westerners are more of an enigma than objects of disgust. In Ngũgĩ wa Thiong'o early novels of the 1960s about the Kikuyu of central Kenya's first encounters with colonialists, Europeans are compared to butterflies. In *The River Between,* a precolonial prophet foretells the arrival of a people "with clothes like butterflies" (Ngũgĩ 1965, 2, 19, 148). If butterflies are considered a sublimated analogue to the soaring winged soul in classical Greece and Egypt (Berenbaum 1995, 558; Clarke 1995, 86), in Ngũgĩ's novel they serve a different not-so-beautiful purpose: as a natural and seemingly unstoppable swarm. The repetition of a condensed summary of this butterfly prophecy in *The River Between* suggests that the coming of the Europeans had been preordained.[20] The prophecies indicate an already-posthuman presence in precolonial cultures, through which the society can accurately predict the feature. Even if the society is blamed for exiling their prophet Mugo and not listening to his divinatory voice, there is little the people could have done to block the butterflies (and the Europeans they represent) from coming into the country.

Unlike in Marais's study of actual insects, there is a hint in Ngũgĩ's anticolonial novels that the reason we need to learn about the insect colonialists is to trap and destroy them. In other words, we need to understand the colonialist through his institutions, as only Africans with a modern education can liberate the continent from colonizers. This is a common motif in the African literature of the 1950s and 1960s even when it does not use the same insect metaphors that Ngũgĩ summons in his works: a feeling that the colonized people need to acquire colonial education to eventually drive the colonialists out.[21] The texts are from a class of Africans who are trained in missionary schools. While criticizing Western religions and education as part of the colonial project, the writers avoid fully denouncing modern institutions. According to the texts from this period, Africans can repurpose colonial practices and harness them as tools against colonial oppression. In spite of the stated desire to annihilate colonialism, it is clear from the context in *The River Between* that the butterflies the prophet dreams about are metaphorical, and the violence toward European colonizers should not necessarily be extended to the actual insects. Constructed through memory, Mugo's prophecy could have been restructured to represent the colonialist in viler terms using an insect considered destructive, but the society chose a butterfly. Ngũgĩ uses this belief to enhance the dramatic irony; in seeing the European as a beautiful and innocuous insect, the society, like the Igbo that Achebe presents in *Things Fall Apart,* does not fully apprehend the destructiveness of colonialism. Is he, then, saying that the butterflies should be destroyed because they are not as innocent as they appear? At this stage in his writing career, Ngũgĩ had not adopted the Fanonist model of liberation, which views violence as necessary to remove from power a violent and dehumanizing colonial regime. The novelist does not seek to trigger any destructive violent feelings toward actual butterflies or even the Europeans that he uses the insect to represent. Even at a metaphorical level, violence against the butterflies is ruled out as the best way to counter European colonialism.

Intriguingly, in the novels that advocate the use of violence against colonialism, Ngũgĩ spares the animals he uses in comparisons of colonialism and its institutions. When he praises anticolonial military force in his later works, the Europeans cease to be insects. For example, in the Fanonist *A Grain of Wheat* (1986 [1967]), which views violence against colonialism as therapeutic, Mugo wa Kibiro's image of Europeans morphs from butterflies to an inanimate object, the Uganda railway line built from Mombasa to Kisumu between 1896 and 1906. At one moment, as in *The River Between,* Mugo wa Kibiro is quoted talking about "people with clothes like butterflies" and as "a stranger with a scalded skin" who tells the Kikuyus about "another country beyond the sea where a powerful woman sat on the throne while men and women danced under the shadow of her authority and benevolence" (Ngũgĩ 1986 [1967], 10). The butterfly, mentioned only once in the novel, is more sinister than in *The River Between.* But when it comes to advocating a military solution to colonial oppression in *A Grain of Wheat*, the European is no longer referred to as a butterfly. The details of Mugo wa Kibiro's foresight change to his reference to an "iron snake" (12, 70, 71). Even here it is made clear from the context that Kibiro's "iron snake" is the railway line, crawling "along this plain before climbing up the escarpment on its way to Kisumu and Kampala" (70). In fact, only once is the railway called a "snake" without referring to the material that it is made of, to qualify that the text is not talking about an actual snake. We should note that even this one-time reference to the "snake" happens in an anaphoric reference after a sentence that has already talked about the "iron snake" (12). The semantic incongruity, in which the speaker couples "iron" with "snake," announces to the readers that they should understand the expression as a metaphor.

Nowhere in *A Grain of Wheat* does the novel advocate sabotaging the railway line, although that would be a viable guerrilla tactic. Even if the snake were to be destroyed, as the community tries to do at the very beginning before Europeans overpowered the natives with guns, it is painstakingly made clear that the metaphorical "iron snake" is different from a literal snake. In *The River Between*, even if the butterflies the prophet sees in his dreams will be "flying about over the land, disrupting the peace and the ordered life of the country" (19), one is not expected to be violent toward them. Such a method of overcoming the insects is futile because "you could not cut the butterflies with a panga. You could not spear them until you learnt their ways and movement" (20). The best way to fight colonial oppression, then, is to synthesize Western education with traditional values to produce an anticolonial force at the interstices between European and native values and practices.

STORMY BEGINNINGS, OR INGESTING LOCUSTS FROM THE WEST

In the postcolony, the perceived intemperance of nature has been used as an allegory of the turbulences colonialism and neocolonialism brought in their wake. The clash of cultures in Africa and its diasporas is usually figured as the vortex of a storm, an intemperate natural force that overwhelms the colonized subject. The Guyana-born British poet Grace Nichols expresses this clash of cultures to a black migrant in London in terms of a storm in her "Hurricane Hits England" (1996). Similarly, David Rubadiri's poem "An African Thunderstorm" poignantly captures, through an evocation of violent natural elements, the turmoil and violence gripping an African nation as a result of colonial contact. Rubadiri experiments with modernism and free verse, but his poem derives its power from its acknowledgement of the strength of the environment over humans. In the poem, nature is uncontrollable. In the face of a thunderstorm, humans "toss and turn" and "dart around / in and out / madly" (2004 [1968], 21). The word "madly" stands on its own in the rugged structure of the poem to signal the pandemonium that nature has caused in the human society presented. As a supreme power, nature is not condemned for its violence. This is in accord with what Raymond Williams considers to be the religious conception of nature, where "the emphasis was on the power of natural forces, and on the apparently arbitrary or capricious occasional exercise of these powers, with inevitable, often destructive effects on men" (1976, 186).

In an edited volume of poetry for secondary schools, Rubadiri groups his "An African Thunderstorm" in a category he describes as "poems about village life in Africa, about the people and the animals living 'on the earthen floor' and closely bound to the forces of nature" (1989, 35).[22] Yet although the poem can be read to be literally about the supremacy of the natural elements beyond human control, the work signals to its postcolonial readers that it is an allegory about colonialism:

From the west
Clouds come hurrying with the wind
Turning sharply
Here and there
Like a plague of locusts
Whirling,
Tossing up things on its tail
Like a madman chasing nothing. (2004 [1968], 21)

The wind could literally be westerly here, but we are attuned to reading the coded commentaries on imperialism in such poems about nature. Therefore, the readers will not miss the fact that the wind that causes instability in this community comes from "the west" as indicated in the very first line of the poem. In the same stanza, the wind is likened to "a plague of locusts." This is a common reference to Europeans, whom seers in different communities had foretold in precolonial times using the image of the locust as a pest to concretize the imperialist Europeans' capacity to destroy. Even in foundational novels such as Achebe's *Things Fall Apart* (1962 [1958]), Europeans are figured as a swarm of insects. In the novel, oral histories blur the line between literal and metaphoric understandings of locusts: Achebe writes that "the locusts had not come in many, many years, and only the old people had seen them before" (48)—at once referring to literal insects and metaphoric colonialists. They have been coming in cycles, provoking myths about them: "The elders said locusts came once in a generation, reappeared every year for seven years and then disappeared for another lifetime. They went back to their caves in a distant land, where they were guarded by a race of stunted men. And then after another lifetime these men opened the caves again and the locusts came to Umuofia" (47). The narrator associates locusts with foreigners, but not necessarily Europeans. The fact that such a phenomenon is recurrent, even if uncommon, indicates that the Igbos have interacted with other foreigners before. The society enjoys the insects, symbols of the foreign, as a meal. Even those who had never seen locusts before "knew by instinct that they were very good to eat" (49). We can take the image of the insects in *Things Fall Apart* as a literal reference to swarms of locusts that visit the geographical region under suitable climatic conditions for such visits. But it is not lost on the reader that the literal presence of locusts in the initial section of *Things Fall Apart* foreshadows the coming of the Europeans to Umuofia and to other clans of the Igbo later in the novel. The writer gives verbal clues to link the locusts with Europeans and to suggest that the Igbo community enjoys eating the locusts because it is unaware of the harmful effects of colonial education and religion on African traditions.[23] Achebe uses similar language to describe the arrival of the locusts in Umuofia and the coming of Europeans in Abame, as reported by Obierika, who is closest to serving as Achebe's possible mouthpiece in the novel (Achebe 1962 [1958], 87–88). Obierika quotes the oracle in Abame as declaring the coming Europeans to be "locusts"; the hot-headed Abame people decide to kill the first European because the oracle declares him "their harbinger sent to explore the terrain" (123). The narrator has already used similar words to describe the locusts that settle in Umuofia earlier in the story, calling them "harbingers." He uses "survey" instead of Obierika's "explore" and "land" in the place his "terrain" (49), but the repetition establishes parallelism between the locusts and European invaders.[24]

A similar literal entomophagy in *Things Fall Apart* is seen in poems such as Emmanuel Obiechina's "Locusts" in which the society munches locusts with abandon:

Baskets shall hoist pot-bellied
Over smoking hearth fire,
Gathering soot and rind,
Wetting giant throats
For the feast of crunching. (1976, 23)

Although it does not directly uphold veganism, the poem is critical of this eating of locusts. The scene in which we witness the roasting of the locusts is gross, but the society sees nothing wrong with its action. The poem mocks the people's celebratory mood in feasting on the insects. But it is not because, in the poem, killing animals is wrong. It appears that the poem criticizes the Africans for its unreflective eating of probably the wrong animals. Unlike in *Things Fall Apart,* in Obiechina's poem the locust meal causes no harm; there is gastronomical pleasure throughout the eating. This is at least from the eaters' point of view, as the poem on the whole suggests that it does not endorse this celebration. The movement of the jaws is compared with a Western dance, a performance genre that several African works, such as Ibrahim Hussein's *Mashetani* (The Devils), associate with unreflective Westernization. In Obiechina's poem, references to the dance are repeated in consecutive lines:

Waltz the jaws
Waltz them hard;
Set teeth grinding;
Let jubilant incisors
Head slow molars
On a dance of caterpillars. (Obiechina 1976, 23)

The poem's repetition brings together the joyous, European dance form of the "waltz" with the connotation of an apocalyptic experience of dying locusts laid out in a hot sun. Even though the locusts "drying in the sun" is a source of celebration, their death indicates the society's proclivity to prematurely celebrate the end of an era, even as the destructive forces of the past continue in the present. The expression also captures human destructive potential. The anaphoric repetition of "waltz" signals that what the villagers are doing in the poem parallels a Western practice. Later in the collection, the musicians have "lost" their "song." The modern music played is "dry," and we are entering an existentialist world in which culture is lost "in the dry bottom of sandy valleys / winding everlastingly into void / Of nothingness" (1977, 32). The eating of locusts has a similar ring of celebrating destruction and nothingness. Like modern music, the waltzing eaters of locusts here are lost in premature celebration of an improved socioeconomic condition, thinking of a life in everlasting glut, while the status quo actually persists. It is not surprising, then, that even if the society believes it has conquered the insects by eating them, the poem ends with a reminder that the forces the insects symbolize, most likely colonial conditions, still persist in the present and the future:

> *Some locusts shall have gone,*
> *Lost in the legend of the gut;*
> *Other locusts shall remain,*
> *Swarming the earth, feeding,*
> *Being fed upon.* (1976, 23)

At the time of composing the poem, in 1971, Obiechina would definitely have been aware of Achebe's representation of locusts, which the poet dwells on in a critical survey of tradition in the West African novel (Obiechina 1975, 125, 131). Again, the sense of mockery and irony is unmistakable in the description of the joys of eating the locusts in a collection of poems that bemoans the emasculation of African intellectuals.

The literal locusts cause joy in Achebe's novel and Obiechina's poem because they are a source of nourishment.[25] But *Things Fall Apart* is ambivalent about the European encounter. On the one hand, there is a possible benefit in this imminent encounter, as this symbolic arrival of Europeans comes shortly before Ikemefuna is killed; such devastating destruction of slave lives and the killing of twins that Ikemefuna's death provokes Nwoye to think about are likely to be brought to an end. One the other hand, the modern education and religion the Europeans bring will destroy African cultures. The literal locusts are thus appreciated because they can be eaten, but the metaphorical ones are a source of anxiety because they prefigure Abrahamic apocalypse. In a postcolonial text, the retreat of the symbolic locusts would be a most welcome development because they are imagined as harbingers of death and destruction.[26]

UBIQUITOUS INSECTS AND THEIR QUEER SEXUALITIES

Like Rubadiri, the Swahili poet Haji Gora Haji has explored the power of natural elements in a popular poem titled "*Kimbunga*" (The Hurricane).[27] While

Rubadiri uses modernist experiments, Haji uses traditional Indian Ocean aesthetics to examine the state of mayhem in a particular moment in his nation. "Kimbunga" poems such as Haji's are not about European invasion of Africa; they comment on the problems facing postcolonial African nations, including political instability, poverty, and inflation.[28] If the insect is "zoology's Other," as Charlotte Sleigh observes (2006, 342), then the human subject it is compared with in allegorical and metaphorical language belongs to the lowest human stratum. The insect is at best an annoyance, and the people it is compared to must be a despicable lot.[29] In the postcolony, the undesirable is best imagined as a pestilent insect to be crushed or as a bodily deformity that we can do little about. The insect metaphor complements images of disability to imagine the marginalized social group that needs to be fully exiled from the polity. For example, in another Swahili poem by Mwinyihatibu Mohamed, "Ushoga" (1977, 69–70), gay sexuality becomes *fukufuku*, glossed as a kind of insect that has penetrated every part of the human body.[30] In the collection this poem features in, insects are not held in high esteem. The section devoted to *vidudu* (insects) is shared with *visivyo hai* (nonliving things). The intricate webs of the *buibui* (spider) are used as a metaphor for shaky authoritarian leadership. In this particular poem, the *fukufuku* symbolize death and strangeness, as they are glossed as capable of attacking both humans and plants.

The *fukufuku* metaphor in Mwinyihatibu Mohamed's poem is reiterated in the *kibwagizo* (the refrain at the end of each four-line stanza) not only to emphasize the ubiquity of the undesirable sexual behavior, but to make the poet's observation mnemonic among his audiences, because the line traditionally expresses the most poignant message of the poem in a pithy observation that the audience can join the performer to sing along in chorus. The concluding quatrain reckons that it is hard to understand homosexuality:

Ushoga vyake vitendo, ubongo hinivuruga
Hugeuza watu mwendo, wakabaki magamaga
Alienayo kibendo, ni madhara kuyakoga
Ni fukufuku ushoga, nasi umetuzunguka.

Homosexuality's acts, mind they boggle
It changes people's gaits, and they walk with legs apart,
The fellow with the problem, is hard to stop
Worms homosexuality is, and it surrounds us.

The poem belongs to the *tarbia* or *unne* (quatrain) tradition. Each *mshororo* (line) in the poem has sixteen syllables and two hemistiches. The first three lines of each stanza have a rhyme at the medial pause (eighth syllable in the line) and a different rhyme at the end of the line. In this tradition, the medial rhyme is optional, but the end rhyme is mandatory. However, Mwinyihatibu Mohamed takes great care in choosing his words and rhymes. In the first three lines, the first hemistiches rhyme at the eighth syllable, while the sixteenth syllables in these lines rhyme with each other. The order of the medial and end rhymes is changed in the *kibwagizo* (the last line in the stanza, repeated throughout the poem): the first hemistich in the refrain rhymes with the second hemistich in the previous lines, the last syllable at the caesura of the *kibwagizo* rhymes with the endings of the first three lines, and the medial rhyme in the first three lines moves to the end syllable of the last line in the stanza. This rhyme scheme is maintained throughout the poem. Such a composition calls for great discipline and a delicate balancing act, because, as Mwinyihatibu Mohamed comments in one of his meta-poems about composing poetry, a well-wrought poem is not just a bundle of *mizani* (meter) and *vina* (rhymes); the rhythmic arrangement has to match the semantic and other phonological choices in the poem. The words at the caesura are not easily changeable, but those in other parts of the line can be replaced a bit more easily with another expression with the same number of syllables.[31] Therefore, the word *fukufuku* is deliberately included; it is not needed to maintain the intricate rhyme scheme and meter; even if it were, it could be replaced by several others with an equal number of syllables (e.g., *marufuku*, undesirable or unlawful); the poet uses it because he specifically wants to invoke an insect metaphor that emphasizes the undesirability of homosexuality.

Colin McGinn reminds us that one of the reasons insects disgust humans is that they represent the "intermediate quasi-life" and "seem mindless and heartless . . . but there is no denying their place on the tree of life" (2011, 114). The same can be said of the homosexuality that the poem uses the insects to signify. Indeed, the speaker in the poem is less disgusted by the insects than by homosexuality. As a life-destroying insect, *fukufuku* remains intact in its alterity throughout the poem, but the poem also uses it to mount a challenge to heteronormativity. Reading prison narratives from East Africa that include references to homosexuality, Taiwo Adetunji Osinubi (2014) usefully reminds us not to rush to condemn such texts merely because of an absence of overt LGBT activism. The ambivalences in such narratives suggest a heterogeneous culture, where multiple and contradictory expressions of desire are played out. Even if they deploy a highly disciplined and seemingly conservative metrical pattern and rhyme scheme, the use of which was already established in the early twentieth century, Swahili *mashairi* (poems) are usually fascinatingly full of *utata* (playful ambiguity), such that a poem that sneers at homosexuality and compares it with disgusting insects can also be asking the society to learn to live with this alternative way of self-fashioning.

We should remember that, as Mama Zogbé (aka Mamaissii Vivian Hunter-Hindrew) explains, "typically, if one were to enquire of an African if homosexuality ever existed in African culture, the usual response would be 'no, never!' Many Africans even blame the existence of homosexuality on the Europeans and the Arab invaders, who today dominate the adult male and child homosexual prostitution markets that exists along any African tourist strip" (2007, 577). Conventionally, people in mainland Tanzania would argue that homosexuality does not exist there. It is seen as a practice that happens in the Indian Ocean islands, brought there by foreigners from Asia and the Middle East; the euphemistic word for a homosexual man is Mpemba (one from the Pemba islands), suggesting that homosexuality is not native to mainland Africa or even the other Indian Ocean islands. Indeed, because homosexuality is considered scandalous and disgusting, a Swahili scholar, Kitula King'ei, chooses the other meaning of the word *ushoga* (friendship between women, usually nonerotic) in a Kiswahili parenthetical glossing, unnecessarily repeated when the word appears in the analysis of this particular poem. Homosexuality cannot even be condemned in homophobic outbursts; rather, it is erased from existence. I show below that the poem is about male same-sex relationships, not "urafiki baina ya wanawake" (friendship between women) as King'ei would have us believe (King'ei 1985, 14; 34). But whichever way we interpret Mwinyihatibu Mohamed's "Ushoga," the playful *utata* in the poem does not extend to insects. The society's putative fear of destructive insects is evoked to conjure the uncanny figure of the gay man on the Indian Ocean Mrima coast of Tanzania.

Susan Miller (2004, 14) is right to observe that "disgust imagery is ubiquitous in the language of degradation that feeds inter-group atrocities." As insects, *fukufuku* are disgusting, but as a metaphor for gay people, the repulsive insects are already lodged in our bodies, and we are suspended between action and paralysis. The word *mwendo* in the poem can mean both "gait" and "culture or social direction." In one of these senses, homosexuality has changed people's ways, so that there is social confusion in their *mwendo* (culture). But the word is also used on a microcosmic level to suggest that the gay man walks queerly askew, legs apart. The word *fukufuku*, glossed as an insect that penetrates the human skin, probably a jigger, is also glossed as synonymous with *sondo* (stalk-borer). Thus, the word is supposed to connote the destructiveness of homosexuality, alluding to pests that attack the human body and crops.

The poem's concerns about homosexuality suggest a cultural change carried on through inappropriate individual behavior: when the poet uses a synonym for *fukufuku*, *sondo* (Mohamed, 1977, 26, 42), it is in association with *ushoga* or what is considered feminine behavior, such as gossiping, which men should not engage in. The *ushoga* in these instances is not sexual; rather, its inclusion suggests that any feminine behavior among men, sexual or otherwise, is a problem. In one of these poems, the *mmbeya* (gossip) exhibiting *ushoga* (femininity) is compared with the *chawa* (louse) to explain that such a person is most destructive to the people closest to him. Like a louse, which bites those in whose clothes it hides, *haumi wa kando* [he doesn't bite the one afar]; he talks ill of those closest to him (1977, 42). The author has already celebrated in an anecdotal note preface to the poem that the real person on whom the poem is based received a public beating. This is to suggest that insects and men who apparently behave like women should be violently punished. Playing with the ambivalence of the word *ushoga* and linking the feminized habit of gossiping to destructive insect behavior, the poet insists throughout that homosexuality is a ubiquitous pestilence that society should be worried about. It is not to be condoned, but there is a sense in which attempts to uproot it might destroy the community at large. It is no coincidence, then, that in his poetry Mwinyihatibu Mohamed uses insects to suggest an insidious threat to the social order: in many of his poems, insects figure alongside natural disaster as images of uncontainable threats to society.

WORLD WITHOUT HUMANS

For its part, Haji's enigmatic poem "Kimbunga" shows that turbulent politics affect the powerful more adversely than the powerless. In Zanzibar, the reference to *kimbunga* evokes the hurricane on April 15, 1872, that destroyed the island's navy and two-thirds of clove and coconut plantations. The 1870s were a decade of turbulence in Zanzibar. When the hurricane hit, Zanzibar was still recovering from a cholera outbreak that caused 70,000 deaths in 1869 (Barua 1992, 13), worsened by the overcrowding in slave quarters and on slave boats. Slave trade, eventually banned in 1873, had also been affected by wars in the African hinterlands, and the scramble for Africa that would curtail the powers of the Zanzibari sultanate was looming large.

In artistic representation, that day's *kimbunga* is prefigured as Agamemnon. Lieutenant William Henn's of the Livingstone Search and Relief Expedition depicted it in apocalyptic terms in a sketch published in *Illustrated London News* on June 1, 1872 (see Fig. 2 below). Of the thirteen major illustrations in this edition of the newspaper, the sketch of the effects of the Zanzibar cyclone is the only image without a human being in it.[32] Granted, below this image is another one representing the British consulate, which seems to reassure the reader that the British interests are not threatened; the Union Jack is still flying high. A second flag in the background of the image is not clear, but it serves to show the vitality and endurance of the nonhuman material world vis-à-vis human fragility.[33] In the second image, there are a few humans in front of the towering consulate building. But the absence of humans and animals in Henn's sketch of the effects of the hurricane evokes an apocalypse. Although newspaper illustrations usually require the visual artist to include humans in the frame, this image does not have humans in it. Other images in the issue at least have humans in them, including the front-cover sketch of a ship grounded in Hastings. The most visible in Henn's sketch of Zanzibar are the destroyed buildings and the grounded ships. The vessel that seems to be functional is pushed to the background. The ship is distant, and it is possible that it has no humans in it. The heavens are overcast—an indication that more atmospheric disturbances are looming. Given that this is a painting produced some time after the event portrayed, the omission of humans seems more deliberate than it would be in a photograph. In an image taken with a camera, it is possible that in the referential world there is no human being within the frame of the shot.

The omission of humans as a deliberate artistic choice becomes clear when we consider that the correspondent for the *Times of India* includes humans and animals in his description of the immediate aftermath of the hurricane:

> Human beings were the only animals astir. My parrots, I observed, were sitting on their perches with ruffled feathers, and did not answer to the usual call. Poultry were in the same state and made no noise when touched. I had heard of such manifestations of animal instinct before, and putting all things together, I felt certain that we should soon experience the shock of an earthquake. (Anon. 1872, 3)

Figure 2: *The World Without Us*: A print of Lieutenant William Henn's sketch of the devastation caused by the Zanzibar cyclone as published in *Illustrated London News*, June 1, 1872. Courtesy of the Melville J. Herskovits Library of African Studies, Northwestern University.

From this correspondence, it appears that animals are more prepared for such an environmental catastrophe than humans. The superiority of the humans in the colonial world is called into question, although the report does not address the status of the locals.[34] Humans and animals are omitted from the depiction of the event to emphasize the devastation caused. But like most art from the time and well into the 1990s, the artist misses the connection between the devastation to humans and large-scale geological forces. With the fall in the supply of slaves due to wars in the hinterland and the signing of treaties that restricted slave trade, the main source of export income for Zanzibar was mangroves. They were cut using slave labor and exported in huge numbers as building materials and as firewood to fuel industries in India and the Gulf (Agius 2005, 125). Although it is conceivable that the destruction of the mangrove shield worsened the effects of the winds, the storm and the devastation it left behind are largely seen as in the literature as a cruel act of Mother Nature. It is in works mainly published in the twenty-first century that the postcolonial artists more consciously draw attention to possible destruction of human life on the planet as a result of global warming.[35]

The 1872 cyclone is rarely mentioned in daily conversations in Zanzibar, but it is embedded the region's artistic collective memory. Haji Gora Haji's poem "Kimbunga" is largely read as referring to a cyclone as an allegory of the 1964 Zanzibar revolution in which the Arab-dominated government was overthrown by the local masses. In the form of a *fumbo* (allegorical riddle), the poem does not mention its literal referent. From the opening line, the hurricane happens in Siyu, a coastal town in Kenya, and it appears that the event is in a mythical past. The poem uses a conventional poetic form to refer to past recent political upheavals in Zanzibar, the twentieth-century political hurricanes.

Haji's depiction of the hurricane is different from Mwinyihatibu Mohamed's. The hurricane in Mohamed's poem is predictable, affecting the leaves and sparing the trunk, but Haji's violent winds seem inclined to spare the weak in society. In the first three stanzas, we learn that the winds uproot the sturdy *mibuyu* (baobab trees, *Adansonia digitata*), but spare *minazi* (coconut trees); they sink *meli* (steamships), while *ngarawa* (leaky boats) are spared. Buildings of more than one story collapse, but *vibanda vya malofa* (huts of the lowly) all survive the hurricane. The fourth and the fifth stanzas are more intriguing because they take the reader to a sublime mythical world in which animals and women possess special powers. The third stanza is about a frog, which could suck dry a river:

Chura kakausha mto, maji yakamalizika
Pwani kulikuwa moto, mawimbi yaliyowaka
Usufi nusu kipeto, rikwama limevunjika
Nyoyo zikafadhaika. (Haji 1994, 1)

A frog dried up the river, water got finished up
On the shore was fire, waves on fire
Half a sack of kapok breaks the pushcart
And hearts were troubled.

In Kiswahili literature, the river-drying animal is usually not a frog, as in this stanza, but a *chewa*, a mythical leviathan that humans cannot literally take revenge against. By presenting the frog as an emblem of disaster, does the poem justify this animal's abjection, especially when we consider that a frog, unlike a *chewa*, is a small animal that humans can destroy? To answer this question, it is pertinent to compare this stanza with a scene in Ebrahim Hussein's allegorical play based on the 1964 revolution in Zanzibar, *Mashetani* (Devils), especially because configurations of nature in cultural expression, as Raymond Williams observes, "contains an extraordinary amount of human history" (1980, 67). In Hussein's play, some similar preternatural animal borrowed from Swahili oral literature drains oceans of water. Unlike the small frog in Haji's poem, the *chewa mkubwa* (the big *chewa*) in Hussein's play is presented as mythological, to be found in the seventh ocean. Within the context of Indian Ocean systems of signification, the word *chewa* brings with it an enormous freight of nuanced and shifting meanings. Although sometimes translated as cod (*Epinephelus maculatus*) (Blok 1948, 58), in Zanzibari folklore *chewa* is a mythical animal that also serves the function of the whale in local translations of the Judeo-Christian story of Jonah. In these stories, especially those composed by Bismillahi Rrahmani Rrahim (Almighty God) Himself, *chewa* is not even a whale; it is just a monstrous aquatic being that only exists in the netherworld.[36]

Not a biophysical reality, *chewa* becomes a fictional icon of incomprehensible and all-powerful nature, the ultimate emblem of alterity that cannot be expressed in another language. There seem to be no easy synonyms for *chewa* even in Kiswahili. Thus Jan Knappert, in *Myths and Legends of the Swahili* (1970), offers a largely assimilative translation of the tales into fluent English, but leaves the word "Chewa" as a proper noun without a translation in "The Giant Whale Chewa" (173–74).[37] In Knappert's collection, the story in which Chewa appears is grouped among stories about spirits. In some renditions of the narrative (e.g., Blok's *A Swahili Anthology* and Knappert's *Myths and Legends*), the fictional status of *chewa* is taken a little further: *chewa* is here the ocean floor; on top of *chewa* is a cow with 40,000 legs and 40,000 horns. The cow carries the earth on its many horns (Blok 1948, 58–59; Knappert 1970, 173–74). As in Hussein's play, in Blok and Knappert's renderings, the waves and tides in the ocean arise when some natural force breathes in and out. Thus, Hussein is likely to have borrowed the myth of *chewa* from Zanzibari oral literature about a foundational leviathan to symbolically represent feudal and capitalist exploitation. Readers are supposed to understand that *chewa* is not an actual animal against which they can enact retribution for anything it is claimed to have done.

Hussein's style clarifies further that *chewa* in his play is more mythical than biological. He uses the term *chewa mkubwa,* which is tautological, given that Kiswahili dictionaries, probably acknowledging that *chewa* is a metaphysical leviathan, only gloss the word as *samaki mkubwa* (a big fish). The expression *chewa mkubwa* thus signifies the monstrosity of this aquatic being, which in some dictionaries, such as A. C. Madan's *English-Swahili and Swahili-English Dictionary* (1902, 60), is described as *samaki wa Ulaya* (a European fish). The fish in the play behaves in a similar way to the frog in Haji's poem in its ability to drain oceans of water: "Chewa huyu akivuta pumzi maji yote yanakupwa, maji yote yanaingia kinywani mwake" (Hussein 1971, 28). (This enormous *chewa* draws all the water if he breaths in; all the water drains into his mouth.) Hussein's ocean-draining monster lives in the netherworld. He swallows everything he feels like destroying. We are told that he is not an actual fish*: "na huyu chewa siyo chewa bali shetani"* (and this cod is not a cod, but the devil himself). From the context, we glean that he is a figment of the imagination. He does not appear on stage. The audience is told about him in a summary of an oral narrative that the character has been told by another person.

I have demonstrated elsewhere the tendency of Tanzania's nationalist literature to present nonblack immigrants of the Indian Ocean as evil, including changing the race of Shakespeare's Shylock to connote the supposed greed of Arab and Guajarati immigrants to East Africa (Mwangi 2017, 207).[38] In reading Hussein's representation of the animal in *Mashetani,* it pays to remember that Chewa is described in some versions of the story as *sultan wa samaki* (sultan of the fish) (Blok 1948, 59). Written in the socialist *ujamaa* nationalist mode, Hussein's *Mashetani* is critical of the feudal sultanate of Zanzibar. *Chewa* is therefore to be seen as representing exploitative leadership that needs to be abandoned in favor of a socialist order. It is little wonder that in the play, the monstrous fish is used allegorically in a story by an ideologically conscious underclass grandmother to explain the greed that characterizes capitalist and feudal systems that deserve to be overthrown.

By contrast, the frog in Haji's poem is presented as real, not a fantastical creation from orature. Instead of the usual *chewa,* he uses a frog to suggest the powers of real small animals that symbolize ordinary people in society. Although the incident involving the frog seems to be from the remote past and a far-off place (Siyu), it happened in a verifiable geographical location. Unlike in Hussein's play, the animal represents the powerless, as opposed to the powerful greedy devil in Hussein's play. Nature seems to be an ally of the ordinary folk in Haji's poem, destroying symbols of capitalist exploitation. As in the previous stanzas, before the frog is featured, the masses are represented as less powerful. The hurricane is benevolent to them, but it destroys the more powerful entities. The masses are presented as a frog and the lightweight kapok. Ordinarily they would not dry up a whole river as the frog does, but in this poem they possess an enormous mystical capacity. The whole world is on fire, including the shores and the ocean waves. A half-full sack of the light silken *usufi* (kapok) is able to wreck a *rikwama* (pushcart).

The last stanza is about a *kikongwe ajuza* (an old woman) with mysterious powers to hold all beings captive. The term is tautological because the two words are synonymous; the words are used to maintain the meter and rhyme and to emphasize that the infirm old person is a woman, a symbol of absolute frailty. The old woman has special powers, too, but unlike in the presentation of the frog and the hurricane winds, there is some negative connotation in the description of the woman as destroying *wataokiendekeza* (the ones who oblige her). It is as if destruction comes to those who tolerate the weak, as they later gain mysterious powers to damage the powerful. At the same time, the woman is presented as a symbol of destructive power in the sense that she holds captive other *viumbe* (creatures) and destroys those that are good to her. Siyu, the setting of the poem, is remembered in Indian Ocean historical treatises for its resistance to the expansionist campaigns of Seyyid Said (1790–1856), the sultan of Oman and Zanzibar in the 1840s.[39] Siyu's local chief, Sheikh Mataka ibn Mbaraka (1779–1856), waged a successful guerrilla war against Seyyid Said's attempts to annex Siyu; he succumbed to Seyyid Said's colonialism in 1863. Could the Zanzibari poet, then, be insinuating that Zanzibar should have been more ruthless toward the rival town of Siyu to suppress rebellions and extend Zanzibari colonial dominance across the Indian Ocean societies in East Africa?

Cosmopolitan in its outlook, Haji's poetry is pan-African, showing immense respect for continental Africa and even going so far as arguing that the origin of Kiswahili is mainland Africa, not Indian Ocean islands as Zanzibari ethnonationalists have insinuated. Indeed, from the preceding stanzas of "Kimbunga," the poem cannot be calling for the destruction of the weaker people of Siyu before they gain power to destroy the Zanzibari ruling elites; although apocalyptic on the surface, the poem uses the image of an animal and the hurricane to celebrate the agency of marginalized groups. The word *wataokiendekeza* (spoil with praise) could have been chosen here for rhythmic purposes and also to suggest that the society should not tolerate oppressive regimes. How that comes to be identified with a woman is odd, unless Haji equates women with nature.

Paradoxically, in Haji's poetry, animals are used as metaphors for all that has gone wrong in postcolonial Africa, but there is a sense in which this is used to promote vegan practices. The cat, a metaphor for the exploitative postcolonial leadership, is a cunning thief: "paka nakuwasa wizi, vitoweo usiibe" (cat, I urge you to stop thievery; meat you should stop stealing) (Haji 1994, 22). The *vitoweo* that the cat steals here may well be vegetarian, but in the Zanzibari context, as explained in works by early European missionaries, *kitoweo* is most likely a meat relish.[40] The first thing that the cat steals in the poem is *samaki* (fish). The apostrophe to the cat sounds very much like an address to the ruling elites, especially because other poems in the collection complain about the exploitative habits of the bourgeois nationalists. Here they are told they are digging a grave for themselves because of the corruption that characterizes their regimes. As a thief, the metaphorical cat is advised to see things that do not belong to it as *sumu* (poison) to help it suppress the urge to steal from others. The poem does not criticize eating of meat; it is against eating stolen meat. But as I suggest below, eating meat is linked with enjoying ill-begotten property.

Like the cat, *punda* (donkey) has become worthless because of his comical antics and ingratitude:

Utamjengea banda, akae asitirike
Huona hujampenda, hicho si kifani chake
Kulala kwenye uwanda, ndio starehe yake
Ndio tabia ya punda, kurusharusha mateke
Kuchunga akikushinda, muachiye ende zake. (Haji 1994, 21)

You build him a pen, to live at ease
He sees that you love him not, that being not his talent
Sleeping in the field is his leisure and pleasure
That is the habit of a donkey, throwing kicks about
If unable to domesticate him, let him go his ways. [my translation]

The whole poem is jeremiad against the thankless donkey, which has no memory about the good things that have been done for it. The poem insists that humans cannot force a donkey to work with beatings. Part of the reason the cat is admonished in the other poem is his tendency to steal meat. The donkey is not to be suppressed, because that is not possible. The speaker in the poem prefers a docile and domesticated animal that accepts human will, but his refrain urges the audience to let the donkey free if that is the animal's wish.

CONCLUSION: SMALL GODS OF THE UNIVERSE

Reading Irish poetry, Borbála Faragó remarks that the insect "allegorically represents the post-human and the transhuman, a life form that surpasses humanity's foibles by decentering human notions of supremacy, all the while becoming an alien, predatory force" (2015, 233). But in the texts I have discussed here, the authors do not seek the destruction of the animals. Instead, they represent the problems of small insects as similar to the problems of the downtrodden in society. They actually show that animals sometimes destroy, without our prompting, that which should be destroyed (e.g., procolonial epistemic practices), making them a divine messenger or servant. In these cases, nature is on the side of the colonized.

It has been a tradition in postcolonial writing to show nature as active, what Bruno Latour would call an "actant" that would "modify other actors through a series" of immanent actions (2004, 75). For example, in Jan Carew's *Black Midas* (1958), the overexploited environment gets revenge against humans in events that in ordinary circumstances would be seen as nature-induced deus ex machina. From the beginning to the end, the novel is full of events that would ordinarily be seen as accidents and coincidences, such as the protagonist's grandparents dying at the same time in different places, one killed in a hunting accident. But the novel suggests the ubiquity of nonhuman agency and celebrates the indomitability of nature, itself a character in the novel. Nature is not capricious; an internal logic governs its operations (I elaborate this a little further in the coda of this book). Similarly, the Zimbabwean poet Kristina Rungano invokes the environment in the form of grass, trees, butterflies, and the weather to comment on political and social issues facing her nation and to underline the possibilities of the end of the prevailing confusion. In a collection of poetry entitled *A Storm Is Brewing*, Rungano deploys images of turmoil succeeded by serenity and bounties from nature to underline that the African environment wouldn't harm us despite the enigma that it generates. Human life still seems to fear the world because of the tumult of the past, but the poem foresees absolute peace as people anticipate "the same familiar beautiful Zimbabwe" where nature (symbolized by lightning) is friendly.

When Kofi Awoonor (2014 (1964], 276) represents colonialists as weaverbirds, it is not to attenuate the colonialist destructiveness. The metaphorical birds are seen as extremely destructive of the native culture they have taken over and desecrated. But the work does not call for the destruction of those birds or the literal subjects they metaphorically represent. The reader is supposed to see the colonialists as a nuisance and try to recover the cultures they have destroyed without annihilating the Europeans. The birds are not to be punished with physical death. Indeed, the death of birds is a harbinger of destruction in the era of the Anthropocene, as represented in such works as Nii Ayikwei Parkes's *Tail of the Blue Bird* (2009); literal birds are themselves victims of colonialism. It is apparent, then, that postcolonial writers portray small animals as enigmatic beings, especially when the narrative is set in precolonial times. Even when they are critical of Europeans, whom they compare with insects and small birds, the writers avoid calling for their destruction. They admire some of the qualities of the metaphorical insect; it is not to be destroyed, but carefully negotiated with.

CHAPTER 5

Interspecies Sexual Intimacies

> it is making love to my
> feet: it understands
> my loneliness . . . miaow?
> —"Kitten" by Hone Tuwhare in *Short Back and Sideways* (1992, 17)

The poem from which this epigraph is drawn suggests a love affair between the speaker and a stray kitten. But the poem, by the Māori author Hone Tuwhare (1922–2008), along with several other postcolonial texts, suggests that such intimacy between humans and animals does not involve coitus. Yet at the time of drafting this chapter, sensational stories were arising in the media about Africans (usually men) who had been taken to court for having sex with goats, donkeys, and chickens.[1] Such incidents are treated as crimes under the bestiality laws inherited from colonial penal code in the 1930s. The reports indicate that interspecies sex occurs frequently in these societies. Reports of interspecies sexual intimacies are usually meant to energize homophobic stereotypes about communities under internal colonialism, as happened when former members of the Ogaden National Liberation Front in the Eastern Ethiopian city of Jigjiga publicly confessed (most likely under duress) that "they engaged sheep and goats and [in] some cases donkeys and mules for carnal release" (Omer 2012).[2] Such stereotypes about rival clans abound across Africa, but numerous hard-news reports from South Africa, Kenya, and Nigeria in the last ten years indicate that human-animal sex is more common in the real world than literary texts would have us believe. Espousing an egalitarian ethics, the texts view human-animal sex as hierarchical, whereby the human exploits the animal for self-gratification. That is, without necessarily opposing sexual possibilities outside the oppressive dominant norms, African writers distance themselves from characters who, instead of cultivating an egalitarian orientation to animals and fellow human beings, take advantage of animals for self-gratification based on a misunderstanding of the animals' intrinsic interests.

In Lauren Beukes's *Zoo City* (2010), the relationship between criminals and their animal companions is one of intimacy. But it is an intimacy born of a dystopian condition that, in a carceral state, expels alleged criminals from humanity. In this phantasmagoric tapestry, Beukes signals the rot in postapartheid South Africa—people become more attached to animals than fellow humans because the state and its institutions have expelled outlaws from humanity. Some scholars of animal-human relationships have noted similar responses to animals among humans on the fringes of the society. Comparing zoos with prisons, Drew Leder reveals, in *The Distressed Body*, possibilities of a regenerative intimacy between condemned people and animals (2016, 202–9). The intimacy between animals and humans in Beukes's *Zoo City* is neither spontaneous nor voluntary as in the instances Leder describes at the Jessup Correctional Institution. In Beukes's novel, the pairing is a form of punishment, which involves convicts being matched with animals ostensibly to shame the human wrongdoers. Apparently, this society sees nothing wrong in pairing innocent animals with people it considers criminals and derelicts. Parker Shipton (2007) explores the various manifestations of intimacy in an African society—from emotional to fiduciary. But in this chapter, I use "intimacy" to indicate coital relationships. I recognize that interspecies sex is queer sex, if we define "queer" the way Alexander Doty (1993), Michael Warner (1993), David Halperin (1995), and Carmen Dell'Aversano (2010) view it: as sexual desires and practices that undermine regimes of normative sexuality and mark "all aspects of non- (anti-, contra-) straight cultural production and reception" (Doty 1993, 3). As a literal and discursive resistance to normative social order, interspecies love is the most intense form of sexual liberation because, as Dell'Aversano (2010) explains, it "permanently subverts one's perception of self, of the other and of the world, bringing it out of alignment with homonormativity's priorities, values and performances" (104).[3] Why, then, has a body of writing that is so radical in challenging conventions and hierarchies become conservative in its depiction of interspecies sex, almost to the level of sounding homophobic, or what Dell'Aversano would call "humanormative," whereby proper human sex can only occur between humans (preferably of opposite sex), not with a nonhuman species?[4] We should remember that even when queer theorists (e.g., David Halperin's view of pederasty in *How to Do the History of Sexuality*) celebrate subversion of the heteronormative order, they are critical of practices that reify hierarchies or justify exploitation.[5]

Allusion to human-animal sexuality in postcolonial literature is not uncommon, but it is usually mentioned cursorily in dark jokes. In Patrice Nganang's *Temps de chien* (*Dog Days*), a stray dog sarcastically wants to know if the protagonist dog sleeps with his human owner. In, Alain Mabanckou's *Mémoires de porc-épic* (*Memoirs of a Porcupine*), a porcupine considers raping a girl it has been sent to kill. This amounts to an unspoken psychotic malevolent desire. In Eri's *The Crocodile*, the protagonist, Hoiri, claims in an unuttered insult that the sorcerer that killed Hoiri's wife was conceived when the evil man's "mother mated with a dog" (119). That the insult is unuttered in the represented world ("muttered to himself, clenching his fist tightly") indexes the taboo status of such a dog-human encounter even when the hero of the story is reflecting in anger and disappointment about the killer of his beloved wife. In Camara Laye's *Le Regard Du Roi* (*Radiance of the King*), Clarence's thought that he sees the clairvoyant old woman Dioki having an orgasm with snakes is a probable misrepresentation of a character's action from another character's perspective. The narrating gecko, Eulálio, in Agualusa's *O vendedor de passados* (*The Book of Chameleons* 2008) and the companion animals in Laura Beukes's *Zoo City* (2008) are present when humans have sex, but the animals do not participate in transspecies coital intimacies. In other words, interspecies sex is largely seen as taboo, and if it is said to have happened, its occurrence is regarded as a rumor that cannot be substantiated, or it is presented as an outlandish stage performance. If same-sex desire among animals is recognized, it is presented as unnatural and a consequence of colonial racism.[6]

I start this chapter with an outline of the major problems an African critic faces in the reading of animal-human sexuality before responding to the representation of interspecies sex in Farah's *Secrets* to examine the novel's use of an unreliable narration that leads us to interrogate the efficacy of human-animal sexual desire. Similarly, I examine Zakes Mda's *The Whale Caller*, in which a character experiences orgasm in a performance with a whale but completely misunderstands the interests of the whale that he claims to love. This is contrasted with Witi Ihimaera's *The Whale Rider*, in which interspecies eroticism is kept at an abstract and lyrical level and is never realized as a physical sexual act. Farah's and Mda's works need a close critique, because the failure to grasp the unreliability of their narration has led to misreadings of the texts as endorsements of interspecies sex. An examination of Nana Nyarko Boateng's "Swallowing Ice" reveals the use of animals as objects of lesbian desires that the postcolonial nation has erased from public recognition.

TERROR OF MISREADING ANIMALS

Like Rebecca Cassidy's discussion of the representation of animal-human sex in "Zoophilia" (2012 [2009]), I neither support nor condemn the practice. But there are more methodological problems in writing about the topic as it is presented in postcolonial texts than in the Western texts that Cassidy deals with. Graham Huggan and Helen Tiffin describe the issue of animal-human sex as "vexed" because it is about "an offence which, if not widespread, is much more common than reported" (2010, 212). Therefore, writers and critics are hesitant to discuss it in noncondemnatory terms. In the West, Neil Carr links the hesitancy to research animal-human sexual intimacy to "the very repugnance that most of society has, or at least displays, for bestiality and zoophilia," with researchers avoiding the topic "for the fear of their reputation being tainted by association with it" (2014, 68). The same situation applies in postcolonial societies. I confess that I wanted to reprint here several cartoons depicting animal-human sex, but my interlocutors and I decided that such graphic illustrations would be in bad taste. Relatedly, findings about animal-human sexuality can be misapplied to silence other nonnormative sexualities. Critics may fear that criticizing sex with animals would put them "in the same position as the closed-minded one who scoffed at the very suggestion of interracial marriage during the age of slavery" (Pettman 2011, 86). But condemnation of interracial sex based on coercion, such as the relationship between Professor David Lurie and his student Melanie Isaacs in Coetzee's *Disgrace*, cannot be seen as closed-minded. Most readers in postcolonial societies would not see how criticism of sex with animals is unjustified. The question is whether such sex can be considered consensual or whether it constitutes rape.[7]

Furthermore, the disapproving ways in which human-animal sex is presented in postcolonial texts privilege arguments about heteronormative sex to such an extent that it is imperative to show how the authors undermine heteronormativity, even when they refuse to endorse animal-human sex. Additionally, arguing that animals cannot consent to human-animal sex is itself an anthropocentric view: we assume that the animal should consent in a language we, as human beings, can comprehend. The solution to this problem is to confine ourselves to the representation of these intimacies in the texts and try to account for them, paying attention to the noncoital human-animal intimacies that the texts celebrate.

In postcolonial African texts, sex with animals is commonly used as a stand-in for the most outrageous human actions. But since Western societies have had similar taboos, as outlined by James Serpell in *The Company of Animals* (1996), among others, proscriptions in themselves may not be the main reason for this attitude. In the African texts I read in this chapter, animal-human sex is presented as abhorrent not because animals are thought to be inferior to humans, but because it is seen as hurtful to the animal. Some writers seem to be concerned that humans might be misreading animals as consenting to sex with them. There is also a subtext suggesting that claims that the animals consent to or enjoy sex with humans is analogous to the spurious projection of the colonized as living in full enjoyment of life under colonialism.

The understanding of sexuality in most postcolonial texts seems to be that any liberatory moves among humans should not involve limiting another species' potential. It is humans, with the power to coerce or manipulate animals, who are portrayed as condoning sexual intercourse with animals when the purpose is to liberate humans from suffocating sexual mores. For example, in 2014, East Africa's most popular editorial cartoonist, Godfrey Mwampembwa (Gado), drew a satyr figure (half-pig, half-human) raping a battered cow. Using the human-animal rape motif, the cartoon symbolizes the exploitation of postcolonial societies by their elites.[8] Half-human animals wearing dapper suits and carrying briefcases were common in his cartoons of that period and symbolized the architects of corruption and self-aggrandizement in Kenya. But it was the first time they were represented in a sexual act in a newspaper that espouses family values, which the paper undertook to distinguish itself from its competitors who are regarded as purveyors of sensationalistic yellow journalism. The lead figure and perverted actor in Gado's cartoon is the pig. The hyena, the crocodile, and what appears to be a leopard cheer the rapist on, maybe waiting their turns. The battered cow is labeled "Kenya" and the cash-stuffed briefcase one of the animals is carrying is marked "MP" (member of Parliament).

The victim is purely bovine; only the evil animals are half-men half-animals. One of the animals, whose species is ambiguous, could be holding the briefcase for the MP; the rapist animal is represented as the pig, consistent with a neologism that entered the Kenyan lexicon at that time: combining *MP* and *pig to produce MPig*. Judging from the cartoon, pigs are supposedly as greedy as members of the Kenyan Parliament. However, in the real world, animals do not bring the country to its knees through corrupt deals or by paying themselves outrageous salaries. Rarely do Gado's cartoons include titles within their frames, but in this one "As if milking the cow dry was not enough" is inscribed above the cow and the animal rapists. The title and the identification of the victim-cow as Kenya and the labeling of one of the aggressors as "MP" emphasizes that the images are to be read as an allegorical representation of the country's elites. The cartoon could refer to news items about such crimes against cows, donkeys, and goats across the country at the time. Thus, if there is to be retribution for crimes against the cow (Kenya), it should be directed at the MPs and other leaders looting the country. While criticizing the abuse of the postcolonial nation, Gado's shocking cartoon retains the welfarist ideology common in postcolonial art: it is acceptable for humans to consume animals as long we do it in a humane way. Judging from the cartoon, it is therefore legitimate to milk the cow, but the animal should not be raped. A similar position as Gado's runs throughout most of African texts regarding nonexploitative human-animal relations, even where the notion of species itself is radically questioned.

DISNARRATED CONCEPTIONS OF ANIMAL-HUMAN HYBRIDS

Before I discuss the literary texts, I want to mention briefly some artistic objects that might appear on the surface to contradict my arguments here because they graphically present products of human-animal sex, such as those depicted in Jane Alexander's artwork. Alexander's work is characterized by hybrid mutants who animate her presentation of the porous border between humans and other life forms, showing us that we are not much different from other animals that we consider ourselves superior to. However, human-animal coitus is left to the imagination. We are never shown how the human-animal hybrid mutants came into being, but they are important in calling settled social and political beliefs into question. Consider Alexander's famous *Butcher Boys*. Produced toward the end of formal apartheid in 1994, the *Butcher Boys* sculptural group (1985–1986) fundamentally undermines the racial policies of the South African government. If interracial sex is illegal in that culture, Alexander goes so far as to show that interspecies sex is legitimate. The sculpture consists of life-size human-animal figures seated on a bench. They look corpse-like and signify the end of white privilege. All are male, suggesting the possible end of male power. Alexander's other installation, *Bom Boys*, includes animal-human hybrids of boys with the facial features of rabbits, vultures, and dogs, while *Infantry* presents militaristic white men with the features of African wild dogs to mock the social control

Figure 3: Jane Alexander's *Butcher Boys*, 1985–86. Reinforced plaster, animal bones, horns, oil paint, wood bench.128.5 x 213.5 x 88.5 cm. Collection of Iziko South African National Gallery © Jane Alexander, DALRO (Dramatic, Artistic and Literary Rights Organisation). Photograph by Svea Josephy.

and pack mentality of a racialized society. In others she uses texts in different languages, such as Zulu and Afrikaans, which would ordinarily not be used together in apartheid South Africa. All in all, Jane Alexander's human-animal figures are hyperbolic and do not so much celebrate human-animal sex as ridicule apartheid laws and militarism.[9]

However, praising the changes in human attitudes toward sex over time—whereby sex not leading to conception, formerly regarded as taboo, is now acceptable—the philosopher Peter Singer takes no issue with humans having sex with animals. He sees significant similarities between humans and animals, and these would justify interspecies sex as long as it does not injure the animal: "We copulate, as they do. They have penises and vaginas, as we do, and the fact that the vagina of a calf can be sexually satisfying to a man shows how similar these organs are" (Singer 2001). Before we accept Singer's argument, we might ask whether the calf enjoys the sex to the same degree that humans do. Naama Harel argues that "it is sometimes difficult and even impossible to verify compulsion or consent when nonhuman animals are involved, because they cannot express their will by human speech and in most cases they are not free to choose, being subjected to human masters, either as pets or as farm animals" (2007, 180). Granted, the problem could be the human inability to comprehend animal consent. Postcolonial writers seem cautious about celebrating such consent because colonialism also presented the colonized as happy under colonialism. To presume that animals consent based on signals we are not sure about places us in a similarly precarious position.

Singer argues that in some cases, animals court humans, suggesting that a resulting sexual encounter would be consensual. However, in postcolonial texts, it is humans who impose themselves on animals. Even in the case that Singer cites in his justification of interspecies coitus, it is humans who encroach on the animal's habitat and keep it in captivity. Singer suggests that sex with a calf can be condoned—even cheered—because it breaks down boundaries between humans and animals. From his argument, rejection of sex with animals is part of an outdated attitude that we should abandon:

> The taboo on sex with animals may, as I have already suggested, have originated as part of a broader rejection of non-reproductive sex. But the vehemence with which this prohibition continues to be held, its persistence while other non-reproductive sexual acts have become acceptable, suggests that there is another powerful force at work: our desire to differentiate ourselves, erotically and in every other way, from animals. (Singer 2001)

I have stated throughout this book that animals should be respected not because they are like human beings, but because they deserve their space on the planet. The fact that we can have sex with certain species of animals should not be the basis for elevating them above other animals as Singer suggests. In the postcolonial texts that I discuss below, having sex with animals is a form of self-gratification at the expense of animals, and this activity forms a direct parallel with colonialism.

UNRELIABILITY OF ANIMAL CONSENT: FARAH'S *SECRETS*

Based on postindependence Somalia, Nuruddin Farah's works, especially the acclaimed "Blood in the Sun" trilogy, belong to the overwhelmingly large canon of postcolonial fiction that crystalizes the nightmarish disillusionment with postindependence politics in the Global South. Nations in that part of the world have flown freedom flags for decades, but without gaining any substantive liberty for their citizens, whom their regimes have continued to dehumanize. Abuse of human rights, internecine conflicts, poverty, and corruption are the order of the day. But although texts in local languages express disappointment similar to those written in the languages of former colonizers, it would appear that home-country critics would prefer these transnational novels to project to the rest of the world a more positive image of their societies. Among these readers, pessimism is an enticement to Western audiences, who are still nostalgic about the glories of colonialism; to these critics, by portraying nations newly liberated from colonialism as failing, the novelists are tacitly telling neocolonialists in the rich North that they consider colonialism not to have been such a bad thing after all. It is not surprising that Farah's critics from the Horn of Africa are not particularly amused by their compatriot's humorous scenes in Farah's trilogy. One reason is the writer's "non-Somali" proclivity for dirty prose. The historian Said S. Samatar writes that he and his fellow ethnic Somalis went "pridefully" to a reading by Farah to give moral support to a "native son made good," only to be embarrassed and made uncomfortable by Farah's language (2000, 142). Samatar cannot recall if the novel in question was *Maps*. But he remembers the "graphic description of a stud of a man banging away at a cow" that went on "ad nauseam" (2000, 142). The hyperbolic scene of prurience that Samatar paints gives a detailed description of a man in Farah's audience having to go to the restroom to vomit. This scene could well be partly fictional, because even if there are references to a man who has sex with a hen in *Maps*, nothing described in Samatar's criticism happens in the novel. Or the novel in question may have been a draft of *Secrets* (1998), the last novel in the trilogy. While *Maps* is set during the Ogaden War of 1977–1978, the events in *Secrets* take place just before the Somali civil war of the 1980s.[10]

Samatar recognizes that writers can portray such prurience if they choose to, but in Farah's work he finds no aesthetic purpose in it. To Samatar, the depiction of dirt in James Joyce's *Dubliners* or Ayi Kwei Armah's *The Beautyful Ones Are Not Yet Born* can be explained, but not its use in Farah's work. The words he uses suggest that he would prefer not to see interspecies sex in a novel about his culture, calling it the "growing cancer of bestiality in Farah's recent fiction" (2000, 142). Furthermore, the historian finds Farah's *Secrets* not only inaccurate in its use of language and depiction of rural Somalia, but also boring because of this "cancer." In other words, Farah is engaged in self-orientalism by trafficking in stereotypes and distortions of a non-Western culture to entertain his Western readers. We have already seen that scholars of Islam laud the way the Koran and other holy edicts in the religion call for just treatment of animals. Like other African writers who have given Muslim characters certain negative traits in their depiction of religious hypocrisy—for example, Abdulrazak Gurnah, Sembène Ousmane, and Mariama Ba—Farah is not criticizing Islam in *Maps* and *Secrets* when he refers to scenes of bestiality; rather, he is poking fun at people who profess to be religious but who neglect Islam's strict injunctions.[11]

Contrary to Samatar's arguments, the occurrence of interspecies sex in Farah's *Secrets* has an aesthetic and thematic function beyond merely entrenching stereotypes about Muslims for Western readers. Francis Ngaboh-Smart urges us to read sexual representation "within its appropriate context" as symptomatic of a country that no longer observes necessary taboos (2004, 60). Farah does not endorse interspecies sex; rather, he uses it as a metaphor for a society that is out of joint. In his careful analysis, Ngaboh-Smart correctly asserts that Farah is not merely experimenting with sexual representation. But such a focus is still problematic because it is based on the character Nonno's anthropocentric theories of morality. To Nonno, "since other animals haven't developed their sense of taboo insofar as we understand the notion, it follows that a bull may mate with his mother, a carrion bird feed on the flesh of its own offspring" (202). Such thinking places humans above animals and tries to justify the breaking of taboos, including "rare" cases of cannibalism. The humans in the novel present the main weaknesses that Nonno identifies as the quality of animals—incest and destruction of one's own species.

Nonno is put in the same class as the debauched Fidow and Madoobe. Because Nonno is not Farah's spokesperson and has come under criticism from within the novel as a participant in the very debauchery he criticizes, I propose that, unlike Ngaboh-Smart, we look at the novel's presentation of sexual permissiveness from a primarily stylistic perspective to see that it does not involve a "paste-on" use of sexuality as Samatar claims. The shocking sexual acts are primarily meant to jolt the readers out of their complacency by depicting a world that Ngaboh-Smart sees falling apart because of the moral rot at its core. Farah also points out in an interview that the scene of bestiality is meant to "make everyone sit up and see the ugliness of what was happening" (Jaggi 2012). Therefore, it is not surprising that Madoobe's sex with a heifer, witnessed when the narrator was a child, is described in the prologue of the novel, before the plot leaps forward a generation to when the narrator is a successful businessman in his thirties. The man-heifer sexual act happens at the home of Sholoongo, the narrator's girlfriend. We have already been given a fairly detailed description of the sexual escapades of Sholoongo's half-brother Timir, including a scene in which the boys masturbate. Timir's bisexual acts are foreshadowed; he admits "having done it with other boys before, and to having made love to other women, some of them prostitutes" (15). Incidentally, it is his partner Fidow who is considered bisexual: "Fidow went both ways in matters of sex" (60). This announces that sexual identities are slippery; the narrator is queer even if he does not see himself in those terms.

In the novel, the curious Kalaman wants to find out if incest has occurred between his girlfriend and her half-brother. Instead, he catches their father, Madoobe, having sex with a heifer. The description is fairly detailed:

> Now his nakedness was prominent with an erection. In a moment he was standing behind a heifer, saying something, his voice even. The nearer I got to him and the young cow, the clearer his voice was, only I couldn't decipher his words, maybe he was talking to the cow in a coded tongue, comparable to children's babble. Was he appeasing the cow's beastly instincts by talking to her in a secret language? (16)

Following Carol Adams's view that human-animal sex is coerced sex, Piers Beirne argues that "in seeking to replace anthropocentrism with acknowledgement of the sentience of animals, we must start with the fact that in almost every situation humans and animals exist in a relation of potential or actual coercion" (1997, 325). To him, just as sexual assault against a human being differs from "normal sex," sex with animals implies human coercion and exploitation through economic, physical, and psychological power.

It is curious that Madoobe's sex with the calf is presented as mutually agreed to. But before we accept that sex between Madoobe and the heifer is consensual, it is only fair to put Kalaman's narration to a simple reliability test, as he goes against the norms the text establishes.[12] We sympathize with Kalaman, but we are not expected to share his worldview; we are meant to regard him with some suspicion, especially because he confesses that he is withholding facts. He is not an authoritative narrator; his views do not align with those of the implied or actual author. The question might arise: why do we find Kalaman reliable in other parts of the novel but not in this passage? Noting that the unreliability of the narrator depends on the distance between the speaker and the implied narrator, Booth was the first to admit that "this kind of distance in narrators is almost hopelessly inadequate" (1961, 158). Kalaman can be shown to be unreliable just by focusing on the text. Toying with modernist experimentation (especially the use of multiple and contradictory narrators and mixing unverifiable details from dreams, reveries, and fantasy with reality), *Secrets* is ambivalent on many levels and seems to support the need to remove Farah from the text. It avoids authorial intrusions, and even the veracity of Nonno's philosophical pontifications is dubious, since we learn that his tongue is "wicked" and he "lent" it to "authoritative abuse when he chose to" (169).

However, there are cues in the passage that alert us to the unreliability of Kalaman, mainly based on his lack of authority.[13] Presented as a purveyor of pornography, he is not what the readers would want to see as an equivalent of the author; he is as ridiculous as the people he laughs at. The narrator undermines his own narrative authority by relying on his grandfather Nonno to make philosophical authorial statements that he presents as capsules of infallible truth; other characters who refer to Nonno's so-called wisdom are skeptical about the old man's fudging and "evasive waffle" (173). His point of view on issues is also contradicted when another narrator tells the story, as when in a section narrated in a different voice, we learn from an omniscient narrator that Kalaman suffers some "guilt-ridden sorrow" into which he has introduced a "blame-the-other" element (189). This is a partial confession, because the chapter is focalized through Kalaman in free indirect speech; here the voice of the third-person narrator mingles with that of the subject of the narration. In an earlier section narrated from his mother's point of view, we are told that Kalaman is "wrong" in his assessment of a character who the mother knows very well (180). The mention of Kalaman's incorrect assessment of Arbaco here is superfluous; it is only included to puncture his infallibility as a narrator of the other sections of the novel.

Kalaman is human and male, and his authority to fully understand the feelings of a cow exposed to human coital violence is limited. Stronger animals, animals that can resist similar abuse, do so, as happens when Madoobe tries to rape a donkey. Early in the story, a cow strongly resists Madoobe's approach until it realizes that he has no intention to come into physical contact with it. Suggesting that the sexual act is consensual, Kalaman presents it as part of what appears to be a bizarre religious ritual: "a little later and after a lengthy invocation, he inserted his erection in the heifer, still talking but breathing hard. I might have been listening to a man and woman making love, for the cow was *muttering* something too" (17). The word *mutter-*

ing is italicized to indicate what the heifer does cannot fully translate into human murmuring. Consent does not have to be intelligible to humans, but we should not assume the animal has consented by equating its behavior with human consent. The cow is imagined as "muttering," but it may well not be. Therefore, Kalaman is an unreliable narrator, who at this point does not understand the events that he has just documented.

There is also a high probability that the narrator is exaggerating the details of this incident and many others that critics have pointed out to be scientifically impossible.[14] Even if Madoobe actually has sex with the heifer, as corroborated through other characters, the boy most likely sees the man's erection in the darkness only in his imagination. When he sneaks in on his parents having sex in their bedroom, his mother can hardly see him (sensing only "the exaggerated contours of a head"), even if the night-light is on and a few candles are still burning (166). As a narrator remembering the events long after he experienced them, Kalaman is making up the details. Citing the passage in which Madoobe has sex with the heifer, Samatar wonders about its aesthetic purpose, besides giving the Somalis a bad name in the West by portraying them as a culture given to practicing bestiality.

> One cannot cavil at the employment of bestiality as a thematic technique; after all, a fictionist has his fictional license, but the bestiality here does nothing for the narrative structure. It is merely a paste-on. In any case, if Farah wishes to present the Somalis as a race of recidivist bestialists, it is his authorial prerogative to do so. But then he should not have picked on the poor cow, a minority species in the land, but rather on the proud camel since Somalia is decidedly a camel country.

It seems as if Samatar would have forgiven Farah if the novelist had portrayed a sex scene between Madoobe and a camel. In a structuralist fashion, Samatar seems to believe that signs in a text are arbitrary; any animal could replace any other and serve the same purpose if placed in a similar relation to the whole narrative. As an arbitrary sign, the meaning of a word is stabilized through the contextual conventions that the story establishes. But Samatar fails to see the context in which Farah uses the heifer. By not using a camel as the object of Madoobe's desire, the novelist avoids entrenching stereotypes that link the Muslim communities with deserts and camels. Instead he chooses an animal that would be found everywhere in non-Muslim parts of the world.

INTRINSIC ANIMAL VALUE AND SEX WITH A HEIFER

The camel is the most important animal in the community in which Farah sets his fiction. As Axmed Cali Abokor demonstrates, the camel straddles Somali literature in folktales, proverbs, and songs. The animal is in high demand and is the most valued among all domesticated animals not only for its milk and meat and as a means of transport, but because of its "natural ability to survive in difficult ecological conditions" (Abokor 1987, 3).[15] In his study of the representation of camels, Abokor includes stanzas that indicate that some men would prefer camels to wives. But the relationship is not sexual; it is that the man in one of the poems is "cool towards women fair" because he cannot stand the thought of being separated from his "beloved camels," which would have to serve as a bride price (49). The poems underline the men's desire for women; the reason they are not married is to avoid paying the bride price. One of them indicates that a camel is not a substitute for a woman:

. . . already am old
desires many have I in life
haven't married yet, though
so as not to part with
camels mine beloved. (Abokor 1987, 49)

The use of "though" disambiguates the stanza. It is not that the man does not need a woman in his life; he just places so much value on his camels that he would prefer to remain single. It is also clear that the camel does not serve the sexual role of a woman.[16] Paul Tablino (1999 [1980]) also captures the taboos that govern pastoralist communities' relationships with animals. For example, among the Gabra people of northern Kenya, "a breeding bull . . . is never killed; when he becomes old and at the end, he is left in the desert to die. Nor is a milch-camel ever sold" (297).[17] While these communities are far from the vegan ideal in the sense that they use animals for food, transport, and currency, they ensure that the animals are not abused. In Yvonne Owuor's depiction of such a community in *Dust,* we are told that Akai describes "the camels she loved and their personalities" (2014, 255). They are treated humanely in this culture. Even if Garba men are said to "show little affection to camels and tend to treat them roughly" (Tablino 1999 [1980], 297), we do not see this weakness among the men in Owuor's novel, which credits Tablino's book as one of its sources. Even the most masculinist and violent men in the novel—

the military man Ali Dida Hada, the gang member Odidi Oganga, and his father policeman Nyipir—treat the animals with admirable gentleness. This suggests that the main camel in the novel will neither be killed nor sold; it has already become mythic. It can be argued that this rural community treats animals this way to continue exploiting them for human needs, whereas it is in modern urban spaces that animals and humans are treated in the most inhumane ways.

Like other critics who see inadequate realism in Farah's choice of language and incidents without putting his stylistic choices in the context of the larger narrative, Samatar views Kalaman as Farah's mouthpiece. However, Farah's language is different from that of Kalaman, the unreliable narrator. This character is making up events in narrative time, long after they are supposed to have happened. Contrary to Samatar's views, man-heifer intercourse in *Secrets* serves many functions in the novel. First, it is consistent with the flippant and irreverent tone in the novel's opening passages. The young narrator pokes fun at a puritanical society that punishes corpses left to rot in the sun and imagines even vultures rejecting them. Yet the same society has characters who commit not only masturbation and incest as teenagers, but bestiality as adults. The novel's irreverent tone adds cohesion to a narrative that is related from shifting standpoints and relieves the tensions that arise from the traumatic incidents in the narrative itself. Details of the incident are repeated in this prologue and later in the story, including toward the end, where we learn that Madoobe has been abusing "cows, hens, and ostriches" (224). His death from a donkey kick is mentioned twice to emphasize bewilderment at the idea that an adult man would have sex with an animal (224, 269).

Through repetition of this sexual act and constant references to the motif of secrecy foregrounded in the novel's title, the narrative remains cohesive. It simulates incoherence and chaos without being itself chaotic. In other words, despite the paratactic sentences used throughout to capture disorientation, violence, and fragmentation, the story remains largely cohesive as a narrative about the imminent collapse of Somalia. The presence of the heifer also serves to show the abuse of the innocent people in Somalia, some of whom acquiesce to dictators and clan warlords. The animal is a prototypical constituent of "the environment, the nonvocal animals" who have joined self-preserving humans in allowing "one-man tyranny to thrive in Somalia" (191). The narrator has also already described Sholoongo as his "calf-love" (6) in a chapter that crystalizes his naiveté as a ten-year-old boy in love with a girl who is four years older. The word "calf" semantically connects the innocent children with what is happening to the "heifer" at the hands of an adult male. That the heifer seems to consent to its own abuse is symbolic of a society manipulated through propaganda to do the bidding of politicians. The narrative celebrates the female donkey that kicks Madoobe to death. He "died from injuries to his whatnot, fatal wounds resulting from a kick received from a female donkey" (224). It is no longer mere speculation that he was committing bestiality: "he was found stark naked nude, on his back, his thing at half-mast, half an erection you might say. But dead all the same" (224). The donkey is symbolic of the humans who resist manipulation. We are told that other animals have also been resisting human control: "Maybe animal power is in the ascendancy lately . . . what with elephants trekking across international boundaries to trample the man who massacred their herds, and the she donkeys avenging, killing, if only to reclaim their rights" (224).Transnational in their efforts, these animals are different from the atavistic beasts that the narrator's mother sees in her nightmares about Sholoongo as a brute that destroys the domestic space. In the dreams, Sholoongo "is long-nailed and is endowed with a stout head, protruding teeth, with legs that are abnormally short, with rounded ears which resemble a ratel's" (13). The mother further claims that Sholoongo can change herself into a malevolent animal and is rumored to have been brought up by a lioness after her mother committed suicide. The "animal powers" that she possesses are evil. The mother's nightmares depict the internal strife that Sholoongo is bound to cause in her family. "Hardly have I fallen asleep than I have a night filled with ominous dreams in which ratels chew their way into my viscera, elephants go amok, their huge ears raised in fury, nightly visions in which hippocampus crashes the flimsy fences of my slumber" (14). In reality, the animals toward the end of the story are politically conscious and oppositional in their ideology, but not malicious. Unlike the human navel-gazing that causes political and social strife in Somalia, the animals ignore superficially drawn national boundaries to fight for their rights. They do not seek to destroy human life like the animals in the mother's dreams. Here the animals only seek revenge against humans who "massacre" them. They want to "reclaim" their "rights" that humans have taken from them.

To further enhance cohesion through the repetition of sex-with-animal motif, human sexual encounters and hunting are described in the novel in libidinous animal terms. The bisexual Fidow (aka "King of the River of Leopards") issues "a bellow similar to that of a bull preparing to mate" while trying to kill an "aroused crocodile" (61). His nickname does not mean that he respects animals such as the leopard. The totem suggests that his cheerleaders, who include the narrator, imagine the leopard as aggressive and destructive; it has to be destroyed before it destroys humans. The cheerleaders help him project his own vices onto an animal and proceed to wreak havoc on the environment. The crocodile here is different from the one in Eri's *The Crocodile* (1970), which ambiguously symbolizes the negative aspects of tradition and modernity alike. In Eri's novel, it is the crocodile that attacks humans, but it is usually only a human being disguised as a crocodile. In such a situation, human revenge against the animal might be justified if we bear in mind that the combat is usually with a human being who had taken the form of a crocodile. However, unlike in Eri's novel, in Farah's *Secrets,* we encounter an actual crocodile, not a sorcerer disguised as an animal. Furthermore, Farah presents humans as aggressors in images and utterances that connote rape. Fidow in the novel goes so far as to use chemicals that help him imitate a crocodile in heat to confuse the animals. We should remember, as Wendy Doniger (2004, 727) has noted, that it is possible to confuse animals sexually "not in myth, but real life," even to mistake a human for their sexual partner. In Farah's novel, Fidow plays this kind of trick on the crocodile to confuse it sexually. He is "stark naked" and has smeared his body with the "odor crocodiles emit just before mating" (60). But unlike the animal responses that Doniger documents from various scientific accounts, the crocodile in Farah's story is presented as intelligent. Fidow manages to charm the young crocodiles, but the mother crocodile is suspicious of him. He cannot charm the animal, so he must resort to brutal force to kill it. Fidow is also a religious hypocrite. While the Koran warns against the destruction of the environment, he uses "Koranic prayers overlaid with additional gibberish in Shiidliana" to fight the crocodile (61).

Unlike Charles Mungoshi's story, in which a boy kills a crow and regrets that action later, in *Secret* the ecstasy the boys feel after killing the crocodile is obvious, and it is expressed in sexually laden language. It is suggested that this pleasure is also queer, as in close proximity to the description of this is a scene in which Fidow and Timir engage in anal sex at the river. We should also remember that the same-sex act is described in intensely homophobic language:

> They were in the river and were at it, assuming that no one would see them. It was very early in the morning. Their bodies clinched together like dogs, Fidow behind, Timir in front and half-bent, Fidow in in-and-out motion, Timir submissive. The King of the River of the Leopards came at last. Timir then took his turn mounting Fidow from behind. (61–62)

Although sounding self-righteous, the narrator, as a voyeur, is part of the same-sex act that he disparages. First-person narratives enable authors and narrators to create a close rapport with the reader. They also are much more believable because they have the authority of a first-hand observation of events. Such narrations are also limited because a narrator such as Kalaman in *Secrets* can only report events that he has witnessed. Without his account of the sex act between Fidow and Timir, we would never know about it. Ironically, by reporting it to the reader, Kalaman becomes part of the oppressive surveillance order, having intruded into the private affairs of others. Different methods could have been used. The characters might have described themselves as Timir describes his mutual masturbation with other boys, or they could have recounted how they sleep with prostitutes, or have had another character observe the sexual act and report it to the narrator. From the context, the grossness of the affair emanates not so much from the fact that it involves same-sex desire as in its assumption of privacy and secrecy while it is done in the open. Yet the act is subversive, a part of what Stacy Alaimo would view as "making sexual diversity part of a larger biodiversity" (2010, 55). Condemned as unnatural in most societies, the homosexual act here is performed in full view of all natural elements. Although nature is usually the site in which normative masculinity is affirmed through hunting, in this passage nature is made to bear witness to an act of same-sex desire. It is also suggested that in a homophobic society such as this one, the domestic space is emasculating and constrictive; nonnormative desire can only be performed in the wilderness, away from heteronormative surveillance. The wilderness, then, is more queer-friendly than the domestic space.

In a reading of the *Brokeback Mountain*'s representation of "doggie-style" male same-sex penetration, Nicole Seymour (2013, 114–15) suggests the impossibility of a queer act that is nonanimalistic. This is not to denigrate nonheterosexuality as nonhuman, but to restore the reputation of animals that in various cultures have been designated as inferior to humans. However, given the dog metaphor that is used to describe the sexual act between Fidow and Timir, it is possible that they are not seen as two dogs having sex but that each imagines himself to be having sex with a dog. Furthermore, it is suggested that there is no difference between what Fidow does to the mother crocodile and what Madoobe does to the heifer or what Fidow and Timir do to one another. The scene of the Fidow-Timir same-sex act is closely juxtaposed to the one in which Fidow engages in crocodile poaching. They are all part of "the many [who] get up terribly perverse doings once aroused. Some never change their ways, the Fidows, the Madoobes, and the Nonnos of this world" (224). Throughout the story, Nonno, the narrator's grandfather, is presented as the voice of reason and the author's alter ego. But here he is lumped together with Madoobe and Fidow, indicating that the whole society is rotten. Even the narrator is complicit in the act of plundering the environment, in that he joins Fidow "in the skinning of the crocodile" and retrieves a manikin from the animal's belly (61). We should also remember that after killing the crocodile the previous day, the narrator was the first to use orgasmic language to describe the human victory over the crocodile. He is as gross as Fidow and Timir. Ultimately, while the narrator seems to disapprove of the sex between Fidow and Timir, such acts should be confined to sex among members of the same species.

A WHALE OF AN ISSUE: GLOBAL WARMING AND SEXUAL PREDATION

In Zakes Mda's melodramatic fifth novel, *The Whale Caller* (2005), South African youths perform a Māori dance they learned from a visiting New Zealand rugby team. Similarly, Mda's novel reads like a playful metafictional response to the Māori renaissance novel by Witi Ihimaera, *The Whale Rider* (1987). Alluding to the annual whale-watching festival in the South African town of Hermanus, a major tourist attraction during the southern winter, Mda's novel is about a unique relationship between the eponymous Whale Caller and a whale that he has come to name Sharisha, with whom he is in love. The novel also addresses the plight of the whales in the Southern Hemisphere; although South African whales are protected under the Marine Resources Act of 1998, Mda shows that the animals are still endangered by tourism, global warming, and industrial pollution. As if this were not enough, the character most closely attached to the whales emotionally, the Whale Caller, uses one of the animals for sexual self-gratification. He sees parallels between that whale and an African woman: "the baby likes to ride on Sharisha's back, much like the way African women carry their children" (141).

In the context of former racist regimes of sexuality and desire that would not countenance interracial sex during the apartheid era (citing specious concerns about life and health), a relationship between a man and a whale in the postapartheid era might appear to be a welcome radical departure from the past. The man-whale coupling is mutually erotic (at least from the man's point of view), with the Whale Caller at one point getting "the front and the seat of his tuxedo pants . . . wet and sticky from the seed of life" as he performs for Sharisha (66). Throughout their relationship he imagines that Sharisha is in love with him and is experiencing similar moments of *jouissance* as the love-stricken man plays his kelp-horn to the whale. He uses phallic words such as "penetrate" to describe the effects of the kelp-horn he plays for the whale. He also sees women (represented in the novel by Saluni) as competing with animals for male attention. To the Whale Caller, Saluni and the whale have something in common: they are part of what Rob Nixon describes as "objects of heritage to be owned, preserved, or patronized rather than subjects of their own land and legacies" (2015, 235).

For its part, Ihimaera's *The Whale Rider* is a feminist rewriting of an origin myth that recounts how Kahutia-te-rangi, founder of the Māori nation, came to New Zealand on the back of a *paikea*, a humpback whale that had rescued him from the ocean. Ihimaera draws a parallel between the ancestral Kahutia-te-rangi and a modern Māori girl to whom the current chief will not pass the baton of leadership because tradition reserves this position of power for male heirs exclusively. Parts of the novel are told from a whale's center of consciousness; the philosophical standpoint of the work as a whole is summarized through the words of a whale.

Though told using a Māori human voice, the most lyrical and agential sections of *The Whale Rider* are focalized through the perspective of whales. Indeed, it is wrong to insinuate, as Western scholars, have that the talking animal is confined to the West because of the Western societies' economic development and nostalgia for the past. For example, in an otherwise extremely perceptive essay on animal narration, Karla Armbruster claims that the West is interested in cultural artifacts involving animals because "people in more developed nations encounter fewer and fewer animals in their daily life" (2013, 19). Armbruster's view echoes John Berger's famous observation about the Western interest in artificial mimicry of animals and animal settings, such as the zoo and toys. For Berger, "zoos, realistic animal toys and the widespread commercial diffusion of animal imagery, all began as animals started to be withdrawn from daily life" (1980, 26). In postcolonial Africa, zoos and game reserves are not meant for locals; they target foreign tourists. From reading postcolonial literature, it becomes clear that non-Western societies are equally fascinated by stories involving talking animals; instead, we as readers of these texts should be attentive to the differentiated ways that animals are used in the texts, especially to reveal the impact of legacies of colonialism on the cultures and economies of formerly colonized regions.

Literature is an ocean full of whales. Brayton observes that "whales have become emblematic of the human ability to incorporate the radical alterity of the sea into familiar definitions of the environment—in short, to find ourselves in the space of the Other" (2012, 134).[18] While cetaceans provide a means for thinking about ourselves, their plight also highlights our destructiveness in the Anthropocene era, in which humans have become a central factor in altering the environment. As Jonathan Steinwand explains in a reading of the presence of cetaceans in postcolonial writing, "whales and dolphins became symbols for environmentalist pleas to save the world's ocean ecosystems once it became apparent that the plane's oceans are threatened by pollution, extraction, and catastrophe" (2011, 182). This section seeks to critique Ihimaera's *The Whale Rider* and Mda's *The Whale Caller* in their representation of nature, animals, and women. Although the works are not ecofeminist in a strict sense, their awareness of different forms of oppression opens possibilities for establishing parallels between the circumstances of oppressed humanity and the predicament of animals at the hands of humans. The authors present what might be seen as an indigenous welfare perspective on animals, an outlook that is ultimately deficient because it accepts human exploitation of animals as natural. But they effectively demonstrate the need to treat animals well and to empower women as well.

Given the similarities of Mda's and Ihimaera's novels in their use of the whale motif, it is striking that the theme of the derivativeness of new art runs throughout Mda's novel, with the most admired child artist, Lunga Tubu, being an imitator of world maestros, such as "Luciano Pavarotti, Plácido Domingo and José Carreras" (88). Saluni's songs in the novel are a repurposing of similar ballads heard in city taverns, occasionally changed to suit her audience and occasion. The Bored Twin's songs in the novel are the only works without a precedent. The Bored Twin's ethereal songs are incomprehensible when recorded on tape. The novel suggests that a work of art has to be contaminated with strands and strains of other works of art for it to make sense and generate pleasure beyond the confines of an esoteric audience. In this context, it does not surprise the reader to hear echoes of Ihimaera's work in Mda's novel about whales.

Mda asserts that he had not read Ihimaera's 1987 novel when composing his own, which is the work in which he is most conscientious in his treatment of the theme of animal rights.[19] Some of his other major works—especially *The Heart of Redness*, *The Madonna of Excelsior*, and *Cion*—depict environmental themes, echoing other texts in their allusive language. He uses a similarly polyphonic structure in *The Whale Caller*, but it is in the latter novel that he demonstrates the greatest awareness of animal rights. Arguing that Mda constructs "a powerful ecological allegory" in the novel, Gail Fincham (2011, 125) suggests that Mda, a professor of creative writing at Ohio University, is in dialogue with "a recent flowering of cross-disciplinary ecological criticism and environmental scholarship" in America. The Whale Caller's consciousness communicates what she sees as the "urgency of environmental issues" (2011, 125). While I generally agree with Fincham, I suggest that, if we consider arguments from animal studies theorists and facts about whales themselves, this character that she sees as the consciousness of the novel leaves much to be desired, especially in his lust for the whale. When compared to Ihimaera's treatment of women in *The Whale Rider*, the Whale Caller is condescending toward both animals and women. He also deliberately twists facts about whales to continue their exploitation and to use Sharisha for self-gratification. Mda demonstrates the uphill task that societies such as South Africa face before total freedom can be achieved if people like the Whale Caller represent the fight for animal rights in the real world.

Through the novel's exuberant intertextuality, Mda is not suggesting that animal rights discourses and norms have to be borrowed from other cultures; instead, a society that is sensitive to animals and the environment is likely to have practices similar to those observed in other societies with comparable attitudes. As Wendy Woodward points out, Mda's *The Whale Caller* locates the South African town it presents "within the global ecological predicaments, in which the deterioration of nature and climate change threaten the sustainable future of the planet" (2008, 143; 2009, 333). Just as one text is interlinked with another, it is not even aware of what Mikhail Bakhtin (1981 [1975], 276) saw as an inevitable dialogism in textual and cultural life. Solutions to global predicaments must be sought in concert with societies beyond national boundaries. As the anthropologist Eric Wolf reminded us in the 1980s, "human societies and cultures would not be properly understood until we learned to visualize them in their mutual interrelationships and interdependencies in space and time" (1982, x). In evoking Ihimaera's novel and other cultural texts, Mda's novel implies the interdependence of different parts of the planet, where human activities in one part of the world affect the fate of animals and humans in another.

The similarities in the novels also seem to derive from the fact that both authors draw from African and Polynesian cultures with shared respect for the whale, especially in the wake of colonialism, in which the plight of the colonized parallels the predicament of animals at the hands of industrial modernity. Foregrounding animal rights in a destructive world, both works respond to colonialism and neocolonialism alike; hegemonic human relations are equated with human destruction of the environment. In this hegemonic relationship, industrialized global powers play the most vicious role in destroying whales and the environment in general. The boundary between whales and the colonized people of the Global South in both novels is destabilized, and both categories are shown as victims of the rapaciously colonizing Northern Hemisphere. Unfortunately, postcolonial cultures are imitating the destructiveness of the colonizer, so that hegemonic colonialism is also seen as analogous to the general human violence against the environment. Although modernity has a role in restoring the environment and empowering the colonized, it is through recourse to precolonial traditions that the environment can be fully rescued from destruction.

Yet the two novels are different. In Ihimaera's novel, queer and interspecies sexual desires are embedded in the subtext, whereas Mda's novel makes direct reference to these sexual practices. Saluni sees herself in competition with Sharisha for the Whale Caller's attentions, and the Whale Caller seems to be experiencing erotic gratification from his relationship with the whale. Ihimaera's novel is a Bildungsroman, told mainly from the perspective of the girl protagonist in a way that valorizes gender equality and critiques the precolonial Māori by privileging modernity over patriarchy; Mda's work is mainly focalized from the perspective of a man whose ideas about women are not always flattering and whose relationship to animals has a tinge of male-female sexual exploitation. Furthermore, whereas Ihimaera draws attention to parallels between Māori and biblical myths (e.g., the story of Jonah), and whereas world novels refer to similar myths (e.g. Melville's *Moby-Dick* and its filmic permutations), Mda's novel borrows from Australian aborigines, from human-animal relationships in Papua New Guinea, and from the Khoikhoi of South Africa.[20]

MISREADING THE PARASITE

Through the relationship between the Whale Caller and Sharisha, Mda not only undermines the human/animal divide but shows that the identity of an animal is as protean as that of humans. If the poet Okot p'Bitek's (1966, 34)

Lawino insists that "No leopard/would change into a hyena" and "the long-necked and graceful/giraffe/Cannot become a monkey" to illustrate the absurdity of an African trying to be European in the wake of colonial conquest, Mda's novel demonstrates the possibility of changing a whale's character. Sharisha is a southern right whale, but the Whale Caller claims to have taught the whale to sing like humpback whale.[21] Although we cannot fully accept the Whale Caller's account of his prowess with the animals, there is little doubt that he is able to call the whales with his kelp-horn. The community makes a similar judgment, contrasting him with the whale crier, whose work is to alert the tourists to the presence of whales. It is clear throughout the text that the Whale Caller has a special talent for communicating with the whales and with Sharisha in particular. Okot p'Bitek's Lawino is correct to argue that a hyena cannot become a giraffe because these two animals belong to different species, but the metaphor is not applicable in human relations since Europeans and Africans belong to the same species and can interbreed and learn from one another. While criticizing the West's role in destroying the environment, Mda does not accept the essentialism that Okot p'Bitek displays via metaphors that set one animal against another to concretize differences within the human race. The cultural nationalism of Okot's character demands a call to essentialism, while Mda's postapatheid perspective emphasizes cosmopolitan openness to cultural practices and sexual preferences other than one's own. Mda shows that animal behavior is learned; through the perspective of the Whale Caller, we are shown Sharisha teaching her calf various swimming techniques. As I show presently, the Whale Caller may be deluded in his belief that he is the one who taught Sharisha how to sing like a humpback whale. He gives himself more credit than he deserves for controlling the animal in its natural environment by merely playing his kelp-horn.

The Whale Caller equates the whale lice parasites on Sharisha with those that afflict Saluni, his human female partner. He knows that the so-called whale lice on the callosities of a whale do not have piercing mouthparts to draw blood from the whale. They predominantly feed on the algae and flaking skin of the host whale (Maggi et al. 2012, 246) and do only minor damage to the whale's skin. The Whale Caller is fully aware of this, because he says "whale lice are quite harmless," but he portrays them negatively, claiming that they "can irritate the joy out of a whale" (57).

The Whale Caller has realized that the whale has characteristics similar to those of human beings, but most people would not experience the intense love that the man lavishes on Sharisha because the whale is far different from other nonhuman animals that share characteristics with humans. Following Thomas White's *In Defense of Dolphins* (2007), Lori Marino notes that cetaceans display characteristics that would attract the Whale Caller to the whale:

> Their intelligence, self-awareness, emotional sophistication and social complexity mean that they are similar to us in that we both experience life as persons. But cetaceans (unlike great apes, for instance) look and move differently, lack changes in clearly recognizable facial expressions, communicate in strange modalities, live in a very different physical environment, and seem to possess a level of social cohesion foreign even to us. (Marino 2013, 104)

We therefore admire the Whale Caller for extending his love to a nonprimate animal that other humans around the world are destroying with impunity. However, far from being altruistic, the Whale Caller's love for nonhuman animals is hierarchical and seems to be based on the character's need for sexual self-gratification; he favors one animal more than others because he is erotically attached to it. As Marino explains, whales live in highly complex societies in relationships that "include long-term bonds" (2013, 98). She further explains that, like humans, whales transmit learned cultural behavior, including "dialects," from generation to generation (Marino 2013, 98). And as Marc Bekoff has demonstrated, whales' interspecies play and socialization (Bekoff 2012b) extends to helping babies from other whale species (Bekoff 2012a). But instead of allowing Sharisha to thrive in her society, the Whale Caller would attempt to alienate her from the other whales and claim her love for himself.

The Whale Caller has already established the hierarchy in which Sharisha is regarded as superior to other whales. Humans employ human criteria to decide which type of whale is superior to others. Humpback whales are presented as more musically inclined. The Whale Caller engineers a change in Sharisha so that she can sing like a humpback whale. In entrenching his anthropocentric hierarchy, the jealous Whale Caller implies that the lice that annoy Sharisha have come from the male whales with whom Sharisha has mated, thus stigmatizing the bull whales by way of parasite metaphors that have been used in various imperial contexts to justify subjugation and even genocide. In effect, it appears that even if the Whale Caller supports the rights of animals and admires whales, he values some whales more than others and probably would not be unhappy if the bull whales that mate with Sharisha were exterminated, since they are carriers of vermin. "Parasite" appears three times in the novel, and always as a negative. Its first instance is a metaphor for a grudge:

> A grudge can take its toll on your health. It is like a parasite that feeds on you. At first it gives you a feeling of warmth. The thought that you will get even gives you comfort. Then the ungrateful guest begins to eat your insides. It gets fatter while you are gradually reduced to a bag of bones. It destroys you. (15–16)

This indicates the Whale Caller's belief that in the postapartheid world there is no need to bear a grudge against former exploiters. The next two instances describe the whale lice, which the Whale Caller portrays as exploiting the whale, completely misrepresenting their role in the ecosystem. In his narration:

> Some of the creatures are playing with floating kelp, manipulating it so that the fronds rub over their backs. The Whale Caller knows that they are trying to remove parasites from their bodies. This is indicated by the callosities on the whales, which are pink or orange instead of white, a clear sign of the presence of lice. (40)

This is his interpretation of the whales in their habitat, and it is not necessarily correct. Like a colonialist, the Whale Caller presents himself as benefitting the whale by blowing his kelp-horn:

> He doesn't have to walk far, for there is Sharisha rubbing her head against the kelp. She must be irritated by lice. Normally Sharisha's callosities are free of lice; that is why they are surf white and not pink or orange or even yellow like those of other southern rights. It seems now lice are beginning to infest her, and the Whale Caller suspects it is from the randy males who had their way with her the other day . . . Sharisha does look annoyed. (57)

In the last instance, the Whale Caller attempts to account for Sharisha's beaching: "Poor navigation because she was disorientated by the storm. Who knows? Loss of orientation can even be due to parasites and diseases and interference by ships" (222). There is nothing to prove this point. If we agree with Timothy Morton that "that global warming is so huge and so impossible to see in one single constantly present thing" (2014, 279) until it is too late, we should not expect to witness it on a grand scale or live to tell the tale. In Mda's novel, global warming is evidenced in a smaller event that presages the apocalypse. The whales become stranded both because of changing sea conditions and by global warming caused by industrialization. In a similar stranding in Ihimaera's *The Whale Rider,* the whales, disoriented by water-borne radiation, are driven to certain death on the beach. From 1960 to 1996, France carried out 210 nuclear tests, 193 of these in French Polynesia in the South Pacific. The colonial powers attempted to convince the world that the explosions were clean by denying that the tests "posed any ecological threat to the region" (Brash and Carillon 2009, 39). On July 17, 1974, a test at Moruroa exposed Tahiti (1,250 kilometers away) to 500 times the maximum allowed level of plutonium fallout. The whales in Ihimaera's novel are responding to this fallout and the massive water-borne sound and shock waves produced by these blasts.[22] Forced by radiation from its home waters and migratory routes, the "ancient whale could only despair that the place of life, and the Gods, had now become a place of death" (66). A similar thing could be happening in the Atlantic, but the oblivious Whale Caller, interested only in sex, blames its natural, benign parasites for the stranding. Human activity has caused these apocalyptic strandings, not other members of the ecosystem as the love-stricken Whale Caller would have us believe.

Drucilla Cornell sees the relationship between the Whale Caller and Sharisha as an example of the Heideggarian ideal of dwelling, wherein the Whale Caller's kelp-horn is a "classic example of what Heidegger means by a thing respected in its accordance with its unique capacities to engage with whales as they are in their peaceful co-existence with each other and with their music" (2009, 146). To her, the Heideggerian explosion of technology is to blame for the beaching and death of Sharisha. However, although technology does not save Sharisha, the blame falls either to global warming, whose consequences lead to Sharisha's confusion, or to the Whale Caller, who distracts Sharisha from her whale companions. By contrast, Ihimaera describes the narrator and his mates riding motorbikes and cutting "across country and beach, flying like spears to help save the whales" (106). The spears are simultaneously a symbol of danger and salvation, life and death.

It is remarkable that, as a woman, Saluni is presented as a parasite as well. Her obsession with perfume reminds the reader of Olive Schreiner's parasitic woman in *Woman and Labor,* who stands out because of the way she has "bedecked and scented her person" and who "from youth to age her offspring often owed nothing to her personal toil" (1911, 80). To Schreiner, this kind of urban woman is a "human female parasite—the most deadly microbe which can make its appearance on the surface of any social organism" (1911, 81). Although Saluni is not one of the rich elite women whom Schreiner paints as parasites, she aspires to a bourgeois "civilized" life as a music celebrity. Her ambitions are based on ostentatious consumption without any production. Even in her envisaged music career, she would be a parasite on the Bored Twins, who are better composers than she is and whose voices are better than hers. Schreiner does not condemn modern women as parasitic; rather, she criticizes modern society for wasting women's productive lives by confining them to sexual roles. In Saluni we do not see talent being wasted; she squanders her potential with alcohol and deluded dreams of affluence.

Saluni in reality is a drunkard without an income. She relies on men in taverns to buy her drinks, telling them dubious stories about how she is a love child. At the Whale Caller's cabin, she drinks his methylated spirits and contributes nothing to their mutual economic welfare. When she does contribute to the kitty, it is from her own shrewd exploitation of his labor and talents. While the Whale Caller is admirably content in his simple life and diet, she tries to wrest him from that ascetic existence into her version of "civilization," which is an expensive bourgeois lifestyle that includes eating meat. Saluni and the Whale Caller do not eat meat like the guests in restaurants and shoppers in malls, because they cannot afford to. She also wears clothes made from fur even though she does not need them for warmth. It is the hot season.

Is it possible for humans, then, to host others in the way Sharisha hosts lice and barnacles, so that the others benefit without giving anything in return to the host as long as the hosted other does not do any harm to the host? This society is represented as cynical to the poor, some of whom, like the lice and barnacles, do no harm to the host they rely on for survival. The humble twelve-year-old boy from Zwelihle Township, Lunga Tubu, "comes down to the sea on weekends and public holidays to sing for his supper" (85). He may not benefit the restaurant on whose portico he performs for patrons ten meters away; on the other hand, his performances cause the management or the clientele no trouble. He probably could even be part of the cynical tourist's entertainment, as they enjoy his antics. Yet the headwaiter, a symbol of the post-independence elite, drives Lunga Tubu away. There is no evidence that the tourists would give the waiters the coins they throw at him.

The Whale Caller lacks what Tom Regan sees as the prerequisite of animal rights activism: "making a sustained commitment to rational inquiry" (1983, iii). This type of insistence on rationality has been criticized, in works such as Josephine Donovan's "Animal Rights and Feminist Theory" (1990, 351), as originating from a Cartesian logic that privileges objectivism over emotion. However, we are not being asked to disregard the emotions the novel generates; rather, we should take care not to accept actions based on emotions that harm the animals the characters extend those human emotions to. The emotions the text generates distance us from accepting the Whale Caller's sentimental displays of his affection for Sharisha. Other whales, and probably Sharisha herself, would not endorse the Whale Caller's activities. Throughout the story, the Whale Caller is emotional and sentimental, and although we can sympathize with him in his genuine love for the environment, the narrative urges us to see the limitations of his approach to environmental conservation as one that could lead to catastrophes such as the one that befalls Sharisha at the novel's end.

Saluni is the quintessential symbol of postapartheid South Africa. She is the novel's most outspoken critic of the inequalities that persist after apartheid. Through her, Mda comments on how the tourism trade in Hermanus brings no benefit to the community: "While the town of Hermanus is raking in fortunes from tourism, the mothers and fathers of Zwelihle are unemployed" (86). Ironically, Saluni, the most politically conscious commentator on the postapartheid condition, is the most cynical about animal rights: "In today's world, with all the foolish laws that protect these useless creatures, what do you do with a stubborn whale that refuses to let loose your man's very soul?" (75). Her sexual jealousy culminates in homophobia: "You don't want to admit that you have gone gaga over a male. And you are so big and strong and muscular and . . . hard . . . I hope. Nothing camp about you at all" (58). Earlier, she is vulgar in her descriptions of gay people, probably because she assumes that the Whale Caller is queer: "After all, the constitution of the new South Africa protects gays. It is against the law to discriminate against anyone just because they are fuckin' moffies. This is not the old South Africa where somebody else thought for us" (23). As if this were not enough, to Saluni, civilized living involves the destruction of the environment: "Saluni revives civilized living. Since the tulips of the mansion are still on strike the vase on the table now has grasses and fresh wild flowers, including some fynbos from Hoy's Koppie, which is protected by government environmental authorities, and shouldn't be in anyone's vase" (162).There is a parallel between postapartheid South Africa and the state of affairs that Derrida characterizes in the aftermath of the French Revolution, in which the society, "without emancipating animals in the name of the rights of man and citizen, and speaking in the name of the sovereignty of the people, would invent zoological institutions" (2009, 275). That is, the revolution fails to transform sovereignty and "inaugurates a new form of the same power structure" (Derrida 2009, 290). Mda suggests that little has changed in the postapartheid era because the transformations are superficial. We are not shown animals in laboratories, as in Derrida's description of postrevolutionary France, but in the South Africa that Mda presents, animals continue to be exploited under the new political dispensation. In fact, the conditions of animals in Mda's novel may be worse than in the French lab culture that Derrida describes, because we would expect even those scientists to be respectful of animals. But the twins and Saluni are either torturers of animals or exploit them for food and clothing. The postapartheid regime has written commendable laws to protect animals and minorities. But their rights continue to be abused because, as Braidotti reminds us, what is necessary is ethical respect for the environment, not contractual laws that people can break at will, people such as the tourists and tour operators who break the laws with impunity.

THE POSTCOLONIAL LOVE OBJECT AND QUEER MELANCHOLIA

In Farah's *Secrets* (discussed above), narrative unreliability is grounded in the suggestion throughout the story that Kalaman is a liar in his presentation of human-animal sex; his description of how he saw Madoobe having sex with a calf should be dismissed as just a figment of his homophobic imagination. By contrast, in Nana Nyarko Boateng's short story "Swallowing Ice" (2017), a similar unreliability of the narrator evokes a speculative hope that animal-human sex and other forms of queer self-expression will be acceptable in postcolonial Africa at some point in the future. But at the moment, such a relationship is impossible and even undesirable. It is an alternative to intraspecies queer intimacy, but it is not the desirable way of relating to animals, because interspecies intimacies do not necessarily result in happiness for the subjects involved. The story is about a young woman, Brema, who occasionally has sex with a stray cat she has domesticated. She makes her living as a journalist, writing fake newspaper stories under a penname (Vivian Quack), and one of her stories is about a lesbian couple who got arrested for kissing erotically at Kotoka International Airport, which reflects her anxieties about her own queerness. The cat, Max, dies from what appears to be poisoning.

The sentimental narrator does not know what to do with the cat's body. The title of the story comes from her habit of ingesting the ice with which she has preserved the cat's body, a Freudian act that indicates the narrator's melancholia and wish to incorporate the lost love-object into herself. It is clear from the story that in a pronatal and homophobic postcolonial nation, nonheterosexual love can only be imagined as a future possibility in speculative fictions such as the one the narrator concocts in her attempt to preserve the lost object of desire.

Boateng's story is about a pathological behavior that she does not fully endorse, a tension potentially explained by Sigmund Freud's distinction between healthy mourning for a departed soul and a pathological inability to mourn that drives the victim to depression. In "Mourning and Melancholia," Freud (1917) observes that "mourning is regularly the reaction to the loss of a loved person, or to the loss of some abstraction which had taken the place of one, such as one's country, liberty, an ideal, and so on" (153). A therapeutic response to the loss and trauma, mourning is overcome with time as the mourning subject comes to grips with the fact that the lost person or object is gone for good. The mourning person slowly comes back to the normal state. However, Freud explains that "the distinguishing mental features of melancholia are a profoundly painful dejection, cessation of interest in the outside world, loss of the capacity to love, inhibition of all activity, and a lowering of the self-regarding feelings to a degree that finds utterance in self-reproaches and self-revilings, and culminates in a delusional expectation of punishment" (153). The narrator's melancholy in "Swallowing Ice" turns the loss of the cat into a pathological loss of a stable self. She loathes herself and is full of self-pity as a queer person lost in an abyss of sadness. At first blush, it appears as if her psychic condition results from the cat's death, but in fact it emanates from the loss of an unnamable abstraction. She only uses the cat as an excuse to explain her inconsolable sorrow. This becomes clear when we realize that she was in a state of immense loss even before the cat died. From the context, the actual source of her sorrow resides in the deep niches of her unconscious. It is clear to the reader that the narrator is trying to mourn the loss of freedom in an independent postcolonial nation that fails to recognize her queerness, a Ghana that denies her full citizenship because of her sexual orientation.

Additionally, for Freud, a melancholic individual "feels justified in maintaining the belief that a loss of some kind occurred, but one cannot see clearly what it is that has been lost, and it is all the more reasonable to suppose that the patient cannot consciously perceive what he has lost either. This, indeed, might be so even if the patient is aware of the loss which has given rise to his melancholia, but only in the sense that he knows whom he has lost but not what he has lost in him" (254). This dangerous psychic process leads to suicidal tendencies, whereby, according to David Eng and Shinhee Han, "suicide may not merely be physical; it may also be a psychical erasure of one's identity—racial, sexual, or gender identity, for example" (672). The narrator effaces her identity throughout. Her family is only mentioned in passing at the beginning, and their advice on how to overcome grief is ignored. Her name is likely to be as fake as the pseudonym she uses in her newspaper articles. There is a possibility that the narrator is dead, because as we see in chapter 3, some African texts are focalized by zombies and ghosts to indicate the overwhelming odds facing certain minorities. Alternatively, she could be laughing at her earlier sentimental self who, suffering melancholia at the time the narrated events took place, grieved over a dead feline sexual partner more than she should have.

In most Ghanaian cultures, the community mourns the dead in elaborate therapeutic public displays of loss. As scholars such as Esi Sutherland-Addy (2010) have noted, funerals enable members of the community to overcome grief collectively and to reaffirm their ontological identities.[23] Unlike in Freudian theory, which suggests the need to forget the dead and replace them with someone else, African societies have ways of memorializing the dead that enhance life rather than providing a distraction from the normal routine. Indeed, Western theorists of grief have revised Freud's insistence that healthy mourning involves forgetting the lost object. For example, J. William Worden argues that "we know that people do not decathect from the dead but find ways to develop 'continuing bonds' with the deceased." One of the tasks of mourning, then, "is to find a place for the deceased that will enable the mourner to be connected with the deceased but in a way that will not preclude him or her from going on with life. We need to find ways to memorialize, that is, to remember the dead loved one—keeping them with us but still going on with life" (2009, 35).[24] However, the narrator in "Swallowing Ice" cannot mourn Max publicly as would be expected in Ghana, because of the shame grieving over a feline sexual partner would attract in a pronatal culture that expects young women to have children. In this culture, death does not signify the end of life; it is a part of a journey to the world of spirits. Ideally, Brema should not preserve the body in a fridge, except in cases where she would be expecting mourners to arrive from abroad. She should memorialize Max because, as Stephen Shuchter and Sidney Zizook argue (contrary to Freud), "the continued emotional or spiritual existence of the dead spouse becomes one of the most powerful means of containing the potentially overwhelming emotions of grief" (1986, 303). This means that we should not expect Brema to forget Max. In fact, her story is a work of mourning that helps her cope with her loss. But by not letting go of the cat's body, she overlooks that Max's death marks a transition from the physical world to the spiritual world. Brema's failure to observe these rites not only indicates the alterity of Max as a lover who cannot be mourned collectively and publicly, it captures Brema's alienation from the rest of the society as a woman in a queer sexual relationship with a pet.

In normal circumstances, the cat should not replace Brema's relationships with human beings. As Beck and Katcher observe, "pets do not just substitute for human relationships; they complement and add to them, giving a special and unique dimension to human life" (6). This is the way pets are presented in such works as Doris Lessing's short story "The Old Woman and Her Cat." To her credit, Hetty, the gypsy woman in Lessing's story, does not try to impose herself on the cat when the pet rejects her overture for physical closeness. Even if her family rejects her because she is old and of gypsy stock, Hetty has fairly good relationships with a few other people in her neighborhood. She remains outgoing throughout her life. But in "Swallowing Ice," the narrator enjoys no healthy relationships with other humans, apparently seeing fellow women as a bother. She is aware of her alienation and delusional thoughts in response to a tragedy, and her only redeeming quality is the creative levity with which she depicts her melancholia to the reader. Echoing Farah's Kalaman, Boateng's narrator is given to fantasies and daydreaming. She even confesses that she is a liar:

> I was a journalist; a liar, if you want, but I was never late for anything. I wrote freelance for the *Accra Times*. I didn't like being around people much. They stared at me. My pseudonym was "Vivian Quack"; I made up stories that were presented as actual news. The standards of journalism in Ghana worked perfectly in my favour. People took whatever they read in the papers as facts; other newspapers just copied my stories without acknowledging me or verifying the details. (159)

We expect a journalist to stick to facts. But "Vivian Quack" offers fiction as the reality. She suggests that this is because of the nature of journalism in the postcolonial nation, where media ethics is flagrantly ignored. Brema is named only once and in passing when a couple of Jehovah Witnesses she does not like very much refer to her by her name (161). This is a reference easy to miss (as I did several times) because the narrator encourages the readers not to take the Jehovah Witnesses seriously, but just as bothersome characters who routinely show up at her door every Sunday. Therefore, her identity and that of the fake journalist slide into each other, especially when we consider that she might have given the religious couple a fake name.[25] Going by the newspaper clip offered in the short story, her newspaper articles use a realist objective voice, masking their fictionality. Even when her name is an obvious giveaway, national media outlets reproduce her fictions and circulate them as facts. Although she is a confessed liar, we should not dismiss her story about her love relationship with the cat Max as pure fiction. Indeed, she is presented as a deeper character and more progressive individual than others in the story (e.g., her landlady and a missionary couple), who ordinarily would be seen as enjoying a healthy psychic state. The story suggests that in an intensely homophobic postcolonial nation, one needs to be in a state like the narrator's to progressively undermine homophobia. A melancholic like her, Sigmund Freud would remind us, "has a keener eye for truth than others who are not melancholic" (255).[26] Her expression "if you want" suggests that her stories would be regarded as lies only if looked at from certain epistemic lenses. But even as a fictional writer, through made-up stories the narrator presents us with profound truths about her society and speculates about changes that need to be put in place to ensure a better life.

Vivian Quack's imaginary story about the harassment of lesbians at the airport is plausible because such harassment happens in real life. This is the airport where a sign declares: "Welcome!! Akwaaba!! Ghana warmly welcomes all visitors of goodwill. Ghana does not welcome paedophiles and other sexual deviants. Indeed, Ghana imposes extremely harsh penalties on such sexually aberrant behaviour. If you are in Ghana for such activity, then for everybody's good, including your own, we suggest you go elsewhere" (Otu 2016). The well-known sign does not mention homosexuality directly, but the coded message as understood across Africa is that gays and lesbians are unwelcome in Ghana.

The lesbian couple in Vivian Quack's story would belong to the category of "sexual deviants," who in the sign are equated to "paedophiles." Ghana's Criminal Code 1960 prohibits "unnatural carnal knowledge," and discrimination against LGBTQ people is common in the country. According to Section 104 of the Ghanaian penal code, such "unnatural" acts include "sexual intercourse with a person in an unnatural manner or with an animal."

WELCOME!!
AKWAABA!!
• Ghana welcomes all visitors of goodwill.
• Ghana does not welcome paedophiles and other sexual deviants.
• Indeed Ghana imposes extremely harsh penalties on such sexually aberrant behaviour.
• If you are in Ghana for such activity, then for everybody's good, including you own, we suggest you go elsewhere.

Figure 4: A sign at the Kotoka International Airport in Accra, a space referred to in Boateng's "Swallowing Ice." Courtesy of Bright Gyamfi.

Boateng's story suggests that it should be read in relation to work by Ama Ata Aidoo. In working through the implications of interspecies sexual encounters, the story positions itself relative to the Ghanaian literary canon, especially Ama Ata Aidoo's *Changes* (1991), a copy of which the narrator has in her room. These connections remind us that switching from one condition to another, as occurs in Aidoo's story, does not result in self-actualization even when that change is necessary and inevitable.[27] At the same time, the mention of Aidoo's novel, which is one of the first serious African works to focus on love (vis-à-vis nationalist politics), indicates the story's intention to move away from the common themes in African writing. It goes a step further than Aidoo's novel, which is about unrequited heterosexual love affairs, to meditate on the possibilities of queer human-animal intimacies. In Boateng's story, queer beings (animals and humans) are excluded from society, and their attempts to move outside bounded private queer spaces into the public sphere end in shame and death. Without the advantage of the rural wilderness, queer subjects in urban Africa can only enact their queerness in the absolute privacy of domestic spaces that are not shared by others. With the story about the Ghanaian women who display queer love at the local airport, the narrator recalls Aidoo's *Our Sister Killjoy* (1968), in which a European woman propositions a Ghanaian girl on a tour of Germany. Aidoo's protagonist Sissie has been read as queer because she does not protest the lesbian's proposition and seems attracted to the German woman, though she wishes that this suitor were a man.[28] But this relationship happens in a foreign country, and Sissie displays no lesbian inclinations in her home country. In the incident Boateng's character imagines and writes about in a national publication, in contrast, queer love does not happen in foreign spaces far from home, and neither is it seemingly perpetrated by racially different foreign "perverts"; it takes place in a national airport and it is between two local women who do not repress their sexuality as Aidoo's Sissie does. In Boateng's story that queerness does not have to flourish only away from home.

It is understandable why an African such as Aidoo's Sissie or Boateng's Brema would be reluctant to openly embrace queerness. Kwame Edwin Otu has discussed ways in which queer people in Ghana navigate the difficult terrain of homophobia in their nation. As Otu (2013, 39) points out, queer people in Ghana might not openly identify themselves as queer because of "cultural belonging, ties to the family, and the impacts of fear, shame, ostracism, and punishment from familial ancestors to sexual minorities." Written into existence in the 1960s, Aidoo's Sissie could not openly embrace her sexuality the way the two imagined women do in the story Boateng's character writes. Brema's story suggests that such open embrace of lesbianism is possible in twenty-first-century Ghana. But the fact that the story is presented as a lie from the quack journalist indicates that such openness is only a future possibility. By presenting harassment as a response to this kind of love between two consenting women, the narrator suggests that love between humans and animals might become the only alternative to heterosexuality, because it is hard to detect if done in private. Embedded in the story within the story is the view that lesbian love should be allowed, but instrumental use of animals should be avoided. Through its representation of queerness as a national spectacle and scandal, the journalist Vivian's fictional story invites its readers into a dangerous identification with the moralistic repudiation of queerness as a style of living that should be confined to private spaces, not such hypermodern national facilities as the airport.

The mourning narrator in "Swallowing Ice" suggests that she has recovered from the most intense stages of her melancholy. This is clear when we remember Freud's observation that melancholy is an illness in which the subject is unable or unwilling to let go of the lost object (in this case the dead cat). We see that there is still affection for the dead cat, but there is also disdain for the pain the cat has to some extent unnecessarily caused.[29] With her first-person narration about her past love affair with the pet, the narrator seems to be inviting us to laugh at her sentimental earlier self, a person who failed to escape from the shadow of the cat as an object of sexual desire. Indeed, the pseudonymous Vivian is alienated from herself and society, and it is this alienation that drives her to a desire to connect with nonhuman beings:

> Every day, I prayed for two things: talking trees and a sky that changed colours to correspond with the days of the week—red on Mondays, green on Tuesdays, yellow on Wednesdays, blue on Thursdays, purple on Fridays, pink on Saturdays and black on Sundays. (157)

The nature of her wishes suggests that some of her posthuman desires are unachievable in real life. Brema is lost in a world of fantasies, and she sees mundane things in terms that remind her of her sex with the cat:

> There was a vibration in the room. I checked the edges of my bed to see if my phone was trapped in there. It wasn't. The mattress was a bit smaller than the bedstead. Books and other things I put on my bed often slipped into the tiny space between the bed frame and the edges of the mattress. I got on my knees, looked under the bed, and there it lay, flat on its back just as I lay for Max. He would purr with pleasure when I stroked his stomach each afternoon and every night. (158)

Even if Brema does not interact with other humans, matter vibrates all around her. The sentence describing the cat purring "with pleasure" blurs the boundaries among humans, animals, and technology. In fact, the description is superfluously brought in, not to draw an analogy between it and the vibrating phone; rather, the accidental fall of the phone is contrived to help the narrator describe in some detail her sexual encounter with the cat and to insist that the pleasure-giving between the cat and Brema is mutual. In other words, she does not see herself as exploiting the cat. That Brema has preferred a cat as a transgressive sexual partner rather than a sex toy or a fellow human being indicates her desire to go beyond the expected limits. It is in a flashback that we are told of how she trained the cat:

> Six years ago, when I found him under the mango tree outside my door, his right hind leg was broken. I carried him in and tended to him. One day, we were sleeping when he started licking my fingers; I liked how his tongue felt on my skin, coarse. From then, I would dip my index finger into milk and wet different parts of my body with it—my clitoris and my nipples. Max would lick off the milk and I would dip my fingers back into the milk bowl. I'd pull him up to my stomach and tickle his ears after my body shook, and tears would fall on the sides of my face. (163)

Brema has manipulated the cat through positive-reinforcement training with treats. Indeed, as Beck and Katcher remind us, "the choice to treat an animal as a person is ours, not the animal's. Only human beings can make an animal into a kind of person, just as children make persons out of stuffed toys" (9). It is Brema who turns Max into a kind of human being. We cannot blame Max for unrequited love when the cat leaves Brema's home and dies. The cat does not deserve to be trapped in a relationship with a human being who has failed to connect with other humans.

Unlike in Zukiswa Wanner's "Teddy and the Pussycat" (2015), in which the narrator adopts a friend's cat who later dies in a car accident and is mourned by even the narrator's mother, Brema's love for Max in Boateng's "Swallowing Ice" is not completely altruistic. Wanner's story is written as an autobiography (the narrator is called Zukiswa) about a girl in Zimbabwe who adopts a cat from a white boy who is leaving the country. She names the cat Teddy in honor of her friend. Zukiswa's mother was initially indifferent to the cat but gradually falls in love with him. In spite of her depiction of her mother as a brainwashed colonial subject who values English more than her native Shona language, Zukiswa loves her mother unconditionally, and the story focuses on her mother's transformation through her relationship to the cat. It is a story of love in the middle of racial hate in southern Africa. Zukiswa dislikes a white couple because these old individuals are racists who, "thirteen years after independence, still referred to the country as Rhodesia and the capital they stayed in as Salisbury" (144). The couple would not allow the black teenager "to cross the door-step into their home" (144). Her love for the cat she has named in honor of a white boy contrasts with the hatred of the white couple, symbols of a dying imperialist order in postindependence Zimbabwe. The seventeen-year-old Zukiswa and her mother mourn the cat without raising their grief to melodramatic levels as in Boateng's "Swallowing Ice." It is suggested that probably there would have been more drama if the death happened in the digital era: "While I understood her pain, I am relieved there was no Facebook at that time, because I am pretty certain that she would have filled her album with cat images. As it was, she had taken some photographs with her Nikon, but not all of them came out well when developed" (146). Overall, the story is about love for a cat from unexpected quarters, as Zukiswa did not expect her mother to love Teddy as deeply as she does. The mother, who was "considered ferocious and non-indulgent," became a "pussycat" in the cat's paws, observations made at the beginning and the end of the story to highlight the mother's transformation (143, 146). Certainly, Zukiswa's love for the cat is platonic, and she forgets the cat once she "found out that the rugby captain from Churchill High School had a crush on [her]" (146). This might suggest that young Zukiswa's love for the cat was erotic and could be replaced with romantic attention from a boy once the cat died. But she contrasts her cavalier attitude then with her outlook today as a mature person. The love of the cat should have been deeper, but it remained nonexploitative, although she suspected her mother got to like the cat later because the woman saw in the animal "a second child who needed her" after Zukiswa, an only child, had become independent. There is no suggestion of overt erotic attraction between the cat and the humans.

In contrast, in Boateng's "Swallowing Ice," Brema exploits the cat to fill the gap left by her inability to interact with fellow human beings. In fact, her grief is not a result of the loss of the cat, as she was already unhappy before the cat died. She uses the cat as a replacement for the lost object, which she cannot name. Ultimately the animal rejects her and moves out. She can only manage to hold it captive in death to replace the object of desire she is using the cat to replace. When she turns to the internet for a source of ideas on how to preserve Max's body, she is hit with a hateful response that is not far from the truth:

> "It will decompose because you cannot outsmart Jah, the alpha and omega. Your cat is at stage omega, DEAD, you can never alpha that shit up, loser. The only thing you can save is the bones but pray the dogs don't find them, haha! All you privileged-ass rich folks, instead of focusing on cats, why don't you focus on your kids? Babylon!"—Messiah Son (165).

The anonymity of the narrator's online identity does not offer her any security. But the insensitivity of internet users hurts her to the quick.[30] Instead of offering solidarity for a fellow mourner, the other participants are rude in their responses. She impulsively starts eating the ice with which she has preserved the body of the cat. The ingestion of ice shows her failure to mourn. She wants to incorporate the body of the cat, instead of allowing the cat what Édouard Glissant would call its "right to opacity"—a condition of unknowability that make others different from us and that should be respected as such. This relation to others does not involve assimilating them into us to erase their difference from us. Similarly, one can love an animal without turning that animal into oneself, as Brema wants to do by swallowing ice with which she has preserved Max's body. Yet her online bully is also wrong. The narrator's love for the nonhuman is not grounded in material wealth, as he claims. Even if impractical, the love is honest and spontaneous—using the cat to grieve for another object of queer desire. Overall, she has a keener eye for the truth than those who claim to be healthier and more realistic than her. We still side with her against the supposedly healthy characters, the heteronormative bureaucrats and neighbors who torment her and her imaginary queer Ghanaians. Apparently, it is better to suffer her kind of melancholia than acquiesce to heteronormativity, as this submission to what the society considers normal and healthy is itself a form of illness. Loss of the freedom to be queer is not something one should ever accept and then just move on, but pets should be freed from our human struggles to assert queerness.

ANIMAL LESSONS ON QUEERNESS

I must emphasize a small point here as a way of concluding this chapter. I am not suggesting that animals should never be considered queer. Many scholars of animal sexuality—e.g., Myra Hird, Bruce Bagemihl, Stacy Alaimo, Jennifer Terry, and Bruce Bagemihl—have offered convincing arguments against the view that animal sexualities are exclusively heterosexual and reproductive.[31] Through studies of queer behavior in animals, they offer a strong argument that sexual diversity in the animal world should give us an opportunity to carve out a space in which the sexual diversity among humans is acknowledged and celebrated. We should also remember that some animals breed across family species (Dekkers 1994 [1992], 75–92).[32] But the lingering question is why nonnormative interspecies sexual practices are discouraged in

African texts. I have argued that the texts do not argue against interspecies intimacy as such; they are opposed to penetrative coital violence, especially by male characters. As an antianthropocentric act, the Whale Caller's sex with Sharisha does not involve physical contact with the whale. What Serpell would see as a scandal of interspecies sex does not occur in Mda's novel because although the Whale Caller reaches orgasm in public, it is at a physical distance from the whale. Madoobe's behavior in Farah's *Secrets* contrasts with the way the novels from the region portray similar Cushitic characters that communicate with animals. Consider, for example, Yvonne Owuor's *Dust* (2014). It is a novel that examines the possibilities of nonnormative "casual intimacy" among women (191), a form of intimacy that is also possible among different species of animals, but it does not envision such intimacy occurring between humans and nonhuman animals. Here, as in Farah's works, we encounter a novel of disillusionment with the postindependence social order in Africa, where societies have been reduced to wanton violence. In the society Owuor constructs, communities fight among themselves, and corruption is the order of the day. The positively drawn characters derive their humanity from the ability to communicate with animals. In the beginning of the story, we admire Odidi for his knowledge of camel water songs, which originate in a foreign ethnic community. An ethnic Luo, Odidi interacts across ethnic lines; this is something the Kenyan political class has failed to do. When he performs the songs at the beginning of the novel, he is a criminal about to be shot down in a hail of bullets, but his performances and love for his expectant girlfriend may be the only redeeming virtues left to him.

It is notable that even when performed in a city shopping mall, Odidi's camel water songs seem to belong in the wilderness, a place wistfully called "home" several times in the novel. It is a place far from urban life and remote in time. In the marginalized northern frontiers of Kenya, Ali Dida Hada communicated with animals through the water songs he sang to them. A "desert eulogist, with knowledge of water songs in seven northern-Kenyan languages, Ali Dida Hada is the one who has taught Odidi these songs" (217). Now stationed in Nairobi, Hada's songs belong to his remote past; he and a senior police officer are both involved in a corrupt system. In addition, a warlord at the beginning of the novel is nostalgic for the camel water songs that one of the characters, a man who is about to die, sings for him. The songs are from Ali Dida Hada's past and are in no way a part of the social fabric of the urban center. We are also told that in the remote past, a hyena would escort the patriarch Nyipir home. This may be fantasy, but Ali Dida Hada's songs have the ring of truth; several people have witnessed him serenading the animals. The cattle dog "that had a lot of hyena in its ancestry" (39) suggests the possibilities of interspecies sex. A short time later, we are told of other dogs that are "descendants of a fierce mongrel herding dog with a touch of a hyena" (48). This could be either speculative or true, but the observations about the dogs serve a thematic purpose. No identity is pure and uncontaminated. Even the dichotomy between the colonizer and the colonized is unstable. However, there is a touch of yearning for purity; the hyena is still an undesirable component in the dogs' lineage. Hybridity is inevitable, but purity in the species is desirable.

It is useful to note that these examples show that queerness remains intra-species or at least that human non-normative sexuality should not, for the time being, extend beyond human boundaries. If sex with animals may empower humans to free themselves from the shackles of anthropocentric heteronormativity, our liberation does not translate into the liberation of other species when we use animals to achieve our goals. Sex with animals is presented as similar to the activities of an empire accumulating its wealth at the expense of the nations it occupies. Only citizens of a privileged empire would fail to see the injustice of the circumstances that lead to their privileged life and their liberties. As Nuruddin Farah demonstrates in novels such as *Maps* and *Secrets,* human queerness should not be imposed on animals, and presumed sexual overtures from animals should not be accepted when humans trespass into animal habitats. The few times that regenerative human-animal sex appears in African texts, it remains mythic and does not involve literal physical contact with animals. Therefore, in literal terms, such sexuality does not constitute interspecies intercourse. If it happens, it is with a biologically nonexistent strange thing that cannot be confused with an actual animal.

Coda

More Agency from the Blue

> Just then the cook produced the lunch
> A dish of Fried Hyeneas;
> And Columbo said: 'Will you take Tail?
> Or just a bit of Penis?'
> —T. S. Eliot, *The Letters* (2012 [1927], 718)

> What I've come to learn is that the world is never saved in grand messianic gestures, but in the simple accumulation of gentle, soft, almost invisible acts of compassion.
> —Chris Abani (2008)

In discussing the appearance of animals as agential subjects, this book has focused mainly on the use of animals as emblems in tropes that compare humans with animals. I have also devoted a section to a discussion of the use of animals as narrators and the implication of that usage in giving the speaking animals agency. I want to close by mentioning, if briefly, another technique to be found in postcolonial texts: the use of animal-inspired coincidences to push the plot forward and resolve conflicts. Such uses of animal images and actions in textual emplotments to disrupt culture/nature hierarchies are numerous. I want to use Jan Carew's *Black Midas* (1958) to illustrate this technical use of animal images, especially because their application is tied to ecological postcolonial themes. A brief reading of these events, which from a human perspective are nature-inspired coincidences, will also recapitulate the main arguments I have developed in this book.[1] Although I have cited a few black diaspora texts (especially from Britain and the Caribbean), this book is not about animal studies or posthumanism in diasporic black writing; animality and posthumanism work by such authors as Octavia Butler, Toni Morrison, Julie Dash, and Janelle Monáe have received some critical attention, if not to an exhaustive degree.[2] I use Carew's *Black Midas* here particularly because its hero Shark's character traits relating to the environment are attributed to his African ancestry throughout the novel. Carew uses coincidence to integrate nature as an agential force, probably one far stronger than human agency.

Colonial accounts of the Amazonian fauna, such as John Quelch's *Animal Life in British Guiana* (1901) and Vincent Roth's *Notes and Observations on Animal Life in British Guiana* (1941), offered an overview of animal life without showing the animal's relationship to the colonized populations. Crew seems to draw from history or popular lore in the sense that his "Ocean Shark" also appears briefly in Roth's *A Life in Guiana*, a series of diaries covering Roth's encounters in South America between 1923 and 1935, as an actual gold prospector in the 1920s and "the real bad man of the colony" (2003, 69). Ironically, Quelch's and Roth's accounts do not seem to fully recognize that their criticisms of human encroachment on animal habitats could be leveled against colonialist activities in Guyana and other colonies. Roth criticizes the colonial elite and, to some degree, sympathizes with "Ocean Shark" when he is bullied by European colonialists. However, it is in Carew's novel that the prospector's interconnectedness with the Guyana landscapes is most sympathetically rendered.

In *Black Midas,* Carew humanizes animals to critique the colonial government and to idealize the precolonial rural Guyana that colonialism has been trying to erase. In the novel, animals and nature at large actively resist human destruction, and the critic Kwame Dawes is correct in urging us to read the landscape in the novel as one of the characters Carew writes "with a deep sense of passion and love" (2009, 9). The world that the novelist offers to the reader is animist, presenting nonhuman species and the universe in general as sentient beings, of which humans are but a component.[3] Human characters in the novel are predatory against some elements of the universe, but they are usually punished in events that can only be read as revenge from nature. The characters are also intricately tied to the other-than-human universe; even when the main character receives a modern education that would help him escape, he feels that "the language of the books" could not replace the natural elements associated with village life: "the sun was in my blood, the swamp and river, my grandmother, the amber sea, the savannahs, the memory of surf and wind closer to me than the smell of my own sweat" (42). Through the use of Guyanese creole, the rural characters in the novel are portrayed as fully integrated with nature, which is sympathetic to the good ones among them. Europeans are cold-hearted: there is one who "even seemed not aware of the wind ruffling his ram-goat beard" (14). Although African slaves and Indian indentured laborers are not native to Guyana, they have, unlike European colonialists, adjusted organically to the land, creating a new language through which they relate to one another.

Published in London by Secker & Warburg in 1958, the novel was simultaneously issued in the U.S. by Coward-McCann as *A Touch of Midas* in 1958 and as an abridged school edition in Guyana, also titled *Black Midas*, in 1969. This signals the work's importance, alongside such novels as Achebe's *Things Fall Apart* (1958) and Samuel Selvon's *The Lonely Londoners* (1956), as part of the canon of emergent non-Western anglophone writing of the time. Like many foundational works from Africa and the postcolonial world, *Black Midas* is a Bildungsroman, in which the development of the main character occurs in tandem with that of the nation at large. Told in the first-person narrative voice, it follows the experiences of Aron Smart as he grows up in colonial Guyana. The black boy, also called "Ocean Shark" because of his facial features and aggressiveness, does not know his parents. His nickname destabilizes the animal/human divide in a world where we encounter people who "knew the language of the forest creatures and would talk to them as if they were human" (262) and where, in a hallucination, Shark rides "a donkey to a dead forest where roots and branches of the trees were like human limbs writhing in agony" (19). We have seen that, using magical realism, postcolonial writers show humans and the environment as conterminous. It is hard to separate the people from the environment in the society that Carew presents. This dream, in which Shark falls into "a well of darkness" (19), presages what is going to happen to him in a mining accident. In a prophetic motif common throughout the postcolonial novels we have seen, *Black Midas* suggests that there is a posthuman mind that can foretell, through dreams, events that are going to happen in the future.

The novel revolves around Shark's rise and fall as a prospector. It describes both the Guyana coast and the jungle in the hinterland, contrasting the villages with the corrupt ways of Georgetown. Sounds of birds and animals pervade the environment in Mahaica, Shark's village on the banks of River Mahaica as it enters the Atlantic. One can starve in the city, but not Mahaica, which is presented as an exotic Eden. There are all sorts of animals, and the mangrove forests allow the production of fruits and other foods. The most lyrical passages in the novel describe the environment as having an indomitable vitality. It is a world that cannot be fully colonized, because it triumphs over human endeavors and destructiveness. It takes revenge against humans who try to destroy it out of greed. The death of Shark's father is an accident, and there are several accidents in the novel—the most important events come about by chance. Aron Shark might as well be speaking to us from the dead or at the time he is narrating the story, he has just survived a similar accident that happens at the end of the novel.

I have resisted the representation of non-Western societies as comprising ecologically noble savages. Carew would seem to agree. The drought that strikes Mahaica at the beginning of the novel reveals the earth's revenge against the human community. The colonialist destruction of habitats to grow sugar cane using slave labor, together with the continued destruction of forests through irresponsible mining, could account for the severity of the drought. Animals are part of the plot's forward-movement triggers. At the beginning of the story, Shark does not know how to escape the village of Mahaica to the city, because his grandparents "wrapped themselves around me and I knew no way of fighting against their feebleness" (6). When he quietly wishes they would die, an animal comes to his aid: his grandfather is killed by a jaguar while out on a government-sponsored hunt. It is good to remember that, ordinarily, jaguars rarely attack humans.[4] In the novel, the jaguar only strikes when it, and its habitat, are under threat. Indeed, the jaguar in *Black Midas* is an anticolonial agent, killing the colonized human being who accepts the offer to kill animals for money. What is most interesting about the jaguar-caused death to the internal dynamics of the story is that it appears to be a coincidence. Other similar coincidences happen that night: the grandmother dies in her sleep, without learning of her husband's death, and their parrot Echo dies soon after and is buried in the same space as the narrator's grandparents in the churchyard.

We have seen throughout this book that postcolonial African writers present animals as sensitive, compassionate, and intelligent. Echo's response to the deaths recalls Martha Nussbaum's (2012) observation that animals can be more compassionate than humans.[5] Carew's novel suggests that colonial modernity has debased the locals to such an extent that, unlike the bird that mourns the dead couple to death, humans do not care for one another or their habitat. Most of the beauty lies in the natural environment, and the animals that inspire it—a connection the money-hungry diamond and gold prospectors destroy with their mines and encroaching urbanization: "The sky was a hard buck-crab blue and no wind stirred in the trees. A harpy eagle soared near the sun, waiting to ambush ducks and herons on their way to the savannahs. The boat shivered like a deer with an instinct for flight" (165). This is the last view we get of the Perenong, as Shark moves to Georgetown.[6] As an observant narrator, Shark is critical of colonialists as traitors. He presents Europeans as not fitting in with the Guyanese landscape. But despite his anticolonial sentiments, Shark is himself a colonialist aggressively exploiting the environment to make profits that he, like the other miners, blows in the city.

Carew presents us with a few good people in the villages who still respect fellow human beings and the environment. The narrator (now reformed from his former avarice) contrasts his earlier self with the nonmaterialistic Bullah, the village shopkeeper. Bullah says he would not sacrifice a human being for earthly wealth. Bullah is ready to join Shark in pursuing a pair who have stolen Shark's minerals, but the shopkeeper is reluctant to sacrifice human life to do that. Speaking of his servant Tonic, the shopkeeper tells the narrator: "Me rather lose everything me got than sacrifice he for couple diamond. Is fifteen odd year since he been with me and me grow accustomed to he ways" (93). Miners do not observe this ethic; they force workers into perilous conditions because they give priority to profits over human life and the environment. Shark knows that the old man means it: "I knew Bullah wasn't going any further, diamonds or no diamonds" (94). As the voice of reason in the novel, Bullah's cosmopolitan kindness to strangers extends to animals. Although Tonic and Shark seem ready to destroy animals, Bullah at one point warns Shark against killing an anaconda, underlining the intelligence of that animal. If killed, its mates would retaliate against the human killers. The next anaconda we see in the story is killed, but it is Tonic who does it. Although to the humans the snake seems to be a threat to Tonic's life, the reader feels that the death of the baby anaconda could have been avoided. In killing the snake, Tonic and Shark have yet to attain the wisdom of Bullah, who does not kill animals throughout the story. It is suggested that the animal-killing young men are still growing up; they will stop the habit when they mature.

Hunting and eating meat are suppressed through disnarration, a technique in which something is alluded to have happened in the real world but is not narrated in the story.[7] Hunting and meat-eating happen in the society depicted, but the story treats them as more taboo than sex, which is given a lot of space in the nonabridged edition. We are told that Bullah is an excellent hunter, but we do not see him hunting; instead, he lies about going hunting while he is actually out pursuing criminals. So, there is a sense that he is not a hunter as he claims. Details regarding meat are also redacted from the story: "we took up spoons and shoveled the rice and peas and salt pork into our mouths. Tonic moved away, satisfied" (80). In the story, the narrator and his companions eat the food just to avoid offending Tonic, the cook. Human emotions (Tonic's disappointment) are valued over animal lives, but the animal-as-meat is disnarrated. The details of the eating are minimized in the plot even though we know that eating continued in the story-world. Similarly, there are killings of animals, but it appears that only intellectually underdeveloped children kill animals, as young Shark usually does on his way to work.[8]

As intelligent beings that should not be killed, animals are deployed to propel the plot forward, because they are capable of revenge on behalf of good people. For example, the conflict between Shark and his avaricious uncle, Richard Dolly, is miraculously resolved when an animal kills Richard by chance as he crosses a river: "I stood between Santos and the river because I didn't want to kill Richard Dolly. Suddenly I heard him scream and saw him beating the water with his hands furiously. He screamed again and again" (98). We learn from Santos's analysis that "cannibal fish got he" (98). Richard has been presented throughout the novel as an evil liar and exploiter. The animal avenges Shark's mistreatment at the hands of Richard. Shark had shot his uncle, and the blood from the bullet wound invited the cannibal fish to attack. However, before the fish attacked, it was apparent that Shark has no intention of killing the uncle. He just wants his diamonds back. The shooting happens by chance, and the fish is at hand to finish the job. As if this is not enough, Santos, the only witness who might implicate Shark in the murder, goes mad and commits suicide the following day. The two thieves are destroyed by cosmic forces. In death, they are cheated of their rewards: though the uncle did drown with some diamonds, Santos had swindled him and given him less valuable stones. The animals' and the earth's capacity for revenge reminds us of Braidotti's observation that "exclusive property, or the unalienable right of one species, the human, over all others or of being sacralized as a pre-established given, is posited as process, interactive and open-ended" (2013b, 60). The human is vulnerable to nature extracting revenge for its destruction through capitalistic human activities.

Like most of the works we have discussed in this book, Carew's novel emphasizes the oneness of the village and nature as a model of egalitarianism throughout. At one point, Shark resists killing a young boa constrictor, because "at the moment I felt that the snake and I were one with the sun and the sky and the young grass" (23). He is not afraid when the snake follows him as a companion in the exploring the swamps. Idealistic in his portrayal of a perfect world of harmony between nature and humans, Carew shows that predatory behavior among animals would lead to double tragedy, in which the prey and the predator alike come to grief. This is best shown in a scene in which the young boa constrictor is friendly to the narrator and accompanies him in the swamp. When they encounter an alligator, the constrictor and gator fight one another to the death. The narrator is the beneficiary of this mutual hostility among animals. As I have argued in this book, literature about animals is not meant for an animal audience; it is directed at humans. Carew's scene is an allegorical call for unity among the Guyanese people struggling for self-determination. Humans are the equivalent of colonialists, and the novel suggests that unless there is unity among the subalterns (whom the alligator and constrictor represent), humans and colonialism will continue to thrive at the expense of animals and the colonized. By making humans analogs to colonialism, Carew emphasizes that although we might be vulnerable as colonized subjects, compared to animals we are privileged and should not abuse that privilege.

AGAINST NEGATIVE CRITIQUE

Braidotti advises us to avoid negativity in our critique and instead emphasize affirmative nomadic ethics. I have avoided the temptation to pin blame on authors for their sometimes-vague position on vegan ethics. But I have questioned the characters' lack of clarity about environmental issues that call for action in quotidian practices. Relatedly, I may sound in this book as if I'm arguing against Gary Francione's radical veganism, but even Francione and Chartlon (2015, 2016) accept the necessity of some nonvegan practices as we prepare for the ideal vegan world. For instance, in works criticizing living with animals as pets, Francione and Chartlon reveal they live with shelter dogs, but aspire to a world in which such animals would be restored to the wild.

At the same time, I have proposed abandoning anticolonial images of the ecologically noble savage. So even if a precolonial indigenous community practiced hunting, we should acknowledge that community's conservation methods without justifying hunting today; as Gary Varner (2002) reminds us, the fact that at one point in the past it was acceptable to do certain things does not mean that we can still accept such practices today. Most of the time, the works I have read refuse to take a firm position on ethical issues, leaving the reader to draw personal and speculative conclusions. Non-Westerners who eat all kinds of strange animals are as nonexistent as the cannibal African, who, according to William Arens, exists "prior to and thus independent of evidence" (1979, 22). Even if there might be actual cannibals and people with weird gastronomical proclivities, such as the black monarch in Eliot's poem, they are usually conjured up by the colonizing group to justify subjugation of local values.[9]

Comaroff and Comaroff (1999b) have pointed out that the postcolonial African's recourse to rituals of the past, some of which colonialism worked to erase, "does not imply an iteration of, a retreat into, 'tradition'" (284). Rather, it involves the use of familiar practices to respond to present conditions and reject colonial control. Therefore, given the Eurocentric denigration of African customs as barbaric since the Enlightenment to justify colonialism, I have guarded against the common elitist vegan dismissal of African animal-killing ritual practices. These customs are rooted in post-independence nationalist revaluation of precolonial African cultures. However, we should note that advocates of the animal rituals emphasize the humane treatment of the sacrificed animal. Usually a symbolic gesture to enhance social revival, the rituals are themselves a replacement of earlier forms of sacrifice now seen as too cruel, such as the physical killing of a king in order to replace him with a younger one. The fact that such a ritual is recognized as a merely symbolic act, performed to avoid doing the "actual" thing, gives me hope that the rituals can be replaced with other signifying practices, as has started to happen among the Maasai, who have abandoned the killing of lions as a rite of passage through which young men, for centuries, have had to announce their entry into manhood to the world (Mbaria 2014). Reminiscent of Fanon's rejection of cultural nationalisms that seek to perpetuate precolonial "feudal traditions" in the name of anti-colonial liberation (2004 [1963], 142) and similar critiques of strands of ethnophilosophical thought that romanticize precolonial Africa in nostalgic efforts to recover a paradise lost and resuscitate "anachronistic traditions" (Boulaga 2014 [1977], 230), African writers have since the 1950s criticized belief systems that justified oppressive customs within precolonial African cultures. Such indigenous practices, according to the authors, need to be replaced. However, the change should at least not be imposed externally by institutions associated with the racist dehumanization of Africans as backward and innately atavistic; rather, transformation should preferably come from within the particular society itself.

Precolonial societies are presented in African and black diaspora literature as observers of environmental ethics that respect animals in every way. Benjamin Zephaniah's "Fearless Bushmen" (2000, 16–17), an ode to African precolonial life, presents the "Bushmen" community of southern Africa as the epitome of modesty, solidarity, charity, cosmopolitanism, and preservation of the environment, qualities lacking in Western and Westernized societies. The poet starts with praising the indigenous community's respect for animals in their art:

The bushmen of the Kalahari desert
Painted themselves on rocks
With wildebeests and giraffes
Thousands of years ago.
And still today they say
To boast is sinful
Arrogance is evil. (2000, 16)

Unlike modern cultures, the "Bushmen" as presented in this stanza are symbols of what the modern society should be like. The poem insists that this first nation "still" observe their respect for animals; it is therefore not too late for the modern cultures to emulate such an attitude. It is in a similar depiction of the "Bushmen" that the poem closes:

These hunter-gatherers are fearless
But peaceful,
They will never argue with a mamba snake,
When one is seen heading towards the village
They kiss the Earth
And move to the next village. (2000, 17)

The indigenous African community does not confine its respect for the environment to abstract art. It submits to the will of nature, never competing for resources with animals. It is notable that the word "Earth" in Zephaniah's poem is treated as a proper noun, while "bushmen," a racial slur for the indigenous community, is written in lowercase. The persona deftly speaks of both the modest "Bushmen" and the arrogant modern societies. Members of this indigenous group respect the planet as much as they do a fellow human being, but modern society sneers at the "Bushmen", even though we are shown that they are more humane and gentler than the cowardly modern societies that prioritize war and destruction. In the poem, they avoid unnecessary conflicts not only with fellow human beings, but with the environment:

> *And although some say today that they*
> *Are the earliest hunter-gatherers known*
> *They never hunt for sport*
> *They think that's rude*
> *They hunt for food. (Zephaniah 2000, 16)*

These are the concluding lines in the first stanza of the poem, whose ideal audience is young people; the collection in which it appears is categorized in library catalogs as "juvenile" literature. The lyricism and simplicity of the language attests to the audience's and speaker's youthfulness. The poem rhetorically ends with the image of the "bushmen" moving their settlement to make way for a snake. They would not kill such an animal because it is not part of their diet. While the poet here seems ready to condone hunting, he insists that it should not involve wanton destruction of wildlife and the environment. What the persona in the poem is unaware of, as demonstrated in chapter 2, is that the so-called hunters and gatherers are more gatherers than hunters. As if to capture this, in the visual representation of the "bushmen" on the printed page we have a sketch of the people holding in their hands various fruits, not animal meat.

Just as I would not expect a nonhuman animal to behave and think like me, I know it's impossible to strip myself of my humanism to fully view nonhuman animals as they would view themselves. I am part of the system I am trying to replace. I do not see humanism as necessarily an evil way of looking at the world, as long as it does not promote human exclusivity or human superiority to other life forms and intelligences. Recuperating humanism in posthuman critiques allows us to accept responsibility for the Anthropocene and act to reverse the situation the world is in. To do so, one must question the capital-letter Humanism of the West that Braidotti identifies as "inherently anthropocentric, gendered and racialized in that it upholds aesthetic and moral ideals based on white, masculine, heterosexual European civilization" (2013, 68). Braidotti is interested in replacing the traditional European Humanism with an egalitarian ethic in line with decentered and postanthropocentric subjectivities. I have suggested that postcolonial humanisms also need to be transformed to address the weaknesses marginalized groups have noted in their own philosophies.

The action I recommend regarding better treatment of animals must come from human beings, not animals. We should not force veganism or a political ideology on animals. As we have qualified, we shouldn't expect Mboudjak in Patrice Nganang's *Dog Days* to fight for fellow dogs' rights or to speak on behalf of dogs. It is humans who should stop abusing those rights and start advocating for their companion species. Neither should we expect Rwandan dogs not to eat human corpses during a genocide, as happens in Michael Caton-Jones's film *Shooting Dogs;* it is humans who should avoid such conflicts among themselves.[10] The dogs are not to blame; they are doing the genocide survivors a favor by cleaning up the environment.

RHIZOMATIC ALLIANCES

Rosi Braidotti has observed that the kind of "sustainable nomadic ethics" we have examined include "rhizomatic alliances." "Concrete practice of cross-disciplinary discussions needs to be adopted, with transposable notions moving about, if more ethical behavior is to come to effect. We need to connect more systematically different discursive communities, such as feminists, anti-racists, pacifists, anti-nationalistic and anti-militaristic concerns with philosophical discussions about new forms of subjectivity" (2006, 130–39). This is a continuous process of relationality. We have touched on a few such processes in the readings of the texts. When an animal is used as a metaphor for negative political processes—e.g., the crocodile in Vincent Eri's *The Crocodile*—it is abundantly clear that the animal in the text is an evil human being disguised as an animal. The actual crocodile would rarely attack a human being. In an ideal world, then, animals and humans coexist harmoniously.

Following Chakrabarty and Braidotti, I have insisted on a transdisciplinary reading of animals. I have also borne in mind Wendy Woodward's observation that we should go beyond understanding that animals have a subjectivity and act to change the conditions of animals in the real world. The texts have suggested the solutions to the problems animals face. The lesson that Barbara Smuts learns from reading Coetzee's work on the lives of animals and from her work as a researcher and animal lover is that "treating members of other species as persons, as beings with potential far beyond our normal expectations, will bring out the best in them, and . . . each animal's best includes unforeseeable gifts" (Smuts 1999, 120). We have seen various writers celebrate animal talents and capacities, even if in anthropomorphic terms. Through these magic realist techniques, the writers call on the readers to respect animals the same way they would a respectable human being.

It is good to remember Smuts's argument that we should extend our respect of animals to the actual world. Animals have been given agency in literary texts, yet continue to be exploited in the actual world. Animals' prominence in these texts is thus comparable to the situation Mineke Schipper highlighted in the 1980s, whereby foundational male postcolonial writers put women on a pedestal without necessarily fighting to improve women's material conditions in society. The gendered specificities of such women's struggles are overlooked. This is to say, the female subaltern was no longer absent from foundational postcolonial narratives, dramas, and poetry, but her presence merely shored up male power. Because they serve as stylistic stand-ins for male anxieties, such women characters are not complex individuals, but mythical and symbolic representatives of abstract masculine national desires. Urging us to move away from such a stance, I have argued that we should be careful in our response to animals, to ensure that we are not just using nonhuman entities to just represent human values, desires, and anxieties.

My analysis of African literary texts has demonstrated the thin line between the human and nonhuman in postcolonial literatures. Interpretations of postcolonial texts often change when we consider the animal question, which arises so often in literature but is usually ignored. Furthermore, as scholars of animal studies, we will not be taken seriously outside the Western academy if, whenever we train our binoculars toward the Global South, all we see are animals as described in a predictable canon of white writers.[11] It is crucially important that we extend critical attention to subjects who are not part of this idolized group of white artists—those who are black, female, queer, and nonelite.

NOTES

CHAPTER 1

1. Lori Marino, for example, considers welfarism in laboratory experiments as tantamount to "ethical gerrymandering" (2011). See also Gary L. Francione's "Animals, Property and Legal Welfarism" (1994) and the introductory chapter in Francione's *Rain Without Thunder: The Ideology of the Animal Rights Movement* for a critique of welfarism as compared to animal rights. While welfarism advocates "humane" treatment of animals by reducing "atrocities" against them, Francione recommends a position that "rejects the regulation of atrocities and calls unambiguously and unequivocally for their abolition" (1996, 2).

2. See, for example, Teresa Mbatia's (2015) op-ed article in *Daily Nation*, the most widely circulated paper in East and Central Africa, in which she argues that "conservation divas" and "interest groups composed of affluent Caucasian and Asian Kenyans" use social media to garner foreign support and donor funding at the expense of local interests. A similar critique runs through John Mbaria and Mordecai Ogada's *The Big Conservation Lie* (2017).

3. Rob Nixon similarly suggests, with reference to postcolonial literary critics' indifference to ecological issues, that in postcolonial studies environmental concerns are regarded "at best, as irrelevant and elitist," and that they are manifestly neoimperialist (235). Rob White is also alert to the possibilities of backlash against "hardcore animal rights activists," who may come off to local communities as having "more empathy for nonhuman animals than humans" (2013, 134). See also Martin H. Prozesky's "Well-Fed Animals and Starving Babies" (2009), in which the apartheid regime is presented as giving priority to animals at the expense of black Africans: "loving wild animals more than black babies, they [the white, male lords of apartheid] looked after them by providing the most wonderful nature reserves" (300).

4. Classically, Carrie Rohman has argued that "while recent postcolonial criticism has privileged the categories of race and gender in an effort to articulate our understanding of modernism's imperialist binaries, it has failed to examine the fact that these discourses frequently sought justification through the discourse of species" (2009, 29). Yet

discussion of animalization forms part of the foundational texts of postcolonial theory. Wendy Woodward's *The Animal Gaze* (2008a) goes beyond using white writers (e.g., J. M. Coetzee) as the exclusive animal studies texts in African literature. Another important text is F. Fiona Moolla's *Natures of Africa* (2016), an edited volume of essays covering a wide range of cultural texts, including oral literature and novels. Cajetan Iheka's *Naturalizing Africa* (2017) offers a good model for the study of African literature from an ecological perspective.

5. See, for example, Cynthia Willett's *Interspecies Ethics* (2014) and the sections devoted to animal studies in Graham Huggan and Helen Tiffin's *Postcolonial Ecocriticism* (2010). The only major study that departs from this tradition is Wendy Woodword's *The Animal Gaze* (2008a).

6. See Maneesha Deckha (2018) for a further elaboration of this idea at the intersection of animal studies and postcolonial discourse. Raymond Corbey holds a similar position when he observes in the *Metaphysics of Apes* that during colonialism, "human identity in European societies was articulated in terms of animal alterity" (2005, 29). Donna Haraway also discusses primatology in connection with colonialism, noting that under high colonialism in the 1920s, "knowledge of the living and dead bodies of monkeys and apes was part of the system of unequal exchange of extractive colonialism" (1989, 19). Also see Achille Mbembe's *Critique of the Black Reason* (2017), in which he discusses the continued animalization of the "all the subaltern humanity" across mostly non-white races in the neoliberal era (4), a practice founded on European philosophical thought by such theorists as Georg Hegel and Paul Valéry that tended to dehumanize non-European peoples as inferior to Europeans (10–13). See also Emmanuel Eze's *Achieving Our Humanity,* in which he observes the tendency of European philosophers (e.g., Hume in *Treatise,* in spite of his opposition to slavery and his recognition of the porousness of the divide between humans and animals) to equate non-Western subjects with animals, seeing black people as "more nearly animal than white" and as inferior beings who in some instances could be legitimately sold like a horse or a dog (Eze 2001, 69). From a performance studies perspective, Joshua Williams (2017) reads "metonymic linkage among blackness, sub-humanity, and beastliness [as] an instrument of social control" in colonial Kenya (336).

7. For Agamben in *The Open* (2004), "if, in the machine of the moderns, the outside is produced through the exclusion of an inside and the inhuman produced by animalizing the human, here [in the premodern machine] the inside is obtained through the inclusion of an outside, and the non-man is produced by the humanization of an animal: the man-ape, the *enfant sauvage* or *Homo ferus*, but also and above all the slave, the barbarian, and the foreigner, as figures of an animal in human form" (37).

8. Using Sylvia Wynter and Hortense Spillers, Alexander G. Weheliye ably explains in *Habeas Viscus* (2014) the antihumanism at the heart of racial relations in Western modernity. Weheliye believes it our duty is to probe "how humanity has been imagined and lived by those subjects excluded from this domain" (2014, 8).

9. For a history of the term in Western debates, see Laura Wright's *The Vegan Studies Project* (2015, 2–6).

10. The Rastafarian concept of "Ital" is the closest to "veganism" in African and black diaspora cultures. Nia Yaa outlines its tenets, which include: "Don't eat anything that can walk, swim, fly, or crawl, or anything that has eyes" (2010, 94).

11. Lawrence Buell's term is an ecocritical repurposing of Fredric Jameson's (1981) concept of the political unconscious, which proposes that literary texts symbolically insinuate the political and social problems of the time. Caminero-Santangelo shows how African writers' treatment of sociopolitical themes suggests a desire to couple political resistance with the fight for environmental justice, even if the works fail to address some aspects of the environment (2011, 2014).

12. The opinion that intellectuals should speak for their communities is widespread among postcolonial activists. It is similarly popular in feminism. In a well-known feminist argument, Linda Alcoff (1991) posits that, even if it is difficult to represent marginalized groups from a position of power, and even if such representations might result in reinforcing oppression, it is irresponsible for privileged individuals not to speak on behalf of minorities. In later iterations of this argument, Alcoff includes animals and the environment among the constituents that intellectuals should support, because the nonhumans "cannot speak directly" (2016, 92).

13. For a summary of George's position and the counterarguments to it by various animal rights advocates, see Sheri Lucas's "A Defense of the Feminist-Vegetarian Connection" (2005). Leela Gandhi's *Affective Communities* (2006) describes the role vegetarians played in anticolonial struggles in nineteenth-century Europe and India, while Laura Wright also demonstrates the connection between vegetarianism and anticolonialism in *Wilderness into Civilized Shapes* (2010, 61–62). See also Michael Glover's argument that although cultural nationalists object to veganism because it threatens ritual killing of animals, vegans and anti-racist activists have similar aims: both "are at bottom driven by a concern for justice" (2017, 192).

14. Rob D. White succinctly summarizes the desire of advocates of species justice, who assert that "animals should be accorded respect and acknowledgement as creatures embodying their own intrinsic worth" (2013, 143). Marc Bekoff takes a similar position when he argues that "individuals of all species have inherent and intrinsic value because they exist, and this alone mandates that we co-exist" (2010, 379). There have been disagreements about how this can be realized, as evinced in the heated debates between Gary Francione and Robert Garner (Francione and Garner 2010). While Francione calls for the immediate cessation of animal consumption, Garner prefers gradual change.

15. Giles Deleuze and Felix Guattari describe the various ways humans become "animals" in neototemic practices among "primitive parts" of "Black Africa," including in "crime societies" in which humans assume the characteristics of animals such as crocodiles to destroy other humans. For Deleuze and Guattari, these groups are "minoritarian," "oppressed," and "prohibited" (1987, 247). Both the 1955 sensational account by the

colonial administrator Paul Ernest Joset, whom Deleuze and Guattari rely on, and the later, more balanced studies (e.g., David Pratten's 2007 *The Man-Leopard Murders*) suggest that the destructiveness of the men-leopards is a response to colonial destruction of precolonial social structures. We would expect postcolonial writers to endorse the anticolonial resistance staged by these groups, but in most cases, the men-leopards are presented as epitomes of oppressive sorcery and violence against upright members of the society.

16. In a pretext blurb opening Burrough's novel, we are told that the Leopard Men engage in "gruesome rites" as members of a "savage cult" "deep in the heart of brooding Africa."

17. For a discussion of the violent man-leopards in southeastern Nigeria in the 1940s, see David Pratten's *The Man-Leopard Murders* (2007).

18. Zeb Tortorici and Martha Few have suggested that incorporating the role of animals in the historical developments in question would enable us to "write more comprehensive and less anthropocentric cultural histories" (Tortorici and Few 2013, 3). Julie Livingston and Jasbir K. Puar have lamented that posthuman thought tends to be Eurocentric (2011, 5).

19. Fayaz Chagani (2016) has argued that by excluding nonhuman animals from a moral universe reserved for humans, postcolonial criticism tacitly participates in violence against animals.

20. Abolitionists Gary Francione and Anna Charlton concede in *Animal Rights: The Abolitionist Approach* (2015) the need to take care of the domestic animals under our care at the moment, although "we would be under an obligation not to bring any more into existence" (25).

21. In discussing the need to insist on the importance of the materiality of a woman's body and not to see "woman" as just a linguistic signifier conjured into existence purely through language and human imagination, Braidotti says that such insistence on nature and materiality beyond semiotic reference is "the materialist acknowledgement of a historical location: a starting position of asymmetrical power differentials. This location is not only geopolitical, but also genealogical and time-bound" (2006, 130).

22. Other theorists who have demonstrated the capabilities of plants include the biologist Daniel Chamovitz, who in *What a Plant Knows* (2012) demonstrates that plants can see, smell, feel the sensation of touch, and remember. See also Michael Marder's *Plant Thinking* (2013) and Jeffrey T. Nealon's *Plant Theory* (2016).

23. For the history of the term "posthuman" in animal studies, including the opposition it has received, see Zipporah Weisberg's "The Trouble with Posthumanism" (2014).

24. See also Alexander Weheliye's *Habeas Viscus* (2014) for a systematic critique of the exclusion of nonwhite subjects from the conceptualization of full humanity. In such ideas of who is human, nonoccidental subjects are not yet, to use Weheliye's words, "fully assimilated into the human qua man" (2014, 10). Zakiyyah Iman Jackson (2013) demonstrates this systematic occlusion of nonwhite subjects from the category of the human, a practice that naturally creates distrust among minorities when scholars focus

narrowly on posthuman categories or when Western critics of Enlightenment disregard earlier similar criticisms by non-Western theorists, especially those criticizing the colonial order.

25. Examples of works that make fun of Europeans who are more interested in African animals than they are in Africans include David Rubadiri's poem "Paraa Lodge," about tourists who have erected barriers between themselves and the native Ugandans in order to come closer to nature, from which they ironically also detach themselves without realizing that they are no different than the hippos excreting in the Nile (1971, 138). See also Rubadiri's "Saaka Crested Cranes" republished in his *An African Thunderstorm and Other Poems* (2004 [1968]b, 39). The hypocrisy of such tourists is also captured clearly in Marjorie O. Macgoye's "The African City," where they appear reading *Playboy* in their hotel rooms instead of interacting with Africans: "After all / it is the animals they came to see, not us" (1998, 16). Micere Githae Mugo's "Questioning the Biologist" (1976 [1969]b) indicates that the term "animals of prey" is more accurately used as a descriptor of the rich, because they are evil (2006, 94). Binyavanga Wainaina's "How to Write About Africa" (2006) also satirizes expatriate writers and critics who expect African writers to produce stereotypical figures of black human beings while "animals, on the other hand, must be treated as well rounded, complex characters" (94).

26. Such critics include Cajetan Iheka in *Naturalizing Africa*, in which he argues for the need to "rehabilitate the human" (2017, 158–60). For a similar critique of posthumanist strands that tend to further sideline already-marginalized human beings, see also Eduardo Kohn's *How Forests Think* (2013, 7) and Alexander Weheliye's *Habeas Viscus* (2014, 8).

27. Cary Wolfe's conceptualization of posthumanism is similar in that it aims to "fully comprehend what amounts to a new reality: that the human occupies a new place in the universe, a universe now populated by . . . nonhuman subjects," a reality that demands "the vigilance, responsibility, and humility that accompany living in a world so newly, and differently, inhabited" (2010, 47). For a further discussion of the intersection of posthumanism and critical animal studies, see Helena Pedersen's "Release the Moths" (2011).

28. Neil Badmington (2003, 13) also notes the presence of "Man" in posthuman conceptions of the death of "Man."

29. The term "Anthropocene" was given currency by Paul Crutzen and Eugene Stoermer (2000), when they observed that we have moved from the Holocene epoch to an era where human activities are a "significant geological, morphological force" (17). Anthropocentricism is "an approach to moral theory that takes humanity as its standard: it starts by inquiring into the essence of 'being human' or of 'humanity,' and assumes that human beings are entitled to rights and justice by virtue of this essential humanity. Animals, in this anthropocentric view, achieve moral standing only if they can be seen as possessing or approximating some aspects of this essence of humanity" (Donaldson and Kymlicka 2011, 33).

30. As Simon Gikandi explains the antirealist impulses of postcolonial literature in

general, "It is perhaps not an exaggeration to say that postcolonial theory came into being as a critique of Western theories of representation and that an antimimetic bend undergirds the most prevalent view of postcolonial literature" (2012, 309).

31. See, for example, Kwame Anthony Appiah's famous essay "Is the Post- in Postmodernism the Post- in Postcolonial?" (1991). He argues that postcolonial texts retain some referential elements. Ngũgĩ wa Thiong'o expresses a similar position in *Penpoints, Gunpoints, and Dreams* (1998). Arguing from a Marxist perspective, Ngũgĩ notes that although doubt is integral to art, we as members of the privileged classes or as unwitting endorsers of an inequitable political and financial system should be careful not to endorse oppression. Ngũgĩ holds that we should be "wary of any uncertainties, particularly those preached and promoted by those with state power . . . we should be wary equally of any rhetoric that promotes Hamlet-type indecision about what to think of our societies which produce today baggers of millions on the shoulders of millions of beggars. Or be wary about language use that may blunt human social sensitivity to suffering because begging, for instance, is an exercise in free speech or where democratic freedoms are equated with freedom of finance capital" (1998, 130).

32. See, for example, Dolleen Manning's "The Becoming-Human of Buffalo Bill," in which she finds the concepts problematic to apply in relation to indigenous peoples in the Americas (2014, 188). Irene Gedaloff criticizes "nomadism" on similar grounds, arguing that it suggests "class privilege that allows for the purely joyful and voluntary mobility of the nomad as a high-flying academic, which has very little in common with the forced, or at least more uncomfortable and complicated, trajectories of migrants, exiles, and others who travel 'without tenure'" (1996, 193).

33. In 1996, the physicist Alan Sokal sent a nonsense article filled with over-the-top mimicry of postmodern language to the academic journal *Social Text*, and it was published! It was titled "Transgressing the Boundaries: Towards a Transformative Hermeneutics of Quantum Gravity." Among other things, he wanted to prove that postmodernists are charlatans who misuse the language of science.

34. Kolozova is building on Judith Butler's *Bodies That Matter* (1993) and *Undoing Gender* (2004), which also call for the affirmation of real bodies if we are to claim substantive political power for marginalized groups. For a synthetic commentary on Butler's use of the "real," see Katerina Kolozova's *Cut of the Real* (2014, 72–77).

35. Kolozova concedes that we should avoid the "reductionist" critique of postmodernism because behind Deleuze's and Derrida's postmodern fascination with language there is, for Deleuze, "a rigorous structure of ethical thought," and for Derrida, a "meticulously constructed ontology of unilateral difference and pure affirmation" (Kolozova 2014, 80).

36. Neil Badmington has similarly urged patience: "It is not possible to arrive at a moment of certainty, mastery, satisfaction. Meaning keeps moving, and cultural criticism must learn to hear the 'yes' with the 'no,' to read the dis-functioning alongside the functioning, to announce how every 'supposed system' is at once a deposed system" (2001, 12).

37. Christopher Peterson has also warned us in *Bestial Traces* against what he calls "facile moral judgment" when reading experimental work, in which the author's position is not always clear, such as in the works of J. M. Coetzee (2013, 113).

38. Manuel DeLanda explains this in his examination of new materialism. In social constructivism, DeLanda explains, "general categories do not refer to anything in the real world and . . . to believe they do (i.e., to reify them) leads directly to essentialism. Social constructivism is supposed to be an antidote to this, in the sense that by showing that general categories are mere stereotypes it blocks the move towards their reification. But by coupling the idea that perception is intrinsically linguistic with the ontological assumption that only the contents of experience really exist, this position leads directly to a form of *social essentialism*" (2006, 45–46).

39. Anthony Vital in "Towards an African Ecocriticism" (2008) and "Critical Intersections" (2016) has also called for an interdisciplinary reading of literary language. In this approach, "while it focuses on language, ecocriticism would stay aware of the social relations affected by modernity's pasts—social relations that mediate relations with what we call 'nature'" (Vital 2016, 169–70).

40. This approach has been effective in postcolonial feminist studies. For example, Chandra Talpade Mohanty, in "Under Western Eyes: Feminist Scholarship and Colonial Discourses" (1984), launched an influential approach to women's rights that would be anticolonial at the same time. In such a theoretical frame, an approach to animal studies that is tinged with racism, homophobia, or misogyny would be untenable.

41. Black sexual violence against white women was a common trope in the nationalist literature of the 1950s and 1960s in which such sexual acts, according to Faith Smith, provided "the opportunity both for vengeance and for the assertion of an anti-colonial masculinity that was a threat of emasculation by the colonizer's violation" (2011, 405). Evan Mwangi (2009) provides some analysis of Ngũgĩ's revisions.

42. Kathryn T. Gines (2016 [2014], 24–25) and Anna Carastathin (2016, 15–24) argue that the concept predates Crenshaw's coinage of the term "intersectionality." In their view, similar ideas are evident in nineteenth-century statements on race and gender in work by such black feminists as Anna Julia Cooper and Sojourner Truth. See also Rosemarie Tong and Tina Fernandes Botts's "Women of Color Feminism" (2014, 16–17).

43. Kimberlé Crenshaw calls into question the privileging, by liberal feminists, of white women's experiences. Others who share these views include Hazel V. Carby in "White Woman Listen! Black Feminism and the Boundaries of Sisterhood" (1982) and Chandra Talpade Mohanty in "Under Western Eyes: Feminist Scholarship and Colonial Discourses" (1984). For a critique of intersectionality as essentializing, see Jasbir Puar's "I Would Rather Be a Cyborg Than a Goddess" (2012). See also Jennifer Nash's (2008) discussion of what she views as fundamental paradoxes of the term.

44. In "It's All in the Family" (1998) and *Black Feminist Thought* (1990), Patricia Hill Collins has pointedly emphasized that even if black women's experiences as a marginalized group are specific to that group, there is need to bring on board entities that have experienced similar forms of oppression in ways that recognize cross-cutting interests

among marginalized groups. To her, different systems of oppression "mutually construct one another" (Collins 1998, 63). Nancy Tuana's concept of "viscous porosity" (2008) explains the paradoxical ways entities that are ordinarily thought to be separate are intertwined, such that sexism and racism, for example, reinforce each other.

45. Vivian M. May explains how various forms of power intersect in "dynamic, shifting ways" (2015, 23).

46. Studies that show the interrelatedness of oppressions are too numerous to list here. A few examples will suffice. Helena Pedersen points out that twenty-first-century critical animal studies provides "an intersectional approach to understanding the commonality of oppressions" (2011, 67). This means that different hierarchical ideologies (e.g. racism, speciesism, sexism, ableism, statism, and classicism) reinforce one another, and it is most productive to adopt holistic approaches to fight against them all at once. For an examination of the interface of animal rights and women's rights, see Lisa Kemmerer's *Sister Species: Women, Animal, and Social Justice* (2011), a collection of essays by fourteen activists. Carol J. Adams argues that feminism has long been aware of parallels between the butchering of animals and the oppression of women, who are often figured metaphorically as nonvegetarian food (2015 [1990], 41]). Emily Gaarder's *Women and the Animal Rights Movement* (2011a) also explores the symbolic and real connections between the abuse of women's rights and the abuse of animals. Gaarder reports that women she studied saw not only "the symbolic connections between women and animals, but also identified personal experiences they considered to be similar to those of animals in society, including violence, disempowerment, lack of voice, and treatment as objects" (2011b, 149). The introduction to Josephine Donovan and Carol J. Adams's edited volume, *The Feminist Care Tradition in Animal Ethics: A Reader* (2007), offers a usefully synthetic summary of women thinkers' arguments about animal and women's liberation since the nineteenth century. Alice J. Hovorka (2015) explores intersections of feminism and animal studies, while in their various similar discussions, Richard Twine (2001) and Maneesha Deckha (2008; 2012) include race, colonialism, and culture in feminist intersections with animal studies. In "Postcolonial Feminism" (2015), Deckha asserts that postcolonial feminism cannot be fully liberatory until it becomes posthuman and accepts nonhuman others. Also, see Kathryn Kirkpatrick's argument against ignoring animal rights in postcolonial and feminist scholarship (2015, 3). Syl Ko points out the danger of comparing oppressions of physical bodies as if they happen separately; the conceptual root of oppression of different groups is the tendency to code these groups, their subjectivities, and geographical locations as inferior and, therefore, "less than human," where "*human* is defined as superior and ideal white species" (2017, 89). The items in A. Breeze Harper's edited volume *Sistah Vegan* (2010) present the interlocking nature of oppression from the perspectives of African America female vegans.

47. Kim Roberts, in "Interlocking Oppressions" (2006, 605), and Sherryl Vint in *Animal Alterity* (2010, 135–36) see a correlation between violence toward women and children and abuse of animals. See also Kelly Oliver's *Animal Lessons,* where she argues that "in so far as it leaves intact traditional concepts of man and animal and the traditional

values associated with them, it [the masculinist presuppositions of humanism] cannot transform our ways of thinking about either" (2009, 19).

48. Angela Y. Davis (2016, 100) also underlines the interface between the struggles for human dignity and animal rights when she draws parallels between "race, gender and sexual non-conformity" and "racial bestialization." Sexist racial attack using animal metaphors is an assault "not only against humans but against the animals as well." For another recent reiteration of such connectedness, see Carol J. Adams and Lori Gruen's "Groundwork" (2014): For them, consists of constructs that "work in solidarity with those struggling against gender oppression, racism, homophobia and transphobia, environmental injustice, colonialism, speciesism, and environmental destruction" (35).

49. Following Jane Elliott and Derek Attridge, Olakunle George suggests in *African Literature and Social Change* (2017, 16) that there are fundamental concerns in African literature that new approaches to the literature must attend to.

CHAPTER 2

1. Other foundational figures in negritude include Aimé Césaire (Martinique) and Léon-Gontran Damas (French Guiana). Souleymane Bachir Diagne's *African Art as Philosophy* (2011 [2007]) offers a detailed philosophical meditation on Senghor's negritude, including Senghor's response to Rimbaud's poetic references to blackness and animality (90). For a discussion of negritude in the context of contemporary theories of cosmopolitanism, see Nadia Yala Kisukidi's "Nostalgia and Postcolonial Utopia in Senghor's Négritude" (2014). Reiland Rabaka (2015) explains the different strands of negritude as philosophical and artistic movement.

2. There is no need to belabor the blind spots in Western philosophers' attitudes toward animals; Kelly Oliver, Rosi Braidotti, and Matthew Calarco have done that quite well on our behalf, uncovering what Oliver calls "the latent humanism in antihumanist texts," enabling us to "witness the ambivalence toward animality and animals that has defined Western philosophy and culture" (Oliver 2009, 5). The ambivalence that Oliver notes in her study of Western thinkers is found in postcolonial writing as well, whereby a text differs from itself and there are multiple contradictions in the society presented.

3. As a child, Senghor reveals in the interview, "I was already raising doves in a cage" and in the palace, where he is the head of state, "trees, flowers, birds" surround him as he tries to replicate his passion for animals in his rural past as the son of a peasant woman.

4. See, for example, Adam Ashforth's notion of "negative *ubuntu*." This is the occult belief in the Soweto township that "a person can survive only to the extent that others in the community choose *not* to destroy him or her. How they might do so is less important than the fact that they can. And when they do, whether by physical or by occult violence, the demand for justice inevitably arises" (2005, 86).

5. Kai Horsthemke has, in *Animals and African Ethics*, explored the "gulf that exists between *botho/ubuntu* and concern for animals" (2015, 84), demonstrating what he

views as abuse of animals in traditional animal sacrifice rituals, such as the *Ukweshwama* of the KwaZulu-Natal region of South Africa. However, as Horsthemke also notes, recent strands of *ubuntu* in works by proponents such as Odora Hoppers, Mogobe B. Ramose, and Malegapuru William Makgoba emphasize ecological responsibility and humane treatment of animals. See also S. O. Oyewole's (2003) call for environmentalists to go beyond natural sciences and consider indigenous beliefs and practices. Since 2010, proponents of *ubuntu* have emphasized its respect for animals and the environment, which was only mentioned in passing in most of the early discussions of *ubuntu;* earlier discussions focused mainly on the human. For arguments that animal concerns are part of *ubuntu*, see Chuwa's *African Indigenous Global Bioethics* (2014, 18). Munyaradzi Mawere also outlines the role of *ubuntu* and other traditional knowledge systems in environmental conservation (2014), while Danford T. Chibvongodze views *ubuntu* as "an intimate relationship between humans and the natural environment" (2017, 157). Kapya John Kaoma's discussion of *ubuntu* in *God's Family, God's Earth* includes a brief discussion of how "the African dependence on the world of plant, insect, and animal species for remedies to social and psychological problems seems to confirm the unity and involvement of all living species in human life" (2013, 99). He suggests that Africans are aware that in some cases their recognition of the power of nature can lead to overexploitation of some species that humans need as remedies to social and psychological problems, including love potions made from animals. See also Edwin Etieyibo's "Ubuntu and the Environment" (2017), in which the thrust of the argument is that although foundational positions on *ubuntu* might appear anthropocentric, the values *ubuntu* propagates encourage a better attitude toward the environment than the exploitative individualistic system Western capitalism fosters.

6. In his *Nonviolence to Animals, Earth, and Self in Asian Tradition*, Christopher Key Chapple (1993) has described in detail the reverence that Hindu and Buddhist philosophical texts extend toward nonhuman animals. Tracing the evolution of the Indian concept of *ahimsa* (nonviolence) over time, Chapple argues that the concept started in ancient Asia, giving birth to Jainism and Buddhism and influencing certain Hindu practices, including the classical yoga school. The term's meanings have morphed, but ingrained in *ahimsa* is "not a political discipline or even a social theory, but the emotion of the horror of killing (or hurting) a living creature," as the earliest Vedic texts attest (Doniger 2009, 10).

7. William M. Adams's "Nature and the Colonial Mind" (2003) discusses in some detail the impact of colonialism on nature and precolonial conservation efforts, while Louise Fortmann and Calvin Nihra's "Local Management of Trees and Woodland Resources in Zimbabwe" (1992), for example, showcases some of the indigenous conservation practices in precolonial Africa. Most creative writers imagine the possibility of recuperating precolonial strategies of conserving nature and blending them with modern conservation practices.

8. Several scholars have argued that pre-Enlightenment and precolonial societies deemphasized the differences between animals and humans. For example, Mircea Eli-

ade argues that, before the European conquest of the postcolonial world, local people understood that life was multifaceted. They imitated animal gaits and appearances to underscore "a new dimension of life: spontaneity, freedom, 'sympathy' with all the cosmos" (1964 [1963], 460). For an outline of the way animals are regarded in the ancient cultures of France, Egypt, Mesopotamia, Mesoamerica, the Aztec empire, India, and Australia, see chapter 4 of Christopher Key Chapple's *Yoga and the Luminous* (2008). For a discussion of the postenlightenment emergence of the priority status currently accorded to humans vis-à-vis animals in Western cultures, see Laurie Shannon's *The Accommodated Animal* (2013). Akeel Bilgrami (2014) also outlines the postenlightenment conception of nature as an entity separate from the human in order to rationalize the exploitation of natural resources. Elsewhere, Bilgrami (2008) sees nationalists such as Mahatma Gandhi to be aligned with anti-Enlightenment European philosophers because Gandhi, in his *Hind Swaraj*, sees useful parallels between modern India and pre-Enlightenment Europe.

9. Leonard Chuwa expresses a similar position when he explains the African's reverence for the biosphere, including animals and nonliving components of the cosmos: "Since religion permeates all aspects of life in the culture of Ubuntu, there is no formal distinction between the sacred and the secular, between the religious and non-religious, between the spiritual and the material areas of life . . . morality permeates all aspects of life and environment. It matters how one treats wildlife or even non-living parts of creation" (Chuwa 2014, 57). Madondo M. Museka (2012) also argues for a conservation model that recognizes that in most African societies humans, nature, and the spiritual world are interdependent. Also see Munyaradzi Mawere's "Buried and Forgotten But Not Dead" (2012) for the argument that in precolonial Africa environmental conservation was based on the spiritual belief that humans and the environment are inseparable. From the perspective of African traditional religion, see Kofi Opoku, who argues that Africans treat animals as sacred beings because we share "the same faculties, and the same experience of life and death" (2006, 351). Similarly, localizing Christianity into African communities in northern Cameroon, theologian Jean-Marc Éla sees the African practice of the new faith to be best expressed through an indigenous belief in n the human entanglements with the nonhuman universe: "In our flesh all is united—tree and animal, water and wine, light and fire, word and bread—all assumed together by the incarnate Word" (Éla [1988] 2009, 43).

10. The term "ecological noble savage" is the shorthand for precolonial indigenous communities with conservation ethics embedded in their management of natural resources to enhance biodiversity. For the history of the term and debates about whether those communities practiced environmental conservation, see Raymond Hames's "The Ecologically Noble Savage Debate" (2007).

11. See, for example, Witi Ihimaera's *The Whale Rider* about the Māori of New Zealand and R. K. Narayan's *A Tiger for Malgudi* about Hindu mysticism.

12. There are numerous rich discussions of Asian and European traditions' treatment of animals. Quick examples include essays in the volume edited by Jeremy Bell

and Michael Naas, *Plato's Animals* (2015) and Neil Dalal and Chloë Taylor's *Asian Perspectives on Animal Ethics* (2014). Graham Harvey's wide-ranging *Animism: Respecting the Living World* (2006) engages the Ojibwe, Māori, and Australian Aboriginal philosophies, practices, and beliefs. Eduardo Viveiros de Castro's *From the Enemy's Mouth* is a detailed study of the Araweté community of the Amazonian region that includes an explanation of the thin line between animality, spirituality, and humanity in the local community (1992 [1986]). See also Viveiros de Castro's *Cannibal Metaphysics* (2014). Viveros de Castro's (1998) concept of "multinatural perspectivism" posits that, according to Amerindian cosmologies, there are multiple natures and that nonhuman elements consider themselves persons (and humans to be animals). In such a cosmogony, humanity is positional and can be assumed by other-than-human beings; everything is therefore human. Eduardo Kohn's *How Forests Think* offers a useful summary of the Amazonian perspective (2013, 95–97).

13. Braidotti's conception of the posthuman academy is similar to Fritjof Capra's "new vision of life," which "no well-established framework, either conceptual or institutional" is able to accommodate (Capra 1982, 265).

14. The maxim is also expressed as *ubutu ngumuntu abantu* (Zulu) or *motho ke motho ka batho* (Sotho). See Tom Bennett and James Patrick's "Ubuntu: The Ethics of Traditional Religion" (2011, 238).

15. Samuel A. Paul's words coincide with Buntu Mfenyana's. See also Villa-Vicencio (2009, 115). Buntu Mfenyana describes *ubuntu* along the nature-culture divide, as "the quality of being human . . . which distinguishes a human creature from an animal or spirit" (1986, 19).

16. Although he endorses Lessem's idea that "East and West have been able to meet because both are somewhat individualistic as opposed to the more communalistic Africa and Latin America," Barbara Nussbaum (2009, 106–8) reveals points of contact between some Western philosophy and Eastern practices.

17. For an outline of the criticism of *ubuntu* in South Africa, see Kai Horsthemke, *Animals and African Ethics* (2015, 80–92), and Doreen Eva Van Norren's "The Nexus between Ubuntu and Global Public Goods" (Norren 2014, 257–60).

18. For a discussion of *ubuntu* as an "inclusive" philosophy and practice, see Mnyaka and Motlhabi's "Ubuntu and its Socio-Moral Significance" (2009, 74). Using Steve Biko's idea of an African sense of community, Munyaka and Motlhabi emphasize that *ubuntu* means "being neighbourly and is imbued with a strong social consciousness" (2009, 73). Martin H. Prozesky (2009, 301–5) sees *Ukama* and *Ubuntu* as mutually defining concepts.

19. For typical examples of this romanticization, see, for example, J. Baird Callicott (1994) in *Earth's Insights* and Richard Brent Peterson in *Conversations in the Rain Forest* (2000), each of whom sets African attitudes toward the environment apart from European anthropocentrism.

20. Richard T. De George (1994) also sees anthropocentrism as a property of the rational and science-oriented European mindset. In his view, "only an anthropocentric

ethics is compatible with" the "presuppositions of science and technology." Thus, in the West, "polluting streams is not wrong because of what it does to the river or fish, but because of what it does to human beings. Endangering or eliminating species of animals or vegetable life is not wrong because of what it does to those species but because of what it does or might do to human beings, given the interconnections of the ecosystem that supports life" (De George 1994, 21).

21. Some anthropologists believe non-Western societies to be opposed to conservation. See, for example, Mary Douglas's 1954 essay on the Lele people of Kasai in the present-day Democratic Republic of Congo, in which she considered these people to be, in their anthropocentrism, completely opposed to conservation efforts of any kind because of their belief that animals are primarily meant for human use (1999 [1954], 16).

22. One of the proverbs is "That which scratches the wild animal, also scratches the human being." Mutwa interprets the proverb to mean that "if you do evil to wild animals, evil will ultimately rebound on your fellow human beings" (19). Another proverb from the Tswana community states that "He who buries the tree will next bury the wild animal, and after that bury his own ox, and ultimately bury his own children." To Mutwa, the proverb "indicates that people were aware, even in the ancient times, of the interdependence of living creatures upon this Earth, and that if you harm one, you harm others and in the end yourself" (19).

23. Michelè Pickover also sees animal liberation as "a natural progression of our humanity, embodying the concept of *ubuntu*" (2005, 171).

24. Drucilla Cornell's position is based on a qualification about *ubuntu* from a South African feminist judge, Justice Yvonne Mokgoro. See Mokgoro's "uBuntu and the Law in South Africa" (2012, 317–23).

25. Hanneke Stuit has examined in some detail the strategic commodification of *ubuntu* in South Africa (2016, 167–211).

26. Matthew Calarco offers a careful interpretation of Levinas's failure to transcend anthropocentrism despite his positive portrayal of the dog, which, in his view, is also a victim of the Nazis. Other scholars who have questioned Levinas's conclusion about the dog include Peter Atterton, Edward Casey, Alphonso Lingis, and David Wood.

27. For an elaboration of Nussbaum's ideas on animal capabilities, see her *Frontiers of Justice: Disability, Nationality, Species Membership* (2006, 325–407). Nussbaum avers that "all animals are entitled to continue their lives, whether or not they have such a conscious interest, unless and until pain and decrepitude make death no longer a harm" (2006, 393).

28. Written in the 1970s, the novel uses words that would today be considered pejorative (e.g., "tribe," "Bushmen," and "Masarwa"). Despite the awkwardness of some of my sentences, I avoid the use of the derogatory terms or use scare quotes, because almost all the current alternatives to "Masarwa" (e.g., "San") also have depreciatory undertones. In *Tears for My Land* (2010), Kiela Kiema explains the inappropriateness of the most of the terms used to name the group.

29. For a discussion of the use of similar animal tropes to dispossess the Irish in Victorian art, see Perry Curtis's *Apes and Angels* (1971, 45).

30. See also Alf Wannenburgh (1979, 28–29) for the observation that the "Bushmen" are more vegetarian than meat-eaters, preferring "a wide range of edible roots, bulbs, berries, fruits, melons, nuts and wild vegetables" (29).

31. Tom Bennett and James Patrick see refusal to engage with gay people as an act that "contradicts the whole idea of Ubuntu" (2011, 242).

32. Mazrui goes so far as to suggest that racism, individualism, and insularity are attributes of people in the colder Northern Hemisphere, people who experience the demands of harsh winters. However, he is quick to exonerate indigenous populations in cold pre-Columbian North America from these undesirable traits of Germanic Europeans. For his part, Baird Callicott argues that to the African, "the individualistic moral ontology of utilitarianism and its associated concepts of enlightened self-interest, and the aggregate welfare of social atoms, each pursuing his or own idiosyncratic 'preference satisfaction' seems foreign and incomprehensible" (1994, 158).

33. Nkrumah follows Anthony William Amo, reputed to be the first African philosopher to teach at a university.

34. Examples of writing in this disillusioned mode are too numerous to name here. Examples include Wole Soyinka's *The Interpreters* (1965), Achebe's *No Longer at Ease* (1960) and *A Man of the People* (1966), Ayi Kwei Armah's *The Beautyful Ones Are Not Yet Born* (1968), and Ama Ata Aidoo's *No Sweetness Here* (1969).

35. See Philippe Descola's *Beyond Nature and Culture* (2013 [2005]) and Graham Harvey's *Animism: Respecting the Living World* (2005). Marshall Sahlins offers a summary of the arguments in "On the Ontological Scheme of *Beyond Nature and Culture*" (2013).

36. For an outline of the various religion-based perspectives on animals, see Paul Waldau's "Religion and Animals" (2006, 69–83) and Erica Fudge's *Animal* (2002, 16–18).

37. For an erudite and beautifully written reading of Zakes Mda, see Jennifer Wenzel's *Bulletproof* (2009). In *Wilderness into Civilized Shapes* (2010), Laura Wright also provides an astute ecocritical reading of Mda's representation of the Xhosa culture, especially in relation to the Xhosa cattle killing in the 1850s.

38. Kitunda explains that killing a hyena is taboo among the Kamba because hyenas are ritual animals, "killed only if their predatory activities grow out of proportion" (Kitunda 2011, 133).

39. Usually paraphrased as "animals are good to think with," Lévi-Strauss's original is more playful: "Les espèces sont choisies non commes bonnes à manger, mais comme bonnes à penser" (1962, 128).

CHAPTER 3

1. The term *orature* was coined by Pio Zirimu in the early 1970s and given currency in a paper he co-wrote with Austin Bukenya, "Oracy as a Tool for African Development" (1986). See the explanation of the term and its origins in Ngũgĩ wa Thiong'o's *Penpoints, Gunpoints, and Dreams* (1998, 111). When I use the term "folk-

lore" here, it is not in a pejorative sense to connote lack of sophistication (as it does in African literary studies), but to suggest that art can belong to the "folk," the ordinary people. To align orature with the folk is to deemphasize individualism and to appreciate it as communal work. In this sense, while the oral artist displays individual talent, the performer is also, as Janheinz Jahn puts it, a "representative of all" members of the society (1961, 163).

2. Since the 1990s, African feminist scholars have exposed the misogyny and other forms of hegemony in indigenous expressions. Examples include work by Penina Mlama (1995), which exposes the hegemony of populist traditional practices, especially for nationalist purposes. Mlama notes the tendency of the people in positions of power in African societies to use oral literature to maintain those power positions. See also Micere Githae Mugo's *African Orature and Human Rights,* which concedes that although oral literature upholds principles of justice, it has "its moments of backwardness, for, some of it could be sexist, pro-patriarchal in values that deified the male principle and subdued the female, praiseworthy of wars and conquests etc." (1991, 38). Artistic works that portray the abuse of oral literature by the powers that be include Achebe's *A Man of the People* (1996).

3. For a discussion of the interface of postcoloniality and magical realism see Stephen Slemon's "Magic Realism and Post-Colonial Discourse" (1988, 9–24) and Ato Quayson's "Fecundities of the Unexpected" (2002). Brenda Cooper (1998) and Quayson (2009) also explore the interface from Africanist perspectives. Alternative terms for this practice include "animist realism" (Garuba 2003).

4. Wendy Doniger (1999) has a similar argument about precolonial India, in which she shows that inherent in Hindu texts is a deep respect for animals. In *The Big Conservation Lie,* John Mbaria and Mordecai Ogada (2017) bemoan the tendency in conservation circles to assume that indigenous Africans are against conservation efforts: "a casual examination of folklore, beliefs, and proverbs across Africa reveals a very intricate tapestry unerringly woven around the abundant biodiversity that people interacted with on a daily basis" (187). See also Tanure Ojaide's defense of precolonial African societies as organic environmentalists: unlike Europeans, who viewed animals and the environment as objects to make profits from, "the traditional African sees non-human beings as neighbors with whom to live harmoniously" (2018, 52).

5. He criticizes Marx and Engels's view of peasants in *Penpoints, Gunpoints, and Dreams* (Ngũgĩ 1998, 108),

6. The others in this series are Bathitoora ya Njamba Nene (1984), translated as *Njamba Nene's Pistol* (1986d), and *Njamba Nene na Cibu Kĩng'ang'i* (Njamba Nene and Chief Kĩng'ang'i/Njamba Nene and Chief Crocodile, 1986).

7. "Mĩhang'o ya Mbia" and "Mĩhang'o ya Mbeca" would translate as "aggressive hunt for money," as "mbia" (money) is synonymous with "mbeca."

8. We encounter in the Chilean Alejandro Zambra's *The Private Lives of Tree* trees with humanlike qualities similar to those in Ngũgĩ's *Njamba Nene and the Flying Bus.* But the trees in Zambra's novel do not speak in the real world. They are the products of a

character's imagination, in a story within another story that the character, Julián, creates to entertain his stepdaughter, Daniella.

9. In *The Ends of Allegory*, Sayre N. Greenfield has noted "how little allegory inheres in the text itself and how much depends upon the process of reading" (1998, 15).

10. A version of the story Micere Githae Mugo has collected from the Ndia community does not include this trial (1991, 26–29). Although shorter than Kenyatta's, it dwells in more detail on the harmony between animals and humans before the elephant evicted his host. The section narrating the ingratitude of the elephant is compressed seemingly to foreground the lost harmony between elephants and humans and to downplay the animal-human conflict.

11. Chinua Achebe was sufficiently impressed by the story to include it as "Gentlemen of the Jungle" (Kenyatta 1985) in *African Short Stories* (Achebe and Innes 1985). His statement in *Home and Exile* (2000) endorsing Kenyatta was made in the late 1990s at a time that Kenyatta's kleptomaniac tendencies as Kenya's first head of state (1963–1978) were well known. It is baffling that Achebe, a fierce critic of postindependence governance in *A Man of the People* (1966), *The Trouble with Nigeria* (1983), and *Anthills of the Savannah* (1987), would fail to see the dictatorial aspects in Kenyatta's character, after he detained Achebe's fellow writer Ngũgĩ wa Thiong'o without trial in 1977. The staunchly anticolonial Achebe is oblivious to the fact that Kenyatta was especially notorious in condoning poaching. Glen Martin has asserted that as a Mau Mau leader in the 1950s, Kenyatta "sustained his fighters in the field by killing elephants for both their meat and their tusks" (2012, 28). While some might defend this in an anticolonial context, giving priority to national liberation, Kenyatta continued the practice after becoming Kenya's first president of in 1964. According to Martin's interviews, Kenyatta allowed the continued sale of ivory after independence, issuing licenses to "favored ex-freedom fighters and allies" (Martin 2012, 29). Because of its obsession with classical colonialism, Achebe's approach fails to acknowledge such character flaws exhibited by a postindependence nationalist.

12. Achebe even identifies Malinowski, Kenyatta's mentor in writing *Facing Mount Kenya*, as a "celebrated anthropologist" (2000, 63). This is in spite of the fact that scholars such as Trinh T. Minh-ha find Malinowski's work to be almost of the same type of colonial apologia as Elspeth Huxley's, who was Malinowski's student at the London School of Economics at around the same time as Kenyatta (Minh-ha 1989, 74–76).

13. Early European ethnologists such as Werner noted the profusion of motifs referring to these economic activities in Wapokomo oral literature.

14. Werner finds it a curiosity that the Wapokomo would not kill monkeys and baboons for destroying crops; it is the European colonialists who do the killings (1913, 382). She also notes that the Wapokomo would protect crocodiles from extinction (361). She even claims that the Wapokomo had a different view of the finch, but research also showed that the Wanyika communities (to which Wapokomo belong) would neither kill nor eat finches, even if they were not regarded as totems or considered sacred (426).

15. Admittedly, this view is not consistent for Komora. His later work, *Sons of Sango*

(1973), is a cultural nationalist text that seeks to document the orature of his Pokomo society by sometimes celebrating stories about violence against animals.

16. For arguments against domestication of animals, including as pets, see Gary Francione and Anna E. Charlton's *Animal Rights: The Abolitionist Approach* (2015) and "The Case Against Pets" (2016). They argue that "non-human animals have a moral right not to be used exclusively as human resources, irrespective of whether the treatment is 'humane,' and even if humans would enjoy desirable consequences if they treated non-humans exclusively as replaceable resources." Shelter animals can only live with humans as "*refugees*," who "should not have existed in the first place" (Francione and Charlton, 2016).

17. This is a common trope. For example, Francis Imbuga's feminist play *Aminata* includes a proverb in which small animals are deluded into thinking they are eating big ones while they are actually eating fellow small animals. To the headman in the play, Aminata is "the egret that pulls ticks from a bull's back and thinks it is eating the bull" (1989, 15). He means that she has bitten off more than she can chew by challenging the patriarchal traditions he represents. We are not supposed to agree with the speaker of this line, a foil to the heroine, but the proverb captures the notion of oppression among small animals.

18. The Swahili word for "brotherhood" (*udugu*) is not gendered. Wamitila describes Komora's story as "displaying a folkoristic approach to political themes" (1997, 121).

19. In Euphrase Kezilahabi's *Mzingile,* the ideal world captured in the Kiswahili novella's dénouement is where, after all the conflicts in the world have been resolved, no animal will eat another animal's flesh: "Wanyama wamerudi katika upya wao! . . . Humo bondeni . . . tuliona wanyama wengi wakichunga kwa pamoja. Wote walikuwa wakila majani, hata simba, fisi na chui. Twiga na ngamia walikuwa wakitazamana kwa tabasamu. Simba na kifaru walikuwa wakifanya mchezo wa kupimana nguvu. Wanyama wadogowadogo walikuwa wakichunga pembeni kidogo" (1991, 69). [The animals reverted to their newness . . . in the wilderness . . . we saw many animals grazing together . . . they were all eating leaves, even the lion, hyena, and leopard. The gazelle and the camel eyed each other, all smiles. The lion and the rhino played together, sizing each other's strength. Smaller animals grazed at the edges.]

20. Jacques Derrida coined the word *animot* to express the inadequacy of the word "animal," which lumps together all living creatures that are not human. For Derrida, we should recognize that "there is already a heterogeneous multiplicity of the living" and "one will never have the right to take animals to be the species of a kind that would be named the Animal, or animal in general" (2008 [2006], 31).

21. Although the Swahili word for human being (*binadamu*) is gender-free, the *binadamu* in the story is graphically represented in the background as a militaristic male with a spear (16).

22. According to Stephen Budiansky: "Domestic dogs, sheep, goats, cattle, and horse far outnumber their wild counterparts. The global population of sheep and cattle today each exceeds one billion; their wild counterparts teeter on the brink of extinction" (1992, 61).

23. This is similar to the views expressed by David Lack in *The Natural Regulation of Animal Numbers* (1970, 88–106) and Stephen St. C. Bostock in *Zoos and Animals* (1993, 64). For Bostock, it is "only too true that captive animals often live longer than wild ones; for many animals, it must be true that only with man's protection have they any chance of dying of (as we say) old age" (1993, 64). Bostock argues that that zoos can protect animal rights. For a critique of arguments that support keeping animals in zoos (e.g., for amusement, education, scientific research, and preservation of endangered species), see Dale Jamieson's "Against Zoos" (2006, 134–40). She concludes that "because what zoos teach us is false and dangerous, both humans and other animals will be better off when they are abolished" (Jamieson 2006, 142).

24. In *African Perspectives on Colonialism,* Boahen lists L. H. Gann, P. Duignan, Margery Perham, P. C. Lloyd, and D. K. Fieldhouse as representative of the "many European and Eurocentric" historians who have claimed that the impact of colonialism was more positive than negative (1987, 94). Their position, he notes, is strongly contradicted in works by Marxist and materialist critics of colonialism, including Walter Rodney and T. B. Kabwegyere. In this book, Boahen discusses what he considers as the positive aspects of colonialism, which are deemphasized in his later posthumous book, *African Perspectives on European Colonialism* (2011).

25. See also Eileen Julien's *African Novels and the Question of Orality* (1992). She emphasizes that the modern novel adapts orature to modern sensibilities. The works should be read "not as a natural derivation of an oral tradition but as a meaningful reappropriation of an oral narrative genre" (Julien 1992, 157).

26. This contrasts with the treatment of the wilderness in Ogot's *The Promised Land.*

27. Except where otherwise indicated, all the translations are mine.

28. In a dictionary of Kiswahili proverbs, Kitula King'ei interprets the proverb to mean "kitendo cha ukarimu hakisahauliki" (a good deed is never forgotten). The proverb is "himizo tuwe wakarimu" (a call to us to be kind) (King'ei 2009 [1989], 366).

29. For a survey of the sociological use of orature in African writing, see Emmanuel Obiechina's *Culture, Tradition, and Society in the West African Novel* (1975 25–41) and "Narrative Proverbs in the African Novel" (1992).

30. In *Bullet Proof,* Jennifer Wenzel (2009) follows Walter Ong in reading African writing as an afterlife of orature. The process of transforming oral art is not confined to orature-to-writing changes. Even the art in oral mode is always changing. Mara Goldman is therefore correct when she reminds us that oral literature involves transformation of materials depending on the occasion and audience. Among the Maasai, whose oral art she studies, narratives from the past are "modified by the narrator differently for different contexts" (97).

31. The myth cannot be based on fact because, as Juliet Clutton-Brock observes in *A Natural History of Domesticated Mammals* (1999), the animals referred to in the story behave differently from livestock; livestock thrive in groups and have a social structure that "predisposes them to leadership by a herdsman" (73). By contrast, the animals in the story that Chege tells Waiyaki and that Henry ole Kulet's changes in *Vanishing Herds*

(2011) are different socially and "were not domesticated in the ancient world" (Clutton-Brock 1999, 73).

32. Roland Barthes (1972 [1957] 143) notes the tendency in the modern petit-bourgeois society to use myths to elide all difference and make unfair power relationships appear as the natural order of things.

33. For the Samburu version of the story that portrays women as bad managers of livestock, see James Wachira's "Discourses in Samburu Oral Animal Praise Poetry" (2011, 124). In another study of the Samburu, Wachira observes that the community does not have a word for "wild animal," as "for the Samburu, all animals are creatures whose cooperation they [the humans] need" (2016, 115).

34. Ole Kulet makes a similar choice in *Blossoms of the Savannah* (2008) and *Elephant Dance* (2017), which examine the themes of gender, corruption, and environmental justice. They both won the Jomo Kenyatta Prize for Literature on publication, and *Blossoms* was selected as a text in Kenyan schools in 2018.

35. In a critique of this position, which he revises later, Alasdair Cochrane sees nothing wrong in changing nonhuman animals into man-made artifacts, because "the implicit assumption behind this thinking is that what is natural must be considered morally good and worth preserving as it exists presently" (2014, 158).

36. Many plays inspired by orature dramatize animal life and speech in anthropomorphic terms. An example of a play that features animal characters is the Egyptian Tawfiq Al-Hakim's absurdist *The Fate of the Cockroaches*, a popular work in sub-Saharan African universities. It opens with a scene in which cockroaches talk to one another. However, the play is human-centered in that much of the humor and irony in the scene derives from the mistaken views of the cockroaches about the dirty bathtub they consider to be their vast kingdom. The cockroaches are used to allegorize the downtrodden human populations in postindependence Egypt.

37. The narrating animal features in Tolstoy's "The Horse" and Kafka's "A Report to the Academy" and "Investigations of a Dog," as well as in contemporary stories such as Patrick Neate's *The London Pigeon Wars* (2003). Grace Nichol's "Cat Rap" (2005) is a humorous poem that alludes to T. S. Eliot's cat poems to subtly comment on race among black immigrants in Britain. An influential text in this subgenre is R. K. Narayan's *A Tiger for Malgudi*, a novel about the relationship between an Indian ascetic and a narrating tiger. See Wendy Woodward's essay on animal narrators for a list of works that use this device (2016, 235).

38. Nganang has said that both oral sources and modern texts have influenced the composition of the novel (Reid 2006, 212).

39. In March 1985, the Cameroonian government made it illegal to import, possess, sell, distribute, or circulate a book of essays by Ruben Um Nyobé, *Le problème national kamerounais* (1984; The National Problem in Cameroon). Nganang himself was in 2017 detained by the Biya government for criticizing it in op-ed articles, and although he carried a Cameroonian passport, was deported to the United States, where he is based.

40. For an analysis of Honwana's narrative, see Wendy Woodward's *The Animal Gaze* (2008a, 114–16). She devotes a chapter to dogs, discussing Honwana's story alongside works by J. M. Coetzee, Olive Schreiner, Melina Rork, Es'kia Mphahlele, Herman Charles Bosman, and Njabulo Ndebele. For a survey of the figure of the dog in the Southern African literature, see Woodward's "Social Subjects" (2008b, 235–62).

41. For example, to Sylvia Wynter (1990), we need to consider how visibility is achieved or given and what the subject achieves from the visibility.

42. For a powerful critique of this phenomenon, see Ketu Katrak's "Indian Nationalism, Gandhian Satyagraha, and Representations of Female Sexuality" (1991), Sangeeta Ray's *En-Gendering India* (2000), and Mineke Schipper, "Mother Africa on a Pedestal" (1987).

43. Charles Hockett lays out the design properties of a language that denies animal communication the property of prevarication (ability to tell lies) and self-reflexivity (ability to communicate about the modes of communication).

44. Reading Virginia Woolf, Cuddy-Keane defines the "auscultizer" as the agential characters doing the listening in a text (2013 [2000], 71). It is from what they hear that the story is sifted to the reader.

45. Rebecca Walkowitz (2006) has discussed in detail the subversive use of triviality in cosmopolitan fictions.

46. For example, a similar approach is seen in works based on Indian folklore, such as Suniti Namjoshi's *Aditi and the One-Eyed Monkey,* in which even the dragon that causes droughts is not killed at the end of the story. The dragon brings about ecological disasters "for fun" and because it gets "bored flying around all by myself. Besides, I like attention" (72). It is an enemy of the environment, and we might wish it to die. But the girl Aditi and her animal friends (the one-eyed monkey and an ant) negotiate with the dragon to stop its destructive habits. The dragon even flies the adventurers in the story home, and the earlier acts of animal-on-animal violence come to an end, with the dragon becoming the nurse for the lion's cubs.

CHAPTER 4

1. Charlotte Sleigh has noted that the apathy toward insects in scholarship is linked to funding. To justify funding, the researchers "needed to convince their audiences that insects were a serious problem requiring professional attention" (2006, 282). See also Paolo Palladino's *Entomology, Ecology, and Agriculture* (1996).

2. Popular since the 1920s, *taarab* is an East African genre of sung poetry that draws on the musical traditions of the Bantu cultures of the region as well as work from North Africa, the Middle East, and the Indian subcontinent. For a discussion of the cultural politics inherent in this music, see Mwenda Ntarangwi's *Gender, Performance and Identity* (2001) and Kelly Askew's *Performing the Nation* (2002).
why the people presented in theultural politics inherent in this music. read as a symbol. with why the people presented in the

3. Several scholars have discussed the representations of insects as symbols of hu-

man relationships and actions. See, for example, Bruce Clarke's *Allegories of Writing: The Subject of Metamorphosis* (1995, 84–87); Kathleen Ferris's *James Joyce and the Burden of Disease* (1995); Cristopher Hollingsworth's *Poetics of the Hive* (2001); Charlotte Sleigh's *Ant* (2003); David Spooner's *The Insect-Populated Mind* (2005); James Carney's "The Buzzing of B" (2012); Angela Moorjani's "The Dancing Bees in Samuel Beckett's *Molloy*" (2013); and Sheng-mei Ma's *Asian Diaspora and East-West Modernity* (2012).

4. In Roy's novel about postcolonial India, insects and other small animals consume the books of the "Imperial Entomologist Pappachi," reducing the "organized information" in them to "yellow lace" (155). For some readings of the insects in the novel, see chapter 10 of Dirk Wiemann's *Genres of Modernity: Contemporary Indian Novels in English* (2008, 259–61).

5. Anias Mutekwa uses Eve K. Sedgwick's triangular model to see the relationship between the brothers as "homosocial" (2013, 357). According to Mutekwa, they boys bond in a homosocial relationship to oppress the crow.

6. Generally, in Bantu metaphysics, we are supposed to see "human and all other forms of contingent life as a gift, an unmerited token of divine magnanimity" (Ruwa'ichi 1990, 106). Such an attitude should be extended to the crow in the story.

7. Studies linking big-game hunting to imperialism include J. A. Mangan and Callum McKenzie's *Militarism, Hunting, Imperialism* (2010) and Joseph Sramlek's "Face Him Like a Briton" (2006),

8. Franz K. Stanzel observes that the meaning of a first-person narrative derives from "the references and relationships between the fictional world and the figure of the authorial narrator and from the resulting tensions in values, judgments, and kinds of experience" (1971 [1955], 28).

9. In *Animal Liberation* Peter Singer has also recommended vegetarianism as one of the available ethical options in ensuring animal rights (2009 [1975], 160). Hunting for food is what Varner calls "subsistence hunting," that which is "aimed at securing food for human beings" (1998, 100). Gary L. Francione (2010, 17) reads Tom Regan as an advocate for animal welfare who would accept the killing or domestication of animals in certain circumstances. He is equally critical of Peter Singer for regarding "animal life as having less value than human life" (2010, 10).

10. Musaemura Zimunya reads the boys in a similar way. Their act is "irrational" and "monomaniacal," amounting to a "grotesque rite of passage"; the crow, on the other hand, is "innocence incarnate" (Zimunya 1982, 63).

11. In a popularly quoted declaration, Alice Walker pronounces that "the animals of the world exist for their own reasons. They were not made for humans any more than black people were made for white, or women created for men" (14).

12. Elsewhere, using the English moral philosopher R. M. Hare's ethics, Varner argues that "just as technological advances may have made it inappropriate for Inuits to continue practicing infanticide, technological advances may make it inappropriate for people in affluent, developed nations to use animals in ways that would have been appropriate in earlier times" (2010, 38).

13. Zhuwarara associates the boys' superstitions with "traditional African beliefs" (32).

14. A particularly compelling example of the child as representative of prelapsarian innocence can be found in Camara Laye's narrator in *The African Child.*

15. In "Why Look at Animals," John Berger advances a similar view by contrasting the kindness to animals in preindustrial Europe with the hostilities toward nonhuman animals in modern societies. However, Nicole Shukin notes in *Animal Capital* (2009, 33–34) that we should be careful to see the figure of animal as both historical and contingent, rather than universal and totalizing as implied in Berger's observation.

16. Building on Levi-Strauss, Philippe Descola (2013 [2005], 292–94) sees totemism as an ontology that compares humans with animals, but does not treat animals as humans.

17. For instance, Marais insinuates that termites have a central command system in which the queen serves as the brain, but Deborah Gordon's research reveals that this is not the case. She argues that while artistic representations of ants impose on the insects the kind of social hierarchies found in human societies, "a real ant colony operates without direction or management" (2010, 59). But Gordon also sees an ant colony as analogous to a brain (1999, 143). While Marais sees the queen as the centralized brain, Gordon's analogy sees individual insects as playing the role of neurons.

18. Wehner (2003) is among the students of insects who later demonstrated that, although the ant has a small brain, the insect is able to solve complex problems.

19. Carolyn Korsmeyer (2011) argues that that disgust, alongside other discomforting feelings, can be transformed in literary works into an expression of aesthetic beauty.

20. See a similar summary in Ngũgĩ's *Weep Not, Child* (1964, 25–26).

21. Examples include Achebe's *Arrow of God,* in which Ezeulu famously concedes, in spite of himself, that change is inevitable and his sons should go to school and be his "eyes there" because "the world is a Mask dancing. If you want to see it well you do not stand in one place" (Achebe 1986 [1964], 44–46).

22. The line "On the Earthen Floor" is from Oswald Mbuyiseni Mtshali's poem "Inside my Zulu Hut" (1989 [1974], 36), which celebrates the African's connectedness to the natural world.

23. In *A Dance of Masks,* Jonathan Peters (1978, 100–1) also reads the descent of the locusts on Umuofia as symbolizing the imminent arrival of Europeans in the Igbo land. See Obiechina's "Narrative Proverbs in the African Novel" (1992), in which he argues that "it is as if by opening the mythic 'caves' from which the locusts emerge, the 'stunted men,' the Igbo equivalent of the fates of Greek mythology, also open up a pestilential phase of events that would consume the hero and quicken the tempo of the fall of the old dispensation" (209). Also see Mac Fenwick's "Realising Irony's Post/Colonial Promise" (2010 [2006], 104–6). Abiola Irele's (2000) analysis of the novel also notes the ambivalence the locusts in the story.

24. The narrator in *Things Fall Apart* personifies the locusts, saying, "At first, a fairly small swarm came. They were the harbingers sent to survey the land" (48).

25. For a survey of the use of images of insects as food in different cultural texts, see Sarah Gordon's "Entomophagy: Representations of Insect Eating in Literature and Mass Media" (2006, 342–62).

26. For another example, see Micere Mugo's poem "Locusts Retreating," in which exuberant optimism is expressed in the form of retreat of imagined locusts (Mugo 1976 [1969]a, 60).

27. In the Indian Ocean, the phenomenon *kimbunga* designates is called a "cyclone," but it is widely translated as "hurricane." I use the latter for convenience. As a *taarab* song, the peom is called "Kitendawili" (Riddle). See Kimani Njogu (2004, 42–45).

28. For example, Mwinyihatibu Mohamed, a poet from Tanga in Tanzania, has a similarly titled poem about the rising cost of living in Tanzania and the failure of the postcolonial leadership to provide a solution to the problems facing the citizens (1977, 87).

29. Mahmood Mamdani, in *When Victims Become Killers: Colonialism, Nativism, and the Genocide in Rwanda* (2001), explains the role of colonial and postcolonial dehumanization of Rwandans in sparking and legitimizing acts of violence against the Tutsi, whom the Hutu, according to Mamdani, saw as a foreign racial category. For a brief discussion of the speciesist use of animal images to shore up racism, see Jacklyn Cock's *The War Against Ourselves* (2007, 138–39). She criticizes antiracists who remain anthropocentric, arguing that "they were only concerned with their own species" and "it is this lack of concern that allows the abuse of animals to continue" (139). Christopher Hollingsworth has also explained the wide usage of insect metaphors to label marginalized groups (2006).

30. For a biography of Mwinyihatibu Mohamed, see M. M. Mulokozi and T. S. Y. Sengo's *History of Kiswahili Poetry* (1999, 46–47).

31. For a discussion of the changing conventions in Kiswahili poetic traditions and their ideological implications, see Joshua Madumulla, Elena Bertoncini, and Jan Blommaert, "Politics, Ideology, and Poetic Form: The Literary Debates in Tanzania" (1999, 314–16). In his *Swahili Beyond the Boundaries*, Alamin Mazrui discusses in detail the aesthetic and political debates surrounding various forms of Swahili poetry (2007, 45–82). See also Mulokozi and T. S. Y. Sengo's sociological exposition on Swahili prosody in their *History of Kiswahili Poetry* (1999, 86–89).

32. The others without a human being in them are a crossword chessboard, a coat of arms, and a croquet mallet.

33. For a detailed discussion of such vitality, see Jane Bennett's *Vibrant Matter* (2009).

34. *Illustrated London News* reports that 200 local people were killed.

35. Examples of such work include Amitav Ghosh's *The Hungry Tide* and Chachage's *Makuadi wa Soko Huria*, Farah's *Crossbones*, and Helon Habila's *Water on Oil*.

36. Some of the work in which chewa features is presented as compositions by God. See for example "Utenzi wa Nabii Yunus" by M. Burhan Mkelle (1978, 1–16). The animal is called *tewa* in this rendition of the story of Jonah from the Quran. But it is glossed in standard Kiswahili as *chewa*.

37. According to Laurence Venuti, assimilative translations are those that smooth out the original so much that a reader of the translated text would not be able to tell that it was originally in a different language.

38. See also Faisal Fatehali Devji's "Subject to Translation: Shakespeare, Swahili, Socialism" (2000, 181–89) for a discussion of race in Nyerere's translation.

39. For a survey of the poetry emerging from this rivalry between Siu and Zanzibar, see Jan Feidel and Ibrahim Noor Shariff's "Kibabina's 'Message about Zanzibar'" (1986, 496–524).

40. For an example of nonvegetarian treatment of *kitoweo*, see Edward Steere's *Swahili Tales, as Told by Natives of Zanzibar* (1870, 20).

CHAPTER 5

1. See, for example, Jackson Biko's catalog of incidents in which Kenyan men have their way with animals in "What Are We Doing to Ourselves?" (2013).

2. The report describes the Reer-Isaaq subclan as having "a liking for sheep and goats, while the Reer Abdille (another subclan) feels at ease with equines—horses, mules and donkeys" (Omer 2012).

3. Similar conceptions of "queerness" as practices, affiliations, and frames of thought that are in a space of opposition to the dominant order are found in most works by queer theorists, including David Halperin in *Saint Foucault* (1995) and Cathy Cohen's "Punks, Bulldaggers, and Welfare Queens" (1997).

4. For Carmen Dell'Aversan, "just as heteronormativity grotesquely maintains that any member of the 'opposite sex' is more appropriate, suitable and attractive as a sexual partner than any member of one's own, humanormativity maintains that *all* members of one species (*Homo sapiens*) have more in common with one another than any of them can have with any member of any other species" (2010, 76). She argues that it is to maintain humanormativity that queer animal-human relations are most strongly opposed.

5. Halperin defines "pederasty" as a hierarchical, nonreciprocal, and nonegalitarian sexual practice involving "the male sexual penetration of a subordinate male—subordinate in terms of age, social class, gender style, and/or sexual role" (2002, 113). It is "sex as hierarchy, not mutuality, sex as something done to someone by someone else, not a search for shared pleasure" (115).

6. For example, in Mwangi Gicheru's *The Mixers* (1991), cows in heat display same-sex desire because in a racist society the bulls of black natives, the only available heterosexual mates, cannot be allowed to mingle with the cows of the white expatriates.

7. Interested readers can download the cartoon from Gado's website: http://gadocartoons.com/wp-content/uploads/2013/05/May-27-12-Milking-and-F%EF%80%A1@ing-the-cow-dry.jpg

8. Critics who view sex with animals as tantamount to sexual assault include Piers Beirne (1997; 2002; 2009), Karen Davis (2001), and Margo DeMello (2012). For an outline of the relationship between misogyny and sexual exploitation of animals, see Carol

J. Adams's "After MacKinnon: Sexual Inequality in the Animal Movement" (2001).

9. For the images, see Hatje Cantz's *Jane Alexander* (2002), which includes contextual discussions of the art, as does the more theoretically inclined Pep Subirós's *Jane Alexander: Surveys* (2011). Kobena Mercer's "Postcolonial Grotesque" (2013 [2011]), first published in Subirós's volume, examines the optimism inherent in Alexander's hybrids. See also John Peffer's *Art and the End of Apartheid* (2009, 63–67), a reading of Alexander's *Butcher Boys* (2011).

10. F. Fiona Moolla's *Reading Farah* (2014) and John Masterson's *The Disorder of Things* (2013) are among the recent work examining Nuruddin Farah's writing. In *Different Shades of Green,* Byron Caminero-Santangelo (2014, 60–74) gives *Secrets* an ecocritical reading.

11. In this, Farah parallels Carol Adams's observation, in *The Sexual Politics of Meat* (2015 [1990], xx), on the legitimization of the use of pornographic ads to awaken meat-eaters from their complacency. For an elaboration of the linkage between pornography and meat-eating, see Carol Adams's *The Pornography of Meat* (2003).

12. Wayne C. Booth (1961) identifies as reliable one who "speaks for or acts in accordance with the norms of the work (which is to say the implied author's norms), unreliable when he does not" (158–59).

13. Susan Lanser's *The Narrative Act* (1981) identifies two levels of authority: the mimetic and the diegetic. Under the diegetic authority she isolated such aspects as authorial equivalence and gender and racial privilege; mimetic authority covers reliability and competence of the narrator. In Farah's novel, the narrator possesses neither of these levels of authority.

14. Said Samatar (2000, 142) says he called his doctor to ask if what Farah describes in this sentence is possible: "When I couldn't breathe because my nasal passages were clogged, my father took my nose in his mouth and, at a single drag, sucked the unease out of me, phlegm and mucus and all."

15. See also Mohamed Adillahi Rishash's (1988) discussion of the philosophical and literary importance of the camel in Somali literatures. In the survey of the camel motif in proverbs, work songs, love songs, dances, and other genres of performance art among the Somali, Rishash concludes that "camel herding" has "shaped the Somalis' destiny and greatly influenced the attitudes towards themselves and towards others," as camels, "like gold, are the standard unit for measuring everything that is of value in life" (1988, 66). For a discussion of the use and misuse of camels and other animals under colonialism, including Somali camels, see James Louis Hevia's *Animal Labor and the Colonial Warfare* (2018), in which he shows that the West was largely ignorant about camels and treated them in cold-blooded utilitarian terms.

16. Ibrahim al-Koni *Gold Dust* (2016 [1990]) presents an intimate relationship between a man and his camel. Although the novel blurs the boundary between the human and the camel, the intimacy is not sexual.

17. In *When Men Are Women,* John Colman Wood also notes that among the Gabra "camels are seldom killed for meat" (1999, 54).

18. In the fifth chapter of his *Shakespeare's Ocean* (2012, 105–35), Brayton offers a useful survey of the depiction of whales in the Western literary canon.

19. Personal interview: "No, I don't know that writer's work."

20. In a personal interview, Mda says: "I know I do mention the Dreaming that I learned about from the Aborigines when I was in Adelaide, Australia (they are not Māori) and the shark callers of Papua New Guinea that I learned about from my girlfriend who used to live with them there. The only other indigenous people that I think I mention (though I don't remember very well, it's more than 10 years since I had contact with that book) are the Khoikhoi of South Africa."

21. Imbuga's reference to a folktale about "the rabbit which wished to lay eggs" in *Aminata* (1988, 35) underscores the belief in traditional African societies that it is unwise to want to change from the customary order of things. But the feminist play about the role of a modern woman in society is against this belief and portrays the character who refers to the story as stuck in the past. The story is disnarrated, only being referred to in passing.

22. Gerald Hensley's *Friendly Fire: Nuclear Politics and the Collapse of ANZUS, 1984–1987* (2013) and Malcolm Templeton's *Standing Upright Here: New Zealand in the Nuclear Age* (2006) outline the protests against nuclear testing in New Zealand at around the time Ihimaera wrote *The Whale Rider*.

23. See also Marleen de Witte's "Of Corpses, Clay, and Photographs" for a description of the Ashanti notions of death (2011, 181–85).

24. This is an addition Worden makes to the first edition of the book published in 1982. The earlier version followed the Freudian model of grief and mourning.

25. By calling herself Brema, the narrator is probably signaling to the evangelist couple that they should stop bothering her because she follows a different Protestant tradition, as "Brema" is the name Ghanaians from the Volta region call followers of Bremen Mission. See Lewis H. Gann and Peter Duignan's *Rulers of German Africa* (1977, 164).

26. Freud observes that, when in "heightened self-criticism" a person suffering melancholia "describes himself as petty egoistic, dishonest, lacking in independence, one whose sole aim has been to hide the weaknesses of his own nature, it may be, so far as we know, that he has come pretty near to understanding himself" (1966, 255). In her *Positive Illusions*, Shelley E. Taylor points out that "the mildly depressed appear to have more accurate views of themselves, the world, and the future than do normal people" (1989, 213). While distinguishing melancholia from depression, Julia Kristeva maintains in *Black Sun* (1989 [1987]) a similar position to Freud's about the creative impulses of melancholia, especially in her commentaries on Holbein, Nerval, and Dostoyevsky.

27. In Aidoo's *Changes* (1991), the protagonist Esi divorces her husband after an incident of marital rape and remarries Ali Kondey, a charming polygamous philanderer, who offers material gifts but little love. While endorsing change from an abusive marriage, the story suggests that the changes Esi makes are not substantial.

28. For such interpretations of Sissie as a queer character who is reluctant to identify herself as lesbian, see, for example, Onuora Benedict Nweke's "Homosexual Tendencies

and Unconscious Determinants" (2009). Hildegard Hoeller's "Ama Ata Aidoo's Heart of Darkness" (2004), and Brenna M. Munro's "States of Emergence: Writing African Female Same-sex Sexuality" (2017).

29. See Eric G. Wilson's *The Melancholy Android* (2006, 26) for an explanation of the mixture of love and hate in a melancholic individual.

30. Pramod Nayar (2010) observes, "the anonymity of identities in cyberspace enables queer people to find a space where . . . [they] can communicate and form a community without fear of 'discovery.' The Internet allows personal preferences to circulate without revealing the physical address or identity of the advertiser" (133).

31. They are responding to the argument exemplified by Lundblad when he claims that "animals must be driven essentially, if not exclusively, by heterosexual and violent instincts" (2010, 748). Aldo Poiani's *Animal Homosexuality* (2010) is a detailed discussion of nonnormative sexuality among nonhuman animals.

32. Midas Dekkers's *Dearest Pet* (1994 [1992]) is one of the texts that covers the representations of human-animal sex in Western cultures, broadly and in detail.

CODA

1. It is worth noting that coincidence is not a device exclusive to literatures of the Global South. James Joyce saw it as "a characteristic of his tendency towards an expansive inclusivity in his approach to writing" (Jordan 2010, 1). Julia Jordan (2010) offers a detailed examination of the use of chance in modern British writing, but she also draws on the use of the technique in classical works. Indeed, no technique is exclusive to Western or non-Western literatures; it is how well it is used and the contextual functions it serves that matter

2. See, for example, analyses of posthumanism in African American writing in such works as Kristen Lillvis's *Posthuman Blackness and the Black Female Imagination* (2017) and Cristin Ellis's *Antebellum Posthuman* (2018). Bénédicte Boisseron's *Afro-Dog: Blackness and the Animal Question* (2018) explores animality in black Francophone writing.

3. As we have already seen, postcolonial scholars (e.g., Mbiti 1990 [1969], 7–8) find the term "animism" inappropriate, even derogatory. I use it here in the nonderogatory sense Descola (2009, 150) uses it, whereby humans (the Amazonian communities in his case) regard themselves as sharing characteristics of their interiorities with nonhuman entities. Tim Ingold's *The Perception of the Environment* (2000) also sees circumpolar societies as exhibiting "animist" understanding of the world as "home to innumerable beings whose presence is manifested in this form or that, each engaged in the project of forging a life in a way peculiar to its kind. But in order to live, every such being must constantly draw upon the vitality of others" (113). For an essay on indigenous nature-culture reciprocity, including a review of texts that claim that indigenous populations participated in the despoliation of the environment, see Michael E. Harkin's "Swallowing Wealth" (2007).

4. Writing from colonial Guyana, Vincent Roth recounts that "in the Colony, . . . as

in many other places, attacks on adult human beings are of exceedingly rare occurrence" (1941, 136). The instances Roth narrates about humans being attacked by a jaguar involve the people encroaching on the animals' natural habitat.

5. Recent scholarship on animal mourning includes essays in *Mourning Animals: Rituals and Practices Surrounding Animal Death* (2016), which focus on the way humans mourn animals; Barbara J. King's *How Animals Grieve* (2013), a study of how various animals (e.g., birds, elephants, apes) respond to death; and Jane Desmond's *Displaying Death and Animating Life* (2016), which includes a discussion on the possibility that animals mourn. In Carew's *Black Midas,* the parrot Echo's emotional capacity to mourn is clearly recognized.

6. The love scenes are omitted from the school edition of the novel, abridged for Longman by Sylvia Wynter in 1969.

7. The term "disnarration" was coined in 1980 by Gerald Price to designate silences in a text whereby the narrator skips details about events that are supposed to have happened in the referential world. A related term is "unnarration," coined by Robyn Warhol, to describe a situation where the narrator indicates that he or she cannot tell us what happened, although the narrative indicates that that event took place.

8. The same imperative is used in Ng'ang'a Mbugua's *Angels of the Wild,* in which we know people eat meat, but they are never shown eating it. The protagonist Birgen, with whom the novella's young target and ideal audience would identify, skips a meal in which meat is served. The dishes he likes the most are "all manner of fruits, food and drinks in the refrigerator" at his uncle's home (Mbugua 2015, 8). The "food" is likely to be nonvegan, but the text suppresses that fact. He may also have skipped the meat dish because of eagerness to leave for a game drive, not because of vegan beliefs. However, the nonvegan reasons are suppressed in the narrative.

9. Peter Hulme argues it is possible that the cannibals presented in the text may have existed, but it mainly a product of the colonial imagination. See also Greg Pollock's "The Cannibal-Animal Complex in Melville, Marx, and Beyond," (2010, 10).

10. Titled *Beyond the Gates,* the 2005 film presents dogs eating corpses during the Rwanda genocide of 1994. The UN peacekeepers are forbidden from killing the marauding militants, so the peacekeepers kill the dogs. For a discussion of the film, see Nigel Eltringham's "Showing What Cannot Be Imagined" (2013) and "Besieged History?" (2008).

11. This is similar to the reason why Maneesha Deckha asks animal studies theorists to consider race and culture in their work if they are to avoid being accused of ethnocentricism and elitism (2012, 534).

BIBLIOGRAPHY

Abani, Chris. 2008. "On Humanity." TED Talk. https://www.ted.com/talks/chris_abani_muses_on_humanity

Abokor, Axmed Cali. 1987. *The Camel in Somali Oral Traditions*. Translated by Axmed Arten Xange. Mogadishu, Somalia: Somali Academy of Sciences and Arts in Cooperation with Scandinavian Institute of African Studies, Uppsala, Sweden.

Achebe, Chinua. 1962 [1958]. *Things Fall Apart*. London: Heinemann.

Achebe, Chinua. 1965. "English and the African Writer," Transition 75/76: 342-349.

Achebe, Chinua. 1966. *A Man of the People*. London: Heinemann.

Achebe, Chinua. 1975. *Morning Yet on Creation Day: Essays*. London: Heinemann.

Achebe, Chinua.1983. *The Trouble with Nigeria*. Enugu, Nigeria: Fourth Dimension.

Achebe, Chinua. 1986 [1964]. *Arrow of God*. London: Heinemann.

Achebe, Chinua. 1987. *Anthills of the Savannah*. London: Heinemann.

Achebe, Chinua. 2000. *Home and Exile*. Oxford, UK: Oxford University Press.

Achebe, Chinua, and Catherine Lynette Innes, eds. 1985. *African Short Stories*. London: Heinemann.

Adams, Carol J. 2003. *The Pornography of Meat*. New York: Continuum.

Adams, Carol J. 2011. "After MacKinnon: Sexual Inequality in the Animal Movement." In *Critical Theory and Animal Liberation*, edited by John Sanbonmatsu, 257–76. Plymouth, UK: Rowman & Littlefield.

Adams, Carol J . 2015 [1990]. *The Sexual Politics of Meat: A Feminist-Vegetarian Critical Theory*. New York: Bloomsbury Academic.

Adams, Carol J., and Lori Gruen. 2014. "Groundwork." In *Ecofeminism: Feminist Intersections with Other Animals and the Earth*, edited by Carol J. Adams and Lori Gruen, 7–36. New York: Bloomsbury.

Adams, William. 2003. "Nature and the Colonial Mind." In *Decolonizing Nature: Strategies for Conservation in a Post-colonial Era*, edited by William M. Adams and Martin Mulligan, 16–50. London: Earthscan.

Aesop. 1882. *The Book of Fables*, edited by Horace Elisha Scudder. Boston: Houghton.

Agamben, Giorgio. 2006. *The Open: Man and Animal*. Urbana: University of Illinois Press.

Agius, Dionisius A. 2005. *Seafaring in the Arabian Gulf and Oman: The People of the Dhow*. New York: Routledge.

Agualusa, José Eduardo. 2008 [2004]. *The Book of Chameleons*. Translated by Daniel Hahn. New York: Simon & Schuster.

Aidoo, Ama Ata. 1979 [1968]. *Our Sister Killjoy: or, Reflections from a Black-Eyed Squint*. New York: NOK.

Aidoo, Ama Ata. 1993 [1991]. *Changes: A Love Story.* New York: Feminist Press.

Akomo, Maritha. 1985. "The Girl Who Turned into a Dog." In *Kenyan Oral Narratives: A Selection, e*dited by Wanjiku Mukabi Kabira and Kavetsa Adagala, 37–39. Nairobi: East African Educational Publishers.

Al-Hakim, Tawfiq. 1973. *Fate of a Cockroach and Other Plays.* Translated by Denys Johnson-Davies. London: Heinemann.

Alaimo, Stacy. 2000. *Undomesticated Ground: Recasting Nature as Feminist Space*. Ithaca, NY: Cornell University Press.

Alaimo, Stacy. 2010. "Eluding Capture: The Science, Culture and Pleasure of 'Queer' Animals." In *Queer Ecologies: Sex, Nature, Politics, Desire*, edited by Catriona Mortimer-Sandilands and Bruce Erickson, 51–72. Bloomington: Indiana University Press.

Alam, Qaiser Zoha. 1994. *The Dynamics of Imagery: The Image in Indian English literature*. New Delhi: Atlantic Publications.

Alcoff, Linda. 1991. "The Problem of Speaking for Others." *Cultural Critique* 20 (Winter 1991–92): 5–32.

Alcoff, Linda. 2016. "Feminism, Speaking for Others, and the Role of the Philosopher: An Interview with Linda Martín Alcoff." *Stance* 9: 85–104.

Anon. 1872. "Terrible Cyclone at Zanzibar." *North Otago Times* XVIII, no. 750 (July 26): 3. http://paperspast.natlib.govt.nz/cgi-bin/paperspast?a=d&d=NOT18720726.2.32

Anyangwe, Carlson. 2011. *Criminal Law in Cameroon: Specific Offences*. Mankon, Bamenda: Langaa Research and Publications.

Appiah, Kwame Anthony. 1991. "Is the Post- in Postmodernism the Post- in Postcolonial?" *Critical Inquiry* 17, no. 2: 336–57.

Applegate, Katherine. 2012. *The One and Only Ivan*. New York: HarperCollins.

arap Chepkwony, A. K. 2003. "African Religion and Science." In *African Culture, Modern Science and Religious Thought,* edited by P. Ade Dopamu et al., 152–62. Ilorin: African Centre for Religions and the Sciences.

Archard, David. 1993. *Children: Rights and Childhood*. London: Routledge.

Arens, William. 1979. *The Man-Eating Myth*. Oxford, UK: Oxford University Press.

Århem, Kaj. 1987. *Milk, Meat, and Blood: Diet as a Cultural Code among the Pastoral Maasai*. Uppsala, Sweden: African Studies Programme, Dept. of Cultural Anthropology, University of Uppsala.

Armah, Ayi Kwei. 1969 [1968]. *The Beautyful Ones Are Not Yet Born*. London: Heinemann.

Armbruster, Karla. 2013. "What Do We Want from Talking Animals? Reflections on Literary Representations of Animal Voices and Minds." In *Speaking for Animals: An-*

imal Autobiographical Writing, edited by Margo DeMello, 17–33. New York: Routledge.

Armstrong, Philip. 2002. "The Postcolonial Animal." *Society and Animals* 10, no. 4: 413–19.

Armstrong, Philip. 2008. *What Animals Mean in the Fiction of Modernity*. London: Routledge.

Asante, Molefi Kete. 2015. *The History of Africa: The Quest for Eternal Harmony*. New York: Routledge.

Askew, Kelly Michelle. 2002. *Performing the Nation: Swahili Music and Cultural Politics in Tanzania*. Chicago: University of Chicago Press.

Awoonor, Kofi. 2014 [1964]. "The Weaverbird." In *The Promise of Hope: New and Selected Poems, 1964–2013*, 276. Lincoln: University of Nebraska Press.

Badmington, Neil. 2003. "Theorizing Posthumanism," *Cultural Critique* 53 (2003): 10–27.

Bagemihl, Bruce. 1999. *Biological Exuberance: Animal Homosexuality and Natural Diversity*. New York: St. Martin's.

Bakaluba, Jane. 1975. *Honeymoon for Three*. Nairobi: East African Publishing House.

Baker, Steve. 1993. *Picturing the Beast: Animals, Identity and Representation*. Manchester, UK: Manchester University Press.

Baker, Steve. 2002. "What Does Becoming-Animal Look Like?" In *Representing Animals*, edited by Nigel Rothfels, 67–98. Bloomington: Indiana University Press.

Bakhtin, Mikhail M. 1981 [1975]. *The Dialogic Imagination*. Austin: University of Texas Press.

Bal, Mieke. 1990 [1985]. *Narratology: Introduction to the Theory of Narrative*. Translated by Christine van Boheemen. Toronto: University of Toronto Press.

Barad, Karen. 2011. "Nature's Queer Performativity." *Qui Parle: Critical Humanities and Social Sciences* 19, no. 2: 121–58.

Barnes, Ashleigh. 2015. *Feminisms of Discontent: Global Contestations*. New Delhi: Oxford University Press.

Barua, Dhiman. 1992. "History of Cholera." In *Cholera*, edited by Dhiman Barua and William B. Greenough, 1–36. New York: Plenum Medical Book.

Beach, David. 1977. "The Shona Economy: Branches of Production." In *The Roots of Rural Poverty in Central and Southern Africa*, edited by Robin Palmer and Neil Parsons, 37–65. London: Heinemann.

Beck, Alan M., and Aaron H. Katcher. 1996. *Between Pets and People: The Importance of Animal Companionship*. West Lafayette, IN: Purdue University Press.

Beirne, Piers. 1997. "Rethinking Bestiality: Towards a Concept of Interspecies Sexual Assault." *Theoretical Criminology* 1, no. 3: 317–40.

Bekoff, Marc. 2010. *The Animal Manifesto: Six Reasons for Expanding our Compassion Footprint*. Novato, CA: New World Library.

Bekoff, Marc . 2013. "Some Closing Words Moving Ahead with Heart, Peace, and Compassion." In *Ignoring Nature No More: The Case for Compassionate Conservation*, edited by Marc Bekoff, 379–88. Chicago: University of Chicago Press.

Bell, Jeremy, and Michael Naas. 2015. *Plato's Animals: Gadflies, Horses, Swans, and Other Philosophical Beasts*. Bloomington: Indiana University Press.

Boisseron, Bénédicte. 2018. *Afro-Dog: Blackness and the Animal Question*. New York: Columbia University Press.

Bennett, Jane. 2009. *Vibrant Matter: A Political Ecology of Things*. Durham, NC: Duke University Press.

Bennett, Tom, and James Patrick. 2011. "Ubuntu, the Ethics of Traditional religion." In *Traditional African Religions in South African Law*, edited by Tom W. Bennett, 223–42. Cape Town: University of Cape Town Press.

Berenbaum, May R. 1995. *Bugs in the System: Insects and Their Impact on Human Affairs*. Reading, MA: Addison-Wesley.

Berger, John. 1980. "Why Look at Animals?" In *About Looking*, by John Berger, 3–26. London: Writers & Readers.

Beukes, Lauren. 2008. *Moxyland*. Auckland Park, South Africa: Jacana Media.

Beukes, Lauren. 2010. *Zoo City*. Auckland Park, South Africa: Jacana Media.

Bhabha, Homi K. 1994. *The Location of Culture*. London: Routledge.

Bhengu, Mfuniselwa John. 2006. *Ubuntu: The Global Philosophy for Humankind*. Cape Town: Lotsha.

Bilgrami, Akeel. 2014. *Secularism, Identity, and Enchantment*. Cambridge, MA: Harvard University Press.

Blok, H. P. 1948. *A Swahili Anthology with Notes and Glossaries*. Vol. 1. Leiden: A. W. Sijthoff.

Boahen, A. Adu. 1987. *African Perspectives on Colonialism*. Baltimore, MD: Johns Hopkins University Press.

Boahen, A. Adu. 2011. *African Perspectives on European Colonialism*. New York: Diasporic African Press.

Boateng, Nana Nyarko. 2015. "Swallowing Ice." In *Lusaka Punk and Other Short Stories*, edited by Caine Prize for African Writing, 157–66. Northampton, MA: Interlink Books.

Booth, Wayne C. 1961. *The Rhetoric of Fiction*. Chicago: University of Chicago Press.

Boulaga, F. Eboussi. 2014 [1977]. *Muntu in Crisis: African Authenticity and Philosophy*. Trenton, NJ : Africa World Press.

Braidotti, Rosi. 1997. "Meta(L)Morphoses." *Theory, Culture & Society* 14, no. (2): 67–80.

Braidotti, Rosi. 2005. "Affirming the Affirmative: On Nomadic Affectivity." *Rhizomes* Iissue 11/12. Web. http://www.rhizomes.net/issue11/braidotti.html#_ftn1

Braidotti, Rosi. 2006. *Transpositions: On Nomadic Ethics*. Cambridge, UK: Polity.

Braidotti, Rosi. 2008. " In Spite of the Times the Postsecular Turn in Feminism," *Theory Culture & Society*. 25(6): 1–24.

Braidotti, Rosi. 2011. *Nomadic Theory: The Portable Rosi Braidotti*. New York: Columbia University Press.

Braidotti, Rosi. 2013a. "Becoming-World." In *After Cosmopolitanism*, edited by Rosi Braidotti, Patrick Hanafin, and Bolette Blaagaard, 8–27. New York: Routledge.

Braidotti, Rosi. 2013b. *The Posthuman*. Hoboken, NJ: Wiley.

Branch, Daniel. 2011. *Kenya: Between Hope and Despair, 1963–2011*. New Haven, CT: Yale University Press.

Brash, Celeste, and Jean-Bernard Carillet. 2009. *Tahiti and French Polynesia*. London: Lonely Planet.

Braun, Elisabeth. 2003. *Echoes from the Wild: Fiction, Fact, Legend and Myth of Africa's Favourite Animals*. Windhoek, Namibia: Out of Africa Publishers.

Brayton, Daniel. 2012. *Shakespeare's Ocean: An Ecocritical Exploration*. Charlottesville: University of Virginia Press.

Brennan, Timothy. 1997. *At Home in the World: Cosmopolitanism Now*. Cambridge, MA: Harvard University Press.

Broodryk, Johann. 2006. *Ubuntu: Life Coping Skills from Africa*. Randburg, South Africa: Knowres.

Brown, Jane K. 2007. *The Persistence of Allegory: Drama and Neoclassicism from Shakespeare to Wagner*. Philadelphia: University of Pennsylvania Press.

Brown, Laura. 2010. *Homeless Dogs and Melancholy Apes: Humans and Other Animals in the Modern Literary Imagination*. Ithaca, NY: Cornell University Press.

Budiansky, Stephen. 1992. *The Covenant of the Wild: Why Animals Chose Domestication*. New Haven, CT: Yale University Press.

Buell, Lawrence. 2001. *Writing for an Endangered World: Literature, Culture, and Environment in the U.S. and Beyond*. Cambridge, MA.: Belknap Press of Harvard University Press.

Buell, Lawrence. 2011. "Ecocriticism: Some Emerging Trends." *Qui Parle: Critical Humanities and Social Sciences* 19, no. 2: 87–115.

Bujo, Bénézet. 2009. "Ecology and Ethical Responsibility from an African Perspective." In *African Ethics: An Anthology of Comparative and Applied Ethics*, edited by Munyaradzi Felix Murove, 113–28. Scottsville, South Africa: University of KwaZulu-Natal Press.

Bukenya, Austin S., Muigai Gachanja, and Jane Nandwa. 1997. *Oral Literature: A Senior Course*. Longhorn, Nairobi.

Bulliet, Richard W. 2005. *Hunters, Herders, and Hamburgers: The Past and Future of Human-Animal Relationships*. New York: Columbia University Press.

Burkett, Paul. 2014. *Marx and Nature: A Red and Green Perspective*. New York: Haymarket.

Burroughs, Edgar Rice. 1962 [1935]. *Tarzan and the Leopard Men*. New York: Ballantine.

Butler, Judith. 1993. *Bodies that Matter: On the Discursive Limits of "Sex."* New York: Routledge.

Butler, Judith. "Desire." 1995. In *Critical Terms for Literary Study*, edited by Frank Lentricchia and Thomas McLaughlin, 369–86. Chicago: University of Chicago Press.

Butler, Judith. 2004. *Undoing Gender*. New York: Routledge.

Calarco, Matthew. 2008. *Zoographies: The Question of the Animal from Heidegger to Derrida*. New York: Columbia University Press.

Calarco, Matthew. 2011. "Identity, Difference, Indistinction." *CR: The New Centennial Review* 11, no. (2): 41–60.

Calarco, Matthew. 2015. *Thinking through Animals: Identity, Difference, Indistinction.* Stanford, CA: Stanford University Press.

Callicott, J. Baird. 1989. *In Defense of the Land Ethic: Essays in Environmental Philosophy.* Albany: State University of New York Press.

Callicott, J. Baird. 1994. *Earth's Insights: A Survey of Ecological Ethics from the Mediterranean Basin to the Australian Outback.* Berkeley: University of California Press.

Caminero-Santangelo, Byron. 2011. "Never a Final Solution: Nadine Gordimer and the Environmental Unconsciousness." In *Environment at the Margins*, edited by Byron Caminero-Santangelo and Garth Myers. 1–21, Athens: Ohio University Press.

Caminero-Santangelo, Byron. 2014. *Different Shades of Green: African Literature, Environmental Justice, and Political Ecology*: Charlottesville: University of Virginia Press.

Caminero-Santangelo, Byron. 2015. "Witnessing the Nature of Violence: Resource Extraction and Political Ecologies in the Contemporary African Novel." In *Global Ecologies and the Environmental Humanities: Postcolonial Approaches*, edited by Elizabeth Deloughrey, Jill Didur, and Anthony Carrigan, 226–41. New York: Routledge.

Caminero-Santangelo, Byron, and Garth Myers. 2011. "Introduction." In *Environment at the Margins*, edited by Byron Caminero-Santangelo and Garth Myers, 213–34. Athens: Ohio University Press.

Cantz, Hatje. 2002. *Jane Alexander.* Ostfildern-Ruit, Germany: Daimler Chrysler Award for South African Sculpture.

Capra, Fritjof. 1982. *The Turning Point: Science, Society, and the Rising Culture.* New York: Bantam.

Carew, Jan. 1958. *Black Midas.* London: Secker & Warburg.

Carney, James. 2012. "The Buzzing of B: The Subject as Insect in Beckett's *Molloy.*" In *Beckett Re-Membered: After the Centenary*, edited by James Carney et al., 224–37. Newcastle-upon-Tyne: Cambridge Scholars Publishing.

Carr, Neil. 2014. *Dogs in the Leisure Experience.* Wallingford, Oxfordshire: CAB International.

Cassidy, Rebecca. 2012. "Zoosex and Other Relationships with Animals." In *Transgressive Sex: Subversion and Control in Erotic Encounters*, edited by Hastings Donnan and Fiona Magowan, 91–112. New York: Berghahn Press

Cavell, Stanley, et al. 2008. *Philosophy and Animal Life.* New York: Columbia University Press.

Césaire, Aimé, 2001 [1955]. *Discourse on Colonialism.* Translated by Joan Pinkham. New York: Monthly Review Press.

Chagani, Fayaz. 2016. "Can the Postcolonial Animal Speak?" *Society & Animals* 24, no. 6: 619–37.

Chakrabarty, Dipesh. 2009. "The Climate of History: Four Theses." *Critical Inquiry* 35, no. 2: 197–222.

Chapple, Christopher Key. 1993. *Nonviolence to Animals, Earth, and Self in Asian Traditions*. Albany: State University of New York Press.

Chapple, Christopher Key. 2005. "Yoga and Ecology." In *Encyclopedia of Religion and Nature*, edited by Bron Taylor, 1782–86. London: Continuum.

Chapple, Christopher Key. 2008. *Yoga and the Luminous: Patañjali's Spiritual Path to Freedom*. Albany: State University of New York Press.

Chen, Mel Y. 2012. *Animacies: Biopolitics, Racial Mattering, and Queer Affect*. Durham, NC: Duke University Press.

Chibvongodze, Danford T. 2016. "Ubuntu Is Not Only about the Human! An Analysis of the Role of African Philosophy and Ethics in Environment Management." *Journal of Human Ecology* 53, no. 2: 157–66.

Chinkanda, N. E. 1994. "Ubuntu in Terms of Socio-Welfare Field." Workshop paper, Ubuntu School of Philosophy, Ubuntu Center, Pretoria.

Chuwa, Leonard Tumaini. 2014. *African Indigenous Ethics in Global Bioethics: Interpreting Ubuntu*. New York: Springer.

Claassens, Anika. 1986. "People and Whites." *The Black Sash* 28, no. 4: 18.

Clarke, Bruce. 1995. *Allegories of Writing: The Subject of Metamorphosis*. Albany: State University of New York Press.

Clarkson, Carrol. 2014. *Drawing the Line: Toward an Aesthetics of Transitional Justice*. New York: Fordham University Press.

Clavaron, Yves. 2012. "Writing the Postcolonial Animal: Patrice Nganang's *Temps de Chien*." *Contemporary French and Francophone Studies* 16, no. 4: 553–61.

Clifford, James. 1986. "On Ethnographic Allegory." In *Writing Culture*, edited by James Clifford and George E Marcus, 98–121. Berkeley: University of California Press.

Cochrane, Alasdair. 2012. *Animal Rights without Liberation: Applied Ethics and Human Obligations*. New York: Columbia University Press.

Cochrane, Alasdair. 2014. "Born in Chains? The Ethics of Animal Domestication." In *The Ethics of Captivity*, edited by Lori Gruen, 156–73. Oxford, UK: Oxford University Press.

Cock, J. 1980: *Maids and Madams: A Study in the Politics of Exploitation*. Johannesburg: Ravan Press.

Coetzee, J.M. 1997. "The Turner Lectures on Human Values." Princeton University October 15–16, 1997. http://tannerlectures.utah.edu/_documents/a-to-z/c/Coetzee99.pdf.

Coetzee, J.M. 1999. *Disgrace*. New York: Penguin.

Coetzee, J.M. 2003. *Elizabeth Costello*. New York: Viking.

Cohen, Cathy. 1997. "Punks, Bulldaggers, and Welfare Queens: The Radical Potential of Queer Politics." *GLQ: A Journal of Lesbian and Gay Studies* 3: 437–65.

Comaroff, Jean, and John L. Comaroff. 1999a. "Alien-Nation: Zombies, Immigrants, and Millennial Capitalism." *CODESRIA Bulletin* 4, no. 3: 17–27.

Comaroff, Jean, and John L. Comaroff. 1999b. "Occult Economies and the Violence of

Abstraction: Notes from the South African Postcolony," *American Ethnologist* 26, no. 2: 279–303.

Connor, Steven. 2013. "Making Flies Mean Something." In *Beckett and Animals*, edited by Mary Bryden, 139–52. Cambridge, UK: Cambridge University Press.

Cooper, Brenda. 1998. *Magical Realism in West African Fiction: Seeing with a Third Eye.* London: Routledge.

Cornell, Drucilla. 2002. "Exploring Ubuntu--Tentative Reflections." http://www.fehe.org/index.php?id=281

Cornell, Drucilla. 2009. "Is Technology a Fatal Destiny?: Heidegger's Relevance for South Africa and for All 'Developing' Countries." In *Refusal, Transition and Post-Apartheid Law*, edited by Karin Van Marle, 141–52. Stellenbosch, South Africa: Sun Press.

Cornell, Drucilla. 2012. "A Call for a Nuanced Constitutional Jurisprudence: South Africa: Ubuntu, and Reconciliation." In *Ubuntu and the Law: African ideals and Post-Apartheid Jurisprudence*, edited by Drucilla Cornell and Nyoko Muvangua, 324–32. New York: Fordham University Press.

Cosslett, Tess. 2006. *Talking Animals in British Children's Fiction: 1786–1914.* Aldershot, UK: Ashgate.

Creedon, Genevieve. 2014. "Analogical Animals: Thinking through Difference in Animalities and Histories." *Configurations* 22, no. 3: 307–35.

Crenshaw, Kimberlé W. 1989. "Demarginalizing the Intersection of Race and Sex: A Black Feminist Critique of Antidiscrimination: Doctrine, Feminist Theory and Antiracist Politics." *University of Chicago Legal Forum* 1, no. 8: 139–67.

Crenshaw, Kimberlé W. 1991. "Mapping the Margins: Intersectionality, Identity Politics, and Violence against Women of Color," *Stanford Law Review* 43, no. 6: 1241–99.

Cronon, William. 1996. "The Trouble with Wilderness; or, Getting Back to the Wrong Nature." In *Uncommon Ground: Rethinking the Human Place in Nature*, edited by William Cronon, 69–90. New York: Norton.

Cross, Leslie J. 1949. "In Search of Veganism—2." *The Vegan* 5, no. 3: 15–17.

Crutzen, Paul J., and Eugene F. Stoermer. 2000. "The Anthropocene." *Global Change Newsletter* 41: 17–18.

Cuddy-Keane, Malba. 2013 [2000]. "Virginia Wolf, Sound Technologies, and the New Aurality." In *Virginia Woolf in the Age of Mechanical Reproduction*, edited by Pamela Caughie, 69–96. New York: Routledge.

Curtis, Perry. 1971. *Apes and Angels: The Irishman in Victorian Caricature.* Washington, DC: Smithsonian Institution Press.

D'Amato, Janet, and Alex D'Amato. 1971. *African Animals through African Eyes.* New York: J. Messner.

Dalal, Neil, and Chloë Taylor, eds. 2014. *Asian Perspectives on Animal Ethics: Rethinking the Nonhuman.* New York: Routledge.

Davis, Angela Y. 2016. *Freedom Is a Constant Struggle: Ferguson, Palestine, and the Foundations of a Movement.* Chicago: Haymarket Books.

Dawes, Kwame. 2009. "Introduction." In *Black Midas*, by Jan Carew, 7–18. Leeds: Peepal Tree.

De George, Richard T. 1994. "Modern Science, Environmental Ethics and the Anthropocentric Predicament." In *Philosophy, Humanity and Ecology: Philosophy of Nature and Environmental Ethics*, edited by H. Odera Oruka, 15–29. Nairobi: ACTS.

de Waal, Frans. 1996. *Good Natured: The Origins of Right and Wrong in Humans and Other Animals*. Cambridge, MA: Harvard University Press.

de Witte, Marleen. 2011. "Of Corpses, Clay, and Photographs: Body Imagery and Changing Technologies of Remembrance in Asante Funeral Culture." In *Funerals in Africa: Explorations of a Social Phenomenon*, edited by Michael Jindra and Joël Noret, 177–206. New York: Berghahn.

Deckha, Maneesha. 2008. "Intersectionality and Posthumanist Visions of Equality." *Wisconsin Journal of Law, Gender, Society* 23, no. 2: 249–67.

Deckha, Maneesha. 2012. "Toward a Postcolonial, Posthumanist Feminist Theory: Centralizing Race and Culture in Feminist Work on Nonhuman Animals." *Hypatia* 27, no. 3: 527–45.

Deckha, Maneesha. 2018. "Postcolonial." In *Critical Terms for Animal Studies*, edited by Lori Gruen, 280–93. Chicago: University of Chicago Press.

Dei, George J. S. 1989. "Hunting and Gathering in a Ghanaian Rain Forest Community." *Ecology of Food and Nutrition* 22, no. 3: 225–43

Dekkers, Midas. 1994. *Dearest Pet: On Bestiality*. London: Verso.

Deleuze, Gilles. 1968. *Différence et répétition (Difference and Repetition)*. Paris: Presses Universitaires de France.

Deleuze, Gilles, and Félix Guattari. 1987. *A Thousand Plateaus: Capitalism and Schizophrenia*. Translated by Brian Massumi. Minneapolis: University of Minnesota Press.

DeMello, Margo. 2012. *Animals and Society: An Introduction to Human-Animal Studies*. New York: Columbia University Press.

DeMello, Margo. 2016. *Mourning Animals: Rituals and Practices Surrounding Animal Death*. East Lansing: Michigan State University Press.

Derrida, Jacques. 2008 [2006]. *The Animal That Therefore I Am*, edited by Marie-Louise Mallet. Translated by David Walls. New York: Fordham University Press.

Descola, Philippe. 1996. "Constructing Natures: Symbolic Ecology and Social Practice." In *Nature and Society:. Anthropological Perspectives*, edited by Philippe Descola and Gisli Palsson, 82–102. New York: Routledge.

Descola, Philippe. 2001. "The Genres of Gender: Local Models and Global Paradigms in the Comparison of Amazonia and Melanesia." In *Gender in Amazonia and Melanesia: An Exploration of the Comparative Method*, edited by Thomas Gregor and Donald Tuzin, 91–114. Berkeley: University of California Press.

Descola, Philippe. 2009. "Human Natures." *Social Anthropology/Anthropologie Sociale* 17, no. 2: 145–57.

Descola, Philippe. 2013 [2005]. *Beyond Nature and Culture*. Translated by Janet Lloyd with a foreword by Marshall Sahlins. Chicago: University of Chicago Press.

Desmond, Jane. 2016. *Displaying Death and Animating Life: Human-Animal Relations in Art, Science, and Everyday Life*. Chicago: University of Chicago Press.

Devji, Faisal Fatehali. 2000. "Subject to Translation: Shakespeare, Swahili, Socialism." *Journal Postcolonial Studies* 3, no. 2: 181–89.

Diagne, Souleymane Bachir. 2011 [2007]. *African Art as Philosophy: Senghor, Bergson, and the Idea of Negritude*. London: Seagull Books, 2011.

Dixon, Bob. 1978. *Catching Them Young 1: Sex, Race and Class in Children's Fiction*. London: Pluto Press.

Dodge, Ernest Stanley. 1976. *Islands and Empires: Western Impact on the Pacific and East Asia*. Minneapolis: University of Minnesota Press.

Donaldson, Sue, and Will Kymlicka. 2011. *Zoopolis: A Political Theory of Animal Rights*. Oxford, UK: Oxford University Press.

Doniger, Wendy. 1999. "Reflections." In *The Lives of Animals*, edited by J. M. Coetzee, 93–106. Princeton, NJ: Princeton University Press.

Doniger, Wendy. 2004. "The Mythology of Masquerading Animals, or, Bestiality." *Social Research* 62, no. (3): 751–772.

Doniger, Wendy. 2009. *The Hindus: An Alternative History*. Oxford, UK: Oxford University Press.

Donovan, Josephine, and Carol J. Adams. 2007. "Introduction." In *The Feminist Care Tradition in Animal Ethics: A Reader*, edited by Josephine Donovan and Carol J. Adams, 1–20. New York: Columbia University Press.

Douglas, Mary. 1966. *Purity and Danger*. Harmondsworth, UK: Penguin, 1966.

Douglas, Mary. 1999 [1954]. "The Lele of Kasai." In *Implicit Meanings: Selected eEssays in Anthropology*, by Mary Douglas, 8–33. London: Routledge.

Douglass, Paul. 1983. "Eliot's Cats: Serious Play Behind the Playful Seriousness." *Children's Literature* 1, no. 1: 109–24.

Dourish, Paul. 2008. "Points of Persuasion: Strategic Essentialism and Environmental Sustainability." *Workshop on Pervasive Persuasive Technology and Environmental Sustainability* (Sydney, Australia). http://citeseerx.ist.psu.edu/viewdoc/download?-doi=10.1.1.362.4500&rep=rep1&type=pdf

DuBois, Thomas A. 2003. "Oral Tradition," *Oral Tradition* 18, no. 2: 255–57.

Duffy, Rosaleen. 2010. *Nature Crime: How We're Getting Conservation Wrong*. New Haven, CT: Yale University Press.

Duke, Norman C. "Mangroves." 2011. *Encyclopedia of Modern Coral Reefs: Structure, Form and Process*, edited by David Hopley, 655–63. Dordrecht: Springer.

Dunayer, Joan. 1995. "Sexist Words, Speciesist Roots." In *Animals and Women: Feminist Theoretical Explorations*, edited by Carol J. Adams and Josephine Donovan, 11–23. Durham, NC: Duke University Press.

Dunayer, Joan. 2001. *Animal Equality: Language and Liberation*. Derwood, MD: Ryce Publishing.

Dunayer, Joan. 2004. *Speciesism*. Derwood, MD: Ryce Publishing.

Dundes, Alan. 1990. "The Hero Pattern and the Life of Jesus." *In Quest of the Hero*, edited by Otto Rank et al. Princeton, NJ: Princeton University Press.

Edwards, Tasha. 2010. "I Am Sistah Vegan." In *Sistah Vegan: Black Female Vegans Speak on Food, Identity, Health, and Society*, edited by A. Breeze Harper, 82–83. New York: Lantern Books.

Éla, Jean-Marc. 2009 [1988]. *My Faith as an African*. Translated by John Pairman Brown and Susan Perry. Maryknoll, N.Y.: Orbis Books

Eliade, Mircea. 1963. *Shamanism: Archaic Techniques of Ecstasy*. Princeton, NJ: Princeton University Press.

Eliot, T. S. 1939. "Macavity: The Mystery Cat." In *Old Possum's Book of Practical Cats*, by T. S. Eliot, 45–47. London: Faber and Faber.

Eliot, T.S. 2012 [1927]. *The Letters of T. S. Eliot*. Volume 3, *1926–1927*, edited by John Haffenden. London: Faber.

Ellis, Cristin. 2018. *Antebellum Posthuman: Race and Materiality in the Mid-Nineteenth Century*. New York: Fordham.

Eltringham, Nigel. 2008. "Besieged History? An Evaluation of *Shooting Dogs*." *Environment and Planning D: Society and Space* 26, no. 4: 740–46.

Eltringham, Nigel. 2013. "Showing What Cannot Be Imagined: *Shooting Dogs*' and *Hotel Rwanda*." In *Framing Africa: Portrayals of a Continent in Contemporary Mainstream Cinema*, edited by Nigel Eltringham, 113–34. Oxford, UK: Berghahn Books.

Eng, David L., and Shinhee Han. 2000. "A Dialogue on Racial Melancholia." *Psychoanalytic Dialogues* 10, no. 4: 667–700.

Enright, D. J. 1961. "Robert Graves and the Decline of Modernism." *Essays in Criticism* 11, no. 3: 319–37.

Eri, Vincent. 1973 [1970]. *The Crocodile*. Victoria, Australia: Penguin.

Etieyibo, Edwin. 2017. "Ubuntu and the Environment." In *The Palgrave Handbook of African Philosophy*, edited by Adeshina Afolayan and Toyin Falola, 633–57. New York: Palgrave Macmillan.

Evaristo, Bernardine. 2014. *Mr. Loverman: A Novel*. New York: Akashic.

Eze, Emmanuel C. 2001. Achieving Our Humanity: The Idea of the Postracial Future. New York: Routledge.

Fanon, Frantz. 2008 [1952]. *Black Skin, White Masks*. New York: Grove Press.

Fanon, Frantz. 2004 [1963]. *The Wretched of the Earth*. New York: Grove Press.

Faragó, Borbála. 2015. "Transnational-Transanimal: Reading the Insect in Migrant Irish Poetry." In *Animals in Irish Literature and Culture*, edited by Kathryn Kirkpatrick and Borbála Faragó, 231–43. Basingstoke, UK: Palgrave Macmillan.

Farah, Nuruddin. 1986. *Maps*. New York: Pantheon.

Farah, Nuruddin. 1998. *Secrets*. New York: Arcade Publishers.

Farah, Nuruddin. 2011. *Crossbones*. New York: Riverhead Books.

Federal Republic of Cameroon. 1965. *Penal Code, Book 1 and 2*. Buea, Cameroon: Government Printing Press.

Feidel, Jan, and Ibrahim Noor Shariff. 1986. "Kibabina's 'Message about Zanzibar': The Art of Swahili Poetry." *Research in African Literatures* 17, no. 4: 496–24.

Fenwick, Mac. 2010 [2006]. "Realizing Irony's Post/Colonial Promise: Global Sense and Local Meaning in *Things Fall Apart* and 'Ruins of a Great House.'" In *Chinua Achebe's Things Fall Apart*, edited by Harold Bloom, 99–114. New York: Bloom's Literary Criticism.

Ferris, Kathleen. 1995. *James Joyce and the Burden of Disease*. Lexington: University of Kentucky Press.

Festa-Bianchet, Marco. 2013. "Why Evolutionary Biology Is Important for Conservation: Toward Evolutionarily Sustainable Harvest Management." In *Ignoring Nature No More: The Case for Compassionate Conservation*, edited by Marc Bekoff, 125–36. Chicago: University of Chicago Press.

Fleissner, Robert F. 1981. "About the Mews: Catching Up with Eliot's Cats." *Thalia* 4, no. 2: 35–39.

Fletcher, Joseph F. 1966. *Situation Ethics: The New Morality*. Philadelphia: Westminster Press.

Fortmann, Louise, and Calvin Nhira, 1992. "Local Management of Trees and Woodland Resources in Zimbabwe: A Tenurial Niche Approach." Occasional Paper 43. Centre for Applied Social Sciences, University of Zimbabwe.

Foster, John Bellamy. 2000. *Marx's Ecology: Materialism and Nature*. New York: Monthly Review Press.

Francione, Gary L. 1994. "Animals, Property and Legal Welfarism: 'Unnecessary' Suffering and the 'Humane' Treatment of Animals." *Rutgers Law Review* 46, no. 2: 721–70.

Francione, Gary L. 1996. *Rain without Thunder: The Ideology of the Animal Rights Movement*. Philadelphia: Temple University Press.

Francione, Gary L. 2010. "The Abolition of Animal Exploitation." In *The Animal Rights Debate: Abolition or Regulation?*, edited by Gary L. Francione and Robert Garner, 1–102. New York: Columbia University Press.

Francione, L. Gary, and Anna E. Charlon. 2015. *Animal Rights: The Abolitionist Approach*. Newark, NJ: Exempla Press.

Francione, L. Gary, and Anna E. Charlon. 2016. "The Case against Pets," *Aeon Newsletter*. https://aeon.co/essays/why-keeping-a-pet-is-fundamentally-unethical.

Francione, Gary L., and Robert Garner. 2010. "A Discussion between Francione and Garner." In *The Animal Rights Debate: Abolition or Regulation?*, edited by Gary L Francione and Robert Garner, 175–269. New York: Columbia University Press.

Frankental, Sally, and Owen Sichone. 2005. *South Africa's Diverse Peoples: A Reference Sourcebook*. Santa Barbara, CA: ABC-CLIO.

Franklin, Julian. 2005. *Animal Rights and Moral Philosophy*. New York: Columbia University Press.

Freud, Sigmund. 1966. *Standard Edition of the Complete Works of Sigmund Freud*. Translated by James Strachey. London: Hogarth.

Fudge, Erica. 2002. *Animal*. London: Reaktion Books.

Gaarder, Emily. 2011b. "Connections, Contexts, and Conclusions." In *Women and the Animal Rights Movement*, edited by Emily Gaarder. New Brunswick, NJ: Rutgers University Press.

Gaarder, Emily. 2011a. *Women and the Animal Rights Movement*. New Brunswick, NJ: Rutgers University Press.

Gandhi, Leela. 2006. *Affective Communities: Anticolonial Thought, Fin-De-Siècle Radicalism, and the Politics of Friendship*. Durham, NC: Duke University Press.

Gann, Lewis H., and Peter Duignan. 1977. *The Rulers of German Africa, 1884–1914*. Stanford, CA: Stanford University Press.

Garner, Robert. 2013. *A Theory of Justice for Animals: Animal Rights in a Nonideal World*, Oxford University Press.

Garuba, Harry. 2003. "Explorations in Animist Materialism: Notes on Reading/Writing African Literature, Culture, and Society." *Public Culture* 15, no. 2: 261–85.

Gedalof, Irene. 1996. "Can Nomads Learn to Count to Four? Rosi Braidotti and the Space for Difference in Feminist Theory." *Women: A Cultural Review* 7, no. 2: 189–201.

George, Kathryn Paxton. 2000. *Animal, Vegetable, or Woman? A Feminist Critique of Ethical Vegetarianism*. Albany: SUNY Press.

George, Kathryn Paxton. 1994. "Should Feminists Be Vegetarians?" *Signs* 19, no. 2: 405–34.

George, Olakunle. 2017. *African Literature and Social Change: Tribe, Nation, Race*. Bloomington: Indiana University Press.

Ghosh, Amitav. 2005. *The Hungry Tides*. Boston: Houghton Mifflin.

Gicheru, Mwangi. 1991. *The Mixers*. Nairobi: Longhorn Kenya.

Gikandi, Simon. 2012. "Realism, Romance, and the Problem of African Literary History." *MLQ* 73, no. 3: 309–28.

Gikandi, Simon. "Theory, Literature, and Moral Considerations." *Research in African Literatures* 32, no. 4: 1–18.

Gilmana, Eric L. 2008. "Threats to Mangroves from Climate Change and Adaptation Options: A Review." *Aquatic Botany* 89, no. 2: 237–50.

Ginzburg, Carlo. 1980. "Morelli, Freud and Sherlock Holmes: Clues and Scientific Method." *History Workshop* 9: 5–36.

Ginzburg, Carlo. 1991. *Ecstasies: Deciphering the Witches' Sabbath*. Translated by Raymond Rosenthal. New York: Pantheon Books.

Glissant, Édouard. 1996 [1981]. *Caribbean Discourse: Selected Essays*. Translated by Michael Dash. Ann Arbor: University of Michigan Press.

Glissant, Édouard. 1997 [1990]. *Poetics of Relation*. Translated by Betsy Wing. Ann Arbor: University of Michigan Press.

Glover, Michael. 2017. "Animals Off the Menu: A Racist Proposal?" In *Animals, Race, and Multiculturalism*, edited by Luís Cordeiro-Rodrigues; Les Mitchell, 175-99. Cham, Switzerland: Palgrave Macmillan.

Goldman, Marlene. 1997. "Go North Young Woman: Representations of the Arctic in the Writings of Aritha van Herk." In *Echoing Silence: Essays on Arctic Narrative*, edited by John Moss, 153–62. Ottawa: University of Ottawa Press.

Goldstein, Judith L. 2004. "The Origin of the Specious." *differences: A Journal of Feminist Cultural Studies* 15, no. 1: 24–47.

Goldstein, Mara. 2011. "Keeping the Rhythm: Encouraging Dialogue, and Renegotiating Environmental Truths: Writing in the Oral Tradition of a Maasai *Enkiguena*." In *Environment at the Margins*, edited by Byron Caminero-Santangelo and Garth Myers, 95–120. Athens: Ohio University Press.

Gordon, Deborah M. 1999. *Ants at Work*. New York: Free Press.

Gordon, Deborah M.. 2010. "Colonial Studies." *Boston Review (*September-October): 59–63.

Gordon, Sarah. 2006. "Entomophagy: Representations of Insect Eating in Literature and Mass Media." In *Insect Poetics*, edited by Eric C. Brown, 342–62. Minneapolis: University of Minnesota Press.

Gowdy, Barbara. 1998. *The White Bone*. Toronto: HarperFlamingo Canada.

Grace, Sherrill. 2002. *Canada and the Idea of North*. Montréal: McGill–Queen's University Press.

Greenebaum, Jessica Beth. 2016. "Questioning the Concept of Vegan Privilege: A Commentary," Humanity and Society 41, no. 3: 355–72.

Greenfield, Sayre N. 1998. *The Ends of Allegory*. Newark: University of Delaware Press.

Gross, Aaron. 2012. "Introduction and Overview: Animal Others and Animal Studies." In *Animals and the Human Imagination: A Companion to Animal Studies*, edited by Aaron Gross and Anne Vallely, 1–24. New York: Columbia University Press.

Gross, Aaron, and Anne Vallely, eds. 2012. *Animals and the Human Imagination: A Companion to Animal Studies*. New York: Columbia University Press.

Gruen, Lori. 2013. "Entangled Empathy: An Alternative Approach to Animal Ethics." In *The Politics of Species: Reshaping Our Relationships with Other Animals, edited* by Raymond Corbey and Annette Lanjouw, 223–31. Cambridge, UK: Cambridge University Press.

Gruen, Lori. 2015. *Entangled Empathy: An Alternative Ethic for Our Relationships with Animals*. New York: Lantern Books.

Gruen, Lori, and Robert C. Jones. 2016. "Veganism as an Aspiration." In *The Moral Complexities of Eating Meat,* edited by Ben Bramble and Bob Fischer, 153–71. Oxford, UK: Oxford University Press.

Gyekye, Kwame. 1987. *An Essay on African Philosophical Thought: The Akan Conceptual Scheme*. New York: Cambridge University Press.

Gyekye, Kwame. 2004. *Beyond Cultures: Perceiving a Common Humanity*. Accra, Ghana: Ghana Academy of Arts and Sciences.

Habila, Helon. 2011. *Oil on Water: A Novel*. London: Penguin Books.

Haji, Haji Gora. 1994. *Kimbunga: Tungo za Visiwani* (Cyclone: Compositions from the Islands). Dar es Salaam: Chuo Kikuu cha Dar es Salaam, Taasisi ya Uchunguzi wa Kiswahili.

Halperin, David M. 1995. *Saint Foucault: Towards a Gay Hagiography*. New York: Oxford University Press.

Halperin, David M. 2002. *How to Do the History of Homosexuality.* Chicago: University of Chicago Press.

Hames, Raymond. 2007. "The Ecologically Noble Savage Debate." *Annual Review of Anthropology* 36: 177–90.

Haraway, Donna J. 1989. *Primate Visions: Gender, Race, and Nature in the World of Modern Science.* New York: Routledge.

Haraway, Donna J. 1992. "The Promises of Monsters: A Regenerative Politics for Inappropriate/d Others." In *Cultural Studies,* edited by Lawrence Grossberg, Cary Nelson, and Paula Treichler, 295–337. London and New York: Routledge.

Haraway, Donna J. 1997. *Modest_Witness@Second_Millennium. FemaleMan©_Meets_Oncomouse©.* London and New York: Routledge.

Haraway, Donna J. 2003. *The Companion Species Manifesto: Dogs, People, and Significant Otherness.* Chicago: Prickly Paradigm.

Haraway, Donna J. 2007. *When Species Meet.* Minneapolis: University of Minnesota Press.

Harel, Naama. 2007. "The Liminal Space between the Species in Peter Høeg's *The Woman and the Ape.*" In *Beyond the Threshold: Explorations of Liminality in Literature,* edited by Hein Viljoen and Chris Van Der Merwe, 79–89. New York: Peter Lang.

Harel, Naama. 2010. "Post-Speciesist Utopias and Dystopias." *Interdisciplinary Humanities* 27, no. (2): 111–20.

Harel, Naama. 2013. "Investigations of a Dog by a Dog: Between Anthropocentrism and Canine-Centricism." In *Speaking for Animals: Animal Autobiographical Writing,* edited by Margo DeMello, 49–59. New York: Routledge.

Harkin, Michael E. 2007. "Swallowing Wealth: Northwest Coast Beliefs and Ecological Practices." In *Native Americans and the Environment: Perspectives on the Ecological Indian,* edited by Michael E. Harkin and David Rich Lewis, 211–32. Lincoln: University of Nebraska Press.

Harkin, Michael E., and David Rich Lewis. 2007. *Native Americans and the Environment: Perspectives on the Ecological Indian.* Lincoln: University of Nebraska Press.

Harper, Amie. 2010. "Race as a 'Feeble Matter' in Veganism: Interrogating Whiteness, Geopolitical Privilege, and Consumption Philosophy of 'Cruelty Free' Products." *Journal for Critical Animal Studies* 8, no. 3: 5-27.

Harper, A. Breeze, ed. 2010. *Sistah Vegan: Black Female Vegans Speak on Food, Identity, Health, and Society.* New York: Lantern Books.

Harvey, Graham. 2006. *Animism: Respecting the Living World.* New York: Columbia University Press.

Head, Bessie. 1971. *Maru.* London: Heinemann.

Head, Bessie. 1986. "Bessie Head in Gaborone, Botswana: An Interview," by Linda Susan Beard, *Sage* 3 no. 2: 44-47.

Hediger, Ryan. 2013. "Our Animals, Ourselves: Representing Animal Minds in *Timothy* and *The White Bone.*" In *Speaking for Animals: Animal Autobiographical Writing,* edited by Margo DeMello, 37–47. New York: Routledge.

Hensley, Gerald. 2013. *Friendly Fire: Nuclear Politics and the Collapse of ANZUS, 1984–1987.* Auckland, New Zealand: Auckland University Press.

Hevia, James Louis. 2018. *Animal Labor and Colonial Warfare*. Chicago: University of Chicago Press.

Hobley, C. W. 1894. "People, Places, and Prospects in British East Africa." *Geographical Journal* 4, no. 2: 97–123.

Hoeller, Hildegard. 2004. "Ama Ata Aidoo's *Heart of Darkness*." *Research in African Literatures* 35, no. 1: 130–47.

Hollingsworth, Cristopher. 2001. *Poetics of the Hive: The Insect Metaphor in Literature.* Iowa City: University of Iowa Press.

Hollingsworth, Cristopher. 2006. "The Forces of the Entomological Other: Insects and Instruments of Intolerant Thought and Oppressive Action." In *Insect Poetics*, edited by Eric C. Brown, 262–77. Minneapolis: University of Minnesota Press.

Horsthemke, Kai. 2015. *Animals and African Ethics*. Basingstoke, UK: Palgrave Macmillan.

Huggan, Graham, and Helen Tiffin. 2010. *Postcolonial Ecocriticism: Literature, Animals, Environment.* London: Routledge.

Hulan, Renée. 2002. *Northern Experience and the Myths of Canadian Culture.* Montréal: McGill–Queen's University Press.

Hulme, Peter. 1998. "Introduction: The Cannibal Scene." In *Cannibalism and the Colonial World*, edited by Frances Barker, Peter Hulme, and Margaret Iversen, 1–38. Cambridge, UK: Cambridge University Press.

Hussein, Ebrahim N. 1969. *Kinjeketile*. Dar es Salaam: Oxford University Press.

Hussein, Ebrahim N. 1971. *Mashetani*. Dar es Salaam: Oxford University Press.

Huxley, Elspeth Joscelin. 1961 [1959]. *The Flame Trees of Thika: Memories of an African Childhood.* Harmondsworth, UK: Penguin Books.

Huxley, Elspeth Joscelin. 1962 (1959). *On the Edge of the Rift.* New York: William Morrow and Company.

Imbuga, Francis. 1988. *Aminata.* Nairobi: East African Educational Publishers.

Ingold, Tim. 2000. *The Perception of the Environment: Essays on Livelihood, Dwelling and Skill.* New York: Routledge.

Irele, F. Abiola. 2000. "The Crisis of Cultural Memory in Chinua Achebe's *Things Fall Apart*." *African Studies Quarterly* 4, no. 3: 1–40.

Jackson, Zakiyyah Iman. 2013. "Review: Animal: New Directions in the Theorization of Race and Posthumanism." *Feminist Studies* 39, no. 3: 669–85.

Jaggi, Maya. 2012. "Nuruddin Farah: A Life in Writing." *The Guardian*, September 21. http://www.theguardian.com/culture/2012/sep/21/nuruddin-salah-life-in-writing

Jahn, Janheinz. 1961. *Muntu: An Outline of the New African Culture*. Translated by Marjorie Grene. New York: Grove Press.

Jameson, Fredric. 1981. *The Political Unconscious: Narrative as a Socially Symbolic Act.* Ithaca, NY: Cornell University Press.

Jameson, Fredric. 1986. "Third-World Literature in the Era of Multinational Capitalism." *Social Text* 15 (Autumn): 65–88.

Jamieson, Dale. 2006. "Against Zoos." In *In Defense of Animals: The Second Wave*, edited by Peter Singer, 132–43. Malden, MA: Blackwell.

Johnson, Gary. 2012. *The Vitality of Allegory: Figural Narrative in Modern and Contemporary Fiction*. Columbus: Ohio State University Press.

Jones, Donna V. 2010. *The Racial Discourses of Life Philosophy: Négritude, Vitalism, and Modernity*. New York: Columbia University Press.

jones, pattrice. 2010. "Afterword: Liberation as Connection and Decolonization of Desire." In *Sistah Vegan: Black Female Vegans Speak on Food, Identity, Health, and Society*, edited by A. Breeze Harper, 187–201. New York: Lantern Books.

jones, pattrice. 2014. "Eros and the Mechanisms of Eco-Defense." In *Ecofeminism: Feminist Intersections with Other Animals and the Earth*, edited by Carol J. Adams and Lori Gruen, 91–106. New York: Bloomsbury.

Jordan, Julia. 2010. *Chance and the Modern British Novel: From Henry Green to Iris Murdoch*. London: Continuum.

Julien, Eileen. 1992. *African Novels and the Question of Orality*. Bloomington: Indiana University Press.

Junod, Henri-Philippe. 1938. *Bantu Heritage*. Johannesburg: Hortors.

Kabira, Wanjiku Mukabi. 1992. "The Oral Artist and the Gender Dimension." In *Reflections on Theories and Methods in Oral Literature*, edited by Okoth Okombo and Jane Nandwa, 57–73. Nairobi: Kenya Oral Literature Association.

Kabira, Wanjiku Mukabi. 1993. "Images of Women in Gikuyu Oral Narratives." PhD dissertation, University of Nairobi.

Kabira, Wanjiku Mukabi. 1994. "Gender and Politics of Control: An Overview of Images of Women in Gikuyu Oral Narratives." In *Understanding Oral Literature*, edited by Austin Bukenya, Wanjiku M. Kabira, and Okoth Okombo, 77–84. Nairobi: Nairobi University Press.

Kabira, Wanjiku Mukabi, and Masheti Masinjila. 1997. *ABC of Gender Analysis*. Nairobi: Forum for African Women Educationists.

Kant, Emmanuel. 1951 [1790]. *Critique of Judgment*. Translated by J. H. Bernard, New York: Hafner Press.

Kaoma, Kapya John. 2013. *God's Family, God's Earth: Christian Ecological Ethics of Ubuntu*. Zomba, Malawi: Kachere.

Katrak, Ketu. 1991. "Indian Nationalism, Gandhian Satyagraha, and Representations of Female Sexuality." In *Nationalisms and Sexualities*, edited by Andrew Parker, Mary Russo, Doris Sommer, and Patricia Yaeger, 395–406. New York: Routledge.

Kemmerer, Lisa. 2011. *Sister Species: Women, Animals, and Social Justice*. Urbana: University of Illinois Press.

Kenyatta, Jomo. 1985 [1938]. "The Gentlemen of the Jungle." In *African Short Stories*, edited by Chinua Achebe and Catherine Lynette Innes, 36–39. London: Heinemann.

Kiema, Kuela. 2010. *Tears for My Land: A Social History of the Kva of the Central Kalahari Game Reserve, Tc'amnquoo*. Gaborone, Botswana: Mmegi Publishing House.

King, Barbara J. 2013. *How Animals Grieve*. Chicago: University of Chicago Press.

King, Harrison. 2016. "Reading, Teaching Insects: Ant Society as Pedagogical Device in Rabbinic Literature." In *Beastly Morality: Animals as Ethical Agents*, edited by Jonathan K. Crane, 157–73. New York: Columbia University Press.

King'ei, Geoffrey Kitula. 1986. *Mwongozo wa* Malenga wa Mrima*: Mwinyi Hatibu Mohamed* [A Guidebook to Mwinyi Hatibu Mohamed's *Malenga wa Mrima].* Nairobi: Heinemann Educational Books.

King'ei, Geoffrey Kitula. 2009 [1989]. *Kamusi ya Methali za Kiswahili* [Dictionary of Kiswahili Proverbs]. Nairobi: East African Educational Publishers.

Kirkpatrick, Kathryn. 2015. "Introduction." In *Animals in Irish Literature and Culture*, edited by Kathryn Kirkpatrick and Borbála Faragó, 1–10. Basingstoke, UK: Palgrave Macmillan.

Kisukidi, Nadia Yala. 2014."Nostalgia and Postcolonial Utopia in Senghor's Négritude." In *Media and Nostalgia: Yearning for the Past, Present and Future*, edited by Katharina Niemeyer, 191-202. Basingstoke, UK: Palgrave Macmillan.

Kitunda, Jeremiah M. 2011. "'Love Is a Dunghill. . . . And I'm the Cock that Gets on It to Crow': Ernest Hemingway's Farcical Adoration of Africa." In *Hemingway and Africa*, edited by Miriam B. Mandel, 122–48. Rochester, NY: Camden House.

Knappert, Jan. 1970. *Myths and Legends of the Swahili.* Nairobi: Heinemann Educational Books.

Knappert, Jan, and Liesje Knappert. 1985. *Islamic Legends: Histories of Heroes, Saints and Prophets of Islam.* Vol. 2. Leiden: Brill.

Ko, Syl. 2017 [2016]. "We Can Avoid the Debate about Comparing Human and Animal Oppressions, If We Simply Make the Right Connections." In *Aphro-ism: Essays on Pop Culture, Feminism, and Black Veganism from Two Sisters,* by Aph Ko and Syl Ko, 82–87. New York: Lantern Books.

Kohn, Eduardo. 2013. *How Forests Think: Toward an Anthropology Beyond the Human.* Berkeley: University of California Press.

Kolozova, Katerina. 2014. *Cut of the Real: Subjectivity in Poststructuralist Philosophy.* New York: Columbia University Press.

Komora, Yuda. 1971. *Usininyonye.* Nairobi: Longman.

Komora, Yuda. 1973. *Sons of Sango.* Nairobi: East African Publishing House.

Korsmeyer, Carolyn. 2011. *Savoring Disgust: The Foul and the Fair in Aesthetics.* New York: Oxford University Press.

Kristeva, Julia. 1989 [1987]. *Black Sun: Depression and Melancholia.* Translated *by* Leon S. Roudiez. New York: Columbia University Press.

Kropotkin, Petr Alekseevich. 1924 [1922]. *Ethics: Origin and Development.* Translated by Louis S. Friedland and Joseph R. Piroshnikoff. New York: Lincoln MacVeagh.

Kulet, Henry ole. 1971. *Is It Possible?* Nairobi: Longman.

Kulet, Henry ole. 1972. *To Become a Man.* Nairobi: Longman.

Kulet, Henry ole. 2008. *Blossoms of the Savannah.* Nairobi: Longhorn.

Kulet, Henry ole. 2011.*Varnishing Herds.* Nairobi: Longhorn.

Kulet, Henry ole. 2017. *Elephant Dance.* Nairobi: Longhorn.

Lanser, Susan. 1981. *The Narrative Act: Point of View in Fiction.* Princeton, NJ: Princeton University Press.

Latour, Bruno. 2004. *Politics of Nature: How to Bring the Sciences into Democracy.* Cambridge, MA: Harvard University Press.

Lévi-Strauss, Claude. 1962. *Le Totemisme aujourd'hui.* Paris: Presses Universitaires de France.

Lévi-Strauss, Claude. 1963 [1962]. *Totemism.* Translated by Rodney Needham. Boston: Beacon Press.

Lezra, Esther. 2014. *The Colonial Art of Demonizing Others: Global Perspectives.* New York: Routledge.

Lillvis, Kristen. 2017. *Posthuman Blackness and the Black Female Imagination.* Athens, Georgia: University of Georgia Press.

Lingis, Alphonso. 2007. "Avian Intelligence." In *Knowing Animals,* edited by Laurence Simmons and Philip Armstrong, 43–56. Amsterdam: Brill.

Lord, Albert B. 1960. *The Singer of Tales.* Cambridge, MA: Harvard University Press.

Lucas, Sheri. 2005. "A Defense of the Feminist-Vegetarian Connection." *Hypatia* 20, no. 1: 150–77.

Lucashenko, Melissa. 2000. "Black on Black." *Meanjin* 59, no. 3: 112–18.

Luke, Brian. "Violent Love: Hunting, Heterosexuality, and the Erotics of Men's Predation." *Feminist Studies* 24, no. 3 (1998): 627–55.

Lundblad, Michael. 2010. "Epistemology of the Jungle: Progressive-Era Sexuality and the Nature of the Beast." *American Literature* 81, no. 4: 747–73.

Lytwyn, Victor P. 1990. "Ojibwa and Ottawa Fisheries around Manitoulin Island: Historical and Geographical Perspectives on Aboriginal and Treaty Fishing Rights." *Native Studies Review* 6, no. 1: 1–30.

Ma, Sheng-mei. 2012. *Asian Diaspora and East-West Modernity.* West Lafayette, Indiana: Purdue University Press.

Maathai, Wangari Muta. 2006. *Unbowed: A Memoir.* New York: Alfred A. Knopff.

Maathai, Wangari Muta. 2010. *Replenishing the Earth: Spiritual Values for Healing Ourselves and the World.* New York: Doubleday.

MacKenzie, John M. 1988. "Chivalry, Social Darwinism and Ritualized Killing: The Hunting Ethos in Central Africa up to 1914." In *Conservation in Africa: Peoples, Policies, and Practice,* edited by David Anderson and Richard H. Grove, 41–62. New York: Cambridge University Press.

MacKenzie, John M. 1997. *The Empire of Nature: Hunting, Conservation, and British Imperialism.* Manchester, UK: Manchester University Press.

MacKinnon, Catharine A. 2007. *Women's Lives, Men's Laws.* Cambridge, MA: Belknap Press of Harvard University Press.

Madan, A. C. 1902. *English-Swahili Dictionary.* Oxford, UK: Clarendon Press.

Madumulla, Joshua, Elena Bertoncini, and Jan Blommaert. 1999. "Politics, Ideology, and

Poetic Form: The Literary Debates in Tanzania." In *Language Ideological Debates*, edited by Jan Blommaert, 307–41. Berlin: Mouton de Gruyter.

Maggi, Ricardo G., Craig A. Harms, Edward B. Breitschwerdt. 2012. "Bartonellosis: An Emerging Disease of Humans, Domestic Animals and Wildlife." In *New Directions in Conservation Medicine: Applied Cases of Ecological Health*, edited by Richard Ostfeld, A. Alonso Aguirre, and Peter Daszak, 239–56. Oxford, UK: Oxford University Press.

Malamud, Randy. 1998. *Reading Zoos: Representations of Animals and Captivity*. New York: New York University Press.

Malinowski, Bronislaw. 1989 [1967]. *A Diary in the Strict Sense of the Term*. Stanford, CA: Stanford University Press.

Mamdami, Mahmood. 2001.*When Victims Become Killers: Colonialism, Nativism, and the Genocide in Rwanda*. Princeton, NJ: Princeton University Press.

Mangan, J. A., and Callum McKenzie. 2010. *Militarism, Hunting, Imperialism. "Blooding" the Martial Male*. New York: Routledge.

Mann, Harveen S. 1994. "U.S. Multiculturalism, Post-Colonialism, and Indo-Anglian Literature: Some Issues of Critical Pedagogy and Theory." *The Journal of the Midwest Modern Language Association* 27, no. 1: 94–108.

Manning, Dolleen Tisawiiashi. 2014. "The Becoming Human of Buffalo Bill." *In Intensities and Lines of Flight: Deleuze/Guattari and the Arts*, edited by Athonio Calcagno, Jim Vernon, and Steve G. Lofts, 187–206. London: Rowman and Littlefield International.

Marais, Eugène N. 1971 [1925]. *The Soul of White Ants*. Translated by Winifred de Kok. London: Jonathan Cape.

Marino, Lori. 2011. "Ethical Gerrymandering in Science." *Journal of Animal Ethics* 1, no. 2: 199–21.

Martin, Glen. 2012. *Game Changer: Animal Rights and the Fate of Africa's Wildlife*. Berkeley: University of California Press.

Masaka, Denis, and Tompson Makahamadze. 2013. "The Proverb: A Preserver of Shona Traditional Religion and Ethical Code." *Journal of Pan African Studies* 6, no. 5: 132–43.

Masolo, D. A. 1994. *African Philosophy in Search of Identity*. Bloomington: Indiana University Press.

Massumi, Brian. 2002. *Parables for the Virtual*. Durham, NC: Duke University Press.

Masterson, John. 2013. *The Disorder of Things: A Foucauldian Approach to the Work of Nuruddin Farah*. Johannesburg, South Africa: Wits University Press.

Matsuda, Mari. 1996. "Standing with My Sister, Facing the Enemy: Legal Theory Out of Coalition." In *Where Is Your Body? and Other Essays on Race, Gender, and the Law*, by Mari J. Matsuda, 61–71. Boston: Beacon Press.

Mawere, Munyaradzi. 2012. "Buried and Forgotten but Not Dead: Reflections on 'Ubuntu' in Environmental Conservation in South Eastern Zimbabwe." *Afro-Asian Journal of Social Science* 3, no. 2: 1–20.

Mawere, Munyaradzi. 2014. *Environmental Conservation through Ubuntu and Other Emerging Perspectives.* Mankon, Cameroon: Langaa Research and Publishing.

May, Vivian M. 2015. *Pursuing Intersectionality, Unsettling Dominant Imaginaries.* New York: Routledge.

Mazrui, Alamin M. 2007. *Swahili Beyond the Boundaries: Literature, Language, and Identity.* Athens: Ohio University Press.

Mazrui, Ali. 1994. "From Sun Worship to Time Worship: Towards a Solar Theory of History." In *Philosophy, Humanity and Ecology: Philosophy of Nature and Environmental Ethics*, edited by H. Odera Oruka, 165–76. Nairobi: ACTS.

Mbaria, John. 2014. "Why Morans are No Longer Killing Lions." *The East African*, March 29. https://www.theeastafrican.co.ke/magazine/Why-morans-are-no-longer-killing-lions/434746-2261776-yg5c56/index.html

Mbaria, John, and Mordecai Ogada. 2017. *The Big Conservation Lie.* Auburn: Lens & Pens Publishing.

Mbembe, Achille. 2001. *On the Postcolony.* Berkeley: University of California Press.

Mbembe, Achille. 2003. "Necropolitics." Translated by Libby Meintjes. *Public Culture* 15, no. (1): 11–40.

Mbembe, Achille. 2004. "Subject and Experience." In *Experience: For a Different Kind of Globalization,* edited by Nadia Tazi, 3–18. Johannesburg: Double Storey Books.

Mbembe, Achille. 2017. *Critique of the Black Reason.* Translated by Laurent Dubois. Durham, NC: Duke University Press.

Mbigi, Lovemore. 1997. *Ubuntu: The African Dream in Management.* Randburg, South Africa: Knowledge Resources.

Mbiti, John S. 1969. *Poems of Nature and Faith.* Nairobi: East African Publishing House.

Mbiti, John S. 1970. *Concepts of God in Africa.* New York: Praeger Publishers.

Mbiti, John S. 1971. *The Crisis of Mission in Africa.* Mukono: Uganda Church Press.

Mbiti, John S. 1990 [1969]. *African Religions and Philosophy.* Oxford: Heinemann International.

Mbugua, Ng'ang'a. 2015. *Angels of the Wild.* Nairobi: One Planet.

McGinn, Colin. 2011. *The Meaning of Disgust.* New York: Oxford University Press.

McHugh, Susan. 2004. *Dog.* London: Reaktion Books.

McKenna, Erin. 2013. *Pets, People, and Pragmatism.* New York: Fordham University Press.

Mda, Zakes. 2006. *The Whale Caller: A Novel.* New York: Farrar, Straus and Giroux.

Mda, Zakes. 2018. *Justify the Enemy: Becoming Human in South Africa*, edited by J. U. Jacobs. Pietermaritzburg: KwaZulu-Natal University Press.

Mda, Zakes. 1965 [1957]. "*The Colonizer and the Colonized.* Boston: Beacon Press.

Mercer, Kobena. 2013 [2011]. "Postcolonial Grotesque: Jane Alexander's Poetic Monsters." *Nka: Journal of Contemporary African Art* 33: 80–90.

Mfenyana, Buntu. 1986. "Ubuntu, Abantu, abeLungu." *The Black Sash* 28, no. 4: 18–19.

Miller, Christopher L. 1985. *Blank Darkness: Africanist Discourse in French.* Chicago: University of Chicago Press.

Miller, Susan B. 2004. *Disgust: The Gatekeeper Emotion.* Hillsdale, NJ: Analytic Press.

Milne, Anne. 2013. "The Power of Testimony: The Speaking Animal's Plea for Understanding in a Selection of Eighteenth-Century British Poetry." In *Speaking for Animals: Animal Autobiographical Writing*, edited by Margo DeMello, 165–77. New York: Routledge.

Mitchell, W. J. T. 2003. "Foreword." In *Animal Rites: American Culture, the Discourse of Species, and Posthumanist Theory*, edited by Cary Wolfe, ix–xiv. Chicago: University of Chicago Press.

Mizelle, Brett. 2015. "Unthinkable Visibility: Pigs, Pork, and the Spectacle of Killing for Meat." In *Rendering Nature: Animals, Bodies, Places, Politics*, edited by Marguerite S Shaffer and Phoebe S. K. Young, 263–86. Philadelphia: University of Pennsylvania Press.

Mkelle, M. Burhan. 1978. "Utenzi wa Nabii Yunus." *Swahili: Journal of the East African Swahili Committee* 48, no. 2: 1–16.

Mlama, Penina. 1995. "Oral Art and Contemporary Cultural Nationalism." In *Power, Marginality and Oral Literature*, edited by Graham Furniss and Liz Gunner, 23–34. Cambridge, UK: Cambridge University Press.

Mnyaka, Mluleki, and Mokgethi Motlhabi. 2005. "The African Concept of Ubuntu/Botho and Its Socio-Moral Significance." *Journal Black Theology: An International Journal* 3 no. 2: 215–37.

Mohamed, Mwinyihatibu. 1977. "Ushoga." In *Malenga wa Mrima*, edited by Shihabuddin Chiraghdin, 69–70. Dar es Salaam: Oxford University Press.

Mokgoro, Yvonne. 2012. "uBuntu and the Law in South Africa." In *Ubuntu and the Law: African Ideals and Post-Apartheid Jurisprudence*, edited by Drucilla Cornell and Nyoko Muvangua, 317–23. New York: Fordham University Press.

Moolla, F. Fiona. 2014. *Reading Nuruddin Farah: The Individual, the Novel and the Idea of Home*. Suffolk, UK: James Currey.

Moolla, F. Fiona, ed. 2016. *Natures of Africa: Ecocriticism and Animal Studies in Contemporary Cultural Form*. Johannesburg, South Africa: Wits University Press.

Moorjani, Angela. 2013. "The Dancing Bees in Samuel Beckett's *Molloy:* The Rapture of Unknowing." In *Beckett and Animals*, edited by Mary Bryden, 165–76. Cambridge, UK: Cambridge University Press.

Mootoo, Shani. *1996. Cereus Blooms at Night*. Vancouver: Press Gang Publishers.

Moradewun Adejunmobi. 2014. "The Infrapolitics of Subordination in Patrice Nganang's Dog Days." *Journal of Contemporary African Studies* 32, no. 4: 438–52.

Morton, Timothy. 2010. *The Ecological Thought*. Cambridge, MA: Harvard University Press.

Morton, Timothy. 2014. "The Liminal Space between Things." In *Material Ecocriticism*, edited by Serenella Iovino and Serpil Oppermann, 269–79. Bloomington: Indiana University Press.

Mtshali, Mbuyiseni Oswald. 1971. *Sounds of a Cowhide Drum: Poems*. Johannesburg: Renoster Books.

Mtshali, Mbuyiseni Oswald. 1989 [1974]. "Inside my Zulu Hut." In *Growing Up with*

Poetry: An Anthology for Secondary Schools, edited by David Rubadiri, 36. Oxford: Heinemann.

Mudimbe, V. Y. 1994. *The Idea of Africa.* Bloomington: Indiana University Press.

Mudimbe, V. Y. 1988. *The Invention of Africa: Gnosis, Philosophy, and the Order of Knowledge.* Bloomington: Indiana University Press.

Mugambi, J. K. N. 1992. *Critiques of Christianity in African Literature: With Particular Reference to the East African Context.* Nairobi: East African Educational Publishers.

Mugo, Micere Githae. 1976 [1969]a. "Locusts are Retreating." In *Daughter of My People Sing ,* by Micere Githae Mugo, 59–60. Nairobi: East African Literature Bureau.

Mugo, Micere Githae. 1976 [1969]b. "Questioning the Biologists." In *Daughter of My People Sing Sing,* by Micere Githae Mugo, 26. Nairobi: East African Literature Bureau.

Mugo, Micere Githae. 1978. *Visions of Africa: The Fiction Oof Chinua Achebe, Margaret Laurence, Elspeth Huxley and Ngũgĩ wa Thiong'o.* Nairobi: Kenya Literature Bureau.

Mugo, Micere Githae. 1991. *African Orature and Human Rights.* Roma, Lesotho: Institute of Southern African Studies.

Mulokozi, M. M., and T. S. Y. Sengo. 1995. *History of Kiswahili Poetry.* Dar es Salaam: Institute of Kiswahili Research.

Mungoshi, Charles. 1989 [1980]. *The Setting Sun and the Rolling World: Selected Stories.* Boston: Beacon Press.

Munro, Brenna M. 2017. "States of Emergence: Writing African Female Same-sex Sexuality." *Journal of Lesbian Studies* 21, no. 2: 186–203.

Murove, Munyaradzi Felix. 2004. "An African Commitment to Ecological Conservation: The Shona Concepts of Ukama and Ubuntu." *The Mankind Quarterly* 15, no. 2: 195–215.

Murove, Munyaradzi Felix. 2014. "Ubuntu." *Diogenes* 59, nos. 3–4: 36–47.

Museka, Madondo M. 2012. "The Quest for a Relevant Environmental Pedagogy in the African Context: Insights from Unhu/Ubuntu Philosophy." *Journal of Ecology and the Natural Environment* 4, no. 10: 258–65.

Mutekwa, Anias. 2013. "From 'Boys' to 'Men'? African and Black Masculinities, Triangular Desire, Race, and Subalternity in Charles Mungoshi's Short Stories." *Social Dynamics: A Journal of African Studies* 39, no. 2: 353–67.

Mutwa, Credo. 1996. *Isilwane: The Animal.* Cape Town: Struik Publishing.

Mwalyosi, R. B. B. 1993. "Management of the Rufiji Delta as a Wetland." In *Wetlands of Tanzania: Proceedings of a Seminar on the Wetlands of Tanzania, Morogoro, Tanzania, November 27–29, 1991,* edited by G. L. Kamukala and S. A. Crafter, 115–24. Gland, Switzerland: IUCN.

Mwangi, Evan Maina. 2009. *Africa Writes Back to Self: Metafiction, Gender Sexuality.* New York: SUNY Press.

Mwangi, Evan Maina. 2017. *Translation in African Contexts: Postcolonial Texts, Queer Sexuality, and Cosmopolitan Fluency.* Kent, Ohio: Kent State University Press.

Nagel, Thomas. 1974. "What Is It Like to Be a Bat?" *The Philosophical Review* 83, no. (4): 435–50.

Nagel, Thomas. 2013. "Pecking Order: John Gray's *Silence of Animals.*" *New York Times,*

July 5. http://www.nytimes.com/2013/07/07/books/review/john-grays-silence-of-animals.html

Namjoshi, Suniti. 1985. *The Conversations of Cow.* London: Women's Press.

Namjoshi, Suniti. 1993 [1986]. *Aditi and the One-Eyed Monkey.* Boston: Beacon Press.

Namjoshi, Suniti . 1993. *Saint Suniti and the Dragon*. North Melbourne, Australia: Spinifex.

Nandwa, Rebecca. 2005. *Mnyama Mwenye Huruma* (A Merciful Animal). Nairobi: East African Educational Publishers.

Nandwa, Rebecca. 2007. *Kibuyu cha Miujiza* (*A Miraculous Gourd*). Nairobi: East African Educational Publishers.

Nash, Jennifer. 2008. "Re-Thinking Intersectionality." *Feminist Review* 89, no. 1: 1–15.

Nayar, Pramod K. 2010. *An Introduction to New Media and Cybercultures*. Malden, MA: Wiley-Blackwell.

Ndebele, Njabulo S. 2007 [1999]. "Game Lodges and Leisure Colonialists: Caught in the Process of Becoming." In *Fine Lines from the Box: Further Thoughts about Our Country*, by Njabulo S. Ndebele, 99–105. Roggebaai, South Africa: Umuzi.

Neate, Patrick. 2003. *The London Pigeon Wars*. London: Viking.

Ngaboh-Smart, Francis. 2004. *Beyond Empire and Nation: Postnational Arguments in the Fiction of Nuruddin Farah and B. Kojo Laing*. Amsterdam: Rodopi.

Nganang, Patrice. 2006 [2001]. *Dog Days: An Animal Chronicle*. Translated by Amy Baram Reid. Charlottesville: University of Virginia Press.

Ngũgĩ wa Thiong'o. 1964. *Weep Not, Child*. London: Heinemann.

Ngũgĩ wa Thiong'o. 1965. *The River Between*. London: Heinemann.

Ngũgĩ wa Thiong'o. 1972. *Homecoming: Essays on African and Caribbean Literature, Culture and Politics*. London: Heinemann.

Ngũgĩ wa Thiong'o. 1977. *Petals of Blood*. London: Heinemann.

Ngũgĩ wa Thiong'o. 1981. *Writers in Politics: Essays*. Nairobi: Heinemann.

Ngũgĩ wa Thiong'o. 1982a. *Devil on the Cross*. Nairobi: East African Educational Publishers.

Ngũgĩ wa Thiong'o. 1982b. *Njamba Nene na Mbaathi ĩ Mathagu* (Njamba Nene and the with Wings/*Njamba Nene and the Flying Bus*). Nairobi: East African Educational Publishers.

Ngũgĩ wa Thiong'o. 1983. *Barrel of a Pen: Resistance to Repression in Neo-Colonial Kenya*. Trenton, NJ: Africa World Press.

Ngũgĩ wa Thiong'o. 1986a. *Decolonising the Mind: The Politics of Language in African Literature*. London: Heinemann.

Ngũgĩ wa Thiong'o. 1986b [1967]. *A Grain of Wheat*. London: Heinemann.

Ngũgĩ wa Thiong'o. 1986c. *Njamba Nene and the Flying Bus*. Translated by Wangui wa Goro. Nairobi: East African Educational Publishers.

Ngũgĩ wa Thiong'o. 1986d. *Njamba Nene's Pistol*. Translated by Wangui wa Goro. Nairobi: East African Educational Publishers.

Ngũgĩ wa Thiong'o. 1986e. *Njamba Nene na Cibu King'ang'i*. Nairobi: East African Educational Publishers.

Ngũgĩ wa Thiong'o. 1988. *Matigari*. London: Heinemann.

Ngũgĩ wa Thiong'o. 1998. *Penpoints, Gunpoints, and Dreams*. Oxford: Claredon Press.

Nichols, Grace. 2005. "Cat Rap." In *Everybody Got a Gift: New and Selected Poems*. London: A. & C. Black.

Nichols, Grace. 1996. "Hurricane Hits England." In *Sunrise*, by Grace Nichols. London: Virago.

Nixon, Rob. 2005. "Environmentalism and Postcolonialism." In *Postcolonial Studies and Beyond*, edited by Ania Loomba, Suvir Kaul, Matti Bunzl, Antoinette Burton, and Jed Esty, 233–51. Durham, NC: Duke University Press.

Nixon, Rob. 2011. *Slow Violence and the Environmentalism of the Poor*. Cambridge, MA: Harvard University Press.

Njogu, Kimani. 2004. *Reading Poetry as Dialogue: An East African Literary Tradition*. Nairobi: Jomo Kenyatta Foundation.

Nkrumah, Kwame. 1964. *Consciencism*. New York: Monthly Review.

Nocella, Anthony J. 2012. "Challenging Whiteness in the Animal Advocacy Movement." *Journal of Critical Animal Studies* 10, no. 1: 142–54.

Norren, Doreen Eva Van. 2014. "The Nexus between Ubuntu and Global Public Goods: Its Relevance for the Post-2015 Development Agenda." *Development Studies Research* 1, no. 1: 255–66.

Notzke, Claudia. 1994. *Aboriginal Peoples and Natural Resources in Canada*. North York, Ontario: Captus Press.

Ntarangwi, Mwenda. 2001. *Gender, Performance and Identity: Understanding Swahili Cultural Identity through Songs*. Trenton, NJ: Africa World Press.

Nussbaum, Barbara. 2009. "Ubuntu: Reflections of a South African on Our Common Humanity." In *African Ethics: An Anthology of Comparative and Applied Ethics*, edited by Munyaradzi Felix Murove, 100–12. Scottsville, South Africa: University of KwaZulu-Natal Press.

Nussbaum, Martha C. 2006. *Frontiers of Justice: Disability, Nationality, Species Membership*. Cambridge, MA: Harvard University Press.

Nussbaum, Martha C. 2012 [2009]. "Compassion: Human and Animal." In *Species Matters: Humane Advocacy and Cultural Theory*, edited by Marianne DeKoven and Michael Lundblad, 139–72. New York: Columbia University Press.

Nweke, Onuora Benedict. 2009. "Homosexual Tendencies and Unconscious Determinants." *Lagos Notes and Records* 15, no. 1: 118–37.

Nyamnjoh, Francis B. 2005. "Madams and Maids in Southern Africa: Coping with Uncertainties, and the Art of Mutual Zombification." *Afrika Spectrum* 40, no. 2: 181–96.

Nyamnjoh, Francis B. 2006. *Insiders and Outsiders: Citizenship and Xenophobia in Contemporary Southern Africa*. London: Zed Books.

Nyman, Jopi. 2003. *Postcolonial Animal Tale from Kipling to Coetzee*. New Delhi: Atlantic.

Nyman, Jopi. 2014a. "Ethical Encounters with Animal Others in Travel Writing." In *Travel and Ethics: Theory and Practice*, edited by Corinne Fowler, Charles Forsdick, and Ludmilla Kostova, 108–27. New York: Routledge.

Nyman, Jopi. 2014b. "Horse as Significant Other: Discourses of Affect and Therapy in

Susan Richards's *Chosen by a Horse: How a Broken Horse Fixed a Broken Heart*," *HUMaNIMALIA* 5, no. 2: 68–86.

Nyman, Jopi. 2016. "Re-Reading Sentimentalism in Anna Sewell's Black Beauty: Affect, Performativity, and Hybrid Spaces." In *Affect, Space and Animals*, edited by Jopi Nyman and Nora Schuurman, 65–79. Abingdon, UK: Routledge.

Nyobé, Ruben Um, 1984. *Le problème national Kamerounais.* Paris: L'Harmattan.

Obiechina, Emmanuel N. 1975. *Culture, Tradition and Society in the West African Novel.* Cambridge, UK: Cambridge University Press.

Obiechina, Emmanuel N. 1976. "Locusts." In *Locusts,* by Emmanuel Obiechina, 23. Greenfield Center, NY: Greenfield Review Press.

Obiechina, Emmanuel N. 1992. "Narrative Proverbs in the African Novel." *Oral Tradition* 7, no. 2: 197–230.

Odhoji, Benjamin M. O. 2009. "The Body as a Figurative Code in Luo Popular Culture, Vernacular Literature, and Systems of Thought." *Postcolonial Text* 5, no. 3. http://postcolonial.org/index.php/pct/article/view/865/992

O'Flaherty, Wendy Doniger. 1995. *Other Peoples' Myths: The Cave of Echoes.* Chicago: University of Chicago Press.

Ojaide, Tanure. 2018. *Literature and Culture in Global Africa.* New York: Routledge.

Okpewho, Isidore. 1992. *African Oral Literature: Background, Character, and Continuity.* Bloomington: Indiana University Press.

Olivelle, Patrick. 2013. "Talking Animals: Explorations in an Indian Literary Genre." *Religions of South Asia* 7: 14–26

Oliver, Kelly. 2009. *Animal Lessons: How They Teach Us to Be Human.* New York: Columbia University Press.

Omer, Muktar M. 2012. "The Jigjiga Desecration: Sordid Tales of Bestiality Sock Community." *Bulsho News.* http://bulshonews.com/2012/11/the-jigjiga-desecration-sordid-tales-of-bestiality-shock-community-by-muktar-m-omer/

Omusamia. 1985. "Simbi and Nashikufu." In *Kenyan Oral Narratives: A Selection,* edited by Wanjiku Mukabi Kabira and Kavetsa Adagala, 1–7. Nairobi: East African Educational Publishers.

Opoku, Kofi. 2006. "Animals in African Mythology." In *A Communion of Subjects: Animals in Religion, Science, and Ethics,* edited by Kimberly Patton and Paul Waldau, 351–59. New York: Columbia University Press.

O'Reilly, Nathanael. 2010. "Introduction: Australian Literature as a Postcolonial Literature." In *Postcolonial Issues in Australian Literature*, edited by Nathanael O'Reilly, 1–14. Amherst, NY: Cambria Press.

Oruka, H. Oruka. 1994. *Philosophy, Humanity and Ecology: Philosophy of Nature and Environmental Ethics.* Nairobi: ACTS.

Orwell, George. 1967. *Shamba la Wanyama [Animal farm]. Translated by* Fortunatus Kawegere. Dar es Salaam: East African Publishing House.

Osinubi, Taiwo Adetunji. 2014. "Hostile Witnesses and Queer Life in Kenyan Prison Writing." *Eastern African Literary and Cultural Studies* 2014: 1–15.

Otu, Kwame Edwin. 2013. "Reluctantly Queer. Sassoi and the Shifting Paradigms of Masculinity and Sexual Citizenship in the Era of Neoliberal LGBTIQ Politics." In *Democratic Renewal versus Neoliberalism: Towards Empowerment and Inclusion*, edited by Claudio Lara Cortés and Consuleo Silva Flores, 33–49. Santiago, Chile: Consejo Latinoamericano de Ciencias Sociales.

Owuor, Yvonne Adhiambo. 2014. *Dust.* New York: Knopf.

Oyewole, S. O. 2003. "African Cultural Response to Ecological and Environmental Concerns." In *African Culture, Modern Science and Religious Thought*, edited by P. Ade Dopamu, 368–71. Ilorin, Nigeria: ACRS.

p'Bitek, Okot. 1966. *Song of Lawino*. Nairobi: East African Publishing House.

p'Bitek, Okot. 1970. *African Religions in Western Scholarship*. Kampala: East African Literature Bureau.

Palladino, Paolo. 1996. *Entomology, Ecology, and Agriculture: The Making of Scientific Careers in North America, 1885–1985*. Amsterdam: Harwood Academic Publishers.

Pandian, Anand. 2012. "Pastoral Power in the Postcolony: On the Biopolitics of the Criminal Animal in South India." In *Animals and the Human Imagination: A Companion to Animal Studies*, edited by Aaron Gross and Anne Vallely, 79–112. New York: Columbia University Press.

Parkes, Nii Ayikwei. 2009. *Tail of the Blue Bird*. London: Jonathan Cape, 2009.

Patton, Paul. 2010. *Deleuzian Concepts: Philosophy, Colonization, Politics*. Stanford, CA: Stanford University Press.

Paul, Samuel A. 2009. *The Ubuntu God: Deconstructing a South African Narrative of Oppression*. Eugene, OR: Pickwick Publications.

Pedersen, Helena. 2011. "Release the Moths: Critical Animal Studies and the Posthumanist Impulse." *Culture, Theory and Critique* 52, no. 1: 65–81.

Peffer, John. 2009. *Art and the End of Apartheid*. Minneapolis: University of Minnesota Press.

Pepetela. 1985. *O Cao e os Caluandas (The Dog in Luanda)*. Lisbon: Publicacoes Dom Quixote.

Pepetela. 2002. *Return of the Water Spirit*. Translated by Luís R Mitras. Oxford, UK: Heinemann.

Peters, Jonathan A. 1978. *A Dance of Masks: Senghor, Achebe, Soyinka*. Washington, DC: Three Continents Press.

Peterson, Christopher. 2013. *Bestial Traces: Race, Sexuality, Animality*. New York: Fordham University Press.

Peterson, Richard B. 2000. *Conversations in the Rainforest: Culture, Values, and the Environment in Central Africa*. Boulder, CO: Westview Press.

Pettman, Dominic. 2011. *Human Error: Species-Being and Media Machines*. Minneapolis: University of Minnesota Press.

Pick, Anat. 2011. *Creaturely Poetics: Animality and Vulnerability in Literature and Film*. New York: Columbia University Press.

Pickover, Michelè. 2005. *Animal Rights in South Africa*. Cape Town: Double Storey.

Plumwood, Val. 1995. "Human Vulnerability and the Experience of Being Prey." *Quadrant* 29, no. 3: 29–34.

Plumwood, Val. 1996. "Being Prey." *Terra Nova* 1, no. 3: 32–44.

Plumwood, Val. 2002. "Decolonisation Relationships with Nature." *PAN: Philosophy Activism Nature* 2: 7–30.

Plumwood, Val. 2012. *Eye of the Crocodile*, edited by Lorraine Shannon. Acton: Australian National University Press.

Poiani, Aldo. 2010. *Animal Homosexuality: A Biosocial Perspective*. Cambridge, UK: Cambridge University Press.

Pollock, Greg. 2010. "The Cannibal-Animal Complex in Melville, Marx, and Beyond." *HUMaN I M A L I A* 2, no. 1: 9–31.

Pratten, David. 2007. *The Man-Leopard Murders: History and Society in Colonial Nigeria*. Bloomington: Indiana University Press.

Preston, Priscilla. 1959. "A Note on T. S. Eliot and Sherlock Holmes." *Modern Language Review* 54: 397–99.

Price, A. Grenfell. 1963. *The Western Invasions of the Pacific and Its Continents: A Study of Moving Frontiers and Changing Landscapes, 1513–1958*. Oxford: Clarendon Press.

Prince, Gerald. 1992. *Narrative as Theme: Studies in French Fiction*. Lincoln: University of Nebraska Press.

Prozesky, Martin H. 2009. "Well-Fed Animals and Starving Babies: Environmental and Developmental Challenges from Processes and African Perspectives." In *African Ethics: An Anthology of Comparative and Applied Ethics*, edited by Munyaradzi Felix Murove, 298–307. Scottsville, South Africa: University of KwaZulu-Natal Press.

Puar, Jasbir K. 2012. "'I Would Rather Be a Cyborg than a Goddess': Becoming-Intersectional in Assemblage Theory." *philoSOPHIA* 2, no. 1: 49–66.

Quayson, Ato. 1997. *Strategic Transformations in Nigerian Writing: Orality and History in the Work of Rev. Samuel Johnson, Amos Tutuola, Wole Soyinka and Ben Okri*. Oxford, UK: James Currey.

Quayson, Ato. 2002. "Fecundities of the Unexpected: Magical Realism, Narrative, and History." In *The Novel. Vol. 1: History, Geography, and Culture*, edited by Franco Moretti, 726–56. Princeton, NJ: Princeton University Press.

Quayson, Ato. 2009. "Magical Realism and African Literature." In *The Cambridge Companion to the African Novel*, edited by Abiola Irele, 159–76. Cambridge, UK: Cambridge University Press.

Quelch, John Joseph. 1901. *Animal Life in British Guiana*. Georgetown, British Guiana: The Argosy.

Quilligan, Maureen. 1992 [1979]. *The Language of Allegory: Defining the Genre*. Ithaca, NY: Cornell University Press.

Rabaka, Reiland. 2015. *The Negritude Movement : W.E.B. Du Bois, Leon Damas, Aime Cesaire, Leopold Senghor, Frantz Fanon, and the Evolution of an Insurgent Idea*. Lanham, MD: Lexington Books.

Raglon, Rebecca and Marian Scholtmeijer, 2007. "'Animals are Not Believers in Ecology': Mapping Critical Differences between Environmental and Animal Advocacy Literatures," *ISLE* 14, no. 2: 122–39.

Ramose, Mogobe B. 1999. *African Philosophy through Ubuntu.* Harare, Zimbabwe: Mond Books.

Ramose, Mogobe B. 2005 [2002]. "The Philosophy of Ubuntu and Ubuntu as a Philosophy." In *Philosophy from Africa: A Text with Readings*, edited by H. Coetzee and A. P. J. Roux, 270–80. New York: Routledge.

Ramsuck, Barbara N. 1990. "Cultural Missionaries, Maternal Imperialists, Feminist Allies: British Women Activists In India, 1865–1945." *Women's Studies International Forum* 13, no. 4: 309–21.

Ratelle, Amy. 2014. *Animality and Children's Literature and Film.* New York: Palgrave Macmillan.

Ray, Sangeeta. 2000. *En-Gendering India: Woman and Nation in Colonial and Postcolonial Narratives.* Durham, NC: Duke University Press. Press.

Reader, John. 2011. *Missing Links: In Search of Human Origins.* Oxford, UK: Oxford University Press.

Redford, Kent H.1991 "The Ecologically Noble Savage." *Cultural Survival Quarterly* 15, no. 1:46–48.

Regan, Tom. 2004 [1983]. *The Case for Animal Rights.* Berkeley: University of California Press.

Reid, Amy Baram. 2006. "Afterword: Reading Around Nganang's Yaoundé." In *Dog Days* by Patrice Nganang, 211–30. Charlottesville: University of Virginia Press.

Rheinberger, Hans-Jörg. 2015. "Difference Machines: Time in Experimental Systems." *Configurations* 23, no. 2: 165–76.

Rishash, Mohamed Adillahi. 1988. "Camel Herding and Its Effect on Somali Literature." In *Camels in Development: Sustainable Production in African Drylands, edited* by Anders Hjort af Ornäs, 53–66. Uppsala, Sweden: Scandinavian Institute of African Studies.

Ritvo, Harriet. 1987. *The Animal Estate: The English and Other Creatures in the Victorian Age.* Cambridge, MA: Harvard University Press.

Roberts, F. Allen. 1995. *Animals in African Art: From the Familiar to the Marvelous.* New York: Museum for African Art.

Roberts, Kim. 2006. "Interlocking Oppressions: The Nature of Cruelty to Nonhuman Animals and Its Relationship to Violence Toward Humans." In *A Communion of Subjects: Animals in Religion, Science, and Ethics,* edited by Kimberly Patton and Paul Waldau, 605–15. New York: Columbia University Press, New York.

Rodgers, Diane M. 2008. *Debugging the Link between Social Theory and Social Insects.* Baton Rouge: Louisiana State University Press.

Rohman, Carrie. 2009. *Stalking the Subject: Modernism and the Animal.* New York: Columbia University Press.

Roth, Vincent. 1941. *Notes and Observations on Animal Life in British Guiana, 1907–1941: A Popular Guide to Colonial Mammalia.* Georgetown, British Guiana: The Daily Chronicles.

Roth, Vincent. 2003. *A Life in Guyana, Volume 1: A Young Man's Journey, 1889–1923*. Leeds, UK: Peepal Tree.

Roughgarden, Joan. 2004. *Evolution's Rainbow: Diversity, Gender, and Sexuality in Nature and People*. Berkeley: University of California Press.

Roy, Arundhati. 1998. *The God of Small Things*. Toronto: Vintage Canada.

Rubadiri, David. 1989. *Growing Up with Poetry: An Anthology for Secondary Schools*. Oxford: Heinemann.

Rubadiri, David. 1971. "Paraa Lodge." In *Poems from East Africa*, edited by David Cook and David Rubadiri, 138. London: Heinemann Educational Books.

Rubadiri, David. 2004 [1968]a. "An African Thunderstorm." In *An African Thunderstorm and Other Poems*, 21–22. Nairobi: East African Educational Publishers.

Rubadiri, David. 2004 [1968]b. "Saaka Crested Cranes." In *An African Thunderstorm and Other Poems*, 39. Nairobi: East African Educational Publishers.

Rungano, Kristina. 1984. *A Storm is Brewing: Poems*. Harare, Zimbabwe: Zimbabwe Publishing House.

Russell, Denise. 2014. "Capturing the Songs of Humpback Whales." In *Captured: The Animal within Culture*, edited by Melissa Boyde, 108–30. Basingstoke, UK: Palgrave Macmillan.

Ruwa'ichi, Thaddeus. 1990. *The Constitution of Muntu: An Inquiry into the Eastern Bantu's Metaphysics of Person*. Berne: Peter Lang.

Rydström, Jens. 2003. *Sinners and Citizens: Bestiality and Homosexuality in Sweden, 1889–1950*. Chicago: University of Chicago Press.

Sahlins, Marshall. 2014. "On the Ontological Scheme of Beyond Nature and Culture." *HAU: Journal of Ethnographic Theory* 4: 281–90.

Saito, Kohei. 2017. *Karl Marx's Ecosocialism: Capitalism, Nature, and the Unfinished Critique of Political Economy*. New York: Monthly Review Press.

Samatar, Said S. 2000. "Are There Secrets in Secrets?" *Research in African Literatures* 31, no. 1: 137–43.

Sandilands, Catriona. 1999. *The Good-Natured Feminist: Ecofeminism and the Quest for Democracy*. Minneapolis: University of Minnesota Press.

Saule, Ncedile. 1996. "Images in Some of the Literary Works of SEK Mqhayi." PhD thesis, University of South Africa, Pretoria.

Savage, Sam. 2006. *Firmin*. Minneapolis: Coffee House Press.

Schipper, Mineke. 1987. "Mother Africa on a Pedestal: The Male Heritage in African Literature and Criticism." *African Literature Today* 15: 35–53.

Scholes, Robert E., James Phelan, and Robert L Kellogg. 2006 [1966]. *The Nature of Narrative*. Oxford, UK: Oxford University Press.

Schreiner, Olive. 1911. *Woman and Labor*. New York: Frederick A. Stokes Company.

Scott, James. 1990. *Domination and the Arts of Resistance: Hidden Transcripts*. New Haven, CT: Yale University Press.

Selvon, Samuel. 1956. *The Lonely Londoners*. London: Allan Wingate.

Sembène, Ousmane. 2013 [1965]. "You Look at Us as If We Were Insects." In *Modern Art in Africa, Asia, and Latin America: An Introduction to Global Modernisms*, edited by Elaine O'Brien, 94–97. Malden, MA: Wiley-Blackwell.

Sembène, Ousmane.1995 [1960]. *God's Bits of Wood*. Translated by Francis Price. Oxford, UK: Heinemann.

Senghor, Léopold Sédar. 1964. *Liberté 1: Negritude et Humanisme*. Paris: Éditions du Seuil.

Senghor, Léopold Sédar. 1976 [1965]. *Prose and Poetry*, edited by John O. Reed and Clive Wake. London: Heinemann Educational.

Senghor, Léopold Sédar. 1993. *Liberté V, le dialogue des cultures*. Paris: Seuil.

Senghor, Léopold Sédar. 2010 [1970]. "Negritude: A Humanism of the Twentieth Century." In *Perspectives on Africa: A Reader in Culture, History, and Representation*, edited by Roy Richard Grinker, Stephen C. Lubkemann, and Christopher Steiner, 477–83. Malden, MA: Blackwell.

Serpell, James. 1996. *In the Company of Animals: A Study of Human-Animal Relationships*. Cambridge, UK: Cambridge University Press.

Seshadri. Kalpana. 2012. *HumAnimal: Race, Law, Language*. Minneapolis: University of Minnesota Press.

Seymour, Nicole. 2013. *Strange Natures: Futurity, Empathy, and the Queer Ecological Imagination*. Urbana: University of Illinois Press.

Shannon, Laurie. 2013. *The Accommodated Animal: Cosmopolity in Shakespearean Locales*. Chicago: University of Chicago Press.

Shaw, Carolyn Martin. 1995. *Colonial Inscriptions: Race, Sex, and Class in Kenya*. Minneapolis: University of Minnesota Press.

Shipton, Parker. 2007. *The Nature of Entrustment: Intimacy, Exchange, and the Sacred in Africa*. New Haven: Yale University Press.

Shoro, Katleho Kano. 2017. *Serurubele: Poems*. Cape Town: Modjaji Books.

Shuchter, Stephen R., and Sidney Zisook. 1986. "Treatment of Spousal Bereavement: A Multidimensional Approach." *Psychiatric Annals* 16, no. 5:295–305.

Shukin, Nicole. 2009. *Animal Capital: Rendering Life in Biopolitical Times*. Minneapolis: University of Minnesota Press.

Simons, John. 2002. *Animal Rights and the Literary Representation*. Basingstoke, UK: Palgrave Macmillan.

Singer, Peter. 2001. *Nerve*,. http://www.utilitarian.net/singer/by/2001.htm

Singer, Peter. 2009 [1975]. *Animal Liberation: The Definitive Classic of the Animal Movement*. New York: Harper Perennial.

Sleigh, Charlotte. 2003. *Ant*. London: Reaktion Books.

Sleigh, Charlotte. 2006. "Inside Out: The Unsettling Nature of Insects." In *Insect Poetics*, edited by Eric C. Brown, 281–97. Minneapolis: University of Minnesota Press.

Slemon, Stephen. 1988. "Magic Realism as Post-Colonial Discourse." *Canadian Literature* 116 (Spring): 9–24.

Smith, Faith. 2011. "Caribbean Literature and Sexuality." In *The Routledge Companion to Anglophone Caribbean Literature*, edited by Michael A. Bucknor and Alison Donnell, 403–11. New York: Routledge.

Smith, Julie A. 2011. "Beyond Dominance and Affection: Living with Rabbits in Post-Humanist Households." *Society and Animals* 11, no. 2: 181–97.

Smuts, Barbara. 2001. "Encounters with Animal Minds." *Journal of Consciousness Studies* 8, nos. 5–7: 293–309.

Smuts, Barbara. 1999. "Reflections." In *The Lives of Animals*, edited by Amy Gutmann, 107–10. Princeton, NJ: Princeton University Press.

Snyder, Gary. 2004. *The Practice of the Wild: Essays*. Washington, DC: Shoemaker & Hoard.

Spear, Thomas. 1993a. "Introduction." In *Being Maasai: Ethnicity and Identity in East Africa,* edited by Thomas Spear and Richard Waller, 1–37. London: James Currey.

Spear, Thomas. 1993b. "Being 'Maasai,' But Not 'People of Cattle': Arusha Agricultural Maasai in the Nineteenth Century." In *Being Maasai: Ethnicity and Identity in East Africa,* edited by Thomas Spear and Richard Waller, 120–36. London: James Currey.

Spiegel, Marjorie. 1988. *The Dreaded Comparison: Human and Animal Slavery.* Philadelphia: New Society Publishers.

Spivak, Gayatri Chakravorty. 1987. *In Other Worlds: Essays in Cultural Politics*. New York: Routledge.

Spivak, Gayatri Chakravorty. 1988. "Introduction." *Selected Subaltern Studies, edited* by Ranajit Guha and Gayatri Chakravorty Spivak, 3–32. New York: Oxford University Press.

Spooner, David. 2005. *The Insect-Populated Mind*. Oxford, UK: Hamilton Books.

Steere, Edward. 1870. *Swahili Tales, as Told by Natives of Zanzibar*. London, Bell & Daldy.

Steiner, Gary. 2005. *Anthropocentrism and Its Discontents: The Moral Status of Animals in the History of Western Philosophy*. Pittsburgh: University of Pittsburgh Press.

Steiner, Gary. 2013. *Animals and the Limits of Postmodernism*. New York: Columbia University Press.

Steinwand, Jonathan. 2011."What the Whales Would Tell Us: Cetacean Communication in Novels by Witi Ihimaera, Linda Hogan, Zakes Mda, and Amitav Ghosh." In *Postcolonial Ecologies: Literatures of the Environment*, edited by Elizabeth M DeLoughre and George B. Handley, 182–99. New York: Oxford University Press.

Stuit, Hanneke. 2016. *Ubuntu Strategies: Constructing Spaces of Belonging in Contemporary South African Culture*. New York: Palgrave.

Subirós, Pep. 2011. *Jane Alexander: Surveys (from the Cape of Good Hope)*. Long Island City, NY: Museum for African Art.

Suk, Jeannie. 2001. *Postcolonial Paradoxes in French Caribbean Writing: Césaire, Glissant, Condé.* Oxford, UK: Clarendon, 2001.

Sutherland-Addy, Esi. 2010. "The Funeral as a Site for Choreographing Modern Identities in Contemporary Ghana." *Ghana Studies* 12/13: 217–48.

Sutton, Mark Q., and E. N. Anderson. 2014. *Introduction to Cultural Ecology.* Lanham, MD: AltaMira Press.

Syambo, Benedict K. 1995. *Mwongozo wa* Shamba la Wanyama [Guide to *Animal Farm]*. Nairobi: East African Educational Publishers.

Tablino, Paul. 1999. *The Gabra: Camel Nomads of Northern Kenya*. Nairobi: Pauline Publishers 1999.

Tadjo, Véronique. [1993] 1997. *Mamy Wata and the Monster.* Abidjan: Nouvelles Editions Ivoiriennes.

Talle, Aud. 2010. "Living beyond AIDS in Maasailand: Discourses of Contagion and Cultural Identity." In *Morality, Hope and Grief: Anthropologies of AIDS in Africa,* edited by Hansjörg Dilger and Ute Luig, 148–72. New York: Berghahn.

Taylor, Shelley E. 1989. *Positive Illusions: Creative Self-Deception and the Healthy Mind.* New York: Basic Books.

Templeton, Malcolm. 2006. *Standing Upright Here: New Zealand in the Nuclear Age.* Wellington, NZ: Victoria University Press.

Terry, Jennifer. 2000. "'Unnatural Acts' in Nature: The Scientific Fascination with Queer Animals." *GLQ: A Journal of Lesbian and Gay Studies* 6, no. 2: 151–93.

Thomas, Elizabeth Marshall. 1993. *The Hidden Life of Dogs.* New York: Pocket Star Books.

Thornber, Karen. 2012. *Ecoambiguity: Environmental Crises and East Asian Literatures.* Ann Arbor: University of Michigan Press.

Tiffin, Helen. 2014. "What Lies Below: Cephalopods and Humans." In *Captured: The Animal within Culture,* edited by Melissa Boyde, 152–74. Basingstoke, UK: Palgrave Macmillan.

Trinh, T. Minh-Ha. 1989. *Woman, Native, Other: Writing Postcoloniality and Feminism.* Bloomington: Indiana University Press.

Tuana, Nancy. 2008. "Viscous Porosity: Witnessing Katrina." In *Material Feminisms,* edited by Stacy Alaimo and Susan Hekman, 188–213. Bloomington, Indianapolis: Indiana University Press.

Tutu, Desmond. 1999. *No Future Without Forgiveness.* London: Rider.

Tuwhare, *Hone.* 1992. *Short Back and Sideways: Poems and Prose.* Auckland: *Godwit* Press.

Valverde, Mariana. 2002. "Justice as Irony: A Queer Ethical Experiment." *Law & Literature* 14, no. 1: 85–102.

Varner, Gary E. 1998. *In Nature's Interests? Interests, Animal Rights, and Environmental Ethics.* New York: Oxford University Press.

Varner, Gary E. 2010. "A Harean Perspective on Humane Sustainability." *Ethics & the Environment* 15, no. 2: 31–49.

Vegan Society. 2014 [1979]. *Memorandum of Association of the Vegan Society.* https://www.vegansociety.com/sites/default/files/The%20Vegan%20Society%20Memorandum%20and%20Articles%20of%20Association%202014.pdf

Vint, Sherryl. 2010. *Animal Alterity: Science Fiction and the Question of the Animal.* Liverpool: Liverpool University Press.

Vital, Anthony. 2005. "Situating Ecology in Recent South African Fiction. J. M. Coetzee's *The Lives of Animals* and Zakes Mda's *The Heart of Redness." Journal of Southern African Studies* 31, no. 2: 297–313.

Vital, Anthony. 2008. "Toward an African Ecocriticism: Postcolonialism, Ecology and *Life & Times of Michael K." Research in African Literatures* 39, no. 1:87–121.

Vital, Anthony. 2016. "Critical Intersections: Ecocriticism, Globalised Cities and African Narrative, with a Focus on K. Sello Duiker's *Thirteen Cents.*" In *Natures of Africa:*

Ecocriticism and Animal Studies in Contemporary Cultural Forms, edited by F. Fiona Moolla, 166–86. Johannesburg, South Africa: Wits University Press.

Viveiros de Castro, Eduardo. 1992 [1986]. *From the Enemy's Point of View: Humanity and Divinity in an Amazonian Society*. Translated by Catherine V. Howard. Chicago: University of Chicago Press.

Viveiros de Castro, Eduardo. 1998. "Cosmological Deixis and Amerindian Perspectivism." *Journal of the Royal Anthropological Institute* 4, no. 3: 469–88.

Viveiros de Castro, Eduardo. 2014. *Cannibal Metaphysics: For a Post-Structural Anthropology*,. Translated by Peter Skafish. Minneapolis, MN: Univocal.

Wachira, James Maina. 2011. "Discourses in Samburu Oral Animal Praise Poetry." M.Phil. thesis, Department of Literature, Theatre and Film Studies, Moi University, Kenya.

Wachira, James Maina. 2016. "Animal Oral Poetry and the Samburu Desire to Survive." In *Natures of Africa: Ecocriticism and Animal Studies in Contemporary Cultural Forms*, edited by F. Fiona Moolla, 97–117. Johannesburg: Wits University Press.

Wainaina, Binyavanga. 2006. "How to Write about Africa." *Granta* 92: 92–95.

Waldau, Paul. 2006. "Religion and Animals." In *Defense of Animals: The Second Wave*, edited by Peter Singer, 69–83. Malden, MA: Blackwell Publishing.

Walker, Alice. 1988. "Foreword." In *The Dreaded Comparison: Human and Animal Slavery*, by Marjorie Spiegel, 13–14. Philadelphia: New Society Publishers.

Walkowitz, Rebecca. 2006. *Cosmopolitan Style: Modernism beyond the Nation*. New York: Columbia University Press.

Wamitila, Kyallo Wadi. 1997. "Reading the Kenyan Swahili Prose Works: A Terra Incognita in Swahili Literature." *AAP* 15: 117–25.

Wannenburgh, Alf. 1979. *The Bushmen*. New York: Mayflower.

Wanner, Zukiswa. 2015. "Teddy and the Pussycat." In *Stray: An Anthology of Animal Stories and Poems*, edited by Hellen Moffett and Diane Awarbuck, 143–46. Cape Town: Hands-On Books.

Warner, Marina. 1994. *From the Beast to the Blonde: On Fairy Tales and Their Tellers*. London: Chatto and Windus.

Weheliye, Alexander G. 2014. *Habeas Viscus: Racializing Assemblages, Biopolitics, and Black Feminist Theories of the Human*. Durham, NC: Duke University Press.

Wehner, R. 2003. "Desert Ant Navigation: How Miniature Brains Solve Complex Tasks." *Journal of Comparative Physiology* 189: 579–88.

Wenzel, Jennifer. 2009. *Bulletproof: Afterlives of Anticolonial Prophecy in South Africa and Beyond*. Chicago: University of Chicago Press.

Wenzel, Marita. 2009. "Zakes Mda's Representation of South African Reality in *Ways of Dying*, *The Madonna of Excelsior* and *The Whale Caller*." In *Word and Image in Postcolonial Literatures*, edited by Michael Meyer, 125–46. Amsterdam: Rodopi.

Werner, Alice. 1913. "Some Notes on the Wapokomo of the Tana Valley." *Journal of the Royal African Society* 12, no. 48: 359–84.

Werner, Alice. 1964. "Wanyika." In *Encyclopaedia of Religion and Ethics: Mundas-*

Phrygians, edited by James Hastings, John A. Selbie, and Louis H. Gray, 424–27. New York: C. Scribner's Sons.

Western, David. 1997. *In the Dust of Kilimanjaro.* Washington, DC: Island Press.

White, Rob D. 2013. *Environmental Harm: An Eco-Justice Perspective.* Bristol, UK: The Policy Press.

Wiemann, Dirk. 2008. *Genres of Modernity: Contemporary Indian Novels in English* Amsterdam: Rodopi.

Wiersum, K. F. 2004. "Forest Gardens as an 'Intermediate' Land-Use System in the Nature-Culture Continuum: Characteristics and Future Potential." *Agroforestry Systems* 61: 123–34.

Williams, Joshua. 2017. "The Lifelike Dead: Staging the Nonhuman in Colonial Nairobi." *Theater and Performance Studies* 69, no. 3: 321–37.

Williams, Raymond. 1976. *Keywords: A Vocabulary of Culture and Society.* London: Routledge.

Wilson, Eric G. 2006. *The Melancholy Android.* Albany: State University of New York Press.

Wolfe, Cary. 2003a. *Animal Rites: American Culture, the Discourse of Species, and Posthumanist Theory.* Chicago: University of Chicago Press.

Wolfe, Cary. 2003b. "Introduction." In *Zoontologies: The Question of the Animal, edited* by Cary Wolfe, ix–xxiii. Minneapolis: University of Minnesota Press.

Wolfe, Cary. 2010. *What Is Posthumanism?* Minneapolis: University of Minnesota Press.

Wood, John C. 1999. *When Men Are Women: Manhood among Gabra Nomads of East Africa.* Madison: University of Wisconsin Press.

Woodward, Wendy. 2008a. *The Animal Gaze: Animal Subjectivities in Southern African Narratives.* Johannesburg: Wits University Press.

Woodward, Wendy. 2008b. "Social Subjects: Representation of Dogs in South African Fiction in English." In *Canis Africanis: A Dog History of Southern Africa*, edited by Lance Van Sittert and Sandra Scott Swart, 235–62. Leiden: Brill.

Woodward, Wendy. 2009. "Whales, Clones and Two Ecological Novels: *The Whale Caller* and Jane Rosenthal's *Souvenir.*" In *Ways of Writing: Critical Essays on Zakes Mda,* edited by David Vell and J. U. Jacobs, 333–353. Scottsville, South Africa: University of KwaZulu-Natal Press.

Woodward, Wendy. 2016. "Human Mask? Animal Narrators in Patrice Nganang's *Dog Days: An Animal Chronicle* and Alain Mabanckou's *Memoirs of a Porcupine.*" In *Natures of Africa: Ecocriticism and Animal Studies in Contemporary Cultural Forms,* edited by F. Fiona Moolla, 235–56. Johannesburg, South Africa: Wits University Press.

Worden, J. William. 2009. *Grief Counseling and Grief Therapy: A Handbook for the Mental Health Practitioner.* New York: Springer.

Wright, Laura. 2010. *"Wilderness into Civilized Shapes": Reading the Postcolonial Environment.* Athens: University of Georgia Press.

Wright, Laura. 2015. *The Vegan Studies Project: Food, Animals, and Gender in the Age of Terror.* Athens: University of Georgia Press.

Wylie, Dan. 2002. "The Anthropomorphic Ethic Fiction and the Animal Mind in Virginia Woolf's *Flush* and Barbara Gowdy's *The White Bone*." *ISLE: Interdisciplinary Studies in Literature and Environment* 9, no. 2: 115–131.

Yaa, Nia. 2010. "What You Cooking, Grandma?" In *Sistah Vegan: Black Female Vegans Speak on Food, Identity, Health, and Society*, edited by A. Breeze Harper, 92–100. New York: Lantern Books.

Yule, George. 2014 [1985]. *The Study of Language*. Cambridge, UK: Cambridge University Press.

Zambra, Alejandro. 2010. *The Private Lives of Trees*. Translated by Megan McDowell. Rochester, NY: Open Letter.

Zeleza, Paul Tiyambe. 1994. *Maasai*. New York: Rosen.

Zephaniah, Benjamin. 2000. *Wicked World*. London: Puffin.

Zephaniah, Benjamin. 2001. *Too Black, Too Strong*. London: Bloodaxe.

Zimunya, Musaemura. 1982. *Those Years of Drought and Hunger: The Birth of African Fiction in English in Zimbabwe*. Gweru, Zimbabwe: Mambo Press.

Zirimu, Pio, and Austin Bukenya. 1986 [1973]. "Oracy as a Tool for African Development." In *The Arts and Civilization of Black and African Peoples 4*, edited by Joseph Ohiomogben Okpaku, 88–105. Lagos: Third Press International.

Zogbé, Mama. 2007. *Origins of the Vodoun Religion in America: The Reclamation of a Suppressed Heritage*. Martinez, GA: Mami Wata Healers Society of North America.

INDEX

Illustrations are indicated by page numbers in ***bold italics***.